THE WHOLE CHILD

NEW TRENDS IN EARLY EDUCATION

THE
WHOLE
CHILD

NEW TRENDS IN
EARLY EDUCATION

JOANNE HENDRICK, Ph.D.

Chairman, Department of Nursery School Education,
Santa Barbara Community College,
Santa Barbara, California

ILLUSTRATED

SAINT LOUIS
THE C. V. MOSBY COMPANY
1975

Cover photograph courtesy Philip Chinn, Denton, Texas

Library of Congress Cataloging in Publication Data

Hendrick, Joanne, 1928-
    The whole child; new trends in early education.

    1. Education, Preschool. I. Title.
LB1140.2.H44   372.21   74-14767
ISBN 0-8016-2142-9

TS/VH/VH 9 8 7 6 5 4 3 2

Preface

This book is intended to equip the beginning teacher of young children with a fundamental point of view and specific skills so that she may function effectively with the children in her care. It cites research where it is possible to do so and resorts to common sense and practical experience with children where research does not provide the answers.

Since it does not appear that we have yet reached the point where we have the final answer on how children learn and why they behave as they do, the book is eclectic in terms of learning theory—sometimes recommending behavior modification as an approach and sometimes urging the reader to identify other reasons for behavior and to work toward the mitigation of behaviors that are malign.

The recommendations for curriculum are based on the assumption that children do indeed pass through stages of development—that growth is an orderly, predictable, sequential process, and that a good teacher or parent can assist the child in growing to his full potential by recognizing these stages and by offering suitable experiences that nurture and challenge him as he develops.

The book is sexist in the sense that it refers to the student as "she." I can only beg the reader's indulgence for this flaw, since writing was simply clearer if one sex was consistently ascribed to the teacher and the other used to identify the child. However, I am well aware that teachers and children come in both genders.

Finally, this book assumes that the function of education is to care for the whole child and help him flourish. For this reason, it focuses on five aspects of the child's self rather than stressing various curriculum topics such as science or outdoor play. It is my belief that once the educational needs of these selves are understood, a specific curriculum follows naturally and is relatively simple to generate.

Writing a book about early childhood education has been exciting—it has been an interesting task for me to set down what I know about this area. If it is also helpful to the beginning teacher and to the children she serves, I will be pleased indeed.

I owe so much to so many people that it is a well nigh

impossible task to mention them all. The contribution of students and parents to my point of view and knowledge has been considerable, as have the innumerable things my staff have taught me. In addition, I am forever in the debt of my mother, Alma Green, who not only began some of the first parent education classes in Los Angeles, but also taught me a great deal about young children and their families.

I am also indebted to Sarah Foot and her wonderful Starr King Parent Child Workshop, which convinced me that my future lay in early childhood education, and to my own children who bore with me with such goodwill while I was learning the real truth about bringing up young people.

As far as the book itself is concerned, I would like to thank Murray Thomas for teaching me, among other things, how to write and John Wilson for convincing me that some things remained to be said and changed in early education. To Chester and Peggy Harris I am forever indebted for a certain realistic attitude toward research, particularly in the area of cognitive development.

My thanks go to Lou Grant and Marilyn Statucki for commenting on the manuscript with such patience and tact. I am also grateful to Dorothy Annable for locating countless books for me and to my typist, Anne Muñoz, for making sense out of an incredible chaos of imaginative typing and illegible scrawls.

Finally, I wish to acknowledge a special debt to Jason Lo'Cicero for his sensitive portraits of young children and to Terry Jones, Head Start Coordinator of Santa Barbara County, who generously granted permission for me to use her collection of Head Start pictures.

JOANNE HENDRICK

Contents

PART NINE

What lies ahead?

References, 307

APPENDICES

PART **ONE**

Beginning to teach

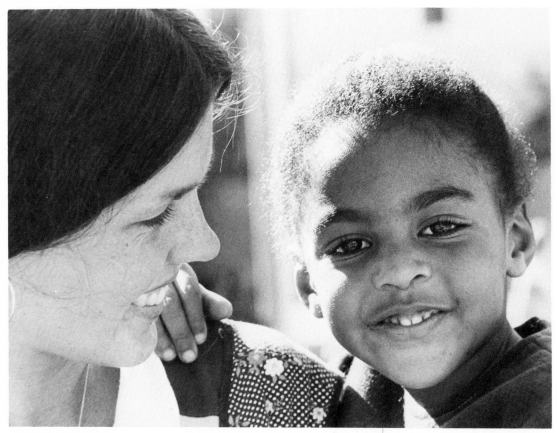

Santa Barbara City College Children's Center

CHAPTER 1

What makes a good day
for children?

There was a child went forth every day,
And the first object he look'd upon, that object he became,
And that object became part of him for the day or a certain part of the day,
Or for many years or stretching cycles of years.

The early lilacs became part of this child,
And grass and white and red morning-glories, and white and red clover, and
    the song of the phoebe-bird,
And the Third-month lambs and the sow's pink-faint litter, and the mare's foal
    and the cow's calf,
And the noisy brood of the barnyard or by the mire of the pond-side,
And the fish suspending themselves so curiously below there, and the
    beautiful curious liquid,
And the water-plants with their graceful flat heads, all became part of him.

The field-sprouts of Fourth-month and Fifth-month became part of him,
Winter-grain sprouts and those of the light-yellow corn, and the esculent
    roots of the garden,
And the apple-trees cover'd with blossoms and the fruit afterward, and
    wood-berries, and the commonest weeds by the road,
And the old drunkard staggering home from the outhouse of the tavern
    whence he had lately risen,
And the schoolmistress that pass'd on her way to the school,
And the friendly boys that pass'd, and the quarrelsome boys,
And the tidy and fresh-cheek'd girls, and the barefoot negro boy and girl,
And all the changes of city and country wherever he went.

His own parents, he that had father'd him and she that had conceiv'd him in
    her womb and birth'd him,
They gave this child more of themselves than that,
They gave him afterward every day, they became part of him.

The mother at home quietly placing the dishes on the supper-table,
The mother with mild words, clean her cap and gown, a wholesome odor
    falling off her person and clothes as she walks by,
The father, strong, self-sufficient, manly, mean, anger'd, unjust,
The blow, the quick loud word, the tight bargain, the crafty lure,
The family usages, the language, the company, the furniture, the yearning and
    swelling heart,
Affection that will not be gainsay'd, the sense of what is real, the thought if
    after all it should prove unreal,
The doubts of day-time and the doubts of night-time, the curious whether
    and how,

3

Whether that which appears so is so, or is it all flashes and specks?
Men and women crowding fast in the streets, if they are not flashes and
  specks what are they?
The streets themselves and the façades of houses, and goods in the windows,
Vehicles, teams, the heavy-plank'd wharves, the huge crossing at the ferries,
The village on the highland seen from afar at sunset, the river between,
Shadows, aureola and mist, the light falling on roofs and gables of white or
  brown two miles off,
The schooner near by sleepily dropping down the tide, the little boat
  slack-tow'd astern,
The hurrying tumbling waves, quick-broken crests, slapping,
The strata of color'd clouds, the long bar of maroon-tint away solitary by
  itself, the spread of purity it lies motionless in,
The horizon's edge, the flying sea-crow, the fragrance of salt marsh and shore
  mud,
These became part of that child who went forth every day, and who now
  goes, and will always go forth every day.

WALT WHITMAN
There Was a Child Went Forth (1871)

Teaching preschool children can be one of the best, most deeply satisfying experiences in the world. Children aged 2 to 5 go through fascinating, swiftly accomplished stages of development. They are possessed of vigorous personalities, rich enthusiasm, an astonishing amount of physical energy, and strong wills. With the exception of infancy, there is no other time in human life when so much is learned in so brief a period (Bloom, 1964).

This phenomenal vigor and burgeoning growth present a challenge to the beginning teacher that is at once exhilarating and frightening. The task is a large one: the teacher must attempt to build an educational climate that enhances the children's development and whets their appetites for further learning. The milieu must also nourish and sustain emotional health, encourage physical growth and muscular prowess, foster satisfying social interactions, enhance creativity, develop language skills, and promote the development of mental ability. Moreover, this must all be garbed in an aura of happiness and affection in order to establish that basic feeling of well-being, which is essential to successful learning.

With such a large task at hand, it is not surprising that the beginning teacher may

wonder somewhat desperately where to begin and what to do. The following material should help the student gain skills and confidence as well as organize what is known about preschool education into a logical whole so that she may become a relaxed and effective teacher of young children.

No doubt the reader is anxious to press on to discussions of discipline or eating problems or teaching children to share— these are valid concerns of all teachers of preschool children. However, it seems wise to take time first for an overview of what should go into a good day for young children. What elements should be included when planning the overall curriculum? Once these elements are clearly in mind, we can turn to a consideration of more specific problems and recommendations.

WHAT GOES INTO A GOOD DAY FOR CHILDREN?

For almost a decade research on approaches to early childhood education has sought to investigate the effectiveness of various kinds of programs in changing the behavior and enhancing the development of young children (Maccoby and Zellner, 1970). The results of these investigations are contradictory. On one hand, the Westinghouse Report (Cicerelli, Evans, and Schiller, 1969) and the Hawkridge study (Hawkridge, Chalupsky, and Roberts, 1968) have found little evidence of change on measures of intellectual ability. In this same tradition, Jencks (1972) has challenged the efficacy of education as an antidote to poverty. On the other hand, Bereiter and Englemann (1966), Hodges, McCandless, Spicker, and Craig (1971), Gray and Klaus (1970), Karnes, Teska, and Hodgins (1970), Lane, Elzey, and Lewis (1971), and Weikart (1967) indicate that preschool programs can be effective change agents. (The reader should be aware that in these studies change has almost always been determined by evidence gathered from standardized measures of mental and verbal ability.)

An examination of these successful programs reveals that they differ in many respects in their philosophy, teaching techniques, and program content. But even though they differ in many ways, analysis by a number of authors (Gordon, 1970; Maccoby and Zellner, 1970) also indicates that successful programs have certain elements in common. It is these elements that are considered in this text; it is left up to the reader to investigate the more unique aspects of particular programs listed in the readings at the end of each chapter and references at the end of the book.

It is heartening to realize that these elements have been identified in rather carefully controlled field research situations. This means that teachers no longer need to base their educational practices solely on instinct or unverified conviction. For the first time, we are able to justify the inclusion of elements of curriculum because research is beginning to provide supportive evidence that they are valuable.

Good human relationships are a fundamental ingredient of a good day*

All good preschool programs are built on the foundation of sound human relationships. Warmth and empathic understand-

---

*Items followed by an asterisk are ones included either on the Maccoby and Zellner (1970) or Gordon (1970) list.

ing have been shown to be effective means of influencing young children's positive adjustment to nursery school (Truax and Tatum, 1966), and it is apparent that genuine caring about the children and about other adults in the program is fundamental to success.

In order for warmth and personal contact to flourish, the day must be planned and paced so there are numerous opportunities for person-to-person, one-to-one encounters. In practical terms, this means that groups must be kept small and the ratio of adults to children as high as possible. Many occasions must also be provided where the children move freely about, making personal choices and generating individual contacts. Such arrangements permit numerous interludes where informal learning experiences can be enjoyed and where human caring can be expressed. The moments may be as fleeting as a quick hug when the teacher ties a pair of trailing laces or as extended as a serious discussion of where babies come from. It is the quality of individualized, personal caring and the chance to talk together that are significant.

The parent should be included as part of the life of the school*

The day is past when parents were expected to pay their bill but leave their children at the nursery school door. Of course, cooperative schools have long demonstrated the feasibility of including the family in the nursery school experience, but today we can also point to mounting research that confirms that inclusion of the parent in the educational process, whether in home tutoring programs or the nursery school itself, results in longer-lasting educational gains for the child (Gray and Klaus, 1970; Gordon and associates, 1969; Weikart and Lambie, 1968).

Since it is possible to include parents in a variety of welcoming, participating ways, which are discussed in a later chapter, it is only noted here that the value of close interaction between home and school is being increasingly documented by research. Therefore, we should do all we can to make this link a strong one.

There should be a balance between self-selection and teacher direction—both approaches are valuable*

Value of self-selection. The idea that young children can be trusted to choose educational experiences for themselves that will benefit them goes all the way back in educational theory to Jean Jacques Rousseau and John Dewey, and at present this concept is experiencing a rebirth in England in the British Infant School, as well as continuing its tenure in the majority of American nursery schools.

Philosophical support for the value of self-selection of activities comes from as disparate sources as the self-selection feeding experiments of Clara Davis (1939) and the psychoanalytic theory of Erikson, who speaks of the preschool child's "sudden, violent wish to have a choice" (1950, p. 252). The virtue of self-selection is that it fosters independence and builds within the child responsibility for making his own decisions. It also provides an excellent way to individualize the curriculum because each child is free to pursue his own interests and to suit himself when he is free to choose.

Value of teacher-determined activities. Despite the virtues and attractiveness of the open environment, research indicates that one should not rely entirely on self-selection. At least in programs designed to serve children who come from poor families, it is now evident that planned, structured experiences that are teacher directed are more effective in producing cognitive gains than are programs lacking this characteristic (Bissell, 1973; DiLorenzo and Salter, 1968). Even though the cognitive self (the part of the child that is concerned with mental activity) is only one aspect of the child's personality, adequate mental development is so closely related to success in school that promising techniques must be taken into consideration when planning a curriculum.

It would be ideal, of course, if all activities were attractive enough that the child would *want* to choose them spontaneously, but there are times when youngsters should participate in learning activities that will enhance their growth even if they are not particularly attracted to them. It isn't fair to let a child graduate from preschool with a degree in trike riding coupled with a deadly inability to put five words together into a coherent sentence.

Good curriculum must be planned with definite objectives in mind*

Evidence is mounting that formulating and carrying out a specific plan for the preschool program is fundamental to success at least when working with economically disadvantaged children. The value of establishing specific objectives has been convincingly demonstrated in programs having such contrasting philosophies as the Piagetian classrooms of David Weikart (Weikart, Rogers, Adcock, and McClelland, 1971) and the learning drill classrooms of Bereiter and Englemann (1966). A study of Mexican-American preschools (Nedler and Sebera, 1971) presents additional evidence that sequenced, planned learning was effective in their program. In addition, all the Planned Intervention Head Start Models required clear definitions of strategies before they could be funded (Klein, 1971).

Yet the value of identifying objectives and formulating plans by which they may be reached is often questioned or ignored by early childhood teachers on the grounds that it may deaden creativity, spontaneity, and opportunities for self-selection (Ebel, 1970; Moskovitz, 1973). As Fowler puts it,

[Teachers fear] the formal, didactic and authority centered forms of teaching prominent in education until the development of the nursery school and progressive education movement early in this century. (1971, p. 30)

Of course, one would not want the formulation of a plan to result in a return to that style of teaching; but at the same time, the beginning nursery school teacher should realize that a curriculum is not something that can be relied on to develop spontaneously as the day marches along. Days must be planned and overall goals identified and implemented to assure educational success.

There are times when the marvelous

welling up of an idea or activity does take place, and these teachable moments are to be sought after and treasured—but this does not happen all the time. Nor does reliance on such events assure that every important area will be covered, that necessary goals will be achieved, or that the needs of individual children will be taken into consideration. Only planning coupled with evaluation can accomplish these objectives.

A good program should be comprehensive

An aspect of planning that deserves special consideration is that curriculum be comprehensive in coverage. An easy way to think about this is to picture the child as being composed of a number of selves —the physical self, the emotional self, the social self, the creative self, and the cognitive self. This book is based in part on this division of the child into selves because experience has shown that various aspects of curriculum fall rather neatly under these headings and that the five selves succeed in covering the personality of the child.

The physical self includes not only large and fine muscle development but also handling routines, since such things as eating, resting, and toileting contribute much to physical comfort and well-being. For the emotional self we consider ways to increase and sustain mental health, to use discipline to foster self-control, to cope with aggression, and to foster self-esteem. Under the heading of the social self are placed ways to build social concern and kindliness, learning to enjoy work, and learning to value the cultures of other people. The creative self covers the areas of self-expression through the use of art materials and creativity as expressed in play and applied in thought. Finally, the cognitive, or intellectual, self is considered in terms of language development, the development of horizontal and vertical curriculum, and the development of specific learning abilities. This last self is the newest one to receive intensive consideration and analysis in early childhood education, and much remains to be learned in this area.

Individualization of instruction is important*

Value of suiting curriculum to each individual child. We have already reviewed research that indicates that the teacher will experience greater success if she identifies her educational goals clearly and carries out activities designed to reach these goals. The real art of teaching lies in her ability to clothe these bare-boned goals in the raiment of individual children's interests and pleasures. Fortunately, the small size and intimacy of preschool groups makes it possible for teachers to know each youngster well and to plan with particular individuals in mind.

Not only should broad goals be personalized to fit the children's interests, but specific goals should be formulated to suit individual children, since every child is different and learns at his own rate. Prompt assessment of the children's skills is invaluable because it can help the teacher identify specific needs of individual children and plan in accordance with these revealed needs.

A simple test to determine whether curriculum is individualized. There are three questions the teacher can use to determine whether the curriculum she offers is individualized:

1. Can she cite some recent instances where curriculum was based on a child's specific interests?
2. Can she point to examples where a child was deliberately provided with opportunities to learn what evaluations had indicated that he especially needed to know?
3. Can she cite some examples where curriculum plans were changed because a child revealed an unanticipated interest or enthusiasm during the day?

A good program has stability and regularity combined with flexibility

Young children need to know what is likely to happen next during the day. This means that the order of events should be generally predictable. Predictability enables the child to prepare mentally for the next event; it makes compliance with routines more likely and helps children feel secure.

At the same time, time schedules and routines should not be allowed to dominate the school. (Sometimes this happens because of a strong-minded custodian or cook. I once knew a school where it was necessary for the children to use only half the space from 10:30 until nap time because of the custodian's routine. Sometimes overconformance to time schedules happens because teachers are creatures of habit and simply don't realize that juice and raisins don't have to be served at exactly 9:15.) Rather than sticking right to the clock, it is better to maintain an orderly, but elastic schedule where play periods can be extended when those moments occur when the majority of the children are involved in activities that interest them intensely.

A good program has variety

Children need many different kinds of experiences as well as changes in basic experiences. Research on the effects of stimulus deprivation (Casler, 1968; Dennis, 1960) and of early stimulation (White, B.L., 1968) has highlighted the value of supplying a variety of experiences even for babies, and variety should certainly be incorporated in a program for preschool children.

Many nursery school teachers think of variety of experience in terms of field trips or covering different topics, such as families or baby animals. But another kind of variety that should also be considered is variety in everyday basic learning experiences. What a difference there is between the school that has the same pet rat and bowl of goldfish all year and the school that first raises a rabbit, then borrows a broody hen, and next has two snakes as visitors. Lack of variety is also shown in schools that offer the omnipresent easel as their major "art" experience or others that set out all the blocks at the beginning of the year and leave it at that.

Children should be offered various levels of difficulty in activity materials. If the nursery school combines age levels during the day so that 3-, 4-, and 5-year-olds play together, it is important to provide materials that are challenging for all the ages within the group. Teachers need to be especially careful to offer materials that are genuinely interesting to the older 4-year-olds and young 5-year-olds. A dearth of stimulating, fresh curricula is the commonest cause of posses of children galloping through block areas and housekeeping corners, spreading destruction as they go.

The curriculum should not only offer a variety of levels of difficulty during every day, it should also become more challenging and move from simple to more complex activities as the year progresses and the children mature and gain competence. The nursery school curriculum should not look the same in May as it did in September.

Children need changes of pace during the day to avoid monotony and fatigue and to maintain a balance of kinds of experiences for them. The most obvious way to incorporate variation of pace is to plan for it in the overall schedule. For example, a quiet snack can be followed by a dance period.

Additional opportunities to meet individual temperamental requirements of children must also be allowed for. The quieter, less gregarious child needs to have a place available where he can retreat from the herd, and the more active youngster needs the escape hatch of moving about when the group has sat beyond his limit of endurance.

Some kinds of programs appear to have special problems associated with pacing. For example, some compensatory programs attempt to cram so much into such a short time (play time, story time, snack, lunch, special activity time, not to mention visits from the psychologist, field trips, and special visitors) that the day goes by in a headlong rush of children being hurried from one thing to the next without the opportunity to savor any experience richly and fully. At the other extreme, some day care programs offer a variety of activities and changes of pace during the morning but turn the children loose in the play yard for 3 interminable hours in the afternoon. Such consistent conditions of hurried stress or unalleviat-

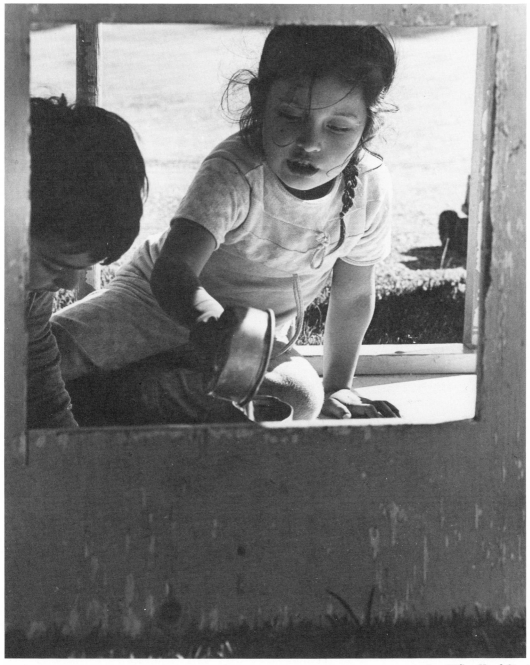

Los Niños Head Start

ed boredom, unless coped with thoughtfully and modified, can ultimately have only a deleterious effect on children.

Learning must be based on actual experience and participation

Anyone who has ever taken a young child to the market knows how strong his impulse is to touch and smell and taste everything he encounters. Although occasionally inconvenient, the child's behavior illustrates a fundamental fact of early childhood learning: children learn best if allowed to use all their senses as avenues of learning. Participatory experience is an essential ingredient in preschool education. This means that the curriculum of the nursery school must be based on real experiences with real things rather than limited to the verbal discussions and pictures commonly (though not necessarily ideally) used when teaching older children.

Because educators of young children from Montessori to Bank Street have emphasized the value of real experience as being fundamental to successful education from the turn of the century, and because Piaget has also stressed the importance of participatory experience in the development of intelligence (Hunt, 1961), one might think that this principle need not be reiterated. However, the current influx of word-oriented rather than action-oriented teaching materials on display in the commercial exhibits of most conferences on early childhood and the fact that these materials continue to sell make it evident that this point must be stated very clearly: young children learn best when they can manipulate material, experiment, try things out, and talk about what is happening as it takes place (Torrance, 1970a; Lombard and Stern, 1970). Talking without doing is largely meaningless for a child of tender years.

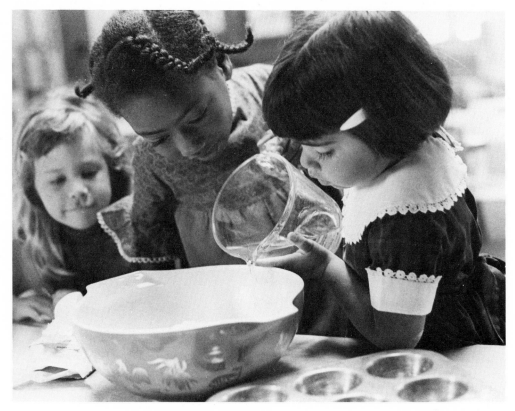

Los Niños Head Start

Play is an indispensable avenue for learning

Another long-held value in early childhood education is an appreciation of play as a facilitator of learning. Although research is still lacking in this area, evidence is beginning to accumulate (Piaget, 1962; Smilansky, 1968) that lends support to something generations of nursery school teachers have learned through experience. Teachers who have watched young children at play know the intent, purposeful seriousness they bring to this activity. Play is the medium used by children to translate experience into something internally meaningful to them. Piaget (1962) agrees with teachers and maintains that children use it as an important symbolic activity, but it serves many purposes beyond this function. Play clarifies concepts, provides emotional relief, facilitates social development, and creates periods of clearly satisfying delight. Sometimes teachers see its value only as a teacher-controlled, structured experience used to achieve a specific educational end (role playing after visiting the fire station, for example), but it is crucial that there be ample time in the curriculum for self-initiated play. It may well be that further research will show play to be the most significant avenue of learning available to young children.

Nursery school should be pleasureful*

Probably the most significant value a teacher can convey to the children in her care is the conviction that school is satisfying fun. This point has been deliberately left until last in order to give it special emphasis in case the reader, having waded through the other elements of a good program, has begun to feel bogged down with the sober-sided responsibilities of running a good program for young children.

Not only should the experience be pleasureful for the children, but it should also be a joy for the adults. Young children have their trying moments, but they are also delightful. They see the world in a clear-sighted way that can lend fresh perspective to the eyes of their teacher, and their tendency to live for the present moment is a lesson to us all. Pleasure, enjoyment, humor, and laughter should be very much a part of each nursery school day.

PUTTING THE ELEMENTS TOGETHER
What does a nursery school day look like that combines these basic elements into a coherent whole?

The setting of a good nursery school is established with children in mind: furniture is scaled to the right size; the building has easy access to the yard; and there is a general air of orderly, yet easy-going comfort and beauty that does not put people off because of its newness or perfection. This kind of atmosphere goes a long way toward making parents feel at home and part of the nursery school family.

When it is necessary to form groups, the children are broken into small assemblies. Story hours and snack tables of four or five children and a grownup, for example, should be the rule in order to facilitate conversation and participation. (My staff refers to this as Hendrick's law: "The larger the group, the smaller the learning.") The daily pace is easy enough and the staff unharrassed enough that there are many intimate little opportunities for teachers to talk with the children individually.

There is a reasonably repetitious scheduling of basic experiences planned to provide alternate periods of quiet and active experience. These periods include a morning welcome for each child as he arrives, a snack in the morning and afternoon, and lunch and rest in the middle of the day.

In between these landmark times, many interesting events take place. These are developed with individual and group goals in mind, and they should include, every day, some activity that is creative, another that is messy, something that is new, something that requires the children to think, some opportunity for the children to engage in meaningful work, and many chances to use books, pictures, poetry, and to listen and be listened to. Intertwined among these activities lie all the situations that the teacher must seize and use as they arise to develop social learnings and emotional strengths in the children.

For at least one generous block of time during the morning and afternoon, materials and possibilities are set out, and the child is expected to take the responsibility of selecting for himself what he wants to pursue. During this time, the teacher moves from one place to another as the occasion demands, talking first with one child, helping another group settle a fight, and getting out a piece of equipment for a third. Another part of the day involves more focussed participation but should not be cast in the mold of fifteen children doing the identical thing in one large group at the same time.

If staffing and weather permit, children have access to inside and outdoors as they prefer. Failing this, large muscle activities are available indoors and smaller muscle and more cognitive and creative materials are available outdoors to avoid the "recess" concept so common in elementary school.

This, then, is the overall framework of a sound preschool day. It includes many diverse things and many diverse people. The miracle of a good school is that, somehow, these all go together to produce a good day for both children and staff.

SUMMARY

After nearly a decade of research, certain elements are emerging that appear to be common to the majority of effective early childhood programs. These include concern for the quality of human relationships, inclusion of the parent as part of the life of the nursery school, a balance of self-selected and teacher-directed activities, the formulation of a well-thought-out plan for the curriculum, and a curriculum that is comprehensive and individualized.

A good nursery school program is basically orderly but also flexible; it provides for variety in experience, levels of difficulty, and pacing; it is based on the principles that learning should be the result of actual experience, that play is a significant mode of learning, and, above all, that nursery school should be a place of joy for both children and staff.

QUESTIONS

1. *Problem:* Suppose a parent said to you, after touring the school, "My heavens, these nur-

sery school fees are high. Why, my baby-sitter charges less than you do, and she comes to the house and does the ironing while she takes care of little Carolyn. I don't see what costs so much about just taking care of little children!" What would you reply?

2. What are some situations in your own educational background where the learning was primarily by means of language and others where there was an emphasis on experience and participation? Which method did you prefer? What were the advantages and disadvantages of each of these approaches?

3. What guidelines would you suggest to help a teacher determine if she is not providing enough free choices or if there is too much structure in the children's day?

4. As a beginning teacher, how do you feel about the prospect of having parents at school? If a mother is helping at school on the day her youngster has a temper tantrum and refuses to come in to lunch, would it be easier to handle this situation if the mother were not there? Do you agree completely that parents should be welcomed at school? Why or why not?

5. Select a basic activity, such as using tricycles or easel painting, which tends to stay the same throughout the year in many schools, and suggest some variations that would add interest and learning to the activity.

REFERENCES FOR FURTHER READING

Historical Resumés of Early Childhood Education

Kessen, W. *The child.* New York: John Wiley & Sons, Inc., 1965. This lively paperback traces the historical development of ideas about children from William Cadogan to Jean Piaget. It includes selections from many authors as well as comments and explanations by Dr. Kessen.

Snyder, A. *Dauntless women.* Washington, D.C.: Association for Childhood Education International, 1972. Cast in the form of numerous short biographies, this book traces the history of early childhood education through the past 175 years. It is highly readable, funny in spots, and contains delightful illustrations.

Weber, E. *The kindergarten: its encounter with educational thought in America.* New York: Teachers College Press, 1969. The development of the kindergarten is traced back to Froebel in the early 1800s. There also are some thoughtful, sound chapters on current trends and implications for early childhood education.

Material on Specific Programs

LaCrosse, E. R., Lee, P. C., Litman, F., Olgilvie, D. M., Stodlosky, S. S., and White, B. L. The first six years of life: a report on current research and educational practice. *Genetic Psychology Monographs,* 1970, **82,** 161-266. A portion of this review of research discusses several of the better-known experimental programs and draws comparisons between them.

Maccoby, E. E., and Zellner, M. *Experiments in primary education: aspects of Project Follow-Through.* New York: Harcourt Brace Jovanovich, Inc., 1970. In this paperback the Follow-Through programs are discussed in terms of their differences and similarities; contains nice, clear-cut discussions of differing philosophies and current educational issues.

Weber, E. *Early childhood education: perspectives on change.* Worthington, Ohio: Charles A. Jones Publishing Co., 1970. Chapters are included that review specific new educational programs for infants, preschoolers, and primary grade children; useful for a quick synopsis of the wide variety of programs that have been investigated in recent years.

Human Relationships

Hymes, J. L. *Teaching the child under six.* Columbus, Ohio: Charles E. Merrill Publishing Co., 1968. This warm, highly readable paperback contains a running discussion of the current "state of the art" in nursery school curriculum and excellent, down-to-earth discussions of what young children are like and what kinds of programs serve them most adequately.

Read, K. H. *The nursery school: a human relationships laboratory.* (5th ed.) Philadelphia: W. B. Saunders Co., 1971. This classic text emphasizes interpersonal relationships in relation to nursery school curriculum.

Planning and Spontaneity

Fowler, W. On the value of both play and structure in early education. *Young Children,* 1971, **27**(1), 24-36. This article contains a balanced, scholarly discussion of the value of structured and unstructured experience in fostering the development of young children.

Play

Hartley, R. E., Frank, L. K., and Goldenson, R. M. *Understanding children's play.* New York: Columbia University Press, 1952. This is a detailed discussion and analysis of the value of many different play materials for young children. Although an older book, this volume is still in print and is of real value to the early childhood teacher.

Putting a Good Program Together

Beyer, E. *Teaching young children.* New York: Pegasus, 1968. Part One contains a delightful narrative account of what an actual nursery school day is like. The book reads like a novel and yet conveys basic principles and values at the same time; highly recommended.

Schedules

Caldwell, B. M., and Richmond, J. Appendix B: a "typical day" for the groups at the Children's Center. In L. Dittman (Ed.), *Early child care: the new perspectives.* New York: Atherton Press, 1968. It is particularly interesting to look at this material because there are schedules printed side by side for infants, toddlers, and preschoolers.

Hildebrand, V. *Introduction to early childhood education.* New York: The Macmillan Co., 1971. Two approaches to scheduling, which should be helpful to the student who desires specific information on this subject, are discussed.

For the Advanced Student

Bissell, J. S. The cognitive effects of preschool programs for disadvantaged children. In J. L. Frost (Ed.), *Revisiting early childhood education: readings.* New York: Holt, Rinehart and Winston, Inc., 1973. In Bissell's reexamination and review of several studies of early childhood programs, she concludes that teacher-directed programs based on defined cognitive and language development goals are more effective in producing cognitive gains for preschool children than are programs that lack these characteristics.

Caldwell, B. M. What is the optimal learning environment for the young child? *American Journal of Orthopsychiatry,* 1967, **37**(1). This is a hard-hitting attack on some assumptions commonly held by child development people and nursery school teachers; stimulating and challenging.

Solomon, P., Kubzansky, P. E., Leiderman, P.H., Mendelson, J. H., Trumbull, R., and Wexler, D. *Sensory deprivation.* Cambridge, Mass.: Harvard University Press, 1965. Although this material deals with experiments conducted on adults, the results of sensory deprivation (the deprivation of experiential sensory input) also have serious educational implications for the development of children.

Santa Barbara County Head Start

CHAPTER 2

How to survive in nursery school
SUGGESTIONS AND GUIDELINES FOR THE FIRST WEEKS OF STUDENT TEACHING

> Supportive interaction between children stems of course from supportive acceptance from adults. A really well-functioning class is not based on rivalry. If children find their daily life satisfying, if their tasks are not too hard and not too easy, if they feel appropriately challenged, and if the teacher is on the whole supportive, trusting and respectful of people, then children will have no need to practice one-upmanship. In a group with a high level of "we" feeling, the individual is helped over the transition of starting new things, because failure has no threat.*

The first weeks of teaching are not easy, but they need not be impossible, either. However, it is wise for the student to make allowances for possible stress and not to be disappointed if she feels more tired than usual, or occasionally disheartened, or bewildered. These feelings will become less frequent as time passes and the children, staff, and routine become more familiar. They also diminish as the student gains more skills and confidence. The following material, which contains some basic principles of teaching and getting along in school, should help the student in this process.

CHOOSING A PLACE TO TEACH

The manner by which students are assigned to their practice-teaching schools varies considerably among colleges.

*From Hirsh, E. S. *Transition periods: stumbling blocks of education.* New York: Early Childhood Education Council of New York City, 1972. P. 7.

Sometimes students are allowed to select their placement from a list of satisfactory schools; sometimes the practice-teaching experience takes place in a demonstration school; and sometimes the student is assigned at the discretion of the supervising teacher.

Regardless of the method of assignment, the student should know there are many kinds of situations in which to work in the field of early childhood education. These can be divided into five main types: the private school, the cooperative, the compensatory program, the day care center, and the demonstration or laboratory school.

Private schools are so named because they do not depend on public funding for support. They are often half-day programs that tend to offer traditional nursery school curriculum based on the individual needs of the children. The program is likely to stress creativity and social and emotional adjustment. Such schools usually serve middle-class families, and they meet a real need for early childhood education in this portion of the community.

Cooperatives usually have fewer professional teachers and more mothers and fathers participating than private schools do, although they are private in the sense that they, too, do not usually have public funds for support. They offer the special enrichment provided by a high adult-child ratio, and the children who attend them also profit from the abundance of ideas furnished by so many different adults. There have been cooperative nursery schools in the United States for many years (Taylor, 1954), and the movement is flourishing anew on many college campuses where young families are banding together to provide care for their children by this relatively inexpensive method. It is still the case that many teachers enter the profession by participating in a well run co-op when their children are small, finding that they love to teach and going on to further training in early childhood education.

Head Start, a federally funded program, is the best known of the *compensatory programs,* since it exists on a nationwide basis. Some states also fund additional preschool programs designed to educate children from families of the poor (Education Commission of the States, 1971). Although termed compensatory because they were originally intended to compensate for lacks in the child's home environment, current investigations have found greater strengths in the homes than had previously been noted, and now the programs seek to honor these strengths as well as to compensate for lags in verbal and mental development.

Day care centers offer day-long child care. They usually serve the children of working mothers, some of whom are fairly wealthy and some of whom are quite poor. Funds for such care are provided both by parents and by state or public agencies. Good day care programs are delightful and valuable because of the leisurely pace and the extended learning experiences that they provide. Mediocre, custodial day care services are still a stain on the conscience of some communities and need to be remedied and modified for the welfare of the children (Keyserling, 1972).

Demonstration or laboratory schools are typically connected with teacher-training institutions or with research programs. They can be wonderful places for young students to begin their teaching, since they are most likely of all the kinds of schools to be child and *student* centered. Ideally, the student should have teaching opportunities in both laboratory and real-life schools so that she receives a balance of ideal and worldly teaching experiences.

SOME COMFORTING THOUGHTS

Do teachers matter? One of the outstanding characteristics of beginning teachers is the caring and involvement that they bring with them to their work, and it is heartening to remember that these characteristics are important factors in achieving success. Weikart (Weikart and Lambie, 1970), for example, found that no matter what kind of curricular model was followed (that of Piaget or Bereiter, or a more traditional model), the involvement of the teacher and her implementation of the curriculum was fundamental to the success of the outcome. Another researcher (Katz, 1969) attributed the failure of a program she studied to the fact that the teachers gave lip service to the curriculum but failed to carry it through in practice. Still another study (Scott, 1969) sought to separate successful from less successful head teachers and found that the successful teachers were characterized as being more spontaneous, in better control of the group, reaching their goals more often, showing more positive emotions, and *being more involved* (italics mine).

So, on days when things may not have gone just right, it may be a comfort to remember that caring and involvement are valuable qualities that the student already possesses and brings with her as positive assets to her teaching. It is, of course, an ancient truth that the more one puts into any experience, the more one gets out— and teaching is no exception.

The master teacher is probably ill at ease,

Santa Barbara County Head Start

too. Sometimes students are so wrapped up in their own shyness that they fail to realize that the teachers they are working with are shy of them as well. They attribute all the awkwardness of the first days on the job to their own insecurities and inexperience. Actually, the master teacher is willing to help, but may also be a little frightened, particularly if she has not had many students before. It will help her help the student if she knows that the student likes her.

One poor experience with a student will not ruin a child's life. Some conscientious new teachers are almost too sensitive to the effect their actions will have on the children. It is true that young children are more vulnerable to influences than older children are, and for this reason everyone attempts to do their very best; but the significance of the single traumatic experience has been overrated. It is usually the continuing approach or climate that molds the child. Therefore, the student need not agonize over one mishandled situation on the grounds that she may have scarred the child for life: this is actually a very unlikely result.

Making mistakes can turn a student into a better teacher. Of course, the student will make mistakes, but so will the teachers she works for. Rather than investing a lot of energy in regretting these errors, it is more healthy and productive for the student to learn by analyzing what went wrong and then deciding how to be more effective the next time. It is also helpful to repeat the experience as soon as possible (rather like getting back on a horse and riding again right away after you've fallen off) so that bad memories are supplanted by better ones.

The following excerpts illustrate how one student struggled and succeeded in profiting from her mistakes.

A Special Project on Dance
EVE ATKINSON

I planned to use records for part of the activity and also to have a time when the children could use instruments to make noise to move to. The first day, I planned to have a dance-type session which would deal primarily with the theme for this month, creek life. I got a record which I have known and loved since I was a child (the Grand Canyon Suite) and planned to use that at first, making a creek with our bodies. I felt that this would combine a lot of fun learning with motor coordination and would also be very interesting to the children.

Actual outcome: first day

To start with, the record player was not available. This didn't worry me too much, since I had already planned to have the children use the instruments for music. . . . [The dance session began well, but then] we went on being all the different animals that lived in the creek, but the group slowly got smaller. I think that they began to get disinterested for many reasons, one being the fact that there was no music, and, since I had to move around with them while I played a tambourine, it wasn't adequate. Also, there was another student in the room, but she did not participate or help. I was all the time having to handle other things besides just the dancing. For example, there was one small girl (3 years old) who needed special care, as she has only been here a few days. She wanted me to hold her, and every time I bent down, she jumped on me and wanted to be picked up and cuddled. I gave her as much as I possibly could without losing the group, but it got to be so bad that I had to leave the room to take her to another area where she might be able to get involved, or at least get the attention she needed. When I came back, the group had completely fallen apart. I think that I simply should have asked the other student to take the child elsewhere instead of my leaving.

Conclusions

I'm rather disillusioned about the activity because I had to alter my plans so much during the morning. I feel that if it were better planned, or perhaps if I had planned for a longer time period of different things, or movements and different types of music (lack of the record player was contributing to this problem), that the first group would have held together better. Next time, I certainly would make sure that I was going to be able to have new things ready. . . . Another thing that I think is necessary is to have an adequate person on hand to take care of any problems which I can't solve without taking my attention away from the group.

Second day

This day worked out lovely! I learned an awful lot about how to go about the activity from the previous day. I made sure I had the record player, and I also made sure Clevonease [the head teacher] would come by and see how I was doing, in case I needed any assistance. I planned everything, and had listened to the music enough so that I knew what we might do when the music varied. I decided not to use any instruments, since they were only in the way yesterday. I wanted to use the same theme each day of this session, and also to have basically the same children, so I again concentrated on the creek.

I first set up the lower room with the tables on one side, and also put out a few cognitive activities on one table. (I put these out because on Thursday I found that when the dancing was done I really needed to have something else that the children could get involved in right away.)

Actual outcome: second day

. . . I put the record back on, as I could see that they were all very enthusiastic about doing it again. The music came to the "sinking" part, and I was surprised that they recognized this and said it was time to go into the water. They did many things without my saying much at all. They were anxious to blow the bubbles and did this several times. At the change in the music, the children began to "swim up," and we reached the part where we start back to where we began. They did this completely through to the end.

Conclusions

I learned enough from the first experience so that I planned better for this one. I knew what I needed to do and to have, and I made sure that I followed through with these things. I realized that I had to really guide the children rather than just say, "Now, dance!" They need direction yet enough freedom to be an individual. . . . I feel it was an excellent experience for both myself and the children, as it flowed smoothly and the children responded so freely.

Now I realize that one person can control a group if all the children are able to get involved and contribute their ideas and feelings, and therefore it is absolutely necessary to make sure that any activity offers opportunities for the children to do this.

Third day

For my final day with this special project, I thought I would try to expand my activity from the second day, using more children. I knew what to say and how to act, since it worked so well on Friday. Unfortunately, things didn't go as I had thought they were going to. . . .

Actual outcome: third day

I began by going around the school and collecting children. I wanted to include those children that I had been with on the previous day, but it seemed as if most of them were very involved in other activities. Because of this, I simply told them I was going to be dancing in the lower room and that I would really like for them to come and join me after they were through. Anyway, I continued to collect children, and unfortunately I ended up with way too many. This was because I overlooked the fact that I would have children coming in the room to join us a little later. Some of the children who had danced with me before remembered what we had done and told the group about it. Then, one boy took off his shoes (this was the beginning of a catastrophe!), and then another child, and before I knew what was happening, the whole room was full of shoes and children with bare feet. I didn't know whether or not to have them all put their shoes on or whether it was better to simply start the dancing. I chose to do the latter, and for a very short while, this was all right to do. We proceeded to do the dance, waking up and stretching. This went fine until the time when we got up and began to move around. There simply were too many children. They all went to some place in the room and began playing games such as monsters and guns, or playing in the housekeeping corner. The group fell apart, and quite a few children went outside (still without their shoes). I had to fetch them back because it was cold outside and have them put their shoes on. This caused quite a difficulty, since the shoes were all mixed up and were all approximately the same. The children didn't know which were their shoes, and besides that, they simply did not want to put them on. By this time, the dancing had gotten completely wiped out, and so was I. The children did not want to put on or even find their own shoes. They were playing chase.

My savior was Kathy Wilson [another teacher at the Center]. She came in and saw the mess and offered her help, so I quickly explained the situation, and she right away said very firmly for each child to find his shoes and to put them on right now! I was amazed at how she got them to respond so quickly, since they right away attempted to get their shoes.

After the goers and stayers had been sorted out, we began the dancing again. It went well this time, with the children reacting creatively and enjoying themselves. A couple had danced with me all through this project, and I think this really gave them a sense of accomplishment. . . .

Conclusions

Too many children! I tried to do something which I simply couldn't do alone. With that many children, there has to be another teacher involved with the children, dancing and helping them. I should have left my plans the same as they were for the second day of the project, instead of planning something much beyond my and the children's capabilities. Also, I shouldn't have started the dancing without the children putting on their shoes first. If there was a small number of children or another teacher, then it wouldn't have mattered that the shoes were off, but as it was, the children weren't staying with the activity long enough to complete it and then to put on their shoes. They were leaving in the middle of it, and this wouldn't have mattered if their shoes had been on. Another thing I learned is that if you are going to let them take off their shoes, then make sure their socks get inside the shoes and also that the shoes are not in one pile but in separate areas of the room. . . .

From this experience I think I have learned a great thing—if something works smoothly, it doesn't mean that you have to attempt something twice as involved next time. I realize, too, that when a group gets into such a mess as this one did, the teacher really must speak out to the children so that the children know you mean business. That is why Kathy got the children to obey—they knew she meant put on their shoes, and they knew she was serious. For me, this was an upsetting defeat, and I felt really inadequate at first. Clevonease and I talked about it, and I learned the reason for taking off the shoes was that there had been a dance in-service session at the Center the day before, and everyone had been barefoot. It was as simple as that; the children remembered it and repeated it. The key to the whole thing though, and Clevonease agreed, was just that I had too many children for the number of adults, which was something like one teacher to thirteen children. It should have been limited to four or five, right from the beginning. After I thought about it for a while, I accepted the fact that one learns from mistakes, and I knew I had learned an awful lot, and so I know it wasn't wasted time but actually very valuable.

[I might add that Eve has since gone on to be a very accomplished young teacher.]

BASIC PROFESSIONAL ETHICS

Now that the student is becoming a member of a profession, it will be helpful to know from the beginning some ethical guidelines that are observed by most teachers.

Strive to be fair to all the children. The most important guideline to observe is that all children deserve a fair chance and a reasonable amount of concern from each teacher. Perhaps the student will recall situations in her own school life where a teacher made a scapegoat of some child and picked on him continually, or where another teacher never seemed to notice some of the youngsters. Although nobody intends to have this kind of thing happen, sometimes it does, and teachers should be warned against behaving this way. Every child is important and is entitled to be valued by his teacher.

Keep personal problems private during the day. Teachers should not discuss their personal problems or emotional difficulties with the parents; nor should they discuss them with other teachers while school is in session. Teachers need to leave personal problems at the door as they begin the day, since the time at nursery school rightfully belongs to the children. The discussion of personal matters should take place after the children have gone home.

Show respect for the child. One important way nursery school teachers demonstrate basic respect for others is by refraining from discussing a child in his presence unless he is included directly in the conversation. Sometimes teachers thoughtlessly talk over the children's heads, assuming that the youngsters are unaware of what is being said. But if the student has ever had the experience of eavesdropping while people were discussing her, she will no doubt remember the special potency of that overheard comment. Anything said about a child in his presence needs to be said with him included. Thus it is more desirable to say, "David, I can see you're feeling pretty tired and hungry," than to cock an eyebrow in his direction and remark to another teacher, "Brother, we sure are in a nasty temper today!"

An even more fundamental aspect of respect between teacher and child can best be described as a valuing of the person: the teacher who truly respects and values the child pauses to listen to him with her entire attention whenever this is possible; she remembers that each child is a unique person and relishes him for his differences from his companions, and she allows him to generate ideas of his own rather than subtly teaching him it is better to unquestioningly accept the teacher's ideas as being best.

This kind of respect is, of course, a two-way street. The teacher who holds the child in such respectful regard sets a model for the youngster, who will in time reflect this same fundamental consideration back to her. This process can be accelerated and strengthened if the teacher quietly makes a point of protecting her own rights as well as the children's. She may say something as simple as, "Now, Margaret, I've listened to you; take just a minute and hear what I want to say," or she may make this same point with another child by saying, "You know, my desk is just like your cubby. I don't take your things out of that, and you must never take anything out of my desk, either."

Observe professional discretion. Still another aspect of respect for people is respect for the family's privacy. Family affairs and children's behavior should not be discussed with people outside the

school who have no need to know about them: even amusing events should never be told unless the names of the children involved are either not mentioned or are changed. Most communities are smaller worlds than a beginning teacher may realize, and news can travel with astonishing rapidity.

In general, student teachers should be wary of being drawn into discussions with parents about their own or other families' children. This kind of discussion is the teacher's prerogative, and it is a wise student who passes off questions about youngsters by making some pleasant remark and referring the parent to the teacher. Nobody is ever antagonized by a student who does this in a tactful way, but disasters can result from well-meant comments by ill-informed or tactless beginners.

In addition, the student should not discuss with outsiders situations she disapproves of at the school where she works. These remarks have an unpleasant way of returning to the source, and the results can be awkward, to say the least. The principle "if you don't say it, they can't repeat it" is a sound one here. It is better, instead, to talk the problem over in confidence with the college supervisor.

Observe the chain of command. In just about every organization there is a chain of command. It is always wise to avoid going over anyone's head when making a comment or request. Understandably, teachers hate being put in a bad light by a student's talking a problem over with the school director before talking it over with the teacher herself.

A related aspect of this authority structure is being sure to get permission before planning a special event such as a field trip or getting out the hoses after a film on water play. Answers to such requests are generally "yes," but it is always best to check before embarking on a major venture.

SOME RECOMMENDATIONS FOR STARTING OUT

Although not always possible, it helps to find some things out before beginning the first student-teaching day. First, it is helpful to talk with the teacher and determine what time she expects the student to arrive and the kind of clothes she recommends for her school. The question of clothing can be something of a crusade among the young today, but the student-teaching placement is not the place to do battle on the subject. Most schools are pretty reasonable and will recommend sensible clothes. Slacks are frequently worn. An apron with a deep pocket is a decided asset. Besides dressing practically, the student should look as bright and pretty as possible, although many of the children will see her as beautiful no matter what she wears.

Some schools have written guidelines they can give the student to read. Time schedules and lists of rules are also very helpful to review. If the school does not have these things written down, the student should ask the teacher how basic routines such as eating and taking children to the toilet are handled, and she should ask about crucial safety rules and for a brief review of the schedule. If the student can come for a visit when the children aren't there, the teacher will have a better opportunity to take her on a tour of the school. During this visit the student can make a special point of finding out where the children's cubbies are, where sponges and cleanup materials are kept, and where various supplies are stored.

PRACTICAL THINGS TO DO TO INCREASE COMPETENCE

Gain confidence in your ability to control the group. Almost invariably, the first thing students want to discuss is discipline. Since this is the point everyone seems most frightened about, it is recommended that the student begin her preparation for work by reading the chapter on discipline in order to ease her mind and help build her skills in this area. This review of theory will help, but observation and practice are the best way to gain competence in handling children.

Get to know the children as soon as possible. One way to become familiar with each child is to make a list of their names from the sign-in sheet and then jot down a few adjectives or facts to remember about each one. Calling the children by name at every opportunity will help, too. It won't take more than a day or two to become well acquainted.

Develop the proverbial "eyes in the back of the head." One of the commonest failings of inexperienced teachers is their tendency to focus on only one child at a time. It is pleasant to sit down and read a favorite book with one or two lovable children and ignore the chaos going on in the block corner. Good nursery school teachers have formed the habit of total awareness. This is true outdoors as well as inside, but to say that the teacher should never plan to settle down with any group would be an exaggeration. Of course, the teacher has to center her attention on specific children from time to time, or there is no satisfaction to the experience for either of them, but she has to keep tuned to the whole room as well. Sometimes such a simple technique as learning to look up frequently will help the student build skills in this area. Another technique is sitting so that the whole room or whole playground can be seen. Many beginning students sit with their backs to half the room—this is simply courting trouble.

Take action in unsafe situations. Since students are sometimes afraid of appearing too restrictive in our liberal nursery school atmosphere, they allow dangerous things to happen because they do not know the rule or school policy about it. The general rule of thumb is that when one is unsure whether the activity is dangerous, it is better to stop it and then check to see what the teacher thinks. Stopping a few activities that are safe is better than letting two children wrestle each other off the top of the slide while the student debates indecisively below. Things will generally look less dangerous to the student as she gains experience and feels less anxious, *but it is always better to be safe than sorry.*

Encourage the growth of independence and competence; avoid overteaching, overhelping, and overtalking. As a general principle, we encourage children in nursery school to do everything they can for themselves.

Santa Barbara City College Children's Center

This is different from the behavior of the teacher who sees her role as doing to and doing for children. It takes self-control to wait while John fumbles for the zipper, insight to see how to assist him without taking over, and self-control not to talk too much while he is learning. But building competencies in the children by letting them do things for themselves increases their self-esteem so much that practicing restraint is worth the effort.

Encourage originality of self-expression. One of the most frowned-on things the student can do is make a model of something for the children to copy when she is working with creative materials. It is easy to be trapped into making someone a snake or drawing a man for another youngster, but early childhood teachers dislike providing such models because they limit the child's expression of his own feelings and ideas. It is better to relish the materials with the children and help them use them for their own purposes.

Keep contacts with the children as quiet and meaningful as possible. Except in a real emergency, the student should walk over to the child to talk with him rather than calling across the room. She should use a low voice and bend down so he can see her face and be less overwhelmed by her size. (An excellent way to find out how big an adult is from a child's point of view is to ask a friend to stand up and teach you something while you remain sitting on the floor. It's enlightening.)

Expect to do menial tasks. No other profession requires the full range of abilities and effort that preschool teaching does. These extend from inspiring children and counseling parents to doing the most menial types of cleanup. Sometimes students do not realize this and so feel imposed upon because they are asked to change a pair of pants or mop the floor or clean the guinea pig, but this kind of work is expected of almost all nursery school teachers as just part of nursery school life. Not only is cleaning up to be expected, but it is also necessary to straighten up continually as the morning progresses. Blocks should be rearranged on shelves and costumes rehung several times a morning to keep the room looking attractive. (Unfortunately, there is no good fairy who will come along and do this.)

Learn from the start to be ingenious about creating equipment and scrounging materials. Nursery schools almost always operate on lean budgets, and every school develops a number of ingenious ways to stretch money and invent equipment. The student can learn a lot from each place she works by picking up these economical ideas from the staff, and she can contribute much by sharing her own ideas about the creative use of materials and new sources of free supplies. She should learn to be on the lookout for so-called waste materials that other businesses throw away; the carpet company's colorful scraps can make handsome additions to the collage box, and rubber tires can be used in fascinating ways to make sturdy play equipment.

Try to be organized. It is very helpful to arrive early on each teaching day so there is time to get everything together in advance for the morning or afternoon. Nothing beats the feeling of security this preparation breeds. Life is also easier if the student checks before going home to find out what will be happening the next time she comes. This makes it possible to read up on fingerpainting or woodworking before having to embark on these activities.

It also helps to know the schedule well enough to tell what is going to happen next as well as what time it is likely to happen. This allows time for cleanup and also helps avoid the disappointment of moving into a new activity just as the group is expected to wash up for lunch.

When help is needed, ask for it. People aren't usually critical if a beginner admits she doesn't know something and has the courage to ask, but they are inclined to resent the student who protects herself by appearing to know everything already. When one is unsure of a policy at the school, it never does any harm to say to the child, "I don't know if it's all right to climb on the fence. Let's go check with Miss Clancy, and then we'll both know."

The chance to chat with the master teacher while cleaning up at the end of the morning, or at some other convenient time of day, is an invaluable time to raise problems and ask questions. During the day itself, students often have to do what the English call "muddling through"—learning by observation and using their own common sense. Nothing disastrous is likely to take place, and teachers are usually too busy to be corralled for more than a sentence or two of explanation while school is in progress.

SOME SPECIAL PROBLEMS

The following problems have come up often enough with students that they deserve discussion. Of course, because each situation is different, recommendations are risky. Nevertheless, the following suggestions may provide solutions that may not have occurred to the student.

What to do if you hate the nursery school to which you are assigned. We have already mentioned that there are several different types of nursery schools and that the same type varies a good deal from school to school. Some schools seem to suit some students, and others fit other students better. Therefore, it is important not to conclude that teaching is not for you just because one placement is less than satisfactory. Maybe a change to another school is the answer to the problem; maybe it isn't. At any rate, the place to begin solving the difficulty is by talking over the reason for the unhappiness with the supervising teacher from the college. This is a more productive as well as more ethical solution than complaining to a friend.

It is also wise to refrain from making snap judgments about a teacher or placement. The first 2 or 3 weeks in any school will be some of the most stressful weeks of the student's career, and it's well to realize that some people react to stress by attacking what is frightening them; others shrink up and feel paralyzed or disillusioned. As time passes, the strain will probably become less, and the school may seem more attractive, a little the way hospital food mysteriously improves as the patient recovers.

What to do if you don't like a child. It's no sin to dislike a child; but it *is* a sin not to admit your dislike, come to terms with it, and try to do something about it. Sometimes what will help most is getting to know him better, since insight often breeds compassion. Sometimes making progress of some sort with him helps. Sometimes figuring out why you dislike him will ease the feeling. With beginning students this can often be traced to the fact that some children challenge adults or put them on the spot. Students who already feel insecure find this behavior particularly trying. Whatever the reason, it is more healthy to risk admitting your dislike to yourself and perhaps to your master teacher if you feel safe with her and then to work toward resolving the problem. Although the suggested remedies may not overcome the dislike completely, they should help. At the very least, it is always possible to be fair and decent to all the children. Probably the liking will come in time.

THE WAY TO YOUR MASTER TEACHER'S HEART

We've already talked about the fact that it takes time to feel at home and to build a friendship with the master teacher. There are three more specific things the student can do that will help generate friendliness. The first is to be prepared to make the small, extra contribution of time and energy *beyond* what is expected. The student who stays the extra 10 minutes on pot luck night to dry the coffee pot is well on her way to becoming a popular member of the staff.

The second thing is to offer help before being asked to lend a hand. Some students are so afraid of being pushy or of making mistakes that they never volunteer. But always having to request help gets very

tiresome for the master teacher, even if the student is willing when asked. It is better to develop an eye for all the little things that must be done and then to do them quietly. Such students are treasured by their master teachers.

Finally, the student should let her enthusiasm show through. The vast majority of nursery school teachers follow their profession because they love it; the rigors of the job and the relatively low pay weed out the others very quickly. The teachers are, therefore, enthusiastic themselves. They're often "born" teachers, and they love teaching students as well as little children. Expressing thanks by being enthusiastic will encourage them to keep on making the extra effort entailed in guiding student teachers.

SUMMARY

The student should grasp three basic principles before beginning to teach in the nursery school: master teachers are human, too; one poor experience won't ruin a child's life; and mistakes can be turned into valuable learning opportunities.

Even beginning students need to observe professional ethics when they are teaching. It is particularly important to respect each child and to preserve the privacy of the families whose children attend the school.

Gaining knowledge of the school's basic routines, schedules, and policies will make the early days of teaching a more comfortable experience for the young teacher. Some practical things to do that will increase the student's competence include gaining confidence in handling discipline situations, getting to know the children, being alert to the whole environment, taking swift action in situations that are dangerous, encouraging the growth of independence and originality of self-expression, making contact with the children as quietly and meaningfully as possible, being organized, and asking for help when needed.

Probably no other time in the life of the nursery school teacher is so exciting, unsettling, and challenging as the first days of student teaching. Teachers are fortunate who manage to retain at least some of this flutter of anticipation throughout their teaching lives.

QUESTIONS

1. Getting started in the first days of student teaching can be a special challenge, and it is helpful to know yourself and your own reactions well enough to be able to control them. How do you anticipate you will cope with the strangeness and unfamiliarity of the student teaching experience when you are just beginning? Close your eyes and think back to the last two or three occasions when you entered a new group and got acquainted. What was your personal mode of adapting? Did you talk a lot? Clam up? Act extremely helpful? Or . . . ?
2. If you were guiding a young, new teacher, what advice would you give her that might help her through her first days of teaching?
3. Do you believe that master teachers and professors are ever nervous or frightened when dealing with students, or do they seem invulnerable to such difficulties?
4. What are some examples in your own experience with teachers where you felt the teacher genuinely respected the people she was teaching? In these instances what were specific ways you felt this respect was demonstrated? How could these approaches be carried over in your own student teaching?
5. List some effective "dos" and "don'ts" for making friends with young children.

REFERENCES FOR FURTHER READING

Overviews

Hymes, J. L. *Early childhood education: an introduction to the profession.* Washington, D.C.: National Association for the Education of Young Children, 1968. In conversational style, Dr. Hymes describes services provided by Head Start, day care, private nursery schools, and so forth, then discusses current problems and needs, and finishes with an enthusiastic statement of the satisfaction inherent in teaching young children.

Tarnay, E. D. *What does the nursery school teacher teach?* Washington, D.C.: National Association for the Education of Young Children, 1965. This pamphlet presents a quick overview of what traditional nursery school education is all about and identifies the underlying educational purpose of nursery school activities. Reprinted many times, it remains one of the best short descriptions of traditional early childhood educational practice.

Books on Specific Kinds of Schools

Beyer, E. *Teaching young children.* New York: Pegasus, 1968. In a delightful description of a nursery school, Beyer reflects the best of the traditional nursery school values and approaches.

Greenberg, P. *The Devil has slippery shoes: a biased biogaphy of the Child Development Group of Mississippi.* New York: The Macmillan Co., 1970. The trials and tribulations of the Child Development Group of Mississippi in the early days of Head Start are described; still the best book that has ever been written about Head Start.

Roby, P. *Child care—who cares? Foreign and domestic infant and early childhood development policies.* New York: Basic Books, Inc., Publishers, 1973. This collection of articles about day care touches on many aspects of this subject.

Taylor, K. W. *Parent cooperative nursery schools.* New York: Columbia University Press, 1954. This older book is filled with practical advice on running a cooperative nursery school.

Achieving Meaningful Contact with Children

Ashton-Warner, S. *Teacher.* New York: Bantam Books, Inc., 1965. The author provides a fascinating description of how she, a beginning teacher, came to know the Maori children and how she developed a system of teaching reading based on what was significant in the children's lives.

Carson, R. *The sense of wonder.* New York: Harper & Row, Publishers, 1956. This book is best summed up by quoting from Mrs. Carson herself. "If a child is to keep alive his inborn sense of wonder . . . he needs the companionship of at least one adult who can share it, rediscovering with him the joy, excitement and mystery of the world we live in."

Helping Children Become Independent

Neill, A. S. *Summerhill.* New York: Hart Publishing Co. Inc., 1960. Although this book describes a progressive English school for older children, it has delighted teachers who teach all ages by its emphasis on trusting the young to act in their own best behalf.

Sources of Inexpensive Materials

Hodgden, L., Koetter, J., Laforse, B., McCord, S., & Schramm, D. *School before six: a diagnostic approach.* St. Ann, Miss.: Central Midwestern Regional Educational Laboratory, 1970. This sturdy compendium of suggestions has an appendix entitled "Trash to Treasures," which is a gold mine of suggestions of inexpensive and free supplies and equipment.

Monahan, R. *Free and inexpensive materials for preschool and early childhood.* Belmont, Calif.: Lear Siegler/Fearon Publishers, 1973. In this invaluable resource are lists of things to send away for, ranging from pamphlets on mental health to educational films and National Dairy Council pictures.

Increasing the Teacher's Self-knowledge

Jersild, A. *When teachers face themselves.* New York: Teachers College Press, 1955. How to face and cope with emotional problems common to members of the teaching profession is discussed in a matter-of-fact, helpful way.

For the Advanced Student

Combs, A. W. (Chm.) *Perceiving behaving becoming: a new focus for education,* Yearbook, 1962. Washington, D.C.: Association for Supervision and Curriculum Development, National Education Association, 1962. This is a wonderfully readable and inspiring overview of the humanistic approach to education; includes articles by Rogers, Maslow, and Kelley and talks about the positive effects of basing curriculum on an attitude of confidence and trust in the student.

PART **TWO**

Fostering physical well-being

Los Niños Head Start

CHAPTER 3

Handling routines in the nursery school

The lunch period should be an occasion for the enjoyment of good food in a social situation. I can remember my first experience as an assistant teacher in an all-day program. Lunch was rolled into the classroom on a wagon. Children (already bibbed) were lying on cots for a pre-lunch rest. Teachers served the plates and summoned the children to the tables. *Everything* on the plate had to be eaten before melba toast chunks were distributed (these were great favorites!) and finally dessert and milk. There was one particularly dismal meal which appeared weekly: a barely poached egg (the white still transparent) sitting on top of some dreary spinach. No one liked it, and one little girl finally refused to eat it. She sat stolidly before the offensive plate, quietly but firmly asserting, "I won't eat it. I hate it. It's not even cooked." The teacher finally removed the plate to the kitchen with the comment that it would be waiting for her after her nap.

After nap, Jill was escorted to the kitchen to be confronted with the cool mess of uncooked egg and spinach. She was told that she could return to the playroom after she had eaten it.

When she returned to the playroom, the teacher asked her if she had eaten her lunch. Jill answered, "Yes, and then I throwed it up." And she had!*

Routines, those omnipresent recurring sequences of behavior, constitute the backbone of the nursery school day and serve as landmarks that divide it into different sections. They typically include the activities of arriving, departing, eating, toileting, and resting.

Adequate handling of routines can foster both emotional and physical health. In recent years teachers have tended to be more aware of the significance of routines in relation to emotional health than aware of the physical significance of good nutrition and adequate rest. But the pasty faces, vulnerability to illness, and low energy levels of many children in compensatory programs now serve to remind us that physical health is vital to well-being and that our young children need these routines to help them build strong bodies as well as stable personalities.

It was surprising to discover that although routines involve a good portion of the day at nursery school and although strong feelings and convictions of what is "right" abound, very little research has been carried out in these areas. What re-

---

*From *Teaching young children* (p. 124), by Evelyn Beyer, copyright © 1968, by Western Publishing Company, Inc., reprinted by permission of The Bobbs-Merrill Company, Inc.

search there is deals with nutrition and the emotional process of attachment and separation rather than with the investigation of alternative ways to handle routines in school. Therefore, the student should understand that the following discussion is based on a concensus of generally followed practice and that the recommendations rest on experience and opinion and are not validated by research.

One other note of caution about routines: if the teacher is unwise enough to go to war with a child on the subject of routines, the child, if he is so inclined, can always win. Thus a child who absolutely won't eat, won't use the toilet, or refuses to go to sleep can win any time he wants to; there is little the teacher can do about it. Fortunately, teachers and children rarely reach this kind of impasse, but it is well to understand that such power struggles can happen and have happened and that the commonest way to bring about such a disaster is to reduce oneself to attempting to force a child to comply with any routine absolutely against his will. It just doesn't work.

The best way to prevent conflicts from developing is to realize that children usually find comfort in reasonable routines that contribute to their physical well-being. It also helps if the teacher determines what the most important learnings are to be derived from each routine and then works toward achieving those goals rather than becoming caught up in "winning" for its own sake. For example, it is more important that a child learn to enjoy food and take pleasure in mealtimes than it is that he clear his plate, wait until everyone is served, or not rap his glass on the table. Bearing this primary goal in mind will reduce the amount of criticism and control that may otherwise mar snack and lunch times.

TRANSITIONS INTO ROUTINES

Handling transition times between play activities and a routine such as lunch can be a little tricky until the teacher gets the hang of it. It always helps to warn once in advance when a change is in the offing. It also helps to remember that transitions do not usually present an opportunity for a real choice (the child is supposed to come, not linger in the yard), so it is best not to ask, "Would you like to come in?" but to say more definitely, "In just a minute it's going to be time for lunch, and we will go indoors. What do you suppose we're having today?" Occasionally, singing a simple song such as "Here We Go a Marching" will also help get children moving in the desired direction.

ROUTINES OF ARRIVAL AND DEPARTURE

It is natural for young children to feel anxious when their mothers leave them at nursery school. This feeling, called *separation anxiety,* appears to be strongest in American children between the ages of 10 to 18 months (Mussen, Conger, and Kagan, 1969). Even beyond this age, however, separation requires time and tactful handling by the staff in order that the child and his mother come to feel comfortable about parting.

Although some research (Schwarz and Wynn, 1971) indicates that many 4-year-olds can adjust rapidly to a school situation without their mothers having to linger, it is not safe to make a blanket rule about this, since there are always individual cases where a child becomes panicky when left behind. This seems to be particularly true for 3-year-olds (Cox and Campbell, 1968) and for retarded children (Kessler, Gridth, and Smith, 1968).

Introducing the child to school gradually

It is common practice and good sense to recommend a visit to nursery school by parent and child for the first day, and then another short stay while the mother leaves briefly, followed by a gradual extension of time as the child's ability to endure separation increases. However, working mothers whose jobs demand that they appear promptly at 8:00, no matter what the nursery school teacher recommends or how hard the child is crying, are not considered in this ideal prescription. If at all possible, special arrangements should be made for such families when their children begin nursery school. A grandmother, father, or aunt might be pressed into service and stay while the child makes friends. Sometimes the mother can bring him by for a visit around lunch time, or the teacher can make a Saturday visit to the home, or the child can come to school with a friend. Any of these arrangements, while not ideal, is preferable to allowing the child to walk in and simply be left in a strange place with strange people for 9 hours on his first day.

Handling outbursts of emotion

It helps to recognize that a child must often deal with three feelings when his mother leaves him (Furman, 1972): grief (the emotion that seems most obvious and logical), fear (also not very surprising) and anger (the emotion that the teacher is least likely to recognize in these circumstances). It is often necessary not only to comfort and reassure the child but also to recognize with him that he feels angry with his mother because she left him at school. I recall one forthright 3-year-old who took real pleasure in biting the mama doll with our toothy rubber hippopotamus as soon as her mother departed. The teacher may also see this angry reaction at being left behind come out at the end of the day when the child insists he wants to stay at school and does not want to go home. If the teacher interprets the true reason for this reaction to his mother, it will help maintain friendly relations all around.

Actually, it is the children who make a forthright fuss as their mothers leave who seem to work through their feelings of loss with the greatest expedition, whereas the child who apparently makes an easy adjustment by becoming instantly involved in activities often becomes downcast a few weeks later as he lowers his defenses; if this happens 3 to 4 weeks after entry to school, the mother is likely to assume something has happened there that makes him want to stay home. The best protection against this conclusion is to explain casually to his mother *before his facade crumbles* that the child may show his grief at a later time and that most chil-dren feel some sadness and loneliness when left at school.

It is also wise to prepare parents for the fact that children may go through a milder attack of separation anxiety again when they return from vacation. Otherwise, this repeated behavior can discourage parents who have had a hard time getting away to start with. Other unexpected circumstances can also trigger anxiety. Last spring the children in our Center walked to the college cafeteria and met their mothers there for lunch. All went well until it came time to part, and suddenly we had several very unhappy children on our hands. The unusual circumstances had made parting difficult once again for our small charges.

But learning to let go is part of becoming mature. A nice balance of comfort combined with a matter-of-fact expectation that he will feel better soon usually gets the child started on the day. Having something at hand that he especially enjoys will help, too. The teacher must take care that she permits the child to form a relationship with her as a bridge to the other children yet at the same time does not encourage this so much that the youngster droops around longer than necessary or becomes a careerist hand holder.

ROUTINES THAT CENTER AROUND EATING
Importance of adequate nutrition

In these days of plastic foods and casual eating habits, it is important to emphasize the value of good food for young children. Too many schools depend on artificial juices and a cracker for snack supposedly on the grounds that the children are well fed at home, but the underlying reasons for serving this kind of food are that it is convenient and cheap. Yet there is a great wave of studies, such as those by Birch and Gussow (1970) and Scrimshaw (1969), that indicate that good nutrition is closely linked to the ability to pay attention and learn.

Although nutritional problems are most severe among the poor, it isn't only the children in compensatory programs who are "orphans of wealth." We must also include our more well-to-do youngsters, some of whom subsist on potato chips, candy bars, and pop. For this reason, daily dietary requirements are listed in Tables 1 and 2. It is almost impossible to meet these requirements unless the nursery school does its part by supplying fruits, vegetables, milk, and other protein during the day.

The way to achieve good nutrition is to serve wholesome, well-balanced snacks and lunches. Dessert should be fruit in some form and should be regarded as a nutritional component of the meal, not a reward to be bargained for. Variety, particularly as the year progresses and the children feel at ease, should be a keynote

Table 1. The basic four (diet pattern to be used every day in the United States and its

Pattern	
1. Milk Children: under 9—2 to 3 cups 9 to 12—3 or more cups 13 to 18—4 or more cups Over 18—2 or more cups	Whole, skim, buttermilk, dry, evaporated (to drink or combine with other foods), cheese, ice cream, yogurt 1 eight-oz. cup of milk = $1^1/_2$ oz. or $1^1/_2$-inch cube Cheddar-type cheese $1^1/_2$ cups cottage cheese 2 cups cream cheese 3 or 4 tablespoons powdered milk† 2 cups ice cream
2. Vegetable-fruit 1 serving citrus or substitute 1 serving dark green or deep yellow vegetable at least every other day 2 servings other fruits or vegetables; potatoes may count as one of these servings	Orange, grapefruit, lemon, lime, tangerine, tomatoes, strawberries, melon, raw cabbage, etc. Adult serving size is $^1/_2$ to $^2/_3$ cup
3. Meat 2 or more servings	Meat, poultry, fish, eggs and their substitutes of legumes, nuts, lentils Adult serving size is cooked lean meat or fish—2 or more oz.‡ or $^1/_2$ cup diced raw lean meat or fish—3 or more oz. eggs—2 medium size legumes—1 cup cooked peanut butter—$^1/_4$ cup (4 T.) nuts—$^1/_2$ cup
4. Cereal-bread 4 or more servings	Whole-grain, enriched or restored: rice, wheat, rye, barley, oats, corn Adult serving is 1 oz. ($^3/_4$ cup) ready-to-eat 1 slice bread (approximately 1 oz.) $^1/_2$ to $^3/_4$ cup cooked breakfast cereal, rice, hominy, cornmeal, Italian pasta $1^1/_2$ oz. baked goods has about 1 oz. flour

* From Howe, P. S. *Basic nutrition in health and disease.* (5th ed.) Philadelphia: W. B. Saunders
† Amount used depends upon size of granule; follow label instructions.
‡ Dividing 1 pound of ground meat into five equal portions would give, when cooked, five servings
Note: Use other foods as desired to meet calorie needs and to increase palatability. Use water or

of the food program. Snacks should be different every day and can be based on seasonal fruits and vegetables to keep budgets within reason.

The teacher should realize that some children eat more than others do. The quantity consumed is a matter of physiological differences and also a function of how fast the child is growing; appetite is also related to emotional states and needs. All of these factors must be considered when deciding whether a child's nutrition patterns are adequate. As long as he remains healthy and his color is good, there is little need to worry about whether he is eating a lot or a little.

nutritive value)*

Principal nutrients in the food groups

The milk group is the best source of calcium and riboflavin.
It also contains protein, phosphorus, carbohydrate, thiamine, and vitamin D (if it has been added); whole milk has fat and vitamin A; vitamin A is sometimes added to nonfat milk products.
Do not substitute calcium tablets, because they do not contain protein or riboflavin.
Do not substitute cream, because it is the fat content of milk.
Do not substitute condensed milk, because it has a very high sugar content.

All vegetables and fruits contain sugar, starch, cellulose, and varying amounts of vitamins and minerals.
Citrus fruits and tomatoes are the principal cources of vitamin C in many diets. Other good sources are cantaloupe, strawberries, broccoli, Brussels sprouts, and raw, green, sweet, or red peppers.
Fair sources of vitamin C include other melons and berries, raw cabbage, asparagus, cauliflower, and the green leaves of collards, kale, mustard, turnips, or spinach.
Dark green or deep yellow vegetables are good sources of vitamin A. The leafy green vegetables contain iron.
Potatoes have thiamine, iron, and vitamin C.
Other fruits and vegetables should not be substituted for the fruits and vegetables which are listed as high in vitamins A and C.

The meat group supplies protein, iron, thiamine, niacin, fat, phosphorus, and some riboflavin.
Liver is an excellent source of vitamin A and iron.
Salt-water fish contains iodine.
Eggs have protein, iron, thiamine, phosphorus, riboflavin, and the yolk has vitamin A and fat.
The protein in legumes is a lower quality than that found in meat, fish, and eggs.
Nuts yield fat, protein, iron, thiamine, riboflavin, and niacin.

All cereals contain starch and some incomplete protein.
Whole grain cereals contain cellulose.
If whole grain, restored, or enriched, the cereal will be a good source of iron, thiamine, riboflavin, and niacin.

Co., 1971.

of approximately 2 ounces. This is due to shrinkage during cooking.
other beverages: adult—6 to 8 cups, child—4 to 6 cups.

Table 2. Recommended food intake for good nutrition according to food groups and the average size of servings at different age levels*

Food group	Servings per day	Average size of servings					
		1 year	*2-3 years*	*4-5 years*	*6-9 years*	*10-12 years*	*13-15 years*
Milk and cheese (1.5 oz. cheese = 1 C. milk) (C. = 1 cup—8 oz. or 240 gm.)	4	$^1/_2$ C.	$^1/_2$-$^3/_4$ C.	$^3/_4$ C.	$^3/_4$-1 C.	1 C.	1 C.
Meat group (protein foods) Egg	3 or more	1	1	1	1	1	1 or more
Lean meat, fish, poultry (liver once a week)		2 Tbsp.	2 Tbsp.	4 Tbsp.	2-3 oz. (4-6 Tbsp.)	3-4 oz.	4 oz. or more
Peanut butter			1 Tbsp.	2 Tbsp.	2-3 Tbsp.	3 Tbsp.	3 Tbsp.
Fruits and vegetables Vitamin C source (citrus fruits, berries, tomato, cabbage, cantaloupe)	At least 4, including: 1 or more (twice as much tomato as citrus)	$^1/_3$ C. citrus	$^1/_2$ C.	$^1/_2$ C.	1 medium orange	1 medium orange	1 medium orange
Vitamin A source (green or yellow fruits and vegetables)	1 or more	2 Tbsp.	3 Tbsp.	4 Tbsp. ($^1/_4$ C.)	$^1/_4$ C.	$^1/_3$ C.	$^1/_2$ C.
Other vegetables (potato and legumes, etc.) *or*	2	2 Tbsp.	3 Tbsp.	4 Tbsp. ($^1/_4$ C.)	$^1/_3$ C.	$^1/_2$ C.	$^3/_4$ C.
Other fruits (apple, banana, etc.)		$^1/_4$ C.	$^1/_3$ C.	$^1/_2$ C.	1 medium	1 medium	1 medium

*From Nelson, W. E., Vaughan, V. C. III, and McKay, R. J. *Textbook of pediatrics.* (9th ed.) Philadelphia: W. B. Saunders Co. 1969. Prepared in collaboration with Mildred J. Bennett, Ph.D., from "Four Food Groups of the Daily Food Guide," Institute of Home Economics, U.S.D.A, and Publication 30, Children's Bureau of the United States Department of Health, Education, and Welfare.

Some basic principles having to do with eating

There is perhaps no area in our social life except the area of sex that has as many restrictions and regulations attached to it as eating does. A class of mine once counted up the rules enforced by their families about mealtimes. We thought of 43 rules within 10 minutes. They ranged from "no dessert until you clear your plate" to "wait until the men are fed before you sit down." We will con-

Table 2. Recommended food intake for good nutrition according to food groups and the average size of servings at different age levels—cont'd

Food group	Servings per day	Average size of servings					
		1 year	2-3 years	4-5 years	6-9 years	10-12 years	13-15 years
Cereals (whole-grain or enriched)	At least 4						
Bread		$^1/_2$ C.	1 slice	1$^1/_2$ slices	1-2 slices	2 slices	2 slices
Ready-to-eat cereals		$^1/_2$ oz.	$^3/_4$ oz.	1 oz.	1 oz.	1 oz.	1 oz.
Cooked cereal (including macaroni, spaghetti, rice, etc.)		$^1/_4$ C.	$^1/_3$ C.	$^1/_2$ C.	$^1/_2$ C.	$^3/_4$ C.	1 C. or more
Fats and carbohydrates	To meet calorie needs						
Butter, margarine, mayonnaise, oils: 1 Tbsp. 100 calories		1 Tbsp.	1 Tbsp.	1 Tbsp.	2 Tbsp.	2 Tbsp.	2-4 Tbsp.
Desserts and sweets: 100-calorie portions as follows: $^1/_3$ C. pudding or ice cream 2-3″ cookies, 1 oz. cake, 1$^1/_3$ oz. pie, 2 Tbsp. jelly, jam, honey, sugar		1 portion	1$^1/_2$ portions	1$^1/_2$ portions	3 portions	3 portions	3-6 portions

tent ourselves here with enumerating only the principles that the majority of nursery school teachers have come to feel are important as they have worked with young children.

Eating away from home can be frightening at first. Sometimes teachers underestimate how frightening it can be for children to eat away from home, but this can be the dreaded crisis of the day for new youngsters. They don't know what the teacher will do if they don't eat everything, and

they may not recognize some of the food either. For this reason, new children should not be urged to eat, and very familiar food should be served during the first weeks when more of the children are feeling shy. When children enter later in the year, it is ideal to have the mother return before snack or lunch if she can because this helps get the child past that first hump of uncertainty.

Eating should be a pleasure. One way to increase pleasure and minimize misbe-

Los Niños Head Start

havior is to make sure the children aren't kept waiting to be fed. When children are hungry and their blood glucose level is low, they are in poor control of themselves; so food should be ready to be served as the children sit down. If it is placed on a low table or nearby shelf, the teacher can start passing it as soon as everyone has arrived.

Eating together should convey a sense of happy family life to the children. There should be time both to eat and to chat. Discipline situations should be avoided whenever possible. It can also be a time to enjoy each other and to help the group by going for seconds, passing food to each other, and cleaning up.

If the food is plain and familiar, and if a lot of it can be eaten with the fingers, the children will eat more. As a general rule, little children are deeply suspicious of casseroles and food soaked in sauces and gravies. They prefer things they can recognize, such as carrot sticks, hamburger, and Jell-O with fruit.

Eating should help a child be independent. When I think of the reason we allow children to serve themselves, I remember the little girl who commented that when teachers are cold they make children put their sweaters on. The same thing is true of eating—when teachers are hungry, they serve the children too much; but if food is passed around the table, each child can take what he desires. It is up to him to choose. He knows how hungry he is, and he knows his preferences far better than his teacher does. Then, too, by serving himself he has the opportunity to learn to observe the social rule, "Take some and leave some."

Having sponges close at hand also helps children become independent because they can mop up their own spills. Advertisements to the contrary, it certainly is easier to clean up food from uncarpeted floors, so it is best to eat over linoleum or even outside when possible.

Nursery school is a good place to develop a taste for new foods. Although the quickest way to teach a child to hate a new food is to make him eat it all up, it is desirable to encourage but not force everyone to take a taste of everything that is served. Generally, the teacher can count on the combination of good appetites and enthusiasm to foster venturesomeness, but sometimes a child will refuse to try something new. One teacher of my acquaintance handles these outright refusals by simply remarking, "Well, when you're older, I expect you'll want to try it," and then she changes the subject.

One of the best ways to encourage children to try a new food is to allow them to prepare it. Cooking is a fine learning experience as well as a pleasure for preschoolers. Making vegetable soup, devilling eggs, or baking whole wheat muffins can introduce them to a whole range of taste experiences that they might otherwise shun.

Negative comments on food such as, "It looks like dog pooh pooh!" should be discouraged. A wave of this kind of talk can sweep through a group of 4-year-olds and actually spoil a meal if not controlled. The policy of "You don't have to eat it, but I won't let you spoil it for other people" is a sound one to enforce.

Foods from different ethnic groups should be served at every opportunity. The white middle-class teacher needs to remember that some foods she has eaten all her life can be dishearteningly unfamiliar to the Indian youngster who is accustomed to mutton and sheep herder's bread or to the Mexican-American child whose staple of diet is the tortilla. Cookbooks and family recipes will help, but a cook in the kitchen who comes from a background similar to that of the children's is best of all.

Eating can be a learning experience. Although the most important goals of the eating situation are to furnish nourishment and pleasure, this experience can provide many opportunities for intellectual learnings, too. The lunch table is a fine place for conversation. Children can be encouraged to talk about their pets, what they did on the weekend, what they like best to eat, and what was fun at school during the morning. The opportunity can also be taken to talk about food, textures, colors, and more factual kinds of information, but some teachers seem to do this to death and forget to stress the more valuable goal of conversational fluency. Eating should first and foremost be fun.

Children with special eating problems

Allergies and other food restrictions. Children who have allergies can have a difficult time in nursery school and so deserve special mention. The allergy that comes up most frequently is the restriction on milk and milk products. When this is the case, the mother should be asked to supply whatever the child requires instead. A simple explanation to the other children that the child's doctor has said he should not drink milk has always been sufficient at our Center. It is wise to be as matter-of-fact as possible in order to avoid making the child feel regretful or persecuted about the restriction.

Sometimes there are other reasons for dietary restrictions. For example, we have had several Black Muslim children and children from vegetarian families in our school, and we always do our best to honor their prohibitions. However, it can be very hard to see a little vegetarian hungrily eyeing the hot dog his neighbor is consuming with gusto. If the problem gets to be too difficult, perhaps the teacher will want to invite the mother to a lunch and ask her what to do about it.

The child who won't eat. Not eating and obesity are luxuries that very few countries in the world can afford, so I suppose we should count our blessings. For most children, soft pedaling the meal situation and allowing a child to skip a meal if he so chooses will gradually solve the problem of not eating. Although it may seem hard hearted, I feel it is a mistake to allow a recalcitrant child to eat later when he realizes that the food is going back to the kitchen. Good food should be set forth; a pleasant opportunity to eat should transpire; and when that time is past, it is past for *everyone* until it is time for snack. This policy should be carried out without vacillation or guilt on the teacher's part. It is up to the child to choose to eat or not eat; it is not the teacher's role to coax, bargain, or wheedle. No one ever starved to death because he missed his lunch.

There are rare occasions when the teacher will come across a youngster who either compulsively insists on eating only a narrowly circumscribed number of foods or who refuses to eat altogether. This behavior is almost always duplicated at home as well. Taking the pressure off and handling mealtimes in a casual manner may not be enough in these special cases, and the condition can be difficult to ameliorate. Under these circumstances, it is important to suggest counseling promptly for the family in order to relieve the situation.

The child who grabs everything. Whereas the noneater is likely to make the teacher anxious, the grabber is likely to make her angry. Some grabbing is due to lack of social experience and consideration of others, and some is due to enthusiasm, hunger, or feelings of emotional deprivation.

The teacher may need to remind the child many times to take some and leave some, as well as recognize his feelings by commenting, "It looks so good to you that you just feel like taking it all, don't you?" It is also sound strategy to make sure the hungry one gets a second helping and that he is delegated to go to the kitchen for refills. When he remembers to leave enough for the other children, his thoughtfulness should be commended.

PROCESS OF TOILETING
Taking children to the toilet

In general, nursery schools use the same toilet rooms for boys and girls. However, there are always exceptions to this rule, such as some schools who serve mostly Mexican-American youngsters, whose families feel strongly that open toileting violates the modesty of the little girls.

The benefits of toileting together are that the children learn to treat sexual differences quite casually. They will ask or comment about differences from time to time, and this provides golden opportunities to give straightforward, simple explanations. Open toileting has the advantage of reducing the peeking and hidden inspections that may go on otherwise. It promotes a healthier attitude toward sexual differences and therefore should be encouraged.

The majority of children of nursery school age can be expected to go to the toilet when they feel the need, but an occasional child will have to be reminded. Rather than lining everyone up at once and insisting that they use the toilet, it is better to remind children while washing up for lunch or before nap that they will be more comfortable if they use the toilet first.

It will encourage children to take this responsibility for themselves if their mothers dress them in pants with elastic tops or other easily managed clothing. It is also sound to remark to occasional children that it certainly feels good to go to the toilet, a point of view with which most of them will concur.

Thoughts about flushing. Some children, most commonly between the ages of 2 and 3, are really afraid of sitting on a toilet while it is being flushed (perhaps they fear vanishing down the hole with their product). Therefore, as a general practice, it is wise to wait until the child gets off before asking him to flush the toilet. We have achieved good cooperation by suggesting to the children that it is thoughtful to flush the toilet so that it is fresh for the next person, rather than constantly reminding, "Don't forget to flush it; go back and flush it."

Handling mishaps. When children wet themselves or have a bowel movement in their pants, they should be changed without shaming or disgust but without an air of cozy approval, either. Such loss of control often happens when children are new to the school, are overly fatigued, or are

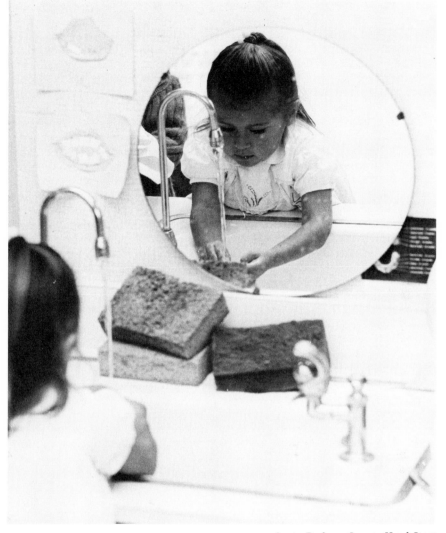

Santa Barbara County Head Start

coming down with something, as well as when children have not yet acquired the rudiments of control. Many children are humiliated by wet underwear, and the teacher should be sensitive to this and help them change in a quiet place. The inexperienced student may find it helpful to know that it is easier to clean a child who has had a bowel movement if the child helps by bending over during the process.

Theoretically, children should always have a dry pair of pants stowed in their cubby, but actually, these are often not there when needed; so it is necessary to have some extras on hand, with "nursery school" written prominently across the seat. It is helpful to have these changes of clothing available in a bureau in the toilet room itself.

Having children toilet trained before admission to school

It has been a common policy among nursery schools in past years to make one of the criteria for admission be that the child has been toilet trained. Today, more schools are accepting children in diapers because the age of admission is going down. It is also true that sometimes women need to work and cannot afford to wait until their children are toilet trained before placing them in day care. At one time our Center had six children in diapers, but that was about five too many. It is easier, and may even be vital if the school is minimally staffed, to have the children toilet trained before they are enrolled, even though it is sometimes necessary to enroll children in diapers.

Children with special problems

Once in a while a mother will worry aloud to the teacher that her child "never" has a bowel movement. By this she usually means he doesn't have a bowel movement every day. This may be his natural pattern of defecation, or it may be true constipation. If the child is constipated, it is best to refer the mother to her pediatrician for help.

The same thing goes for a child who continually leaks out a little bowel movement in his pants. The child is often "clean" at school, but messes a little most of the time at home. Again, this can be a touchy issue and may require help from a pediatrician or, more likely, from a competent psychologist.

HANDLING NAP TIMES

If eating in a strange place with unknown people is disturbing to young children, going to sleep under such circumstances can be even more so. Releasing oneself into sleep is, among other things, an act of trust, and it is not surprising that this can be difficult for a young child to allow during his first days at nursery school. Fortunately, there are some things that the teacher can do to make this task easier for him.

Regularize the routine

Keep daily expectations and the order of events the same when approaching the nap period. That is, try to do things the same quiet, steady way every day. One pattern that works well is to send the children one by one as they finish lunch to use the toilet and wash their hands. Then they are expected to settle down on their cots or mats with a book to look at quietly until all the children are ready to begin resting. Next the room is darkened, and the teacher moves about quietly, helping children take their shoes off, find their blankets, stuffed rabbits, and so forth and setting the books aside. This process should be accomplished with quiet affection combined with the clearly projected expectation that the youngster is going to settle down.

When the children are all snuggled in their blankets, some teachers prefer to read a story, while others sing softly or play a quiet record. It helps to have the children spread out as far from each other as possible and to have them lie head to toe; this reduces stimulation and also keeps them from breathing in each other's face. Restless children should be placed in out-of-the-way corners. Teachers need to be quiet and not talk among themselves, and other people must not be allowed to tiptoe in and out.

It takes two teachers to settle a roomful of children, and it may take as long as half an hour or 45 minutes before the whole school goes to sleep. Some children will need their backs rubbed in a monotonous way to soothe them into slumber.

Allow children to get up as they wake up

Usually after about an hour, some of the children will wake up by themselves and begin to stir about. This gradual awakening is convenient because it means that each child can be greeted and helped to dress one by one, and it presents a nice opportunity for friendly, but quiet chats with the teacher. Children are more likely to wake up in a good mood if they are wakened gradually by the activity around them rather than by having the teacher wake them up. They need time to collect themselves and regain awareness before they begin the afternoon activities. It often works well to have a few staff getting children up and the rest of the adults in the play yard, with snack available as the children desire it and some attractive activity also available that the children may select when they feel ready for it.

How long should children sleep?

It is unfair to the parent to allow a child to sleep all afternoon, unless, of course, he does not feel well. A sleep of an hour or so is about right for most youngsters, but this does not include the time it takes for them to settle down.

Should all children nap?

All children of nursery school age should be expected to lie down and relax for a while in the middle of the day. The need for sleep itself varies considerably with different children, and this difference needs to be taken into consideration. There will be some youngsters, particularly older children who are approaching kindergarten age, who never go to sleep. They should not be expected to lie stiff on their mats for 2 hours. Instead, following a reasonable rest period, they should be permitted to go outside and play under the supervision of a staff member. These more mature children often vastly enjoy helping prepare the afternoon snack. It makes them feel important and pays tribute to their more grown-up status.

Occasionally, there will be a child who needs to rest but who is so high strung and active that he disturbs everyone at nap time. Our staff has concluded that it is more satisfactory to take these youngsters out of the nap room and give them something quiet to do in the director's office than to become involved in angry confrontations, which upset all the children as well as frighten the restless one.

A practical note about cots

Storage of cots can be a real problem in some schools. If the floor is not too drafty, folding mats may be used instead of cots. This works well except for children who wet their beds at nap time. Saran-covered cots are better to use with these youngsters so that the urine drips through and doesn't collect in a puddle on the mat. Linoleum floors are, of course, indispensable for those who wet their beds.

SUMMARY

Routines, which consist of arriving and departing, eating, toileting, and resting, are an important part of the nursery school day. If they are well handled, they can contribute both to the physical health and emotional well-being of young children.

Teachers will experience greatest success in handling routines if they avoid trying to win for the sake of winning, but work instead toward the more worthwhile goals of helping the children become competent, independent people who have healthy attitudes toward their bodily needs and who look forward to eating, toileting, and resting because of the comfort and pleasure associated with these activities.

QUESTIONS

1. What foods do you particularly dislike? Can you remember the reason for your original dislike? Do you feel you learned anything from that situation which could be transferred to the way you handle eating situations at nursery school?
2. List all the rules you can think of that applied to eating, sleeping, or toileting in your own family as you grew up. After recalling the stated rules, think of some of the deeper, unspoken ones that were also observed.
3. *Problem:* You are the staff teacher who is delegated to greet children at the door every morning, and there is one little boy who always begins to whimper as he comes in the door. At that point the father jollies him along and finally gives him a smack on the bottom, telling him firmly, "Little boys don't cry!" You have learned in your student teaching days that it is important for children to express their feelings. How would you handle this situation?
4. Try an experiment wherein you just tell the children for 3 or 4 days that it is time to come in for snack, and then for the next few days try warning them ahead of time that it will soon be time to come in. Is there any difference in the way they respond?
5. *Problem:* Although you never meant to have things arrive at such an impasse, you have inadvertently made such an issue of a child's going to the toilet that he has become so balky about it that he won't use the toilet anymore but wets his pants instead. At this point, what approach would you try next to solve this difficulty?

REFERENCES FOR FURTHER READING

Handling Routines

Furman, R. A. Experiences in nursery school consultations. In K. R. Baker (Ed.), *Ideas that work with young children.* Washington, D.C.: National Association for the Education of Young Children, 1972. This article is an excellent discussion of separation anxiety and how it was handled in the case of a particular little boy; a shrewd, concise discussion.

Hirsch, E. S. *Transition periods: stumbling blocks of education.* New York: Early Childhood Education Council of New York City, 1972. *Transition Periods* contains many wise comments and suggestions about making these potentially troublesome times easier for staff and children.

Janis, M. G. *A two-year-old goes to nursery school: a case study of separation reactions.* New York: National Association for the Education cf Young Children, 1966. A description and analysis of how a very young child adapted to nursery school over a long period of time; should be read with special attention by those who advocate early admission.

Read, K. *The nursery school: a human relationships laboratory.* (5th ed.) Philadelphia: W. B. Saunders Co., 1971. The chapter entitled "Helping Children in Routine Situations" has a detailed discussion of toileting that will be of particular interest to students devoted to the psychoanalytic point of view.

Trieschman, A. E., Whittaker, J. K., and Brendtro, L. K. *The other 23 hours.* Chicago: Aldine Publishing Co., 1969. This is an interesting and thorough analysis of how routines are handled in a therapeutic environment for disturbed school-age boys. Some of the techniques are inappropriate for preschool children, but the explanations, approach, and reasoning that lie behind the recommendations provide excellent examples of how to plan routines to suit the requirements of special children; very interesting reading.

Wilder, A., Sendak, M., and Engvick, W. *Lullabies and nightsongs.* New York: Harper & Row, Publishers, 1965. This exquisite songbook consists entirely of lullabies; beautifully illustrated by Maurice Sendak—a special treasure.

Nutrition

Child Development Staff. *Programs for infants and young children, part II: nutrition.* Washington, D.C.: Appalachian Regional Commission, 1970. A number of food service programs are described in this readable, interesting, inexpensive publication. Many resource centers are listed, and there is an excellent article on infant feeding.

League of Women Voters. *Food for all.* Washington, D.C.: League of Women Voters, 1972. This clear, no-nonsense pamphlet explains food stamp and school lunch programs, including those for preschoolers. It identifies what the community should check to make sure programs are operating according to regulation and discusses how to institute such services in a community that does not have them.

Sunderlin, S., and Wills, B. (Eds.) *Nutrition and intellectual growth in children.* Washington, D.C.: Association for Childhood Education International, 1969. This group of articles summarizes research on the relationship of poor nutrition to mental development.

Cookbooks

Bowser, P., and Eckstein, J. *A pinch of soul: fast and fancy soul cookery for today's hostess.* New York: Avon Books, 1970. The book describes itself as containing "delectable dinners from Bread Pudding with Brandy Sauce to Kentucky Burgoo. Super suppers from African Bean Soup to Congo Chicken. All with very little effort, a lot of style and a pinch of soul." The recipes are very good and are genuine.

Ferreira, N. J. *The mother-child cookbook.* Menlo Park, Calif.: Pacific Coast Publishers, 1969. The recipes in this book have been pretested with nursery school children, and the quantities given are sufficient for 16. It is an invaluable volume that divides recipes according to indoor-outdoor, different kinds of skills, and age groups. It also has some ethnic recipes, including Chinese and Portuguese ones.

Piper, M. R. *Sunset Mexican cookbook.* Menlo Park, Calif.: Lane Magazine & Book Co. The delicious Mexican recipes are written so that Anglos can understand and concoct reasonably authentic Mexican menus.

United States Department of Agriculture. *Project Head Start Community Action Program: food buying guide and recipes.* Washington, D.C.: Office of Economic Opportunity, 1967. This useful, inexpensive guide has many tables listing size of portions and amount to purchase to serve 25 or 50 children; a helpful reference for cooks and kitchen managers to have on hand.

United States Department of Health, Education, and Welfare. *Quantity recipes for child care centers.* Washington, D.C.: U.S. Government Printing Office, 1973. This recipe card file was designed to provide quantity recipes and other information on preparing meals in children's centers. The easy-to-use file cards offer recipes for main dishes, soups, salads, vegetables, and desserts.

For the Advanced Student

Bakwin, H., and Bakwin, R. M. *Behavior disorders in children.* (4th ed.) Philadelphia: W. B. Saunders Co., 1972. This is the classic reference in the field. It lists and discusses innumerable behavior problems, including those associated with eating, toileting, and sleeping, and contains brief discussions of cause, treatment, and suggested further readings in the field.

Kessler, J. W. *Psychopathology of childhood.* Englewood Cliffs, N. J.: Prentice Hall, 1966. This book, written for the serious student who wants to know more about handling special behavior problems, has an entire chapter devoted to eating and toileting problems. The book is more detailed than the Bakwins', but not as broad in scope.

Thomas, S. B. *Malnutrition, cognitive development, and learning.* Urbana, Ill.: ERIC Clearinghouse on Early Childhood Education, 1972. This annotated bibliography of current research in the field of malnutrition is a very good way to obtain an overview and locate references to read in greater detail.

Yarrow, L. J. Separation from parents during early childhood. In M. L. Hoffman and L. W. Hoffman (Eds.). *Review of child development research.* Vol. I. New York: Russell Sage Foundation, 1964. This chapter analyzes and discusses different kinds of parent/child separations and what is known of the effect of such separation on the development of personality.

Photo by Jason Lo'Cicero

CHAPTER **4**

Development of the physical self

Jimmy, for example, was a child of elderly parents. Life in his comfortable home had been filled with listening to music or to stories and quiet play with small blocks or coloring books. When he first came to nursery school, he retreated from the active world in which the children lived. He sat by the victrola, and, if given a choice, would politely refuse to go outside. He didn't care for swinging or climbing or running or jumping—and the children didn't find him fun. After some time the rhythm of swinging seemed to attract him and very slowly he began playing more actively and gaining some motor skills. With skill came confidence and contacts with other children. Jimmy had attended nursery school nearly six months before he could bring himself to try going down the slide. His delight when he succeeded was evident. He used the slide again and again, squealing with joy, calling everyone's attention to his accomplishment. His growth was rapid from this time on. He began to stand up for himself in play. His tenseness diminished and his friendliness increased. He grew more childlike and more of a person in his own right. It had taken him a long time to enjoy the outdoors but when he discovered himself there, he could grow as a child.*

Good food, reasonable toilet procedures, and adequate rest are important factors in maintaining the physical and emotional well-being of young children. Additional factors that affect the physical development of children include health and safety and provision of maximum opportunities for their bodies to grow and develop in the most healthy way.

PROMOTION OF HEALTH AND SAFETY IN THE NURSERY SCHOOL
Basic ways to protect and foster the physical health of children

Beginning teachers who come from middle-class homes sometimes do not re-

*Reprinted by permission from *Let's play outdoors*, by Katherine Read Baker, pp. 9-11. © 1969 by the National Association for the Education of Young Children, 1834 Connecticut Ave., N.W., Washington, D. C. 20009.

alize the necessity for early childhood centers to take the lead in making sure young children have adequate health care. Many families served by preschool centers have very low incomes but do not understand how to make use of free services available to them through Medicare or other health facilities (Gussow, 1970). Families from the lower middle–income bracket are often even harder pressed to find the money that medical care requires. Both of these groups may need advice from the teacher about how to make use of free or inexpensive community health resources. Even more well-to-do families need to be encouraged to make sure their children have health checkups and immunizations. A recent study reveals that only three fourths of the young people in the United States have been immunized against polio and measles, and only four fifths have had diphtheria, whooping cough, and typhoid immunizations. The student should not be lulled into assuming this situation is improving, since the rate of immunizations actually appears to be declining. For instance, the Public Health Service reports that the number of children aged 5 years and younger who received at least three doses of polio vaccine has declined since 1965, when 74.9% were immunized, to only 62.9% in 1972 (U. S. Department of Health, Education, and Welfare, 1973b).

Physical examinations should be required before the child enrolls. Because the preschool is often the first institution that comes into contact with families of young children in a formal way, it is particularly valuable for each school to require preentry physical examinations. This not only protects the other children in the school but also assures that inoculations are brought up to date and that physical examinations are given to many children who might otherwise slip by without them until entry to kindergarten. Some states already make this part of their licensing regulations for day care centers and nursery schools; those that do not should be encouraged to add this requirement to their regulations promptly.

The teacher should be prepared to help parents find health care during the year whenever possible. There are a variety of free health services and examinations available in many communities, and the teacher needs to make it her business to become acquainted with each one so that she can refer families who need their help. These services range from university-sponsored speech and hearing clinics to eye examinations paid for by men's fraternal organizations and the special services offered by the Crippled Children's Society. Sometimes arrangements can be made with training schools to supply health services in return for the opportunity to work with young children. Dental hygienists, for example, may be willing to clean the children's teeth in order to obtain experience with preschoolers.

A good way to locate information about such services is to contact the public health nurses in the community. These people are usually gold mines of practical information about sources of assistance.

The teacher should act as a health screener. An alert teacher can often spot problems that have been overlooked by families and even by pediatricians, who, though expert, lack the teacher's opportunity to see the child over an extended period of time. The teacher should particularly watch for children who don't seem to see or hear well, who are very awkward, who seldom talk, or who are unusually apathetic or excessively active. The behavior may be only an idiosyncrasy, or it may require professional help—and the sooner help is sought the better. (See also Chapter 18 for further details on identification of special problems.)

The teacher should make a health check of every child as he arrives at school each day. This serves the purpose of assuring a personal greeting and provides a quick once-over so that a child who is not feeling up to par may be sent home before his mother departs. Although there are some standard things to check for, such as flushed or too pale faces, rashes, and marked lethargy (Vaughn, 1970), the most important symptom to be aware of is any significant change in the child's appearance. Teachers who see the same children every day get to know how they usually look and behave and can often spot such variations promptly and thus avoid exposing other children in school to the condition. (See also Appendix A for a list of common diseases, their symptoms, and incubation periods.)

The teacher must know what to do when a child becomes ill at school. No matter how careful the teacher and conscientious the parent, an occasional child is going to blossom forth with something during the day. Ideally, the child should be sent home immediately, but in practice this can be very difficult to do. Even when parents have been asked to make alternative arrangements for emergency care, these arrangements sometimes fall through, and the school and youngster have to make the best of it. Most schools try to keep children who are ill apart from the rest; usually the office serves this purpose fairly well. The child should have a place to lie down located as close to a bathroom as possible, and he will need to be comforted and reassured so that he does not feel bereft and lonely.

Because sending a child home from school often embarrasses and angers the parent and hurts the child's feelings as well, it is desirable to be firm but gentle when doing this. Sending something home along with the youngster, such as a little play dough or a book, will help him feel less rejected and make his return to school easier when he is feeling better.

General health precautions should be observed consistently by children and staff. Blowing noses on disposable tissue, washing hands before handling food, and not allowing children to share food, cups, or utensils they have had in their mouths are basic precautions that must always be observed. Most schools make it a practice never to administer medication (including aspirin) without the express request of the physician and parent in writing.

It is also important to be aware of the real temperature of the day and to take jackets off indoors and dress the children warmly enough outdoors, but not too warmly. Particularly in the fall, mothers tend to weigh their children down with too much clothing, and the children may be so absorbed in their play that they can be dripping with sweat and not realize it. The teacher needs to remind them about staying comfortable and to help them adjust their clothing to suit the temperature when necessary.

Maintaining the physical safety of the children

The teacher must never forget that the children in her care are not her own and that supervising them carries a special responsibility. All schools should carry insurance, both to protect them against being sued and also to provide accident coverage for the children. In addition, the entire school needs to be checked continually to make sure it is maintained in safe condition. Broken equipment such as tricycles without pedals and wobbly jungle gyms must be removed or repaired promptly. Sticks, particularly with nails in them, should be discarded. Safety precautions such as using swings with canvas seats should be observed. The danger area around swings must be clearly marked, and children should be taught to wait on the bottom step of the slide (which can be painted red to make it easier to identify).

Disinfectants, ant poisons, scouring powders, bleaches, and antiseptics, which are all commonly found in nursery schools, should be kept on high shelves in the kitchen where children are not permitted or, better yet, in locked cabinets.

In Chapter 2 it was suggested that inexperienced teachers stop an activity if it looks dangerous to them rather than permit an accident to happen. One other safety rule has proved to be generally helpful: the teacher should never lift a child onto a piece of play equipment if he cannot manage to get on it by himself (swings are an exception to this rule). Of course, youngsters sometimes climb up on something, feel marooned, and must be helped down; but that is different from lifting them onto the top of the jungle gym or boosting them onto a tippy gangplank before they are really able to cope with these situations.

The concern for safety has to be moderated by the teacher's good sense and self-control. Children must be protected, but they also need the chance to venture and try things out. This venturesomeness is a hallmark of 4-year-olds in particular. Occasional small catastrophes are to be expected, and the teacher should not become so overly protective that she hovers over the children and remonstrates them constantly to be careful. Instead, she should try to maintain a generally high level of safety combined with the opportunity for the children to experiment with the mild risks that build feelings of competence as they are met and mastered.

HELPING CHILDREN DEVELOP THEIR LARGE AND FINE MUSCLE ABILITIES
Basic principles of development

Before reading about specific ways to foster psychomotor development, the student needs to understand some developmental principles that have important implications for education.

Development occurs in predictable patterns and sequences. Although some investigators are now questioning the concept that chronological age should determine when children are taught various skills (Bruner, 1964; Gagné, 1968; White, 1971), it is still generally agreed that children progress through a predictable sequence of developmental stages (Mussen, Conger, and Kagan, 1969; Sutton-Smith, 1973). This is true of both intellectual development (Piaget and Inhelder, 1969) and physical development. Children usually sit before they stand, stand before they walk, and walk before they run (Gesell, Halverson, Thompson, and Ilg, 1940). In addition, specific skills such as running, jumping, and throwing progress through a number of substages of competency before they emerge as mature physical abilities (Wickstrom, 1970).

Teachers need to be able to recognize these stages of development so they can adjust their curriculum offerings to provide a good balance between opportunities for practice in order to consolidate the skill and opportunities for accepting the challenge of a slightly more difficult activity to go on to.

The course of development moves from head to tail. This *cephalocaudal* principle means that children are able to control the region around their head and shoulders before they can control their hands or feet. This is an easy principle to remember if one recalls that babies can sit up and manipulate playthings long before they are able to stand on their feet and walk. Quite simply, children are able to

Table 3. Stages of motor, visual, and perceptual development*

Approximate time of appearance	Selected behaviors
Gross motor behaviors	
1 year	Walking unaided A rapid "running-like" walk Will step off low objects
2 years	Walking rhythm stabilizes and becomes even Jumps crudely with 2-foot take-off Will throw small ball 4-5 ft. True running appears Can walk sideward and backward
3 years	Can walk a line, heel to toe, 10 ft. long Can hop from two to three steps, on preferred foot Will walk balance beam for short distances Can throw a ball about 10 ft.
4 years	Running with good form, leg-arm coordination apparent, can walk a line around periphery of a circle Skillful jumping is apparent Can walk balance beam
5 years	Can broad-jump from 2-3 ft. Can hop 50 ft. in about 11 seconds Can balance on one foot for 4-6 seconds Can catch large playground ball bounced to him

*Adapted from Cratty, B. J. *Perceptual and motor development in infants and children.* New York: The Macmillan Co., 1970.

Table 3. Stages of motor, visual, and perceptual development—cont'd

Approximate time of appearance	Selected behaviors
Manipulative behaviors	
1-3 months	Separate looking at objects
1-4 months	Alternates his glance from object to hand
2-4 months	One- and two-arm control Looking at objects, i.e., arm waving and other signs of excitement "Corrals" objects, swipes at objects Both hands brought to the front of his body
3-5 months	Gradually brings his hand to an object
4-12 months	Hand preference emerges Mouths objects
5-8 months	Grasps object with palm
6-9 months	Grasps with fingers
6 months plus	Grasps with fingers, examines objects, makes "motor copies" Exploits objects, shakes, hits, etc. "Letting-go" behavior, drops and throws Loses sight of object and searches; object permanence concept
11 months plus	Showing: the beginning of social behavior by using objects
18 months plus	Naming objects: classification concept
Visual and perceptual behaviors	
Birth	Rudimentary fixation, reflexive tracking for brief periods
3 months	Accommodation becomes more flexible, head and eyes coordinate Seeks novel visual experiences Evidences size and shape constancy in perceptual judgments
6 months	Visually tracks through 90° in horizontal and vertical planes Visually alert about 50% of the time, awareness of depth in visual-cliff studies
1 year	Mature pupil fibrillation appears
2 years	
	Distinguishes vertical from horizontal lines
5 years	
	Distinguishes between lateral, vertical, and horizontal lines
7 years	
	b, p, d, q confusions resolved
9 years	
10 years	Can intercept balls thrown from a distance

Continued.

Table 3. Stages of motor, visual, and perceptual development—cont'd

Approximate time of appearance	Selected behaviors
Scribbling and drawing	
1 year	Scribbling emerges, repetitive in radial or circular patterns
2 years	Multiple and single line crossings Variety of scribbling patterns, various positions on a page
3 years	Simple cross may be drawn, using two lines Encloses space; a variety of patterns emerge Figures placed in simple combinations using two figures Aggregates, more than two figures combined
4 years	"Suns" drawn with extra lines, sometimes forming faces Human figures emerge, crudely drawn Crude buildings and houses appear Human figures contain more detail; trunks usually absent; "stick" arms, legs, and fingers Boats and cars crudely drawn Circles and squares may be drawn
5 years	Animals drawn, trees appear in drawings Refined buildings and houses Better drawings of means of transportation; cars, airplanes, boats, etc.
6 years	Triangles drawn reasonably well
7 years	Diamonds drawn
8 years	
9 years	Three-dimensional geometrical figures drawn
10 years	
11 years	Linear perspective seen in drawings
12 years	

reach, grasp, and use their hands with considerable skill before they are able to master the art of skipping or kicking accurately. The curriculum of the preschool should be planned accordingly.

The course of development moves from large to fine muscle control. Large muscle activities have been identified by Guilford (1958), who factor-analyzed activities from motor proficiency tests, as including activities involving static balance, dynamic precision, gross body coordination, and flexibility. Fine muscle activities include such things as finger speed, arm steadiness, arm and hand precision, and finger and hand dexterity. Development from large to fine muscle control means that children gain control over their larger muscles first and then gradually attain control over the finer muscle groups. Thus a child is able to walk long before he is able to construct a table top house of tiny plastic bricks.

The educational implications of this developmental principle for early childhood teachers are that preschool children need ample opportunities to use their large muscles in vigorous, energetic, physical play. It can be torment for young children to have to remain confined too long to chairs and tables. However, since the finer muscle, eye-hand skills are also beginning to develop during this period, activities that stimulate the children to practice these skills should also be offered—but not overdone so that excessive demands are made on the children's self-control.

Use of large muscle activities in the nursery school

Since large muscle work is so dear to the young child and preoccupies so many of his waking hours, we shall discuss it first.

Instructing young children in perceptual-motor activities. Following the studies conducted by Gesell (Gesell and associates, 1940), which stressed the role of maturation in relation to development, nursery school teachers have usually been willing to content themselves with supplying many kinds of equipment and depending on the children's spontaneous use of it to foster their physical development. This attitude toward the development of psychomotor abilities still prevails today, and recent reports of research support the value of this approach. For example, in a study of Hungarian babies, Pickler (1968) found that if the infants were supplied with a reasonably well-equipped environment, they developed adequate motor skills, with no further intervention being necessary. In another study, Hodges, McCandless, Spicker, and Craig (1971) found that their group of 4-year-old "disadvantaged" children was deficient in both large and fine motor skills at the beginning of the project but that both the instructed experimental group and the uninstructed control group had improved so much in large muscle skills by the end of the project that there was no statistically significant difference between trained and untrained children at the year's end.

On the other hand, Leithwood and Fowler's study (1971) indicates that instruction can make a difference in the acquisition of physical skills by young children. They investigated the possibility of improving the gymnastic skills of 4-year-olds through instruction and found that the trained children made three to ten times as much improvement in gymnastics as a nontrained group did.

The growing interest in various programs that purport to develop the perceptual motor skills of young children also reflects interest in systematic training of these skills. However, since many of these claims are not supported by research findings (Kirk, 1972), it is very difficult to sort valid from invalid ideas. Indeed, some programs make such grandiose claims of success that, as Cratty puts it, "Some parents and educators have embraced various 'systems' with the fervor usually seen only in churches of the more demonstrative religious sects" (1970, p. 107).

It is quite important, therefore, to caution the teacher of young children to use common sense and avoid being swept off her feet by unusual-sounding activity programs that make extravagant but untested claims. The truth is that at this time we really don't know very much about the effects of specific perceptual-motor training programs on the development of young children.

Using "movement education" with preschool children. Two approaches that fall best under the term *movement education* appear to be useful, or at least likely to do no harm to young children. One of these approaches, based on the writing of Laban (1960), stresses the relationship of movement to living and learning. It emphasizes the development of body awareness and the way the child perceives himself in relation to space. Proponents of this philosophy are particularly interested in spatial positioning and the perception of time in relation to motion (Gerhardt, 1973).

The second approach, advocated by Cratty (1973), explores the way children can use physical movement to learn a variety of cognitive concepts. This material has the advantage of showing how physical and intellectual activities mesh together. In the past, we have studied the relationship of body to emotion or of emotion to learning, but the subject of body movement as related to mental growth has been ignored. Since we know how important physical activity is for children under the age of 5, this emphasis on movement education in relation to mental development may prove to be fruitful for futher investigation.

On the whole, we can only conclude at this point that we are still unsure whether specific kinds of training in physical development are desirable. If supplied with a good assortment of equipment, most children appear to develop within the normal range. The disadvantage of adding more controlled physical education instruction is that we are still uncertain what the content of such a program should be, although movement education may be a promising possibility. There is also the additional disadvantage that more planned instruction would restrict the amount of time available for free play and exploration by the child.

Providing various kinds of opportunities and equipment for large muscle activities in the nursery school. In general, the school should furnish a large assortment of big sturdy, durable equipment that provides many opportunities for all kinds of physical activity, and it should also provide a teacher who values vigorous large muscle play and who encourages the children to participate freely in this pleasure.

Equipment that is good for crawling through, climbing up, balancing on, and hanging from should be included. The children will need things they can lift, haul, and shove around to test their strength and use to make discoveries about physical properties the equipment possesses. They need things they can use for construction, and they need equipment that provides opportunities for rhythmic activities, such as bouncing and jumping and swinging. In addition, there must be places of generous size for them to carry out the wonderful sensory experiences that involve mud, sand, and water. Finally, they need plenty of space in which to simply move about.

Photo by Jason Lo'Cicero
All Saints by the Sea Nursery School

I have been deliberately nonspecific about suggesting particular pieces of large muscle equipment in the hope that talking about the children's activity requirements will encourage the teacher to consider afresh what might be used to meet these needs. However, for those who wish to pursue this question in detail, two excellent publications provide detailed lists of indoor and outdoor equipment and firms that manufacture it: *Equipment and Supplies* (Sunderlin and Gray, 1968) and *What Do I Need? How Much Does It Cost?* (Grant, 1971).

There currently is an exciting trend toward designing play equipment that is novel, often beautiful, and occasionally cheaper than our more mundane playground furnishings (Lady Allen of Hurtwood, Flekkoy, Sigsgaard, & Skard, 1964; Child Development Group of Mississippi, 1967; Educational Facilities Laboratory, 1972; Friedberg, 1969; Utzinger, 1970).

Equipment need not be expensive to provide sound play value, and several references that give suggestions about how to combine economy with beauty and ingenuity are included at the end of this chapter. It is wise to remember, though, that poorly constructed, cheap equipment can be the poorest kind of economy in the long run. Children are hard on things, and it doesn't pay to buy or make playthings that are flimsy—better to have a bake sale and raise money for better-quality equipment than be stuck with buying two cheap swing sets 2 years in a row.

In general, the more movable and versatile the equipment is, the more stimulating and interesting it will remain for the children. Observation of many schools has convinced me that movable outdoor equipment is one of the things in shortest supply in the play yard; yet it is vital to have plenty of boards, sawhorses, large hollow blocks, ropes, rubber tires, and barrels lest the children feel starved when they cannot complete their more ambitious projects. Schools should budget for more of this kind of equipment every year; there is no such thing as owning too much of it.

Before buying outdoor equipment, however, every teacher should read the discussion by Kritchevsky, Prescott, and Walling (1969) about how to plan and develop play centers that will have maximum attractiveness and play value for young children. Material explaining the English concept of adventure playgrounds should also be investigated (Allen, 1968; Bengtsson, 1972). These wonderfully messy, casual-looking English playgrounds place great emphasis on freedom to try out and explore—the faces of the children in the pictures bear witness to the value of such experience.

Once the equipment has been acquired, it is important to maintain it carefully. Hollow blocks, which are very costly, should be used on grass, not on cement or asphalt, where they will splinter badly when knocked down. Wood equipment has to be sanded and varnished every year to keep it smooth, and over a period of time this treatment can make it beautiful as well. Wooden items must be stored under cover at night. Metal items should be stored under cover when possible to avoid rust or oxidation.

Of course, children's vigorous activities do not need to be restricted to the school yard. Children will be delighted with the chance to visit parks with large open spaces where they can run freely and roll down hills. Many communities have wading pools for preschoolers or special play areas set aside for younger children. Even a trike expedition around the block with a pause at an interesting long set of steps can offer challenges that should not be overlooked, particularly in an all-day program.

Role of the teacher in fostering large muscle play. In addition to providing equipment to enhance large muscle play, the teacher can do much to encourage this kind of activity. Probably most important is that she provide enough uninterrupted time for satisfying play to transpire. Children need time to develop their ideas and carry them through, and if they build something, they need time to use it after they build it.

Outdoor play time at nursery school is not treated as teachers often handle recess in the elementary school. Playtime at nursery school requires the active involvement of the teacher with the children. She does not do this by participating as a companion in their play, but by observing and being alert to ways to make the play richer by offering additional equipment or tactfully teaching an intrusive child how to make himself more welcome to the group. Because her function is to encourage play to continue, she tries to be as facilitative yet unobtrusive as possible.

The teacher needs to keep the environment safe, but at the same time she should keep an open mind about the uses to which equipment can be put. If encouraged, children often come up with original or unconventional uses of materials that are not dangerous and that should be welcomed by the teacher because they are so creative and satisfying to the child. For example, one of our Center children recently got together all the beanbags to use as a pillow in the playhouse, and another youngster used the hose to make a worm tunnel in the sandbox. These harmless creative activities are all too easily squelched if the teacher is insensitive to their value or too conventionally minded.

Finally, the teacher should keep on the lookout for children who are at loose ends and involve them in activities before they begin to run wildly and aimlessly about. She needs to be comfortable with a good deal of noise and to welcome the vigorous activity so characteristic of 4-year-olds because they need this opportunity for vigorous assertion and movement in order to develop fully.

Use of fine muscle activities in the nursery school

Because muscle development moves from large toward finer muscle control as the child matures, it is important to permit a great deal of large muscle activity and play during the nursery school day and also to provide suitable opportunities for fine muscle activity to take place.

What constitutes fine muscle activities. Fine muscle activities include those that are performed with the arms, hands, and fingers, and typically require the coordination of hand with eye. They include almost all "tabletop" activities such as sewing, using peg boards and puzzles, stringing beads, and playing with put-together materials. They also include block building, which taps stacking and balancing skills, pouring and spooning in its many forms, and manipulating art materials, most particularly pencils, brushes, scissors, and crayons. Woodworking is another more vigorous example of small muscle activity. It takes a good deal of skill to hit a nail with something as small as a hammer head.

Things to remember when presenting small muscle activities. Offering a range of challenge in levels of difficulty is particularly important in a group of mixed ages, but even in a relatively homogeneous group of 4-year-olds provision must be made for the fact that the level of fine muscle skill, not to mention the amount of emotional control and ability to concentrate, will vary considerably from child to child. A common flaw in curriculum design is to set out activities that are all on about the same level of difficulty; these will generally be too easy or too hard for some of the

children in the group. Rather than setting out three or four puzzles of 16 pieces each, it will meet the children's range of abilities better if one or two inset puzzles, and perhaps a 7-, 15-, and 22-piece puzzle, are set out and changed as they become boring.

Sometimes it adds interest to offer two levels of otherwise identical material. Large and small wood beads make an interesting contrast; or occasionally, puzzles that have the same picture but vary in the number of cut pieces can be purchased and made available for use. Children enjoy having access to both levels and like to put into words what it is that makes the materials similar and what it is that makes them different.

Fine muscle activities should be of reasonably short duration. It is difficult for young children to hold still very long, much less sit and concentrate on a fine muscle task that requires considerable self-control. For this reason, several activities should be available at the same time, and children should always be free to get up, move around, and shift to more or less taxing experiences as they feel the need. Quiet periods such as story hours or snack times should not be followed by additional quiet, fine muscle play but by more vigorous large muscle activity.

The teacher should watch out for signs of unusual frustration. I once had a little boy in my nursery school who participated with enthusiasm and happiness in almost everything we did, with one notable exception. Whenever he played with floor blocks, he would work a while and then in a rage send them flying. Yet he was drawn to them as a moth to a flame. His mother and I were baffled; he seemed well adjusted and easy going, with only this exception. The staff tried building his skills, investigated whether he was happy at home, and watched to see whether other children interfered with his work and made him angry, but we could find no satisfactory answer. Finally one day his mother arrived beaming at school with the following tale. Alan and his father had been looking out the window the week before, and he had said, "Oh, look Papa, see

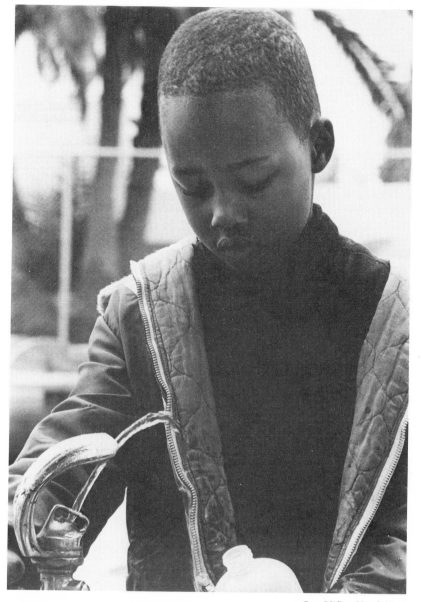

Los Niños Head Start

those two kitties!" But his father had looked and asked "What two kitties?" since he could see only one. "Why, those two little black kitties right over there," quoth Al. Shortly thereafter, when his eyes were examined, the answer to his block problem became clear—he was slightly cross-eyed, just enough so that stacking small blocks was a particularly irritating problem for him to solve, and it was this condition that caused him to send them tumbling down when his self-control was exceeded by the difficulty of the task.

This story may help other teachers remember to be alert to activities that seem to provoke consistent frustrations in some children. This kind of reaction can often be a symptom of a physical problem that warrants further investigation, since early remediation makes correction more likely.

VALUE OF SENSORY EXPERIENCE IN THE NURSERY SCHOOL
Current cultural restrictions on sensory awareness

It has been maintained that 80% of everything we learn comes to us through our eyes, but it seems to me that our society encourages this far more than is necessary. One has only to watch the deodorant and disinfectant ads on television to become aware of the tremendous emphasis on the desirability of smelling only a few choice fragrances. Children are continually taught not to touch things, and as they mature, they are also taught not to touch other people except under carefully restricted circumstances. As for tasting, how many times have you heard a mother warn her child, "Don't put that in your mouth, it's dirty"? The latest victim of the war against the senses appears to be hearing. In self-defense, people seem to be learning to tune out the continual piped-in music of the supermarket and the constant noise of the television set.

Fostering sensory experience

The nursery school teacher needs to contend with this narrowing and restricting of the use of the senses by deliberately

Santa Barbara County Head Start

continuing to utilize all of them as avenues of learning. Children should be encouraged to make comparisons of substances by feeling them and smelling them, as well as by looking at them. Science displays should be explored by handling and manipulation rather than by looking at bulletin board pictures or observing demonstrations carried out by the teacher. Stress should be placed on developing auditory discrimination skills as well as on paying attention to what is said at nursery school, and attention should be drawn to the way things look and to the fact that they may appear quite different from different angles. Learning through physical, sensory participation should be the order of the day.

In particular, the value of personal physical contact should be understood and appreciated. Ashley Montagu (1971) has recently reviewed numerous studies of the beneficial effect of being touched and the relationship of tactile experience to healthy physical and emotional develop-ment. He speaks of "the mind of the skin" and comments that although the skin is the largest organ of the body, it remains one of the most ignored. Lawrence Frank (1971) also makes a very good case for the significance of tactile communication.

Young children need the reassurance and comfort of physical affection from teachers. They need to be patted, rocked, held, and hugged from time to time. Cornelia Goldsmith's statement that a teacher's most important equipment is her lap is as true today as when she said it 20 years ago. The emotional needs of children are basic and timeless, and teachers should remember that one valuable way to convey caring and affection is through a gentle hug or a few cozy moments in a rocking chair.

SUMMARY

The promotion of health and safety is vital to the physical well-being of the young child in the nursery school. During the hours he is at school, it is the teacher's

Los Niños Head Start

Los Niños Head Start

responsibility to see that he follows good health practices and to keep the child as safe and healthy as possible without nagging at him or being overprotective.

In addition, it is desirable to offer equipment and activities that foster large and fine muscle development. Attaining competence in these physical areas enhances the child's self-esteem and provides opportunities for him to gain social expertise as he develops wholesome feelings of vigor and good health.

Equipment for large muscle activities should be versatile, sturdy, and well maintained. The teacher can encourage active play by tuning in on what is happening and being alert to ways to add to its richness rather than by regarding large muscle playtime as a recess period when she can retreat to the office and have a cigarette.

Fine muscle activity is also valuable to offer at nursery school, but it is important to offer an assortment of levels of difficulty and to be sure that such activities do not

continue for too long at a time without relief.

Finally, education should take place by means of all five senses. Our present culture tends to restrict and narrow sensory experience to the sense of sight, but the nursery school teacher should utilize touching, smelling, tasting, and hearing as additional valuable avenues of learning. Above all, she should feel comfortable about touching the children and allowing them to respond to her in similar fashion. These physical expressions of affection and caring play a vital role in fostering the emotional well-being of young children.

QUESTIONS AND ACTIVITIES

1. *Problem:* A little girl has just fallen out of the swing and is brought into the office bleeding heavily from the mouth. Examination reveals that her front tooth is still whole but has cut entirely through her lower lip. As the teacher in charge, how would you handle this emergency? Remember to think about both short- and long-term aspects of the situation.

2. Are there any conditions in the school where you are teaching that are particularly well handled in terms of safety precautions? Are there some possible hazards that warrant attention?

3. Suppose you were beginning a new school and had a budget of $400 for large muscle equipment. In your opinion what would be the most satisfactory way to invest this money? What would you buy and why?

4. Could there be advantages to putting children through a planned series of physical exercises on a regular basis? This might not be calisthenics as such; it might be tumbling or learning ball skills. What might the disadvantages or advantages be to this approach to physical education?

5. Many nursery school teachers appear to avoid physical contact with the children. What do you think might be the reasons for this restraint?

6. What are some examples from your own experience where you are aware that the use of every sense except vision is restricted or curtailed?

REFERENCES FOR FURTHER READING

Health and Safety

American National Red Cross. *Standard first aid and personal safety.* Garden City, N.Y.: Doubleday & Co., Inc., 1973. This valuable reference, which describes how to handle common emergencies, should be available at all nursery schools.

Gussow, J. D. Bodies, brains and poverty: poor children and the schools. *ERIC-IRCD Bulletin,* 1970, **6**(3), 1-20. For a chilling analysis of the effect of poor health on learning, the reader should pursue Gussow's article as well as additional discussions included in the same volume of the *ERIC-IRCD Bulletin.*

Vaughn, G. *Mummy, I don't feel well: a pictorial guide to common childhood illnesses.* London: Berkeley Graphics, 1970. Ever wondered what chicken pox looks like? This book will leave you in no doubt; very useful.

Sequential Physical Development

Cratty, B. J. *Perceptual and motor development in infants and children.* New York: The Macmillan Co., 1970. Cratty's work is a more up-to-date reference than Gesell's and also deals with physical development.

Gesell, A., Halverson, H. M., Thompson, H., and Ilg, F. *The first five years of life: a guide to the study of the preschool child.* New York: Harper & Row, Publishers, 1940. This classic reference details step-by-step development of young children in many areas, including various physical skills. Although published more than 30 years ago, it remains the most comprehensive reference in the field.

Wickstrom, R. L. *Fundamental motor patterns.* Philadelphia: Lea & Febiger, 1970. Wickstrom discusses and illustrates the development of running, jumping, throwing, catching, kicking, and striking skills, beginning with preschool children and extending onward to physical maturity. This is a useful reference for those who are interested in meticulous sequential analyses of these particular skills.

Theories of Perceptual Motor Development

Gearheart, B. R. *Learning disabilities: educational strategies.* St. Louis: The C. V. Mosby Co., 1973. This book has several good chapters that describe the most important schools of thought concerned with perceptual motor development.

Activities For Physical Development

Robb, M. D., Mushier, C. L., Bogard, D. A., and Blann, M. E. (Eds.) *Foundations and practices in perceptual motor learning—a quest for understanding.* Washington, D.C.: American Association for Health, Physical Education & Recreation, 1971. In this series of articles the importance of perceptual motor learning is discussed, and current concerns and the state of the art are reviewed.

Sinclair, C. B. *Movement of the young child: ages two to six.* Columbus, Ohio: Charles E. Merrill Publishing Co., 1973. Sinclair's helpful book about movement education focuses on early childhood; appears to be quite practical. A good list of equipment is included.

Equipment and Buildings

Child Development Group of Mississippi. *From the ground up: ideas for playground and indoor equipment to build for a community Head Start program.* Jackson, Miss.: KIPCO, 1967. This profusely illustrated book is rich in suggestions for indoor and outdoor equipment that can be made by anyone. It is full of money-saving, attractive ideas that have good play value.

Educational Facilities Laboratory. *Found: spaces and equipment for children's centers: a report from the Educational Facilities Laboratory.* New York: EFL, 1972.

Grant, L. *What do I need? How much does it cost?* Santa Barbara, Calif.: Lou Grant, 1971. In this invaluable publication the author bases his recommendations on two lists: equipment essential for opening a school based on a minimum budget and equipment that could be included if the budget is more liberal; also contains catalog citations of where items can be located and the prices of the equipment.

Utzinger, R. C. *Some European nursery schools and playgrounds.* New York: Educational Facilities Laboratory and the Architectural Research Laboratory of the University of Michigan, 1970. In this, as in the Educational Facilities Laboratory work above, one picture is worth a thousand words. Both pamphlets are made up almost entirely of photographs and contain innumerable exciting contemporary ideas for arranging and furnishing nursery schools.

Adventure Playgrounds

Lady Allen of Hurtwood. *Planning for play.* Cambridge, Mass.: The M.I.T. Press, 1968. Lady Allen, a very progressive thinker, was among the first to advocate the development of adventure playgrounds. She describes the purpose of this book as being "to explore some of the ways of keeping alive and sustaining the innate curiosity and natural gaiety of children." It does just that.

Bengtsson, A. (Ed.) *Adventure playgrounds.* New York: Praeger Publishers, Inc., 1972. Crammed with photographs, this publication surveys adventure playgrounds throughout the European community. Pictures are accompanied by an extensive and thorough text, which explains theoretical and practical aspects of how to found, design, and sustain such a playground.

For the Advanced Student

Arnheim, D. D., and Pestolesi, R. A. *Developing motor behavior in children: a balanced approach to elementary physical education.* St. Louis: The C. V. Mosby Co., 1973. Those who would like to acquaint themselves with current approaches to physical education in the elementary school will find this one of the most readable and up-to-date references available.

Cratty, B. J. *Some educational implications of movement.* Seattle: Special Child Publications, 1970. The author presents a readable, sensible discussion of what is known at present about the effects of movement education upon development; contains many bibliographical references.

McGraw, M. B. Later development of children specially trained during infancy: Johnny and Jimmy at school age. In R. N. Singer (Ed.), *Readings in motor learning.* Philadelphia: Lea & Febiger, 1972. This famous study of twins investigated the value of stimulating a very young child to engage in activities to the extent of his ability as compared with the value of allowing his twin to develop without deliberate instruction.

White, B. L. Informal education during the first months of life. In R. D. Hess and R. M. Bear (Eds.), *Early education: current theory, research, and action.* Chicago: Aldine Publishing Co., 1968. Dr. White's chapter should be read along with McGraw's study because it provides a description of a more contemporary investigation of the effects of early stimulation on the development of the infant.

PART **THREE**

Nourishing and maintaining emotional health

Photo by Gene Garrett
Los Niños Head Start

CHAPTER 5

Fostering mental health in young children

In the evaluation of the dominant moods of any historical period it is important to hold fast to the fact that there are always islands of self-sufficient order—on farms and in castles, in homes, studies, and cloisters—where sensible people manage to live relatively lusty and decent lives: as moral as they must be, as free as they may be, and as masterful as they can be. If we but knew it, this elusive arrangement *is* happiness.*

The valuable contribution early childhood programs can make to fostering mental health has been emphasized in the recent report of the Joint Commission on the Mental Health of Children (1970), which points out repeatedly that day care centers, nursery schools, and compensatory programs present outstanding opportunities for carrying out preventive and remedial work in this area.

In an era when at least one in every ten people is destined to spend time in a mental hospital, the importance of such work is clear, and we must give careful consideration to practical things the teacher can do that are likely to foster mental health in the children in her care. For this reason, several chapters of this book are devoted to establishing general therapeutic policies, handling discipline and aggression, and building self-esteem because these are all important aspects of developing emotional health. Additional aspects

of mental health, covered under the development of the social self, include learning to care for other people, cross-cultural education, and taking pleasure in meaningful work.

IMPORTANCE OF DEVELOPING BASIC ATTITUDES OF TRUST, AUTONOMY, AND INITIATIVE IN YOUNG CHILDREN

The most fundamental thing the teacher can do to foster mental health in young children is to provide many opportunities for basic healthy emotional attitudes to develop. Erik Erikson (1959, 1963, 1971) has made a very significant contribution to our understanding of what these basic attitudes are. He hypothesizes that during their life span, individuals pass through a series of stages of emotional development wherein basic attitudes are formed. Early childhood encompasses three of these: the stages of trust versus mistrust, autonomy versus shame and doubt, and initiative versus guilt. Although children in nursery school are likely to be working on the second and third sets of attitudes, it

---

*From Erikson, E. *Young man Luther.* New York: W.W. Norton & Co., Inc., 1958.

65

is important to understand the implications of the first set, also, since Erikson theorizes that the resolution of each stage depends in part on the successful accomplishment of the previous one.

In the stage of *trust versus mistrust,* the baby learns (or fails to learn) that other people can be depended on and also that he can depend on himself to elicit needed responses from them. This development of trust is deeply related to the quality of care that the mother provides and is often reflected in feeding practices, which, if handled in a manner that meets his needs, helps assure the infant that he is valued and important. Although by the time he enters nursery school, the balance between trust or mistrust will have been tipped in favor of one attitude or the other, the need to experience trust and to have it reaffirmed remains with people throughout their lives. This is also true for the other attitudes as they develop.

Therefore, it is vital that the basic climate of the nursery school encourage the establishment of trust between everyone who is part of that community. If the teacher thinks of establishing trust in terms of letting the children know that they can depend on her, it will be fairly easy for her to implement this goal. For example, consistent policies and regularity of events in the program obviously contribute to establishing a trustful climate. Being reasonable also makes it clear to the child that he can depend on the teacher. In addition, if she is sensitive to his individual needs and meets them as they arise, the teacher can confirm the message of his infanthood once again that he is worthy of love and thus further strengthen trust and self-esteem.

In our society the attitudes of *autonomy versus shame and doubt* are formed during the same period in which toilet training takes place. During this time, the child is acquiring the skills of holding on and letting go. This fundamental exercise in self-assertion and control is associated with his drive to become independent and to express this independence by making choices and decisions so often couched in the classic imperatives of the 2-year-old,

"No!" "Mine!" and "Me do it!" Erikson maintains that children who are overregulated and deprived of the opportunity to establish independence and autonomy may become oppressed with feelings of shame and self-doubt, which result in losing self-esteem, being defiant, trying to get away with things, and in later life in developing various forms of compulsive behavior.

The desirable way to handle this strong need for choice and self-assertion is to provide an environment at home and nursery school that makes many opportunities available for the child to do for himself and to make decisions. This is the fundamental reason why self-selection is an important principle in curriculum design. At the same time, the teacher must be able to establish decisive control when necessary, since young children often show poor judgment and can be tyrannized by their own willfulness unless the teacher is willing to intervene.

Gradually, as the child develops the ability to act independently, he embarks on building the next set of basic attitudes. Around the age of 4 or 5, he becomes more interested in reaching out to the world around him, in doing things, and in being part of the group. At this stage, he wants to think things up and try them out; he is interested in the effect his actions have on other people (witness his experimentation with profanity and "bad" language); he formulates concepts of appropriate sex roles; he enjoys imaginative play; and he becomes an avid seeker of information about the world around him. This is the stage Erikson has so aptly named *initiative versus guilt.*

In order to feel emotionally satisfied, a child of this age must be allowed to explore, to act, and to do. Nursery schools are generally strong about meeting the children's need to explore and create, but they often underestimate the ability of older 4- and 5-year-olds to participate in making plans and decisions for their group or to attempt challenging projects. Of course, the teacher must make allowance for the fact that 4- and 5-year-olds are better planners and starters than they are finishers. Satisfaction in completing projects is more likely to be part of the developmental stage that follows this one: the stage of industry versus inferiority, which is characteristic of the child during his early years in primary school. But encouraging the ability to initiate plans and take action will enhance the child's feeling of self-worth and creativity as well as his ability to be a self-starter—all highly desirable outcomes necessary for future development and happiness.

HALLMARKS OF AN EMOTIONALLY HEALTHY YOUNG CHILD

To determine whether the child is in good emotional health, the teacher should ask the following questions about him. If she can answer the majority of them affirmatively, chances are good that he is emotionally healthy.

Is the child working on emotional tasks that are appropriate for his age? We have already talked about the fundamental need for planning a curriculum that provides many opportunities for children to exercise their autonomy and initiative. When looking at individual children, the teacher should ask herself if they are taking advantage of these opportunities. She will find that the majority of them are achieving independence, choosing what they want to do, and generating their own ideas with zest and enthusiasm; but there will be a handful of

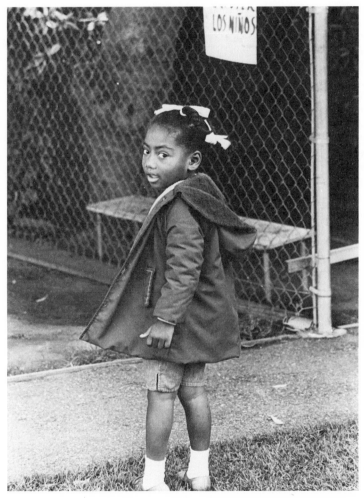

Los Niños Head Start

youngsters who need sensitive help to venture forth. This usually involves taking time to build a strong foundation of trust between the child and teacher and then helping him advance to increased independence as his confidence grows.

Is the child learning to separate from his family without undue stress and to form an attachment with at least one other adult at nursery school? Considerable space was devoted in the chapter on routines to handling separation anxiety in a constructive way because the ability to separate from significant others and form additional relationships is an important skill. The teacher should realize that most children, particularly shy ones and those who are younger, make friends with a teacher at school before they branch out to make friends with other children. The teacher who is aware that this is a typical pattern can relax and enjoy this process without fretting about the child's dependency because she has confidence that in time most children will leave her side in favor of being with other youngsters. This bond between teacher and child may not be as evident in socially able 4-year-olds as it is with younger children, but it should exist all the same. If the child has not formed a relationship with some adult after he has been at school for a while, he should be encouraged to do so. Being attached to the teacher makes it more probable that he will use her as a model or come to her for help when it is needed. Affection between teacher and child is also a fundamental ingredient of good discipline.

At the same time, the teacher has to be sensitive to the quality of the attachment. Oversolicitude for the child's feelings of loneliness or the teacher's own unmet needs for affection can occasionally create a form of dependency that is undesirable because it restricts the child's venturing out and making friends with his peers. This situation should, of course, be avoided. The teacher must learn to tell the difference between a youngster who genuinely needs the emotional support of a close relationship to begin with, and the one who is using her or is being used by her as an emotional crutch.

Is the child learning to conform to routines at school without undue fuss? Of course, conforming to routines varies with the age of the child and his temperament, and teachers anticipate some balkiness and noncompliance as being not only inevitable but healthy. Two-year-olds are particularly likely to be balky and at the same time insist that things can be done the same way every time. However, consistent refusal to conform goes beyond this norm and should be regarded as a warning sign that the child needs help working through this behavior.

Is the child able to involve himself deeply in play? A characteristic of severely disturbed children in mental institutions is that they cannot give themselves up to the experience of satisfying play. Indeed, when they become able to do so, it is encouraging evidence that they are getting ready to be released from the hospital. Being able to play is also very important for more typical children. The child's ability to enjoy participating in play by himself or with other children as he grows older is not only a hallmark of emotional health but appears to contribute to maintaining mental health as well.

Is the child developing the ability to settle down and concentrate? Children may be distractible for a variety of reasons, and no child is able to pay attention under all circumstances. Excitement, boredom, needing to go to the toilet, fatigue, interesting distractions, or not feeling well can all interfere from time to time with any child's ability to concentrate. But occasionally the teacher will come across a child who never seems to settle down: he flits continually from place to place and seems to give only his surface attention to what he is doing. There are a multitude of reasons for this behavior, ranging from poor habits to birth injuries, but a common cause of distractibility is tension or anxiety. Since this behavior can seriously interfere with learning, the teacher should seek to identify the cause and to remedy it as soon as possible.

Is the child unusually withdrawn or aggressive for his age? One of the great advantages teachers have is that by becoming acquainted with hundreds of children over a period of time, they are able to develop sound norms for behavior that make it relatively easy to identify youngsters who behave in extreme ways. Very withdrawn behavior is more likely to be overlooked than aggressive behavior because it is much less troublesome to the teacher, but she should be aware that either response is a signal from the child that he is emotionally out of balance and needs some extra thought and plans devoted to help him resolve whatever is causing him to cope in that manner.

Does the child have access to the full range of his feelings, and is he learning to deal with them in an age-appropriate way? Some children have already learned by the age of 3 or 4 years to conceal or deny the existence of their feelings rather than to accept and express them in a tolerable way. The nursery school teacher can help children stay in touch with the full repertoire of their emotions by showing them that she, too, has all sorts of feelings and that she understands that children have feelings as well, whether these be anger, sadness, or affection. Healthy children should also begin to learn during the preschool years to express their feelings to the people who have actually caused them and to do this in a way that does not harm themselves or others. Learning to do this successfully takes a long time, but it has its roots in early childhood.

PERSONAL QUALITIES THAT WILL HELP THE TEACHER ESTABLISH A THERAPEUTIC CLIMATE IN THE NURSERY SCHOOL*

The nursery school teacher can utilize her personal qualities as well as more practical techniques to foster a therapeutic climate in her nursery school. A *therapeutic climate* consistently allows the active development and maintenance of an atmosphere conducive to mental health. It frees people to develop to their fullest potential as balanced, happy individuals. The personal qualities of a "therapeutic" teacher have a great deal to do with establishing this desirable climate, and for this reason they are discussed below.

Consistency. One way to build a sense of trust between the teacher and the children in her care is for her to behave in ways they can predict and to be consistent about maintaining guidelines and schedules. Thus the children will know what to expect, and will not live in fear of erratic or temperamental responses to what they do. For this reason, emotional stability is a highly desirable trait for teachers of young children to possess. Of course, consistency does not mean that rules must be inflexible, but their enforcement should not depend on the whim of the teacher or the manipulative power of various children.

Reasonableness. Coupled with the steadiness of consistency should go the trait of reasonableness, which I define as "expecting neither too much nor too little from

Santa Barbara City College Children's Center

---

*The work in this section owes much to the humanistic philosophy of Carl Rogers and his client-centered approach to psychotherapy.

children." One practical way to increase reasonableness is to learn the characteristics of the developmental stages when these are discussed in child development courses. The brief developmental summaries presented in this book are intended to remind the student of general developmental characteristics. Knowledge of these characteristics prevents the inexperienced teacher from setting her standards too high or too low. She does not expect a 2-year-old to have the self-control of a 4-year-old. On the other hand, when a 4-year-old starts making demands more typical of a 2, she knows that he is regressing and that she must search for and alleviate the stresses that are causing his retreat.

Courage and strength of character. Particularly when dealing with outbursts of anger, the student will find that courage and the strength of character commonly called fortitude are required to see such oubursts through. Understandably, the embarrassment and insecurity of fearing that the scene may not turn out all right make it easy to placate an angry child or, more usually, to allow him to run off or have his way. But the trouble with allowing this to happen is that the child will repeat the behavior and feel contemptuous of the adult who permits it. Therefore, being courageous and seeing a problem through is worth the struggle when coping with the strong emotional reactions that are so common at the nursery school level.

Trustful confidence. Trustful confidence is the faith the teacher feels that the child wants to grow and develop in a healthy way. Interestingly enough, psychoanalysts maintain that this ability to have trust or confidence in the child's inherent tendency to develop in desirable directions goes back to the individual's own experiences as an infant, when she found she could or could not generally depend on her environment to be a nurturing one. Be that as it may, contemporary research (Rosenthal and Jacobson, 1968) bears out what many teachers and parents have determined empirically: children respond to what is genuinely expected of them by the

people who matter to them. The teacher who optimistically trusts children to act in their own best behalf is likely to obtain this response from most of the children most of the time.

Congruence. The teacher also promotes trustful confidence between herself and the child by being honest with herself and with him about her own feelings. This is what Rogers calls congruence. A congruent person attempts to recognize and accept her own feelings and be truthful about them to other people. Thus a teacher might "level" with one child by saying, "I don't want you to kick me ever again; I feel really angry with you when you do that to me," or with another by saying, "I'm glad to see you today. I've been looking forward to hearing about your new kittens."

However, a note of caution is in order. Rogers advocates revealing such feelings *when it is appropriate to do so.* Children should not be subjected to outbursts of temper or angry attacks by adults in the name of congruence. Uncontrolled outbursts are too disturbing to children, since they know they are relatively helpless and at the mercy of the teacher.

Empathy. Empathy is the ability to feel *as* another person feels, to feel *with* him rather than *for* him. Empathy is valuable not only because it allows the teacher to put herself in the child's place, but also because it helps her identify and clarify for the child how he is feeling. Research supports the value of this quality. A study by Truax and Tatum (1966) has shown that empathic ability combined with the ability to express warmth are effective in fostering positive adjustments to the preschool setting and to peers.

Warmth. Warmth is so important that it deserves special emphasis. The warm teacher lets the children and staff know that she likes them and thinks well of them. Both children and adults flourish in this climate of sincere approval and acceptance. But being warm and accepting does not mean that the teacher just sits around and smiles at the children no matter what they do. There is a difference between expressing warmth and being indulgently permissive, and there are times when the teacher must exert control because a child is unable to. But when she does this for him, she must make it plain that she is taking control because she truly cares for him and not because she wants to obtain power for its own sake or have the satisfaction of winning.

Attaining these qualities

Some of the qualities listed above, such as consistency, fortitude, and reasonableness, can be acquired through practice and experience. The others—empathy, trustful confidence, congruence, and warmth—can often be enhanced by participation in well-run encounter groups or through psychological counseling if they don't seem to "come naturally." Many teachers have found that such experiences have improved both their teaching abilities and their personal relationships.

PRACTICAL THINGS THE TEACHER CAN DO TO HELP YOUNG CHILDREN ACHIEVE HEALTHY EMOTIONAL DEVELOPMENT

Before turning to a discussion of more concrete things the teacher can do to contribute to a therapeutic milieu, the student should remember two principles. One is that young children respond with encouraging quickness to a change in atmosphere or approach. It is possible to quickly bring about positive changes in their feelings and behavior by using appropriate methods.

The other principle has been mentioned before: children are resilient. They bounce back from their own and others' mistakes, and it is unlikely that one imperfect handling of a situation will inflict permanent damage on a child. This is not said to sanction irresponsible actions by the teacher but to reassure her that, when dealing with difficult situations, she should not be unduly hesitant on the grounds she may injure the child. It is the repetition of procedures and the overall quality of the milieu, rather than the single episode, that are likely to enhance or damage.

Develop friendly, close relationships with each family. Nursery school usually marks the occasion in the child's and parents' life when he leaves their protection for the first time on a regular basis. If the school and family establish a feeling of closeness and a shared interest in the child's welfare, it is easier for him to make this transition, since his world is thereby widened rather than split into two pieces.

Teachers are quick to see the advantage that a friendly, comfortable atmosphere means the family is more likely to seek advice from the school. But another advantage should not be overlooked: the teacher is also in a better position to accept advice and suggestions from the parents when a "caring-sharing" atmosphere is established. This two-way respect fosters genuine mutuality and lays the basic foundation for emotional health in the nursery school.

Reduce frustration for the child when possible. Children should not have to spend time waiting for things to happen. Children's needs are immediate, intense, and personal, and the longer they are kept waiting the more irritable they become. Snack should be available as the children sit down, and someone should be outside for supervision as the children are dressed and ready to go out and play. Duplicates of equipment mean that there is generally enough to go around—two or three toy trucks are much more satisfactory than just one. A good assortment of activities must be available so that 3-year-olds are not expected to stack tiny plastic blocks and 5-year-olds do not have to make do with eight-piece puzzles. The day should be planned so that few and moderate demands are made on children at points where they are likely to be tired and hungry.

Of course, the teacher cannot and should not seek to eliminate all frustrating circumstances. Comparative animal studies indicate that a moderate amount of adversity may foster socialization (Elliot and King, 1960; Hess, 1960). But so many interruptions and frustrations happen in even well-run nursery schools (Jackson and Wolfson, 1968) that the elimination of needless sources of frustration makes sense.

Learn to identify and reflect the children's feelings to them, and help them express these feelings to the relevant people. In our society we seem to have reached the conclusion that it is dangerous to allow some emotions to be expressed, the assumption being that if they are expressed they will become stronger, but if we ignore them or deny their presence they will vanish. Actually, the opposite of this premise is psychologically true. Blake's poem puts this neatly:

I was angry with my friend,
I told my wrath, my wrath did end.
I was angry with my foe,
I told it not, my wrath did grow.

Negative emotions that are recognized, accepted, and expressed usually fade, but if not expressed they seem to generate pressure that causes the person to relieve them ultimately in a more explosive or veiled, yet hostile way.

The advantage of helping the child know how he feels is not only that he avoids overwhelming explosions or complicated emotional displacements but also that he learns that all emotions are acceptable and that, therefore, an important part of himself is acceptable. As he matures, this self-knowledge forms a foundation for learning to express feelings in a way that harms neither himself nor other people.

It takes practice and sensitivity to acquire the skills of reflecting the child's feelings to him and helping him express them, but research shows that teachers can learn these skills (Reif and Stollak, 1972). There is more to it than just saying to an angry child, "You're feeling really mad at him, aren't you?" Some examples will help illustrate the technique.

Evelyn says goodbye to her mother and then hangs by the gate, looking after her sadly as she drives away. Her teacher bends down, picks her up, and says, "You look like you wish she'd stay this morning, Evelyn." "I do, I do, I want her to stay—[emphatically] I hate her, that mean old mommy of mine, I hate her, and I wish she'd stay!" "Yeah, I know how it is— you feel sad she's left you, and it makes you mad because you wanted her to stay." "Yes! And I'm never, never going to speak to her

again." (They move toward the nursery school room and go inside.) "And I'm just going to feed her turnips and beans for dinner—turnips and beans, turnips and beans, turnips and beans!" But this is said with decreasing venom and increasing humor as she trails off toward the housekeeping corner to embark on her busy day.

In the following example the teacher, working with an older child, encourages him not only to express his feelings but to deal with the person who is causing the unhappiness.

Jonathan arrives at the woodworking bench very excited by the box of new wood he has spied from across the play yard. He reaches for Henry's hammer as it is laid down and is really surprised when Henry snatches it back. The teacher tells Jonathan that all the hammers are in use and he will have to wait. Jonathan stands on one foot and then the other—his hand obviously itching to snatch Henry's hammer. At this point, rather than trying to redirect him to the swings, the teacher says to him, "It's hard to wait, isn't it? I can see how much you want that hammer." "Yes, it is. I wish old Henry'd hurry." "Well, tell him so. Tell him what you want." "Henry, you old son of a bitch, I want that hammer when you're done." (The boys grin at each other.) The teacher suggests, "Why don't you saw some wood while you're waiting?" "Don't mind if I do," says Jonathan.

In the examples above, the teacher doesn't content herself with the simple statement to Evelyn, "You feel angry," or to Jonathan, "You feel impatient." Instead, she tries to describe to the child what he feels like doing as well as name the feeling for him if she's fairly sure she can identify it. Describing feelings or intended actions is particularly helpful when working with young children because they understand the statement, "You want her to stay," or "It's hard to wait," better than they grasp the label "angry" or "impatient." In addition, description has the advantage that it stands a better chance of being correct and that it is always better to talk about what a person does rather than what he is.

With a younger child or a less controlled one, the teacher may need to go further and reassure him by saying, "It's okay to want to grab it as long as you don't really do it." Sometimes she will need to go even further than that and actually restrain him, saying, "I can see you want to hit Henry, but I won't let you hurt him. Tell him you feel like taking his hammer." It takes many experiences for a young child to reach the level of the children in our examples, but it can be done.

Also, in the examples above, the teacher neither moralized with Evelyn, "Of course you really love your mother," nor offered an involved interpretation to the children of the reasons behind their behavior. Instead, she concentrated on letting the children know that she understood what they felt, that it was all right to talk about it, and that she would help them draw the line between feeling and acting if they needed that help.

There are many additional ways to express feelings through play and through the use of sublimative and expressive materials, which are discussed later on, but the ability to openly acknowledge feelings is the soundest and most fundamental therapeutic skill to use to foster mental health.

Learn to recognize signs of stress and emotional upset in children. Children give many signals besides crying or fussing that indicate emotional stress. Reverting (regressing) to less mature behavior is a very common signal. We are all familiar with the independent 4-year-old who suddenly wants to be babied while recovering from the flu or the child who wets his bed after the baby arrives.

Various nervous habits, such as hair twisting, sighing deeply, nailbiting, or thumb sucking, also reveal that the child is under stress. Increased irritability, sometimes to the point of tantrums, is another indicator, as is lethargy or withdrawing from activities. Sometimes expressions of tension or stress are more subtle and are conveyed only by a strained look about the eyes or a tightened mouth; sometimes stress is expressed in the more obvious form of excessive activity and running about.

In addition to this knowledge of common symptoms, as the year progresses and she gets to know the children well,

the teacher will have the additional advantage of knowing how each child usually behaves, which will make it easier for her to spot changes and identify children who are signalling for special help.

Know what to do for children who are emotionally upset. Emotional upsets have to be handled on a short-term basis and sometimes on a long-term basis as well.

SHORT-TERM, EMERGENCY TREATMENT. The first thing to do for a child who is upset to the point of tears is to comfort him. But the manner of comfort will vary from child to child: some youngsters need to be held and rocked, whereas others do best if allowed to reduce themselves to hiccupping silence while the teacher putters about nearby. Children who are using emotional outbursts as a means of controlling the adult's behavior require still a third response—mildly ignoring them until they subside.

No matter why a child is crying hard, it is a waste of energy to try to reason with him until he has calmed down. However, it can help soothe him to repeat something in a quieter and quieter tone of voice so that he gradually quiets himself to hear what is being said. This may be as simple a sentence as, "When you've stopped crying, we'll talk things over," or, "I'm waiting to help you when you've stopped crying." Occasionally, it can also be helpful to remark matter-of-factly if the occasion warrants, "You know, I will keep on holding you, even when you've stopped crying."

As the child calms down, getting a drink of water or washing his face may also soothe him. It's often effective at this point to talk over the difficulty, but sometimes it's better to wait and discuss it in a casual way later in the day to clarify how he felt or why he broke down. Each situation has to be judged in its own context.

Finally, the teacher should either help the child return and resolve the problem in the group, or if she deems it wiser, she should help him get started on another satisfying activity. Activities that are particularly helpful at such times include swinging, water play, or messy activities such as finger painting or clay. Water play generally seems to be the best choice.

It is always wise before deciding that an emotional upset represents a serious long-term difficulty to wait and see if the child is coming down with something; incipient illness is a frequent source of loss of emotional control. It is also wise to consider whether an approaching holiday could be causing the disturbance. Christmas and Halloween are notorious tension increasers, and we have found in our campus children's center that the weeks before and during college exams are likely to be edgy ones, also. Many episodes of fighting, crying, and other exaggerated responses to minor crises will disappear after such times have passed.

LONG-TERM TREATMENT. If the symptoms of stress do not subside, it is necessary to find out more about what is causing tension in the child. The behavior may be due to something going on at home or to something going on at school, or to a combination of these things.

One helpful way to locate the cause is to think back to the point when the signs of stress appeared and then to confer with the parent about what else changed in the child's life at about the same time. Per-

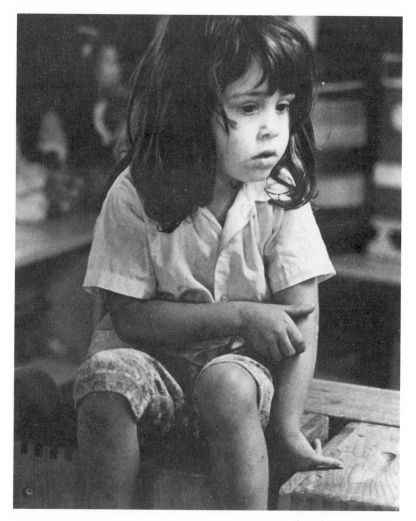

Photo by Gene Garrett
Los Niños Head Start

haps the youngster was moved to another group at nursery school, or his close friend was absent because of chicken pox; perhaps his grandfather died, or his father was away, or houseguests were visiting. Once the cause has been discovered, steps can be taken to help the youngster feel more at ease. Sometimes just recognizing the source helps a lot, without doing anything more.

Other signals of disturbance can be traced to continuing environmental situations. Perhaps discipline policies are erratic at home, or affection is lacking, or the child is excessively fatigued because he watches the late show on television. These are more difficult situations to deal with, but even they can often be successfully resolved by talking with the family.

If the situation is too complicated or difficult to be quickly eased by the teacher's intervention, she must encourage the family to seek counseling from a psychologist or a psychiatrist. The area of guidance and referral is such an extensive one that it cannot be treated in detail here. The reader is invited to pursue the subject further in Chapters 17 and 18.

SUMMARY

The therapeutic nursery school seeks to create as many opportunities as possible for young children to develop their sense of autonomy and initiative in a setting that is reasonable, consistent, trustful, empathic, and warm. Children who are mentally healthy are working on emotional tasks appropriate for their age. They are learning to separate from their families and to conform to school routines without undue stress. They can involve themselves deeply in play, and they are developing the ability to settle down and concentrate. Emotionally healthy children are not excessively withdrawn or aggressive; they have access to the full range of their feelings and are beginning to learn to deal with these feelings in appropriate ways.

The teacher can help the children in her care develop emotionally by forming a good relationship with their families, reducing frustration for them where she can, identifying and reflecting the children's feelings for them and helping them express these to the relevant people, recognizing the signs of stress that signal that help is needed, and handling emotional problems on a short-term and long-term basis when necessary.

QUESTIONS AND ACTIVITIES

1. What are some matter-of-fact ways to express warmth and liking to young children?
2. Looking back on your own education, give an example of a teacher who had unreasonably high expectations for you as a pupil. What was the effect on your learning?
3. What is the difference between feeling sympathy for someone and feeling empathy for him? Which attitude would be the more desirable one to develop when working with young children? Why?
4. With other members of the class set up some role-playing situations that provide opportunities for "children" to express their feelings, and practice phrasing responses from "teachers" that would help the child identify how he feels and show that the teacher understands him.
5. Do you believe it is always wise to be forthright about your own feelings? What limitations might be helpful to remember? On the other hand, can you think of times when it would have been better to take the risk and be more open and frank in your response? What did you do instead of being direct? Do you think that it was a satisfactory solution?
6. What are some examples where you have seen adults ignore, suppress, or mislabel a child's feelings? Could you see how the child was immediately affected by this kind of response? What would you predict might be the long-term effects of a child's experiencing many such responses to his feelings?

REFERENCES FOR FURTHER READING

Developmental Stages and Emotional Needs of Children

D'Evelyn, K. E. *Developing mentally healthy children.* Washington, D.C.: American Association of Elementary-Kindergarten-Nursery Educators, 1970. The pamphlet is written from the rarely presented viewpoint of the positive qualities of mental health that should be fostered in the classroom. The five "musts" included are: the child must know and feel he is an integral member of his class, must know what is expected of him, must become involved with his classmates, must begin to develop self-discipline, and must achieve according to his ability.

Erikson, E. H. *Childhood and society.* New York: W. W. Norton & Co., Inc., 1950. (2nd ed., 1963.)

Erikson, E. H. A healthy personality for every child. In R. H. Anderson and H. G. Shane (Eds.), *As the twig is bent: readings in early childhood education.* New York: Houghton Mifflin Co., 1971. These publications contain original source material that explains in detail Erikson's concepts of the eight stages of man and the emotional attitudes that are of paramount importance at various stages of development.

Moustakas, C. *The authentic teacher: sensitivity and awareness in the classroom.* Cambridge, Mass.: Howard A. Doyle, 1966. This rare book provides many examples of ways teachers can be more aware of mental health principles and can put them into practice in the classroom.

Redl, F., and Wattenberg, W. W. *Mental hygiene in teaching.* (2nd ed.) New York: Harcourt Brace Jovanovich, Inc., 1959. Chapter 4 is particularly valuable because it contains a clear-cut description of the mechanisms by which people (including young children) cope with emotional conflicts. It may be the best description ever written on this subject for teachers to use.

Waatjen, W. B., and Leeper, R. R. (Eds.) *Learning and mental health in the school.* Washington, D.C.: Association for Supervision & Curriculum Development, 1966. This discussion of the values of humanistic psychology emphasizes the development of competency, self-actualization, and "becoming." Ways these values can be incorporated in education are also discussed.

Establishing Sound Emotional Relationships with Children

Axline, V. M. *Dibs: in search of self.* Boston: Houghton Mifflin Co., 1964. This highly readable account, based on a case study of an appealing little boy named Dibs, illustrates what goes on in child-centered therapy and gives many examples of how to respond to children by accepting and reflecting their feelings.

Ginott, H. *Teacher and child.* New York: The Macmillan Co., 1972. This book is also filled with examples of dialogues between teachers and children that illustrate negative and positive methods of talking together. Although it focuses on older children, it would be helpful for any teacher to read.

Murphy, L. B., and Leeper, E. M. *More than a teacher.* Washington, D.C.: U.S. Department of Health, Education, and Welfare, 1970. This down-to-earth pamphlet, which explains very clearly the value of assuming a "mothering," nurturant role when teaching young children, is filled with everyday examples and useful suggestions.

Rogers, C. R. *On becoming a person.* Boston: Houghton Mifflin Co., 1961. Rogers sets forth his philosophy that desirable emotional relationships between people are facilitated by the presence of warmth, congruence, and empathy. *On Becoming a Person* is a good book of his to begin with because it is a collection of articles that can be sampled as the student's tastes and time dictate.

Descriptions of Mental Health Services

Joint Commission on the Mental Health of Children. *Mental health: from infancy through adolescence: reports of Task Forces I, II, and III, and the committees on education and religion.* New York: Harper & Row, Publishers, 1973. Recommendations for improving the mental health of children are given. The special section on education is particularly good, and the material on the preschool child is also valuable.

Looff, D. H. *Appalachia's children: the challenge of mental health.* Lexington, Ky.: University Press of Kentucky, 1971. The author presents a chatty, anecdotal account of how mental health services were implemented in three counties in Appalachia; interesting reading.

United States Office of Education and the National Institute of Mental Health. *Mental health and learning: when community mental health centers and school systems collaborate.* Washington, D.C.: U.S. Department of Health, Education, and Welfare, 1973. The need to facilitate cooperation between mental health services and schools is discussed and some model situations where this is taking place are described.

For the Advanced Student

Joint Commission on the Mental Health of Children. *Crisis in child mental health: challenge for the 1970's.* New York: Harper & Row, Publishers, 1970. The state of mental health and the emotional needs of children at the beginning of this decade are assessed. Evaluations and detailed recommendations made to the United States Congress concerning what should be done to improve the quality of mental health for the children of this country are included, and the important role of day care centers and nursery schools in this area are stressed; surprisingly readable and interesting.

Sigel, I. E., Starr, R., Secrist, A., Jackson, J. P., and Hill, E. Social and emotional development of young children. In J. L. Frost (Ed.), *Revisiting early childhood education: read-* *ings.* New York: Holt, Rinehart and Winston, Inc., 1973. The book of readings is a review of significant research concerned with social and emotional development. This article is particularly valuable because it discusses implications of research for day care at the end of each section.

Goleta Head Start, Santa Barbara

CHAPTER 6

Helping young children establish self-discipline and self-control

A nursery school with our "democratic" atmosphere . . . teaches attitudes, not by preaching or nagging or moralizing, but by demonstrating and encouraging the kinds of attitudes that make for harmony and understanding and tolerance. It teaches control of primitive impulses by clearly limiting and discouraging destructive behavior, and by offering acceptable substitutes as well as opportunities for discussion. It opens the doors of discovery of things and self by alerting children to the wonders of the everyday world, the joys and delights as well as the mysteries of the world around us. It is neither too rigid nor too permissive. It is human and caring.*

Because discipline worries beginning teachers the most, it is usually the subject they want to discuss first when they begin teaching. Sometimes this is because they fear physical aggression or that the children won't like them, but more frequently they fear losing control of the situation because they don't know what to do next. So when teachers say fervently that they want to discuss "discipline," what they usually have in mind is how to control the children or, as one forthright young student put it, "how to get the kids to do what I want."

TWO BASIC GOALS OF DISCIPLINE

Although "getting the kids to do what I want" is undeniably part of the package, should it be all that is encompassed by the

*From *Teaching young children* (p. 144), by Evelyn Beyer, copyright © 1968, by Western Publishing Company, Inc., reprinted by permission of The Bobbs-Merrill Company, Inc.

concept of discipline? The teacher should also have in mind the higher goal of instilling inner self-controls in the child in place of teacher-maintained external ones. Therefore, every discipline situation should not only achieve a workable solution to the current crisis but should also seek to interiorize self-control and self-management. This internalization of control rests on the gradual development of conscience and the development of ego strength. Here, again, the importance of warmth and caring must be emphasized. Research indicates that the development of conscience is associated with warm, nurturing parent-child and teacher-child relationships and with the ability to reason (Mussen, Conger, and Kagan, 1969; Sutton-Smith, 1973). Therefore, throughout this discussion of policy and techniques we must bear in mind that teachers should do all they can to create a warm, nurturing atmosphere and that they should take time whenever possible to offer truthful, brief explanations of what the rules are and why they exist.

In addition to internalizing controls, the teacher should work to teach the child to express his feelings verbally rather than physically. This is, of course, a sophisticated learning that not even nations have grasped completely, since they continue to resort to war. Nevertheless, the roots of this ability can be instilled in early childhood if the teacher and parent make a consistent effort to accomplish this.

HOW TO SET YOURSELF UP FOR A BAD DAY

One of the basic premises of this book is that teachers can set up good or poor environments for themselves and the children to live in. No one intentionally makes trouble for herself by creating a poor environment; yet so many of the situations listed below happen in nursery schools from time to time that it seems appropriate (as well as being fiendish fun) to begin by pointing them out before going on to a more positive discussion of ways to generate acceptable behavior.

TEN EASY WAYS NOT TO REACH THE BASIC GOALS OF GOOD DISCIPLINE

1. Make the children wait a lot, and expect them to sit quietly while they wait, preferably like little ladies and gentlemen with their hands in their laps and their feet on the floor.
2. Be inconsistent: let the children ride their trikes on the grass on days when you don't feel up to par, but take their trikes away when you're feeling better, because it's against the rules to ride on the grass.
3. Be unreasonable: never make allowances for children who are (1) tired, (2) hungry, (3) coming down with something, or (4) getting over something. It will also help ruin the day to have a great many arbitrary rules that are never explained although rigidly enforced.
4. Decide that the way to let children learn for themselves is never to intervene; pay no attention to the possibility that the younger, smaller children are being bullied and that some older ones are actually learning that "might makes right."
5. Be consistent: always punish the children by doing the same thing to them. For example, no matter what they do, make them sit in the office, or don't let them have dessert at lunch.
6. Give up half way through a confrontation, and let the child run off. After all, you're not supposed to leave your work station.
7. Lose your temper and yell at the children. This will frighten them into behaving and will make you feel better.
8. Strike a child; pinch him or jerk his arm when no one is looking. This will also frighten him badly, but maybe he'll behave after that.
9. Ignore the problem; just send the trouble maker off to play with the new teacher. It will help her gain experience.
10. Talk too much. Confuse the child: moralize, shame, or embarrass him, or warn him that you're going to tell his mother! This will help him understand the consequences of his actions and set an example of verbal control for him.

When behaviors such as these are singled out and listed, it is clear how undesirable such approaches are; and yet they are commoner than one would wish them to be in many schools, probably because they reflect discipline practices many teachers experienced in their homes while growing up. If the following principles are put into practice, the need for these more unproductive methods will be reduced.

PRACTICAL THINGS TO DO TO MAKE IT EASIER FOR CHILDREN TO BEHAVE IN ACCEPTABLE WAYS

There are three fundamental things to do to help children in nursery school behave in acceptable ways and to improve the ease and quality of discipline and control in the group: (1) prevent discipline situations when possible; (2) increase the child's feeling of self-worth so that he feels stronger and in better control of himself; and (3) know what to do when a crisis occurs.

Prevent discipline situations when possible

Reward behavior you want to see continued; don't reward behavior you wish to discourage. Children (and adults) repeat behavior from which they obtain satisfaction. This reward doesn't necessarily come in the form of payoffs of chocolate chips or gold stars. Whether teachers realize it or not, they use rewards every time they say "thank you" or "that's a good job," or even when they smile at a child. The value of this technique, which is one form of behavior modification called *positive reinforcement,* has been well proved, (Hilgard and Bower, 1966), and there is no doubt that it is an effective way to deal with recurring discipline and behavior problems. Therefore, when undesirable behavior persists, it is a good idea to take a look at what the child is getting out of it. Preventing the payoff can help eliminate the behavior. It is also very effective to note positive actions on the part of the children and to respond to them with pleasure, since this positive reward, combined with the pleasure inherent in successful accomplishment, is a very potent reinforcer.

When trouble repeats itself, analyze the situation and try changing it rather than nagging at the child. When something happens over and over, in addition to checking up on payoffs, the teacher should also think about changing the situation instead of the child. For example, instead of telling a restless youngster to be quiet all the time, it might be better to let him leave after hearing one story, to ask a volunteer to read to him alone, or even to let him play quietly nearby during story time until he becomes more interested and can be drawn gradually into the group.

Emphasize the positive rather than the negative; always tell the child the correct thing to do. This habit can be formed with a little practice. When using positive directions, rather than saying, "Don't get your feet wet," or "Stay out of that puddle," the teacher says, "Walk around the puddle." She says, "Put the sand in the dump truck," rather than, "Don't throw the sand." This technique is desirable not only because it reduces negative criticism, but also because it directs the child toward something he can do that is acceptable.

Give the child a choice whenever possible; but if he really has no choice, don't give him one. We have discussed in some detail the virtues of developing autonomy in children by providing many opportunities for choices. If a child is given a choice, the teacher should be prepared to honor it. Such questions as, "Do you want dessert?" "Would you rather fingerpaint or play with the blocks?" or "Would you like to pass the napkins today?" are examples of valid choices because it is all right if the child chooses to refuse. Unfortunately, many teachers use "Would you like—" or "Would you please—" or "Okay?" as a polite camouflage for conveying an order. Thus they inquire, "Let's get on the bus, okay?" or "Would you like to put on your sweater?" Young children are likely to retort "No!" when asked such questions, and then the teacher is really stuck. It is better not to ask, "Let's get on the bus, okay?" if the child has to get on the bus anyway, but to try saying, "The bus is here, and it's time to go home. Where do you want to sit?" or "It's cold today. If you want to go out, you will need to put on your sweater." In short, honor choices when given, but give no choice when there is none.

Warn ahead of time to make transitions easier. The teacher should anticipate transitions with the children a few minutes before the activity is due to change. She might say, "It's going to be lunch time pretty soon. I wonder what we're going to have?" Or she might warn, "There's just time for one more painting. Then you can help me wash the brushes, and we'll have a story." Warning ahead gives the children time to wind up what they're doing. Sometimes just walking around the yard and commenting here and there that soon it will be time to go in will serve this purpose. It takes the abruptness out of the situation and makes compliance with routines much easier for the children.

Avoid unnecessary constraints. Even in well-run nursery schools children are constrained from following their own pursuits more often than we may realize. For example, at the University of Chicago Nursery School, Jackson and Wolfson (1968) found that twenty constraining episodes took place every minute of the nursery school day. Although these constraints were not always teacher generated, this study points up the desirability of avoiding them whenever possible in order to reduce the children's feelings of frustration and increase their feelings of absorbed satisfaction.

Have as few rules as possible, but make the ones you do have stick. Unless the teacher is watchful rules will grow up like a thicket around each experience. But if situations are reviewed from time to time, unnecessary restrictions can be weeded out.

On the other hand, some rules are genuinely necessary, and their enforcement is desirable not only because research shows that establishing firm limits, coupled with warmth and a simple explanation of the reason behind the rule, enhances the child's self-esteem (Coopersmith, 1967; Sears, Maccoby, and Levin, 1957), but also because it increases his ability to establish inner controls. Therefore, the teacher does not need to feel uneasy about establishing reasonable restrictions—they are of genuine value to the child. When holding fast to a rule, it is wise to include a brief explanation for it, but it is not necessary and may even be confusing and offensive to go into a lot of preachy detail. Simply saying, "I can't let you bite her because it hurts too much," or "We flush the toilet so it's fresh for the next person," is sufficient. If a reason isn't easy to come up with, it may be a sign that the rule is not important and could be abandoned.

When supervising children, plan ahead. Try to anticipate the point where the children will become uninterested or the play will fall apart, and have alternatives ready to propose that will help the play continue to flourish. An insightful teacher might think, "Now, if I were he, what would I like to do next with those blocks and cars?" Perhaps it would be getting out the arches or the wood strips to make a garage, or maybe it would be constructing ramps for the cars to run down. Tactfully posing several possibilities to the children will serve to continue play and to lengthen concentration as well as keep the children happily occupied and out of trouble.

Keep the day interesting. To combat idleness, the nursery school day needs variety to it—not only variety of pace to avoid the fatigue that leads to misbehavior, but also variety of things to do to maintain interest and fun and to keep the children busy in productive ways. Accomplishing this requires planning and sensitivity, but it is well worth the investment of effort.

Increase the child's feelings of being a valuable, worthwhile person

Self-control depends on ego strength as well as on the conscience, and self-esteem makes the ego stronger. The child who thinks well of himself and feels competent is in a favorable position to assume command and control of himself.

Unfortunately, some children are noticed at nursery school only when they do something wrong. This continual negative relationship with the teacher does not enhance their feelings of self-worth. Even the "worst" child in school doesn't misbehave all the time. A considerable part of his day is spent in acceptable activities, and it is vital that he receive credit for his good behavior as well as control for his transgressions if his self-esteem is to remain intact.

The teacher does not have to gush about how wonderful the child is, but she can say, "Thank you very much for helping me. I appreciate it," or "You did that exactly right," or "I can see you're really trying; next time I bet it will work out for you." These honest expressions of approval will help balance the criticisms and are one of several essential ways to build the child's feelings of self-worth. (For a more complete discussion of helping the child develop self-esteem, see Chapter 8.)

Know what to do when a crisis occurs

Of course, the ideal to work toward even in crisis situations is to teach the children to solve their own problems, since in their adult life they won't always have a teacher present to arbitrate differences. The situations discussed in the following sections, however, are ones where it is evident that the child has to have help to control himself and to be able to take action that is socially acceptable. Even in these situations, the focus should never be on the God-like powers of the teacher to bring about justice, but on development of the child's ability to do this for himself.

When should the teacher step in and control misbehavior? Inexperienced teachers are often unsure of when they should interfere and when they should let children work the situation through between themselves. The general rule of thumb is that children should not be allowed to hurt other people (either children or grownups), to hurt themselves, or to destroy property. This policy leaves considerable latitude for noninterference, but it also sets a clear line for intervention. An occasional teacher is particularly unsure about whether she should allow children to hit her or kick her as a means of "getting their feelings out." Children should not be allowed to attack adults any more than adults should attack children. Aside from the fact that it hurts and can't help but make the teacher angry, permitting such attacks makes the child feel guilty and uncomfortable—he really knows he shouldn't be allowed to do it.

The best way to prevent physical attack if it appears to be imminent is to hoist the child on the hip, with his head forward and his feet stuck out behind. This unglamourous pose, known as the *football carry,* works very well to stave off attack and permit the teacher to carry the child someplace if she has to. Although it is rarely necessary to resort to such measures, it helps to know what to do in a real emergency.

When trouble brews, take action yourself before the child does. Over and over again, I have seen teachers sit on the sidelines and let a situation go from bad to worse until it explodes, and then step in to pick up the pieces. If the situation is one that will have to be stopped at some point, it is much more effective to step in before

trouble starts rather than a minute after blood has been shed.

Prompt intervention makes it more probable that the teacher can use a rational approach with the children; this is a better environment for teaching any skill. Intervening before the fight occurs also prevents either child from receiving gratification from the attack. For example, stepping in before one child bites another takes preternatural quickness but is vital to do because biting feels so good to the biter that no amount of punishment afterward detracts sufficiently from the satisfying reward of sinking teeth into unresisting flesh.

Keep your own emotions under control. One way children learn attitudes is by observing models (Bandura, Grusec, and Menlove, 1967; Bandura and Menlove, 1968). Teachers need to control their tempers, since by doing so they provide a model of self-control for the children to copy as well as because intense anger frightens children. Also, when discipline situations arise, it is not just one child and the teacher who are involved: every child in the room is likely to be covertly watching what is happening and drawing conclusions from it. Therefore, it is often valuable for the teacher to talk over what happened with various children afterward to help them deal with how they felt about it and to clarify and consolidate what they learned from it.

Sometimes, of course, it is simpler to advocate self-control in the teacher than to achieve it. Self-control is made easier by remembering that one is dealing with a child, by deliberately keeping control of oneself and by acknowledging the feeling and saying to the child, "Let's wait just a minute until we're both a little calmer. I feel pretty upset about what you did." The biggest help, though, comes from analyzing scenes and upsets after they have occurred and planning how best to handle them the next time they happen. This experience and analysis builds skills and confidence—and confidence is the great strengthener of self-control. Children sense this assurance in the teacher just the way dogs know who loves or fears them, and children become less challenging and more at ease when they feel the teacher knows how to cope and has every intention of doing so.

Handle disagreements between children fairly. In the chapter on mental health considerable time was spent in explaining how to help children express their feelings verbally. Although this is fairly easy to accomplish when the teacher is dealing with only one child, it is considerably more difficult but just as important when dealing with more than one. When two children are involved, it is a wonderful opportunity to help both of them develop this social skill, and the teacher should urge them to talk things over and to tell each other what they want and how they feel.

It is also essential that the teacher avoid being trapped into rendering judgments about situations she hasn't seen. Four-year-olds are particularly prone to tattle about the misdeeds of others. A polite name for this is *prosocial aggression;* it is a natural, if unappealing stage in the development of conscience. Unless the reported activity is truly dangerous, the best course of action in the case of tattling is for the teacher to encourage the child to return with her and settle the matter himself. She should avoid taking sides or the word of one child because George

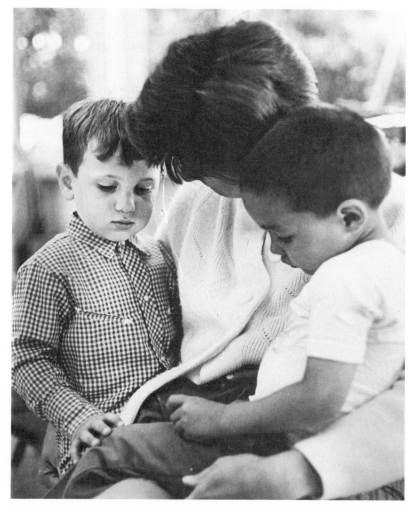

Los Niños Head Start

Washingtons are remarkably scarce in nursery school. When it is a case of who had what first, it may be necessary, if a compromise cannot be reached, to take whatever it is away from both youngsters for a while until they calm down. It is often the child who is crying the loudest who began the fight, although he may appear to need comforting the most. The only thing to do in situations such as this is be fair and deal with both children in a firm but nonjudgmental way. Impartiality is the keynote.

When a fight boils up, it can also be very helpful to call a meeting of the children who are nearby to discuss settling it. The point of such discussions is not to ask the witnesses who was to blame (remember, it takes two to make a fight), but to ask them for ideas and suggestions about how to arbitrate the difficulty. The fighters can often be prevailed upon to listen to what their peers have to suggest, and children often come up with surprisingly practical and fair solutions. Moreover, it is fine experience for them to think about how to get along together and work out solutions based on real life situations.

When a child has gone so far that he has hurt another youngster, he should be allowed to help remedy the injury. Perhaps he can put on the bandage or hold a cold towel on the bump. This constructive action helps him see the consequences of his act, relieve his guilty feelings, and show concern by doing something tangible. I do not believe children should be asked to say they're sorry. Often they aren't sorry, and even if they are, I fear teaching the lesson that glib apologies make everything all right.

Whenever possible, let the punishment fit the crime. Nursery school teachers (and enlightened parents) avoid doling out punishment in its usual forms. Teachers don't spank children, shut them in closets, take away their television privileges, or deny them dessert because they haven't been good. But they do allow another form of punishment when it is appropriate. This is simply permitting the child to experience the natural consequences of his behavior. Thus, the child who refuses to come in for snack is permitted to miss the meal; the child who rebelliously tears a page from a book is expected to mend it; and the youngster who pulls all the blocks off the shelf must stay to help put them away. Even young children can see the fairness of a punishment that fits the crime so aptly and appreciate the justice of a consequence that stems logically from the action. It is not necessary to be unpleasant or moralistic when any of these results transpire; it is the teacher's responsibility only to make certain that the child experiences the logical outcome of his behavior.

What to do when children continue to misbehave. Since children do not always stop throwing sand or grabbing tricycles simply because the teacher tells them to or redirects them to another activity, it is necessary to know what to do when a child continues to misbehave. I call the approach I use the four learning steps in discipline: (1) warning the child, (2) removing him, (3) waiting for him to decide when he is ready to return, and (4) helping him return and be more successful.

1. Warn the child, and redirect him if he will accept such redirection. For example, you might warn a youngster that if he continues to throw sand, he will lose the privilege of staying in the sandbox; then suggest a couple of interesting things he could do with the sand instead of throwing it. It is important to make the child understand that his behavior is up to him. It is *his* choice; but if he chooses to continue, you will see to it that you carry out your warning.

2. If he persists in doing what he has been told not to do, act calmly and promptly. Remove him and insist that he sit beside you, telling him he has lost the privilege of playing in the sand. This is more valuable than just letting him run off. Having him sit beside you interrupts what he wants to do, is a mildly unpleasant consequence of his act, and prevents his substituting another activity that is more pleasant.

3. At step 3, many teachers say something on the order of, "Now you sit

here until lunch is ready," thus shifting the responsibility for the child's behavior to their own shoulders instead of putting the child in command of himself. It is better to say, "Now, tell me when you can control yourself, and I will let you go back," or, more specifically, "When you can keep the sand down, tell me, and then you can go back and play." Some children can actually say they are ready, but others will need help from the teacher, who can ask them, when they look ready, "Are you ready to go back now?" (Perhaps he nods or just looks ready.) "Good, your eyes tell me you are," or "I can see by your nod you are. What would you like to do for fun there?"

4. Finally, it is important to go with the child and help him be successful when he does go back so that he has the experience of substituting acceptable for unacceptable behavior. It will probably be necessary to take a few minutes and get him really interested. Be sure to congratulate the child when he has settled down, perhaps saying, "Now, you're doing the right thing. I'm proud of you!"

Occasionally, the teacher will come across a more glib customer who says hastily when removed from the sandbox, "I'll be good, I'll be good!" but then goes right back to throwing sand when he returns. At this point it is necessary to take firmer action. Have him sit beside you until he can think of something acceptable to do, but don't permit him to go back to the sandbox. You might say, "What you did [be explicit] shows me that you haven't decided to do the right thing; so you'll have to come and sit with me until you can think of somewhere else to play. You've lost the privilege of playing in the sandbox." Then when he decides, go with him or alert another teacher so that he does start on something desirable to do.

Inexperienced teachers sometimes dread these confrontations because they fear that the child will be hostile afterward or actively dislike them for keeping their word and enforcing their authority. However, such confrontations almost invariably build a closer bond between the teacher and the child, who usually seeks her out and makes it evident that he likes her after such encounters.

Most important, notice when children do the right thing, and comment favorably

This entire chapter has been spent talking about preventing or coping with misbehavior. Fortunately, most of the nursery school day does not center around such episodes; many days go smoothly and the children get along happily. When the day is a good one, when the children are obviously making progress, when they mostly talk instead of sock each other, when they share generously and enjoy the opportunities to help each other, let them know that you are pleased with their good behavior. They will share your pleasure in their accomplishments, and this recognition will help perpetuate the growth and self-discipline that they have displayed.

SUMMARY

Discipline should be more than just "getting the kids to do what I want." It should also include development of inner controls in the children and should help them substitute verbal for physical reactions. There are many undesirable ways to control children, but there are also more desirable approaches, which can be subsumed under the general heading of preventing discipline situations when possible, building the child's ego strength and self-control by increasing his feelings of being a worthwhile person, and knowing what to do when a crisis occurs. When a child continues to misbehave, it is particularly important to take him through all four of the steps in learning self-control: (1) warning him, (2) removing him from the activity while keeping him with the teacher, (3) waiting for him to make the decision to return to the activity, and (4) helping him return and be more successful. Consistent use of this approach will be effective in helping children gain control of themselves, thus helping them to become socially acceptable human beings.

QUESTIONS

1. Have you ever had the experience of deciding, theoretically, how you intended to handle misbehavior, and then found yourself doing something different when the occasion actually came up? How do you account for this discrepancy?
2. What is the difference between moralizing and explaining to a child the reason why he cannot be allowed to do something?
3. *Problem:* A child is throwing sand in the sandbox, and you want him to stop. What should you say to put your statement in positive form rather than telling him what not to do; that is, rather than saying "Don't throw the sand"?
4. Select an activity, such as lunch time, and list every rule, spoken and implicit, that you expect children to observe in this situation. Are there any that could be abandoned? Are there any that are really for the teacher's convenience rather than for the purpose of fostering the children's well-being?
5. *Problem:* Elaine, who is $4^1/_2$, is playing at the puzzle table and keeps slipping little pieces of puzzle in her pocket. No one except you sees her doing this. You have already told her twice to keep the puzzles on the table so the pieces won't get lost, but she continues to challenge you by slipping them in her pocket. What should you do next to handle this situation?
6. *Problem:* As you enter the room you see John and David hanging on to a truck, both shouting that they had it first and that they can keep it until they're done with it. How would you cope with this crisis?

REFERENCES FOR FURTHER READING

Setting Limits for Children

Read, K. H. *The nursery school: a human relationships laboratory.* (5th ed.) Philadelphia: W. B. Saunders Co., 1971. Since it is impossible to touch on every point in every book, reading additional material on a subject as broad as discipline can be very helpful. Beginning students will find the chapters "Authority and the Setting of Limits" and "Initial Support through Guides to Speech and Action" very informative.

Establishing Control of the Group

Galambos, J. W. *A guide to discipline.* Washington, D.C.: National Association for the Education of Young Children, 1969. This all too brief pamphlet is filled with practical advice about how to handle such discipline situations as spitting, biting, and kicking. It contains many examples of things to say that will relieve, control, or prevent tense situations in the nursery school.

Murphy, L. B. and Leeper, E. M. *Away from bedlam.* Washington, D.C.: U.S. Department of Health, Education, and Welfare, 1970. Murphy and Leeper's very practical pamphlet discusses in plain terms how to maintain reasonable order and control in a nursery school classroom. It may be obtained from the superintendent of Documents, Washington, D.C.

Theories and Related Methods of Handling Children

Wittes, G., and Radin, N. *Ypsilanti home and school handbooks: helping your child to learn: the nurturance approach.* San Rafael, Calif.: Dimensions Publishing Co., 1969. Wittes and Radin provide a well-thought-out, carefully presented explanation of how to help children learn by using an approach based on love, understanding, respect, and mental stimulation. This booklet is an outline of a course developed for parents. It is very clear and contains many examples and group exercises for learning how to apply the suggestions to children.

Wittes, G., and Radin, N. *Ypsilanti home and school handbooks: helping your child to learn: the reinforcement approach.* San Rafael, Calif.: Dimensions Publishing Co., 1969. Presented in the same fashion as the booklet described above, this one explains reinforcement theory and outlines how to apply it to modify the behavior of young children. Although there are a great many books that deal with this subject, this is one of the best for beginning teachers because it is short, deals with preschool youngsters, and is very clear. In order to obtain a balanced understanding of the values and pitfalls of using behavior modification, I recommend that the student read the article by Lillian Katz, "Condition with Caution," *Young Children,* 1972, **27**, 5, in conjunction with it.

For the Advanced Student

Brown, D. G. *Behavior modification in child and school mental health: an annotated bibliography on applications with parents and teachers.* Rockville, Md.: National Institute of Mental Health, 1971. This reference is helpful for students who wish to explore the subject of behavior modification further, since it lists and summarizes 118 references in this field.

Los Niños Head Start

CHAPTER 7

Aggression: what to do about it*

It is not sufficient that a child simply be kept from doing damage at a given moment. He must develop standards of conduct that will not require constant policing in order to maintain acceptable kinds of behavior. He must come to possess appropriate internal controls. The kinds of aggression he finally learns to use must be appropriate in form and intensity, and they must be used only under acceptable circumstances.

The necessity for control of both action and learning at the same time leads to some difficulties in training children vis-à-vis aggression, for the consequences of a particular practice may be quite different in its short-term and long-term influences. One can introduce pressures to stop the fussing and whining, but this is only half the problem. Does the child learn to do what his mother wants the next time? What does he learn? How does he behave after the pressure is taken off?†

Now that the general subject of discipline has been discussed, it is time to talk about dealing with aggressive behavior in particular. In this context, aggressive behavior means: "actions that are intended to cause injury or anxiety to others, including hitting, kicking, destroying property, quarreling, derogating others, attacking others verbally and resisting requests" (Mussen, Conger, and Kagan, 1969). At the nursery school level we see examples of this kind of behavior manifested when children barge through the room, leaving a bedlam of smashed blocks or ravished housekeeping corners behind them, or when they spend most of their time whooping wildly about being tigers or monsters, or when they deliberately

seek to injure other children by destroying what they are doing, teasing them, or physically hurting them.

UNDESIRABLE WAYS TO COPE WITH AGGRESSION

Teachers and parents deal with acting-out behavior in both useful and not-so-useful ways. Some of the more undesirable methods of responding to such behavior follow.

The authoritarian teacher

At one extreme is the teacher who is a tightly controlling authoritarian. She responds to aggression in children as if expressing her own aggressive tendencies, garbed in the disguise of authority and control, were the only way to meet this problem. In forthright cases, schools dominated by such teachers are likely to be riddled with many rules generally determined by what is convenient for the teacher. "Don't run!" "Don't make noise!"

---

*Revised from *Young Children,* May 1968, **23**(5), 298-305.
†From Sears, R. R., Maccoby, E., and Levin, H. *Patterns of child rearing.* New York: Harper & Row, Publishers, 1957. P. 230.

"Sit down!" "Line up!" "Be quiet!" "Don't easel paint with your fingers!" "Stay clean!" "Don't splash!" "Take turns!" "Tell him you're sorry!"—and a thousand other tiresome injunctions are typical. Punishments used by such teachers are apt to be severe, occasionally to the point of being emotionally destructive or physically painful.

Sometimes a beleaguered teacher feels that controls of this type are necessary because the classes are too large or too obstreperous for her to cope with any other way. Sometimes she believes that this kind of control is what the parents expect and that she'd better conform to this expectation or the children will be withdrawn from school.

More than likely the real reason for her reaction runs deeper than this and has to do with strong patterns carrying over from her own childhood, when little tolerance and freedom were granted to her by the adults in her life. The frustration, resulting hostility, and covert aggression instilled by this treatment are particularly likely to be rearoused when she is confronted by the challenge of a belligerent 4-year-old. Transgressions are often dealt with by stringent punishments, and contests of will are highly probable if this teacher crosses swords with a genuinely spirited child.

What of the aggressive child who exists in this tightly controlled environment? What is the effect of overcontrol on him? For a few youngsters the bright edge of creative expression is dulled. Some children cannot afford to risk nonconforming (which is the essence of creativity) under these circumstances, and so most of their energy is used up holding onto themselves and "doing the right thing." These children have had their spirits broken. They conform—but at what a price!

There are almost bound to be other defiant young souls who continue to challenge or sneak past such a teacher. Common examples of such underground, continued aggression may range from quietly pulling the fur off the guinea pig to being unable to settle down for stories, or consistently destroying other children's accomplishments at the puzzle table or in the block corner.

Still other children internalize the angry feelings generated by authoritarian restrictions and become resistant and sullen or, in rare cases, turn their rage inward to such an extent that they attack themselves and bite their arms or gnaw their hands in a savage way.

In such schools a basic restlessness and tension seems to simmer in the air, and the teacher works harder and harder to hold the line, an exhausting business for all concerned. She tends to operate on the assumption that stronger punishment will result in greater control of aggression, but this is not necessarily true. Evidence from research studies indicates that strong punishment, particularly physical punishment, can actually increase the amount of aggressive behavior (Eron, Walder, Toigo, and Lefkowitz, 1963; Glueck and Glueck, 1950; Sears, Maccoby, and Levin, 1957). The teacher also overlooks the fact that there is a limit to how far she can go to enforce her dicta. What will she do if matters persist in getting out of hand?

The overpermissive teacher

At the other disciplinary extreme is the teacher who feels that "anything goes." Such teachers are often confused about the difference between freedom and license, and they fail to see that true freedom means the child may do as he wishes only as long as he does not interfere with the rights and freedom of other people. This extremely permissive teacher is fairly rare in nursery school because the pandemonium that occurs quickly makes parents uneasy. Apparently the results of this kind of mishandling are more obvious to the unprofessional eye than are the results of overcontrol.

In response to overpermissiveness the children may display behavior that is similar to the response for overcontrol. They may destroy other children's accomplishments or unconcernedly take whatever appeals to them. Sometimes they seem driven to tyrannical desperation trying to find out where the limits are and just how far they must go before the teacher at last overcomes her apathy and stirs herself to action. A common example of children's behavior in these circumstances is defiant teasing and baiting of the teacher by being ostentatiously, provocatively "naughty."

What the children really learn in such overpermissive circumstances is that "might makes right." This is a vicious circle, since the aggressor is often rewarded by getting what he wants and so is more likely to behave just as aggressively next time. Indeed, research indicates that attendance at a "permissive" nursery school does increase aggressive behavior (Patterson, Littman, and Bricker, 1967), and additional research by Bandura and Walters (1963) indicates that the presence of a permissive adult generally facilitates the expression of aggression.

The inconsistent teacher

The third undesirable way to deal with aggressive behavior is to be inconsistent. An inconsistent teacher may be unsure that it is really all right to control children, or she may be uncertain about how to control them; hence she deals erratically with out-of-hand behavior sometimes by enforcing a rule when she thinks she can make it stick and sometimes by sighing and letting the child run off or have his own way.

This approach, too, creates deep unease in children and fosters attempts by them to manipulate, control, and bargain in order to gain special dispensations. Whining, nagging, wheedling, and implied threats by the youngsters are all likely to be prime ingredients in this environment. For example, a 4-year-old may threaten, "If you don't give me that trike right now, I'll have to cry very, very hard, and then I'll prob'ly throw up, and you will have to tell my mother!"

Inconsistent handling may sound merely weak. However, it may actually be the most undesirable approach of all, since it has been found to produce extremely aggressive children (Sears, Maccoby, and Levin, 1957). The reason for this result may be that in the case of inconsistency the reward for aggressive behavior is in-termittent rather than continuous, and it has been effectively demonstrated that an intermittent reinforcement schedule is a very powerful means of causing behavior to continue.

Conclusion

It is fairly easy to see that the teacher who is overcontrolling (authoritarian) or undercontrolling (extremely permissive) or very inconsistent brings special difficulties upon herself when dealing with aggressive behavior. But it is less easy to determine what constitutes a reasonable balance between aggression and control and to decide how to handle this problem in an effective and healthy way. Teachers often feel confused about how and where to draw the line. They think it is important to relish the burgeoning vitality of young children, and so they want to provide vigorous, free, large muscle play, and plenty of it. But most teachers do not think that large muscle activity should be permitted to be expressed at nursery school as endless, aimless, wild running about or terrorizing the quieter children.

Many teachers can go along with the idea that the child has the right to destroy anything he has made so long as it is his own and not someone else's. However, they also believe that direct aggression in the form of throwing things at people, biting, hitting others with objects in hand, outright insolence, and defiance of rules are generally unacceptable. At the same time, they are likely to subscribe to the theory that it is unhealthy to suppress feelings of anger and hostility, which are generally expressed by aggressive behavior.

The problem is how to permit the expression of these feelings in ways that are acceptable at nursery school and in society. The remainder of this chapter provides some basic approaches that will help the teacher solve this problem.

DESIRABLE WAYS TO COPE WITH AGGRESSION
Assess the underlying causes of aggression, and ameliorate them when possible

First, it is helpful to remember that pronounced self-assertiveness is part of the

Los Niños Head Start

developmental picture for 4-year-old boys and girls. Many boys show evidence of this by attempting feats of daring, being physically aggressive, and swaggering about with an air of braggadocio. Girls are more likely to express it by being bossy or tattling in a busybody way on the wrong-doings of other children. But it is important to realize that this rather out-of-hand phase serves a healthy purpose for these youngsters who are busy finding out who they are by asserting their individuality (it is somewhat like adolescence in this regard). Assertiveness, then, can be basically growth enhancing, and for this fundamental reason it should not be crushed or unduly discouraged. However, when it goes beyond a tolerable point, it is necessary for the teacher to intervene.

Besides the influence of the developmental stage, native temperament may have a lot to do with the expression of aggression. Some children can stand more frustration than others can without exploding (Block and Martin, 1955). Sex-linked characteristics also affect its expression. Maccoby (1966) summarizes many studies indicating that in our culture more direct physical aggression is expressed by boys than by girls, and Feshbach (1969) has reported that girls are more likely to employ indirect means of expressing aggressive feelings. But how much of this behavior is due to biological differences and how much to culturally instilled values has yet to be determined.

In extreme cases of aggression, particularly when it is combined with hyperactivity, the possibility of brain damage should be considered, since lack of impulse control may be indicative of such a condition. Medication can produce considerable improvement in such behavior for some acting-out youngsters.

Parental mishandling is the reason most frequently given by teachers as the cause of undue aggression in children, and it is true that rejection, particularly cold, permissive rejection by parents, is associated with aggressive behavior in children (Glueck and Glueck, 1950; McCord, McCord, and Howard, 1961). If this appears to be the case, the teacher should encourage the parents to seek counseling.

It is all too easy for the teacher to slough off her responsibility for aggression in a child by raising her eyebrows and muttering, "He surely must have had a tough morning at home. What do you suppose she did to him this time?" It is more practical to think about how the school environment might also be contributing to the child's belligerent behavior, since this is the only area over which the teacher has any real control. She must take a look at the child and assess how he is relating to the nursery school program. At what time of day does he misbehave? With whom? What circumstances bring on an outburst? Does the child receive more criticism than positive recognition from the staff? Does he have to sit too long at story hour? Does he arrive hungry because of too light and hurried a breakfast and thus need an early snack? Is the program geared to the tastes of little girls and lacking in areas that hold a boy's interest?

There is no satisfactory substitute for this continuing analysis of the causes of aggressive behavior. Working to ameliorate such sources of frustration takes time and determination, but acting-out behavior will yield to treatment in the end, consistent handling does pay off, and the teacher will find in the long run that this is a productive way to come to terms with the problem of aggression.

Utilize direct control when necessary; then teach the child to find alternative ways to get what he desires

Direct control is an essential method of coping with children's aggressive behavior. A child must sometimes be definitely stopped from hurting another person or destroying property. As discussed in the chapter on discipline, it is important that the teacher step in before the child has experienced the gratification of seizing what he wants or of hurting someone. This is particularly true if it is unlikely that the child he has attacked will retaliate. It is also important to intervene promptly because it allows the teacher to act before she is angry herself, and it is highly desirable to present a model of self-control for an aggressive child to imitate.

Once the teacher has put a stop to the undesirable behavior, it is vital that she teach the aggressor a more acceptable way to achieve his ends. The first step is to take time with him to recognize his feelings and talk over what it is he wants. This recognition can be phrased as simply as, "I can see that you're dying to grab that trike," or, "I know how much you want to knock over their blocks when they won't let you play." After acknowledging the feeling, the next step is to supply the reason why such behavior is unacceptable. It is best for the child to state this himself if he can. For example, the teacher might ask, "But what is the rule about trikes?" If the child cannot state the reason, the teacher should do this for him. "Remember our rule? The person who has it first can keep it until she's done with it," or "You can knock down the things you build yourself, but you can't knock down other people's buildings unless they say it's all right." The reason provided should be brief and truthful. Moralizing should be avoided; it only antagonizes the child further.

Following the clear statement of the reason for the restraint, the final step is to help the child work out alternative ways of getting what he wants. Perhaps the aggressor can be encouraged to *tell* the other child that he wants a turn; sometimes a substitute satisfaction can be provided (perhaps another tricycle can be located); sometimes a cooperative arrangement can be developed (the child might deliver blocks to the block builders in one of the trucks); sometimes a diversion can be created ("How about using the swing until Marie is done with the trike?"); and sometimes the child just has to wait until the other youngster is finished, or he has to accept the fact that he is rejected and find someone else to play with.

Whatever alternative is employed, the teacher should see that the child clearly understands that hurting others is not allowed but that this need not mean he must swallow his anger and knuckle

Los Niños Head Start

under; instead, there are a variety of both effective and acceptable ways to get what he wants.

Permit reasonable deviations from the rules

Despite the fact that consistency is important and should generally prevail as a policy, there are exceptions to this rule. We have all seen timid children at school and have rejoiced when they finally ventured to shove back and stand up for their rights. It is important for such children to express these aggressive feelings in some form and come out of their shell as a first step; learning control can come later. The teacher simply has to use her knowledge of the children and her good judgment in these matters.

The teacher must also make allowances for children when they are under special stress. For example, her standards should not be unreasonably high at 11:00 in the morning, since lowered blood sugar levels at that time usually mean lowered self-control. This is the time to practice adroit avoidance of confrontations, since children cannot be expected to control themselves very well under such circumstances. The same thing holds true for children who are recovering from illnesses or undergoing family problems. They may require that special allowances be made for them until they have regained their emotional balance.

Reduce frustrating circumstances when possible

Although controversy continues over whether aggression is an inherent trait (Lorenz, 1966) or a learned behavior (Bandura, 1973), there is considerable evidence that frustration makes the expression of aggression more likely (Otis and McCandless, 1955; Sutton-Smith, 1973; Yarrow, 1948). Thus it makes sense to reduce aggression by reducing frustration where it is possible to do so.

Frustration usually occurs when the child wants something he cannot have, be it the teacher's attention, going outside to play, or the new fire engine. It is not possible to remove all frustrating circumstances from the life of a child, and it would not be desirable to do so anyway, since this would mean that he never has a chance to learn to cope with these feelings. However, there are so many restrictions and frustrations in everyday life that we really do not have to be concerned over the possibility of living in an environment without frustration (Jackson and Wolfson, 1968).

As previously described, the most effective way to reduce frustration is to help the child learn acceptable ways to get what he wants. Another way to reduce frustration is to have a plentiful amount of play equipment available. It is always desirable to have several tricycles, three or four swings, and a number of trucks, toy cars, sandbox shovels, and hammers. Children cannot endure waiting very long, and enough play materials will reduce the agony of anticipation, which can lead to frustration and acting out.

Still another way to reduce frustration is to keep rules to a minimum. The enforcement of the many petty rules cited in the discussion of the authoritarian teacher is one of the quickest ways to build anger in children, because such rules often go hand in hand with unreasonably high expectations of behavior, such as insisting that young children stand in line, sit for extended periods while waiting for something to happen, and never raise their voices.

Finally, two other good frustration preventers, also previously mentioned, are following the policy of warning in advance so that children have the chance to prepare themselves for making a transition to a new activity and providing many opportunities for choices in order to reduce children's feelings of defiance and help them feel that they are masters of their environment.

Provide substitute opportunities for socially acceptable expressions of aggression

The substitution of socially acceptable aggressive activities in place of those that cannot be tolerated is valuable because it is both emotionally satisfying to the child and safe for those around him.

Such activities are best offered, however, before the child reaches the boiling point. It is generally unsatisfactory to march a youngster over to a punching bag after he has hit someone and say, "It's all right to sock this!" By the time this happens, or by the time he gets the boxing gloves on and the fight set up, a lot of the flavor has gone out of the experience. It is better to offer acceptable aggressive activities as part of each day, as well as to make sure they are available when the teacher anticipates that the day will be especially tense either for an individual child who is upset or for the entire group (on Halloween, for example). Fortunately, there are a great many activities that will help. Remember, though, that these activities are substitutes for what the child would really prefer to do. When offering someone a substitute experience, be as free with it as possible, and supply plenty of material, plenty of time, and as few restrictions as you can tolerate.

In general, any kind of large muscle activity that does not have to be tightly controlled is valuable. Nursery school teachers tend to buy play equipment that is too small to take the vigorous activity of 4- and 5-year-old boys. It is always better to invest a few more dollars and buy sturdy, large equipment that will stand up to hard use rather than to continually nag the children, "Don't shake the jungle gym, you'll break it," or "Not too high now!" Try the following specific suggestions.

Jumping on old mattresses spread out on the grass or jumping off jungle gyms or boxes onto mattresses works off energy harmlessly and satisfies a need to be daring as well.

Swinging is particularly effective because the rhythm is soothing and because it isolates the child from his companions and calms him at the same time. If the teacher has time to do some friendly pushing, the one-to-one relationship is easing, too.

Trike riding, climbing, and sliding, or, as a matter of fact, anything that works off energy harmlessly helps.

Activities that provide for vigorous use of the hands in an aggressive yet acceptable manner should also be included. If the teacher joins in with gusto from time to time and uses the material herself, the child will often participate with more spirit.

Beanbags are fine to use for this purpose, but rules should be established about where they are to be thrown. A large wall, maybe with a face on it, is best, and the more beanbags the better. It is no fun to have to stop and pick them up after every three throws. Thirty bags are about the right number.

Punching bags have some use, but it is hard for young children to coordinate really satisfying socks with the bag's tendency to rebound.

Inflatable clowns are somewhat useful, but there may be trouble with maintaining them in airtight condition.

Hammering, sawing, and using the brace and bit, but most particularly hammering and even smashing things, such as old egg cartons, orange crates, or piano cases is quite relieving. Very young chil-dren can use "knock-out" benches for this same purpose.

Large quantities of dough, (not tiny, unsatisfying dabs) are fine aggression relievers. We restrict the tools the children use with it (such as cookie cutters) and encourage the children to stand at the table so that they can work forcefully, using their hands to pound and squeeze and pinch and punish the dough to their heart's content.

In fingerpainting and other types of smearing techniques such as soap painting, emphasis should be placed on richness of color and lots of gooey paint base, be it liquid starch, wallpaper paste, or homemade, very thick, cooked starch.

Once in a while, a particular child finds relief in tearing and crumpling paper. Again, large amounts are better than small amounts.

Although cutting up fruits and vegetables requires considerable self-control (by child and teacher), for some children the controlled opportunity to use a knife can be helpful. It's best to start with things such as bananas, which are easy to cut and which don't wobble around. Mashing potatoes is another good aggression reliever.

Noise is a good outlet for expressing aggression. The aggression-relieving possibilities of sheer noise (at least on the days when the teacher doesn't have a headache) should not be overlooked. It is wise to remember that noise has an infectious effect on the entire group and may accelerate activity too much. However, on the many occasions when things are in good order, I am all in favor of noise! Drums are an all-time, satisfying "best" for noise, but pounding on the piano is good, too. Real music and dancing can be added for those who enjoy it. Sitting on top of the slide and kicking heels hard makes a wonderful, satisfying noise. Yelling and playing loudly, and crying—the louder the better—also serve to work off feelings.

Opportunities for dramatic play can also help the child work off aggressive feelings. Direct participation by dressing up and playing house will let youngsters work through situations that may be troubling them. Anyone who has ever watched an irate young "mama" wallop her "naughty" baby doll will understand the merit of providing this kind of play material as an aggression reliever. Doll house furniture and little dolls are useful, but more so for 4-year-olds than for 3-year-olds.

Sets of fairly large rubber wild animals and hand puppets lend themselves admirably to aggressive play. Interestingly enough, the animal that produces the greatest amount of this play is not the lion or tiger, but the hippopotamus. I have concluded that it is the open mouth and all those teeth that brings this out. It makes me think how angry adults with toothy open mouths must appear to children, particularly since youngsters tend to look up and in!

The best and most relieving thing for out-of-hand children to play with is water. It is deeply relaxing in any form. Washing doll clothes or plastic cars, playing with soap bubbles, or playing with water in the housekeeping area is beneficial.

Whenever weather permits, the best thing of all is a running hose and lots of sand and mud. This combination has led to some of the calmest, happiest days we have ever had in our school, but pouring and playing with water in tubs or basins can also be satisfying. At home, a warm bath can work miracles.

Spitting (in a clearly designated place) helps an occasional child, especially one who has become so angry that he can't talk.

Finally, encouraging very overactive youngsters to take time out to go to the toilet often simmers things down considerably.

Additional techniques to help reduce the amount of aggressive behavior

So much for the specifics. There are also some general techniques that the teacher may find helpful for handling aggression.

Provide kindly, one-to-one attention for acting-out children. A few minutes consistently invested every day with an aggressive child when he is doing positive things (that is, before he gets into difficulties) often works wonders.

Stopping some activities before they start

saves criticism and discipline later. I have learned, for example, to keep an eye out for "angry monster" games or a local variation on the same theme, referred to as "Golden Eagle" by some young friends of mine. When such a game gets too high pitched, the quickest way to bring it under control is to look for the ringleader and get him involved in something else that he particularly likes.

Our staff discourages gun play at our Center. We believe that children can play at better things than killing each other, and it is also true that such play usually leads to overexcited running about. Therefore, when guns are brought to school, they are stored in the cubbies until it is time for the children to go home.

Be on the lookout for combinations of personalities that are currently poisonous, and do what you can to dilute them. Children who egg each other into trouble should not snack together or rest near each other, and other friendships for both children should be encouraged.

Finally, plan, plan, plan! Plan to provide interesting activities that children really like, and plan the daily program with specific children in mind. ("John is coming today, I'd better get out the hammers and saws.") The program must not make undue demands on their self-control and should include acceptable outlets for their energy. As a general principle, consistent opportunities that allow children to achieve mastery and competence in acceptable areas should be provided. Every time a youngster can do something well, whether it's building blocks, doing helpful, meaningful work, creating a painting, or learning to pump on the swing, his aggression has been channeled into accomplishing something constructive.

SUMMARY

Aggressive behavior is defined as action that is intended to cause injury or anxiety to others. This kind of behavior needs careful handling and guidance in the nursery school so that children are not forced to suppress such feelings completely, but learn instead to channel these impulses into socially acceptable activities.

Three approaches to coping with aggression in young children are particularly undesirable, since they are all likely to increase aggressive responses from them. These include authoritarian, overpermissive, and inconsistent methods of dealing with such behavior.

On the more positive side, several approaches for working with acting-out children are effective in reducing and channeling such behavior. Among these are assessing the underlying causes of aggression and ameliorating them when possible, utilizing direct control when necessary, and teaching the child to find alternative ways to obtain his desires. In addition, permitting reasonable deviations from the rules in special cases and reducing frustrating circumstances when possible are helpful. Finally, substituting socially acceptable opportunities for expressing aggression can relieve the child's feelings without jeopardizing the safety and happiness of those around him.

The teacher who applies these principles when handling aggressive behavior will reduce tension within the child and herself by preventing aggressive feelings from building up and will also help the child remain happier, more open, and more ready to welcome life with enthusiasm.

QUESTIONS AND ACTIVITIES

1. Everyone seems to have different "breaking points" in tolerating aggression. For example, one person sees red if a child is insolent, whereas another finds it more difficult to put up with a child who is cruel to animals or who deliberately hurts another child. Compare notes among the people in class about what they feel constitutes acceptable ways to express aggression and where their breaking points are.
2. Some reasons why a teacher might be too authoritarian are suggested in this book. What are some reasons that might lie behind the behavior of the teacher who is too permissive?
3. Keep an eye out during the coming week, and observe and briefly record several situations where children or staff members appeared to be angry. Note what each individual did about this feeling. If the teacher was working with a child, what did she do to help the youngster recognize and express his feelings in an acceptable way?
4. Are there any "discipline" situations in your school that seem to recur? For example, are the children always being told not to tap their glasses on the table while waiting for lunch? Suggest several ways the situation could be changed instead of continuing to "teach the children to behave."

REFERENCES FOR FURTHER READING

Introductory Overviews

McCandless, B. R., and Evans, E. D. *Children and youth: psychosocial development.* Hinsdale, Ill.; Dryden Press, 1973. The chapter entitled "Areas of Psychosocial Conflict" contains a succinct but good overview on the subject of aggression, including a review of the effects of television on aggressive behavior. It concludes with some helpful recommendations about ways to reduce the expression of aggression.

Sears, R. R., Maccoby, E. E., and Levin, H. *Patterns of child rearing.* New York: Harper and Row, Publishers, 1957. This material is based on a research study, but the discussion ranges beyond the usual narrow description of results and presents a penetrating analysis of aggression and its probable antecedents; readable and clear.

Practical Advice about Dealing with the Aggressive Child

Beyer, E. *Teaching young children.* New York: The Bobbs-Merrill Co., Inc., 1968. Evelyn Beyer uses a realistic, anecdotal approach to describe an overly aggressive and an overly withdrawn child. These chapters contain many practical recommendations for managing both kinds of behavior.

Read, K. *The nursery school: a human relationships laboratory.* (5th ed.) Philadelphia: W. B. Saunders Co., 1971. Another good discussion of hostility and aggression is contained in Chapter 17. Katherine Read discusses probable causes of aggression and makes recommendations for accepting and handling hostile feelings. Chapter 17 should be read in conjunction with Chapter 18, "Authority and the Setting of Limits." The tone of the book is somewhat freudian.

Redl, F. *When we deal with children.* New York: The Free Press, 1966.

Redl, F., and Wineman, D. *Children who hate.* New York: The Free Press, 1951.

Redl, F., and Wineman, D. *Controls from within.* New York: The Free Press, 1952. All three of these books are indispensable for understanding the causes of aggression and the means of handling it. Dr. Redl knows a great deal, on both a theoretical and a practical level, about working with angry, acting-out children; highly recommended.

Sheviakov, G. *Anger in children.* Washington, D. C.: American Association of Elementary-Kindergarten-Nursery Educators, 1969. Although written about older children, this pamphlet offers a useful discussion of the causes of anger in the classroom and practical suggestions for coping with angry children.

For the Advanced Student

Bandura, A. *Aggression: a social learning analysis.* Englewood Cliffs, N.J.: Prentice-Hall, Inc., 1973. The author favors the utilization of behavior modification techniques to reduce aggressive behavior; an important reference in this field.

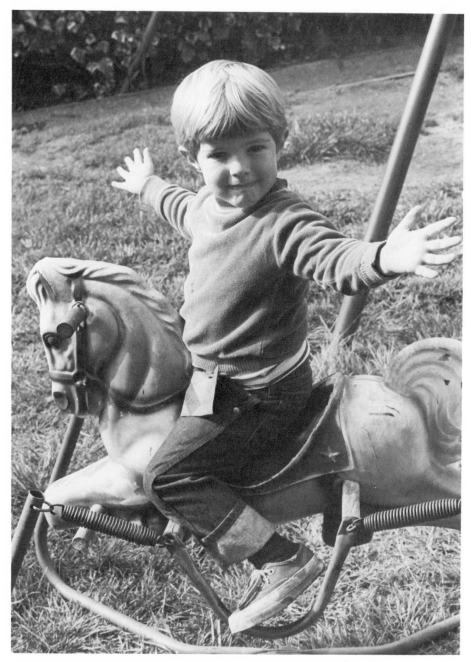

Photo by Jason Lo'Cicero

CHAPTER **8**

Developing self-esteem in young children

Children cannot be fooled by empty praise and condescending encouragement.*

Feeling oneself to be a person who has something worthwhile to contribute to the life around him is an important aspect of being mentally healthy. It is the kind of feeling I have in mind when describing an individual who possesses self-esteem. A person who feels this way about himself is able to venture out into the world, work toward attaining what he hopes for, and welcome life with pleasureful anticipation.

On the other hand, individuals who lack self-esteem fit, to varying degrees, the following description.

Persons who seek psychological and psychiatric help frequently acknowledge that they suffer from feelings of inadequacy and unworthiness (Wylie, 1961). They tend to perceive themselves as helpless and inferior (Rogers and Dymond, 1954), have difficulty in either giving or receiving love (Fromm, 1939), and tend to feel isolated and alone (Coopersmith, 1967). They are likely to feel guilty, ashamed, or depressed, and to derogate their own potential and accomplishments (Coopersmith, 1967). . . . Furthermore, the anxious child's tendency to derogate himself tends to generalize and affect his image of

his bodily integrity and adequacy as well (Ruebush, 1960; Walsh, 1956). A negative self-concept appears to promote defensiveness in the child's reactions to himself and others (Riley, 1966; Ruebush, 1960).*

It is apparent, then, that a good self-concept and self-esteem are highly desirable qualities to foster in young children, since no one wants children to suffer from the feelings described in the paragraph above. What teachers and parents need to understand more clearly is how to help children generate good feelings about themselves that are based on reality.

RELATIONSHIP OF SELF-ESTEEM TO SELF-CONCEPT

Self-esteem and self-concept are very closely related to each other. Self-concept refers to an individual's idea of who he is. His feelings of self-esteem result from his reaction to what he sees himself as being and to his anticipation of being accepted or rejected (Dinkmeyer, 1965). Thus a youngster who is well coordinated, who is sought after by his playmates, and who

*From Erikson, E. *Childhood and society.* (2nd ed.) New York: W. W. Norton & Co., Inc., 1963. P. 235.

*From Mussen, P. H., Conger, J. J., and Kagan, J. *Child development and personality.* New York: Harper & Row, Publishers, 1969. P. 489.

gets along well with his teacher will probably see himself as adequate and will possess good feelings of self-esteem, whereas an overweight high school girl suffering from a poor complexion and few friends may come to think of herself as being unattractive and unlovable and as a result will hold herself in low esteem.

SOURCES OF SELF-ESTEEM

Although individuals should ultimately develop internal resources for generating self-esteem, in the early stages of growth the child's feelings of self-esteem come from the people around him. Parents are very significant influences (Baumrind, 1972; Coopersmith, 1967). As children move out into the larger world, the opinions of other adults, such as teachers, become important, too, as do the opinions of their peers. That society also has an impact is evident from studies indicating that many people of minority group status possess lower self-esteem than others do (Dworkin, 1965; Zirkel, 1971). Because the unhappy effects of persistent prejudice on the self-image and esteem of minority children cannot be overestimated, an entire chapter is therefore devoted to a discussion of ways to sustain or improve the self-image of such youngsters (Chapter 10).

Since there are so many powerful factors that influence the development of self-esteem, teachers should not believe that they can completely alter the way a child sees himself. However, they can establish policies in their classrooms that will help build a child's self-esteem, and they can meticulously avoid employing practices that are likely to have destructive side effects.

COMMON SCHOOL PRACTICES LIKELY TO REDUCE FEELINGS OF SELF-ESTEEM
Using comparison and competition to motivate good behavior

Competitiveness reaches a peak in children around the age of 4 to 5 years (Stott and Ball, 1957), and it is all too easy for the teacher to use this fact to obtain quick results by asking, "I wonder who can get his coat on quickest today?" or by commenting, "See how carefully Shirley is putting her blocks away? Why can't you do it like that?" The trouble with motivating behavior by drawing such comparisons and setting up competitive situations is that only a few children "win" under this system. Even the child who turns out to be "best" and whose self-esteem has presumably been enhanced pays an unfortunate price, since he has obtained his self-esteem at the expense of the other children's well-being.

A more desirable way to use comparison is by invoking it in relation to the child's own past performance. This can be a true source of satisfaction for him when the teacher says, "My goodness, John, you're learning to pump better and better every time you try!" or, "Remember the way you used to bite people? You haven't done that in a long time now. I'm proud of you!"

Overhelping and overprotecting children

A teacher may unintentionally lower a child's self-esteem is by doing too much for him. Thus she rushes in to carry the bucket of water so that it won't slop, or without thinking she puts all the shoes and socks on the children following nap. Helping in these ways has the virtue of saving time and assuring that the job will be done properly as well as keeping the teacher busy. But it is much more desirable to wait and let the child do things for himself, since this allows him to experience the triumph of independence that such achievement brings.

Judging children in their hearing

Children often develop ideas of who they are from hearing what other people say about them. Sometimes this happens in direct form, as when the teacher says impatiently, "Come along now; you're always so slow," or asks, "How can you be so selfish?" Other children are also prone to deliver pronouncements such as, "You pig! You never share anything," or "Hazel is a pooh-pooh pants, Hazel is a pooh-pooh pants!" Labels such as these tend to stick; enough of them plastered on a child can convince him that he is neither liked nor worth much, so he might as well not try.

Sometimes negative evaluations are not delivered directly to the child but are said over his head to someone else instead. "My, aren't we in a terrible temper today!" "I see she's having a hard day again!" "There's no point asking *him*—he always holds on like grim death!" Somehow, overheard comments have a special, painful power to compel belief. The teacher should avoid making them not only for this reason but also because they may hurt a child's feelings and can strengthen a negative self-image. On a more subtle level, talking over a child's head implies that he is not important enough to be included directly in the conversation.

POSITIVE METHODS OF ENHANCING SELF-ESTEEM
Unconditional positive regard

The most effective way to help a child build a basic feeling of self-esteem is, unfortunately, also the most elusive for some teachers to achieve: the ability to feel and project what Carl Rogers terms unconditional positive regard. This kind of fundamental acceptance and approval of each child is not contingent upon his meeting the teacher's expectations of what he should be but simply depends on his being alive, being a child, and being in her group. It implies a kind of optimism about the way the child will turn out, which subtly makes him aware that the teacher has faith that he will grow in sound directions.

There is no substitute for these underlying feelings of trust and confidence in the child. Some teachers are fortunate enough to have developed optimism about people as a result of their own trust-building childhood experiences; some gain it from long experience with children themselves, and some acquire it by means of psychotherapeutic treatment, which helps restore their own confidence as well as their faith in others.

Acceptance of the child as he is also includes accepting his right to be different from the teacher and from the other children. Here again, ethnic and cultural differences come particularly to mind (Chapter 10). A teacher can make a significant contribution to increasing the self-esteem of minority children by unconditionally valuing them herself and by using herself as a model to influence the attitude of the other children.

Honest recognition and praise

Rewarding a child with praise is usually the first way teachers think of to build self-esteem. Unfortunately, sometimes praise is the only method they think of. Actually, it is only one of several ways to enhance a child's feelings of self-worth.

It almost goes without saying that such praise must be sincere in order to be effective. Teachers who use praise continually as a means of reinforcing behavior often dole it out in such a mechanical way that it comes to have almost no meaning at all. On the other hand, some teachers hardly ever take time to comment favorably on what a child has done. They seem to feel that praise weakens character and that individuals should do things simply because it is right to do them; but praise that is merited should be given freely—honest recognition is sweet indeed.

It is just as important to appreciate the effort of children when they have not been successful. They particularly need encouragement at this point, since the reward inherent in successful accomplishment has not been realized. The teacher can say, "I see how hard you've worked at that," or, "I'm proud of you; you really tried," or, "It takes a while to learn to do that. You've really stuck with it; pretty soon you'll learn how."

Respect

Respecting the child is such a high-minded phrase that examples of behavior must be provided in order to see how respect can be implemented in the nursery school. One basic way to show respect is to abide by the child's decision when he has been given a valid choice (also see Chapter 6). When a teacher does this, she is really saying, "What you want is important. I have confidence that you know yourself better than I do, and I count on you to choose what will enhance your existence most."

Another way to show respect and thus sustain the child's self-esteem is to avoid humiliating a child in front of other people. It is best to carry out discipline measures as unobtrusively as possible. Belittling a child's behavior at any time is, of course, fundamentally disrespectful as well as destructive of self-esteem.

A third valuable way to show respect is to pay the child the compliment of explaining the reason behind the rule. Coopersmith (1967), who carried out an extensive study of children possessing high self-esteem, found that parents of such youngsters were firm in their control of them but also took time to explain the reason for their actions. Such reasoning confers respect because it assumes that the child is important enough to be entitled to an explanation and intelligent enough to comprehend it.

Helping the child achieve competence

The practices enumerated thus far are external sources of a child's self-esteem. Although all of them are sound in that they will help build positive self-pictures for children, they have one weakness in common: they all depend on the good will of another person for implementation. Yet the ultimate goal should be the internalization of esteem in order that the individual will not remain permanently dependent on others to supply his feelings of self-worth.

The teacher can help a child develop inner sources of self-esteem by fostering the child's competence. Once he is able to do something well, whether it is practicing diplomacy in the housekeeping corner or using the brace and bit, he has gained a small portion of confidence in himself that does not require the plaudits of others to sustain it.

Robert White (1968, 1972) has suggested that the drive toward competence is a powerfully motivating agent in people's lives. He defines competence as "effectiveness in dealing with the environment." This effectiveness builds a child's self-esteem by helping him feel masterful; thus competence is worth enhancing in young children. Fortunately, there are many opportunities to do this in the nursery school.

Allowing children to experience mastery by making their own choices and by being as independent as possible are two ways to encourage competence that have already been discussed. Coupled with allowing children to do things for themselves goes the establishment of reasonable standards of achievement. For instance, a teacher who wishes to build self-esteem in a newly generous little girl appreciates her helpfulness when she volunteers to pass the snack and overlooks the fact that she has served herself first, just as she thanks the child who has stuffed his boots away in his cubby and refrains from telling him to fix them so the toes point out.

The teacher can also provide many different ways for children to experience success. Sheer variety of activities is important here, since one child may excel at assembling puzzles, whereas another's forte may be hanging by her heels on the jungle gym. It is important, also, not to be too hidebound when selecting curriculum activities, since a youngster may possess a special skill not usually thought of as suitable for nursery school but that, when well used, can confer distinction on him and enrich the lives of the other children. Our Center, for example, recently had a child attending who loved to embroider. She knew several stitches, and two or three of the older children relished learning them from her, although "everyone knows" that embroidery is too difficult for preschool children to carry out successfully.

Creative activities offer excellent opportunities for experiencing competence, since there is so much latitude for individual ability and differentness in these areas. It feels good to make something that is attractive; and if the materials and colors provided by the nursery school teacher are harmonious, most things made by the children will have a satisfying outcome and thus enhance the children's feelings of self-esteem.

It is also worthwhile to provide opportunities that are challenging but not excessively difficult in order to give the children the chance to test themselves against difficulties. The daring-do of 4-year-olds is a prime example of this desire to make things a little bit harder every time they attempt them. (The reader may recall learning the game of jacks and its steady progression from "Rolling Down Broadway" to the more difficult game "Around the World" and finally on to "Eggs in a Basket" and "Shooting Star.") In general, children should always be allowed to attempt more difficult feats as they think of them unless it is evident that they have not anticipated any serious dangers that may be involved.

In addition to competence in activities and motor skills, interpersonal competence is of great importance. The child who feels that he can get along with others, that he is liked by them, and that he generally manages to have his needs met is likely to feel pretty adequate. The following chapter presents a more detailed discussion of how to help children gain skill and competence in interpersonal relationships.

SUMMARY

The nursery school teacher who wishes to increase feelings of self-esteem in the children in her care has at her disposal many ways of accomplishing this. However, practices such as using comparison and competition, being overprotective, and judging children in their hearing should be avoided, since they tend to lower self-esteem.

Esteem-building practices that should be made part of the daily life of the nursery school include the expression of unconditional positive regard, the provision of recognition and praise when warranted, and the expression of genuine respect for every child.

Finally, the attainment of competence should be valued in the nursery school. The more opportunities the child has to acquire instrumental and interpersonal skills, the more likely he is to acquire an inner conviction of his own ability to cope. This inner conviction of basic competence is, in the long run, the most satisfactory builder of self-esteem.

QUESTIONS AND ACTIVITIES

1. Pick a nursery school or family life situation (perhaps a trip to the market) for role playing, and include in it as many possible ways you can think of to deflate and lower the self-esteem of the "children" who are involved.
2. Select a youngster in your school who seems to suffer from low self-esteem. As far as you can tell, what are some principal reasons for this self-image? What could you do to modify it in a more positive direction?
3. Many activities, even for college students, center on externalized sources of self-esteem. Grades are a prime example of external input. What college-related policies appear likely to produce internalized sources of positive self-esteem?
4. This chapter questions the value of using competition to motivate behavior, since competition reduces feelings of self-esteem. Is this necessarily true in all cases? Are there times when competition is both satisfying and desirable?
5. Listen to yourself for several days while you are working with the children. Every day put ten pennies in your pocket, and whenever you hear yourself talking about a child in front of him, transfer a penny to your other pocket. Can you go an entire day without shifting any pennies?
6. Imagine that a new rule has been passed at your school: you may not praise a child for anything during the day, and yet you must increase his self-esteem substantially. How would you go about doing this?
7. Go down your roster, and try to identify opportunities during the past week where each child had the chance to gain competence in some activity. Did each youngster have a chance to accomplish this in some manner?

REFERENCES FOR FURTHER READING

Overviews

Briggs, D. C. *Your child's self-esteem: the key to his life.* Garden City, N.Y.: Doubleday & Co., Inc., 1970. This book, which deals with building self-esteem in children and its influence on the entire life of the child, is written primarily with parents in mind but can also be helpful reading for the teacher.

Gordon, I. J. *Children's views of themselves.* (Rev. ed.) Washington, D.C.: Association for Childhood Education International, 1972. In this sensible pamphlet the author talks about how the concept of self develops and also makes recommendations that the teacher can use to help children develop positive self-concepts in the classroom.

McCandless, B. R., and Evans, E. D. *Children and youth: psychosocial development.* Hinsdale, Ill.: Dryden Press, 1973. The chapter on "The Development of the Self" presents a good overview, including developmental trends and conceptual and philosophical problems involved in studying this concept, and closes with a discussion of some educational implications.

Development of Competence

White, R. W. *The enterprise of living: growth and organization in personality.* New York: Holt, Rinehart and Winston, Inc., 1972. The chapter on competence, which discusses its importance in relation to development, traces its growth through various stages, and talks about why the concept is significant, is excellent. The entire book is first-rate reading.

Factors that Contribute to Poor Self-esteem

Baumrind, D. Socialization and instrumental competence in young children. In W. W. Hartup (Ed.), *The young child: reviews of research.* Vol. 2. Washington D.C.: National Association for the Education of Young Children, 1972. The effect of society's expectations on the self-concepts of little girls is discussed, and how girls are socialized to become instrumentally incompetent is described. A good bibliography is included.

Kirkhart, R., and Kirkhart, E. The bruised self: mending in the early years. In K. Yamamoto (Ed.), *The child and his image: self-concept in the early years.* Boston: Houghton Mifflin Co., 1972. This chapter is helpful primarily because of its review of practices that are likely to reduce self-esteem in young children.

Porter, J. D. R. *Black child, white child: the development of racial attitudes.* Garden City, N.Y.: Doubleday & Co., Inc., 1970. This book has two good chapters on the development of racial self-concepts and on the development of self-esteem among black children. Following this, the implications of the specific research reported in the book are discussed, and recommendations are included for improving the self-image of black children. This book is particularly worthwhile for the nursery school teacher because it concentrates on preschool children.

For the Advanced Student

Coopersmith, S. *The antecedents of self-esteem.* San Francisco: W. H. Freeman and Co., Publishers, 1967. Coopersmith recounts a classic study that sought to identify the factors within the family that influence self-esteem either positively or negatively.

White, R. W. Motivation reconsidered: the concept of competence. In M. Almy (Ed.), *Early childhood play: selected readings related to cognition and motivation.* New York: Simon & Schuster, Inc., 1968. In this classic the author reviews various theoretical approaches concerned with the nature of motivation and then proposes that certain behaviors are motivated by the need to achieve competence; good, scholarly reading.

Zirkel, P. A. Self-concept and the disadvantage of ethnic group membership and mixture. *Review of Educational Research,* 1971, **41**(3), 211-226. Many research articles having to do with the relationship of self-esteem to membership in various ethnic groups are reviewed. The author concludes that the relationship is still unclear because of the variation in methodological approaches.

PART FOUR

Fostering social development

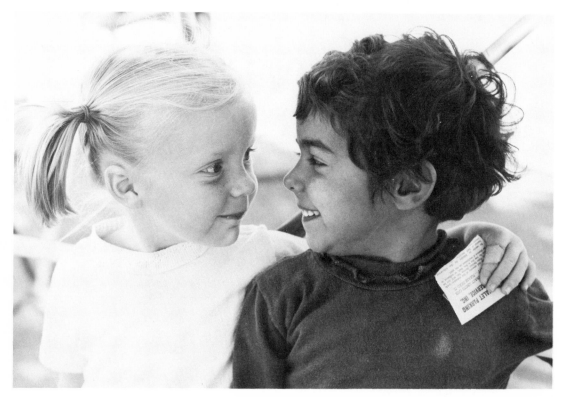

Photo by Jason Lo'Cicero
La Mesa Preschool, Santa Barbara

CHAPTER 9

Developing social competence in young children

This point was brought home to me by the comments of a distinguished Soviet psychologist, an expert on development during the preschool years. He had been observing in an American day-care center for children of working mothers. The center was conducted under university auspices and reflected modern outlooks and methods in early childhood education. It was therefore with some concern that I noted how upset my colleague was on his return.

"I wouldn't have believed it," he said, "if I hadn't seen it with my own eyes. There were four children sitting at a table, just as in our nurseries. But each was doing something different. What's more, I watched them for a whole ten minutes, and not once did any child help another one. They didn't even talk to each other. Each was busy in his own activity. You really are a nation of individualists."*

Early childhood is a time that can be rich in social learnings; it is a dynamic period characterized by many beginnings but few completely attained learnings in the development of social skills and interactions. Although the home is profoundly influential in this area, nursery school teachers can also make a valuable contribution to social development. Before pursuing important social goals for the young children in her care, however, the teacher should review the developmental trends and theories of social growth discussed below, in order for her to know what social behavior to expect from the children.

DEVELOPMENTAL TRENDS IN SOCIAL GROWTH

We know that children advance from solitary play, through parallel play (playing beside but not with another child), to play that involves more direct association and cooperation with their peers (Parten, 1932). Children develop more friends as they move from infancy to kindergarten, and they tend to increasingly select friends who are of the same sex (Hagman, 1933). As they grow older, the number of quarrels between children decreases, but the length of the altercations increases (Dawe, 1934), as does the number of social contacts (Maudry and Nekula, 1939).

---

*From Bronfenbrenner, U. Preface. In H. Chauncey (Ed.), *Soviet preschool education.* Vol. 2. *Teacher's commentary.* New York: Holt, Rinehart and Winston, Inc., 1969. P. 5.

Table 4. Progress indicators of social development, first 3 years*

Behavior item	Age expected
	(Weeks)
Responds to smiling and talking	6
Knows mother	12
Shows marked interest in father	14
Is sober with strangers	16
Withdraws from strangers	32
Responds to "bye-bye"	40
Responds to inhibitory words	52
Plays pat-a-cake	52
Waves "bye-bye"	52
	(Years, months)
Is no longer shy toward strangers	1-3
Enjoys imitation of adult activities (smoking, etc.)	1-3
Is interested in and treats another child like an object rather than a person	1-6
Plays alone	1-6
Brings things (slippers, etc.) to adult (father)	1-6
Shows beginning of concept of private ownership	1-9
Wishes to participate in household activities	1-9
Has much interest in and watches other children	2
Begins parallel play	2
Is dependent and passive in relation to adults	2
Is shy toward strangers	2
Is not sociable; lacks social interest	2-3
Is ritualistic in behavior	2-6
Is imperious, domineering	2-6
Begins to resist adult influence; wants to be independent	2-6
Is self-assertive; difficult to handle	2-6
Is in conflict with children of own age	2-6
Refuses to share toys; ignores requests	2-6
Begins to accept suggestions	3
Has "we" feeling with mother	3
Likes to relive babyhood	3
Is independent of mother at nursery school	3
Tends to establish social contacts with adults	3
Shows imitative, "me, too" tendency	3
Begins strong friendships with peer associates, with discrimination against others in group	3-6

*From Sutton-Smith, B. *Child psychology.* Englewood Cliffs, N.J.: Prentice-Hall, Inc., © 1973. Abridged from L. H. Stott. *The longitudinal study of individual development.* Detroit: Merrill-Palmer School, 1955.

Feelings of rivalry and competition begin to develop and appear to be at an intense level between the ages of 4 and 6 (Greenberg, 1932), although this behavior varies considerably from child to child. Generous behavior tends to increase with age and has been shown to occur even at the preschool level (Hartup and Coates, 1967). Role taking (the ability to put oneself in another's place) also increases as a child becomes older (Flavell, 1966).

Tables 4 and 5 summarize some of the many additional social behaviors that are characteristic of children at various ages.

In addition to these developmental trends, one of Piaget's concepts concerning social and intellectual development has considerable relevance for understanding the social behavior of young children. Piaget (1926) maintains that children in the preoperational stage of development, which includes the nursery

Table 5. Progress indicators of social development, ages 4 through 10*

Behavior item	Age expected (years)
Is assertive, boastful	4
Has definite preference for peer mates	4
Tries to gain attention; shows off	4
Tends to be obedient, cooperative; desires to please	5
Seeks approval; avoids disapproval of adults	5
Shows preference for children of his own age	5
Shows protective, mothering attitude toward younger sibling	5
Is sensitive to parents' and others' moods, facial expressions	6
Has strong desire to be with father and do things together (especially true of boys)	6
Insists on being "first" in everything with peers	6
Bosses, teases younger siblings	6
Has rich capacity to "pretend" in social play	6
Shows compliance in family relations	7
Desires to be "good"	7
Begins to discriminate between sexes	7
Forms close friendships with one of the same sex; the age of "bosom pals"	8
Sex cleavage is definite; girls giggle, whisper; boys wrestle, "roughhouse"	9
The age of "clubs"	9
Sex differences are pronounced: girls show more poise, more folk wisdom, more interest in family, marriage, etc., and in their own personal appearance	10

*From Sutton-Smith, B. *Child psychology.* Englewood Cliffs, N.J.: Prentice-Hall, Inc., © 1973. Abridged from L. H. Stott, *The longitudinal study of individual development.* Detroit: Merrill-Palmer School, 1955.

school years, are primarily egocentric. That is, they see the world from their own point of view and experience considerable difficulty putting themselves in others' places. The teacher should understand that this self-centeredness is typical and is not due to "selfishness" or reprehensible callousness. Rather, it is a developmental stage, and during the time the child is in nursery school, he is in the process of learning to decenter and to see the world from another's vantage point. The nursery school can facilitate this trend in many ways, particularly if the teacher understands the processes by which children become socialized and makes use of these principles in her teaching.

How do children become socialized?

Although opinion remains divided about how children become socialized (Parke, 1972a), it appears that children learn to become like other people and to get along with them as a result of identifying with

and imitating them and also by being reinforced for desirable social behaviors.

Considerable evidence indicates that children learn by observing grownups and other children and that, particularly if the person is nurturing and is powerful, they will seek to be like the model and imitate his behavior (Bandura and Huston, 1961; Mischel and Grusec, 1966). There is also some evidence that indicates that children are more likely to be influenced by behavioral models than by moral preachments (Rosenhan, 1972); so it behooves the teacher to model the behavior she wishes to encourage rather than just talk about it or, worse yet, preach something she does not practice.

There is also considerable evidence that children learn socially acceptable responses as a result of reinforcement (Allen, Hart, Buell, Harris, and Wolf, 1964; Horowitz, 1967). This can be either negative reinforcement in the form of punishment that may suppress behavior

(Parke, 1972b), or positive reinforcement in the form of recognition, praise, or other responses and satisfactions that come from without or within themselves. In addition, a study by Thompson (1944) shows that teachers can facilitate the development of some specific social behaviors by assuming an active, guiding role.

Implications for teaching. We can conclude from these findings that the teacher needs to do more than sit idly by while the children grow and develop: she should assume a role based on active teaching. Since one way children acquire social behaviors is by identifying with models and imitating their behavior, obviously the teacher should provide a good example. In addition, the relationship between her and the child should be based on mutual liking (Bandura and Huston, 1961; Mussen and Parker, 1965).

Because young boys may tend to imitate male models more readily than they do female ones, it is also desirable to include male teachers and volunteers in the nursery school whenever possible.

Since children learn as a result of positive reinforcement, the teacher needs to be sure that children receive satisfaction from acting in socially desirable ways. Sometimes this reinforcement will be in the form of a pleasant comment or expression of affection from herself, but a more desirable approach is for the teacher to point out to the child that it feels good to help other people so that the pleasure stems from this inherent reward rather than from a calculated external one.

SUGGESTIONS FOR TEACHING APPROPRIATE SOCIAL SKILLS

When young children want something, be it attention, assistance, or possession of an article, their need is *immediate, intense, and personal.* Their reactions, therefore, to having to wait or to consider the rights of others can be very strong, and it takes patient teaching backed by fortitude to develop in children the ability to wait a little, to control their feelings to a degree and to consider the rights and desires of others when necessary. All of these skills are central to the process of getting along in a social world. If the teacher remembers to take into account the strength of these immediate, intense, and personal needs as she reads about more specific social learnings, she will gain an added appreciation for the magnitude of the child's task in learning to become a socialized human being.

There are, of course, many more social goals than the seven listed below, but these seven goals have been selected because they are frequently listed by teachers of young children in the United States as being important and as having real social value.

Goal I: Help children learn to be generous and able to share equipment, experiences, and people with others

Although much of the research on social development dates back to the 1930s, there is new interest in identifying effective ways to foster what is sometimes called *prosocial behavior* or *altruism,* and generosity is one of the most investigated areas. This research has indicated that when affection from the teacher is combined with verbal comments about what is happening, the greatest number of charitable responses are produced in children (Midlarsky and Bryan, 1967). Modelling generosity also increases this behavior (Rosenhan, 1972), and paternal nurturing facilitates generosity in boys of nursery school age (Rutherford and Mussen, 1968). Thus we again find support for the recommendation that teaching a prosocial behavior is accomplished most effectively by a teacher who sets a good example and expresses affection while at the same time clarifying what is happening by discussing it with the children.

Help children learn to share equipment. Teaching a specific aspect of generosity such as sharing (a social skill of real concern in nursery school) requires something more than nurturing and setting a good example. It requires carrying through clear-cut policies that are directed toward building the generous impulse within the child rather than relying on externally enforced generosity supervised by the teacher. As one of my students put it,

"I want him to share from his heart, not because I make him do it."

Many teachers try to teach sharing by regulating turn taking. ("You can have it for two minutes, then he can have it for two minutes.") They seem to interpret sharing as meaning that the child has to hand over anything he is using almost as soon as another child says he wants it. Teachers who enforce taking turns on this basis find they are constantly required to monitor and referee the turn-taking themselves. This is not only tiresome but puts the locus of control and decision outside the child rather than within him, and it means that a child may not be permitted to have enough of an experience to be filled up and truly satisfied by it. This builds a kind of watchful hunger and avarice, which should be avoided.

Rather than struggling to institute the policelike control of the previous procedure, the teacher can establish a climate of generosity by making sure that the child has enough of most experiences. Therefore, she does not limit him to two paintings or allow him to ride the trike around the course only three times because another child is waiting. Instead, she follows the rule that the child may keep what he has or do what he is doing until he has had enough of it. This means that children don't have to be calculating and defensive about hanging on to things; and it makes settling arguments easier, because it is relatively simple to base decisions on who was using it first and then to state the rule, "Whoever had it first may keep it until he's done with it."

Once assured that his own rights and desires will be protected, it becomes much easier for a child to share. When another child is waiting, the teacher can point this out, perhaps saying, "John, when you're done with the swing would you remember to tell Helen? She'd like a turn when you're through." The final step in this process is recognizing when he does remember to tell Helen that he is done by commending him and pointing out, "Look how pleased Helen is that you remembered. She's really smiling at you. I guess you're her friend!"

It helps in such situations to have enough equipment available that children do not have to wait and wait. Several easels are better than one, and feeling free to improvise in order to meet peak demands will help, too. For example, if painting is suddenly very popular, setting out paint tables might help, or giving children cans of water and old brushes to paint the fence could satisfy their need and reduce waiting.

Help children learn to share the teacher. Children not only have to learn to share equipment, they also have to learn to share their teacher and her attention with other children. Again, the best model is the generous one, where each gets what he needs rather than each getting an identical, metered amount. This may mean that only one child is rocked while several others play nearby in the block corner rather than every child being rocked a little. As long as each child receives comfort when he needs it, the teacher doesn't have to worry about whether she is being "fair." She can explain to the children that different people get different special things according to what they need, and then, to remind them that this policy applies to everyone, she can cite examples of times when they had special attention.

Some individual satisfactions have to be put off, since it is not possible for one child to monopolize the teacher's attention throughout lunch or story time. To handle such demands the teacher might say, "You know, lunch is for everyone to talk together, but I can see you really want to talk to just me. I promise we'll have time for that while I'm getting you ready for nap."

Goal II: Help children develop empathy

Being able to understand what another person is feeling or why he acts as he does is a valuable social skill. As Flavell says:

Making good inferences about what is going on inside these objects (i.e. other people) permits us some measure of understanding, prediction, and control in our daily interactions with them (Flavell, Botkin, Fry, Wright, and Jarvis, 1968, p. v).

Piaget (1926) has long maintained that

young children are egocentric and are unable to put themselves in the place of another. But recent research (Borke, 1971;
Flavell, 1966), as well as the experience
of many nursery school teachers, indicates that this egocentrism is not an all-
or-nothing condition. As children grow
from 2 to 5, they become increasingly able
to assume roles (Flavell, 1966). They can
also, with training, become more sensitive
to other people's feelings and to the effect
their actions have on these feelings.

Encourage role playing. There are several
things the teacher can do to increase the
awareness of how it feels to be someone
else. One of the most obvious of these is
to provide many opportunities for dramatic and imaginative play involving role taking about what people do. Most nursery
schools maintain housekeeping corners,
which facilitate the role playing of family
life so dear to 3- and 4-year-olds. We have
seen that as children reach 4 and 5 years
of age, their interest in the world around
them increases and extends beyond the
family and the school. For these youngsters, enriched role opportunities can be
offered with accessories for doctors and
nurses, bus drivers, nursery school teachers, or anyone else who is familiar to the
children. For example, we have a fine
time in our children's center with chefs'
hats and coats since our cook, whom the
children adore, always wears such garments when serving lunch. The costumes
need not be complete. Indeed, it seems
wise to leave something to exercise the
children's imaginations; but hats are particularly fun, and it is good to have a variety of them representing different characters.

*Help the child understand how the other
person feels.* Teaching children how other
people *feel* in addition to what they *do* is
more difficult but not impossible. One virtue of encouraging children to tell each
other what they want or how they feel is
that in addition to relieving the speaker's
feelings, it informs the other child about
someone else's emotions and desires. The
other important reason for doing this, according to Piaget, is that children are
freed of egocentrism by experiencing

interactions with other people. The
hypothesis is that both social conflict and
discussion facilitate cognitive growth and
an accompanying ability to put the self in
another's place (Piaget, 1926; Smedslund,
1966).

The teacher can increase empathy for
another's feelings by explaining how a
child is feeling in terms that are personal
to the observing child, relating the feeling
to one that he has also experienced. For
example:

Henry, who has just caught his finger in the
door, is crying bitterly as the teacher holds him
and comforts him. Frankie comes in and stands
watching silently, his thumb in his mouth. He
looks interested and worried, and as the teacher
pats Henry on his back, she explains to Frankie, "Henry hurt his finger in the door. Remember when I rocked on your toe with the
rocking chair?" Frankie nods. "Well, his finger
feels like that." "It hurt," says Frankie. "It hurt
a lot. But we put cold water on it and that made
it stop. Let's put his finger in cold water." The
teacher says, "That's a great idea! Henry, Frankie is telling you something." Frankie says,
"Come on, Hennie, we'll put your finger in
water—that will help." And off they go.

Here, the teacher related Henry's feelings directly to what Frankie already
knew from his own experience. This
helped make the feeling real to him and
also encouraged him to use this insight to
provide practical comfort for his friend.

Goal III: Help the child learn that it feels good to help others

I agree with the Russian's implication
at the beginning of this chapter that
American children are not encouraged to
help their friends as much as they might
be. Providing opportunities for children to
experience the satisfaction and pleasure
that come from helping someone else appears to be a sound way to generate willingness to take prosocial action. Sometimes helping others takes the form of
comforting another child; sometimes it is
as simple as passing the cups at snack;
and sometimes it is as sophisticated as
thinking of an excursion everyone will
enjoy.

Children should be encouraged to help

each other, not only in situations where they can provide comfort, but also in situations where they can assist another child by handing him his coat or showing him how to do something. These opportunities should be handled carefully so that the undesirable effect of comparing children with each other is avoided. For example, rather than saying, "Why don't you do it the way Alan does—he's a big boy," it is better to say, "Alan just learned how to zip his coat. Why don't you ask him to show you how it goes together?" Children are often generous about teaching such skills to each other as long as it doesn't take so much time that they lose patience.

Goal IV: Teach children that everyone at nursery school has rights and that these rights are respected by all

I made the point earlier that children have individual needs and that the teacher should not hesitate to meet these on an individual basis; that is, she should not interpret fairness as meaning that everyone gets exactly the same thing. But children do, in general, have to conform to the same rules. This impartiality of rule enforcement will help children gradually understand that everyone is respected as having equal rights.

Teach children that rules apply to everyone. A good example of this may be seen in handling sharing problems. At the beginning of the year there always seems to be one or two children who seize possession rather than asking and waiting for turns. Of course, the teacher often has to restrain such a youngster from doing this. It is particularly important with this kind of child that she also watch carefully and almost ostentatiously protect the seizer's rights when someone tries to take his trike away, so that he sees that everyone, *himself as well as others,* has his rights of possession protected. This is a very effective way to teach fairness and to help the child see what the rule is and that it applies to every child. The message is, "You may not intrude on their rights, and they can't intrude on yours, either." As the year progresses and the child learns to know and apply these rules himself, he will be-

come increasingly able to enforce them without the teacher's help and thus be able to stand more securely on his own socially.

Teach respect for others' rights by honoring personal privacy. Children enjoy bringing things from home; it's a cheerful link between their families and the school. Since these items are their personal possessions, it should be their choice whether to share them or not. Even the teacher should ask, "May I see it?" before she reaches out to handle a personal possession.

When he does not choose to share something, the child should put it in his cubby. Keeping his possessions there provides an opportunity to teach privacy and personal rights if the rule is enforced that a child may go only in his own cubby, never in anyone else's without permission. Of course, there will be many transgressions of this rule, but the children will learn to honor this policy over a year's time, just as they will learn to stay out of the teacher's desk and out of the staff rest room if these are insisted on.

Goal V: Emphasize the value of cooperation and compromise rather than stressing competition and winning

Competition and winning over others is so much a part of American life that it hardly seems necessary to emphasize them in nursery school, and yet many teachers do so because appealing to children's competitive instincts is such an easy way to get them to do what teachers want. It is particularly easy to employ competition as a manipulative device with older nursery school children. Research shows that rivalry peaks around the age of 5 years (Stott and Ball, 1957); thus using competition to manipulate behavior plays right into a developmental characteristic of the child.

The teacher is using this method when she makes such statements as "Oh, look how well Johnny's picking up the blocks; I bet you can't pick up as many as he can," or "It's time for lunch, children. Whoever gets to the bathroom first can sit by me. Now remember, no running!" Such techniques reward children for triumphing over other children and neglect the chance to teach them the pleasure of accomplishing things together.

Model cooperation yourself. One effective way for the teacher to substitute cooperation for competition is to model it by helping the children herself. Thus when it is time to put away the blocks, the teacher warns in advance and then says, "It's time to put the blocks away. Come on, let's all pitch in. I guess I'll begin by picking up the biggest ones. Henry, would you like to drive the truck over here so we can load it up?" He may refuse, of course, but after a pause, he'll probably join in if the teacher continues to work with the group to complete the task.

Teach the art of compromise. Being able to compromise is another basic part of learning to cooperate. Four-year-olds love to strike bargains and are often able to appreciate the fact that everyone has gained some of what he wants when a fair bargain or agreement is reached. The following episode, which occurred recently at our children's center, is a good example of this.

Jimmy has been pulling some blocks around the play area in the wagon. Finally, tiring of this, he asks the teacher to pull him instead. Just at this moment Alan arrives and wants the wagon. This is too much for Jimmy who, dog-in-the-manger style, suddenly decides he wants to pull it after all. He says, "No, Alan! You can't have it! I'm using the wagon. I'm not done. I want to pull it! Get off!" "My gosh, Jimmy!" says the teacher. "Weren't you just saying you wanted a ride? Here's your chance. Weren't you just asking for someone to pull you?" She pauses to let this sink in. "Maybe if you let Alan have a turn pulling the wagon, he would give you the ride you want." She turns to Alan. "Would you do that, Alan?" She turns to Jimmy, "Would that be okay with you, Jimmy?"

Thus the teacher helped the boys strike a bargain whereby both got what they wanted.

As the children become more socially experienced, the teacher could encourage the boys to think the situation through for themselves rather than intervening so directly herself. Perhaps she might say at that point, "Jimmy, Alan is telling you he really wants to use the wagon, too. Isn't there some way you can both get something good out of this?" If the boys can't conceive of any solution, then she can go on to the more obvious approach outlined above.

Goal VI: Help children discover the pleasures of friendship

Children become more and more interested in having friends as they grow older. By age 5 they are likely to spend more than half their playtime with other children (Valentine, 1956), and friendship bonds between particular children are generally much stronger at this age than they are in younger children (Green, 1933). By second grade it is almost intolerable to be without a friend.

Friendship depends on many variables, including similarity of age, sex, and sociability, as well as the less readily analyzable qualities of personal attractiveness. There also appears to be considerable variation in the capacity and need for close friendships at the preschool age.

It sometimes seems that the only friendships nursery school teachers are aware of are the ones they try to break up between older boys who egg each other on into trouble. Yet there are many desirable relationships, which should be noted and nurtured in the preschool.

Facilitate friendliness by using reinforcement to reduce isolated behavior. Social interaction between children can be increased by the judicious use of reinforcement. This is a particularly helpful technique to employ with shy, isolated children (Allen, Hart, Buell, Harris, and Wolf, 1964). Using this approach, the teacher provides some kind of social dividend whenever the child approaches a group or interacts with them, but withholds such recognition when the child withdraws and plays by himself. (It is hoped that over a period of time the pleasure the youngster finds in being part of the group will replace this more calculated reward.) Note that this approach is just the opposite of the pattern that often occurs in nursery school where the teacher tends to "try to draw the child out" when he retires from the group, thereby rewarding with attention the very behavior she wishes to extinguish.

Increase the social skills of disliked children. Another way to foster friendships and cordial social relationships among children is to teach less likeable youngsters social skills that make them more acceptable to the other children. For example, a child who has learned to ask for what he wants is generally more welcome than one who rushes in and grabs whatever appeals to him.

Pair children together. Pairing children together sometimes helps them make friends. Coming to school in a car pool or going home from school to play together can cement a friendship, as can doing a number of jobs together or sharing an interest in common. In the long run, though, it is up to the child to form the friendship; all the teacher can do is make such possibilities available to him.

Goal VII: Assist children in determining and developing behavior that is appropriate to their sex

The problem of establishing sexual identity. Teachers need to be aware that, during the years of early childhood, children are developing many concepts having to do with sexual identity. This is both a fascinating and touchy subject at present, since stereotypes of what constitutes "appropriate" sex roles for human beings are undergoing change in some segments of our society. (This is not solely the result of the recent Women's Liberation Movement. It is interesting to note that as long ago as 1961, research showed that some traditionally sex-linked pastimes and games were becoming more acceptable to children of both sexes. Sutton-Smith and Rosenberg (1961) compared four studies of games selected by children from 1896 to 1959 and found an increasing similarity between the sexes in game preference. This change seemed primarily due to a shift in play preferences among the girls, who have gradually come to participate more frequently in such activities as swimming, playing tag, and flying kites).

However, it must also be pointed out that research, which deals with what is rather than what might be, indicates that at present there are behavioral traits that differ according to sex. In one comprehen-sive review of research, Maccoby (1966) found that numerous studies showed that boys are more aggressive than girls. On the other hand, girls display a greater need for affiliation, greater interest in people, and more positive feelings for others than boys do. More recent research, which supports these findings, indicates that some differences in behavior between males and females are evident even during the first year of life (Goldberg and Lewis, 1969; Moss, 1967). How much of this behavior is due to the subtly pervasive influence of culture and how much is the result of psychological or physiological predisposition is impossible to say at this time. No doubt some of these behaviors are learned responses and can be modified, since they result from training. Whether this is the case for all behavioral traits usually described as being feminine or masculine remains to be determined, and the next decade of research should produce some intriguing answers about all this.

The questions for the teacher who is caught in the midst of this change are, "How do I respond to this possible shift in values and role descriptions? Is it in the best interest of the children to let my personal convictions of injustice radically affect what I teach in the classroom? Does the restructuring of the male/female concept mean I must avoid all social definitions of what constitutes masculinity and femininity as we think of them at the present time?"

It seems too risky to advocate that sexual roles be abandoned altogether (even if this were possible, which it more than likely is not). Children need to have clear ideas of who they are and of how to behave in ways that will be accepted by other people. In our society these are so closely linked to the sex of the individual that attempting to scrap all such teaching might result in unanticipated and undesirable side effects related to possibly serious confusions about self-image.

But this does not mean that the teacher should do nothing different about teaching sexual roles and establishing sexual identities for the children; it does mean that she should be thoughtful, careful, and not destructive about what she plans to do. At least three factors should be emphasized: providing clear, unembarrassed explanations of sexual differences and similarities, developing wider competence and equal privileges for both sexes, and making sure that she does not suppress and emasculate the boys.

Explaining physiological differences. The most basic approach to clarifying sexual roles lies in teaching simple physiological facts. Open toileting has long been the rule in most nursery schools because, when boys and girls use the same toilets, secrecy about sexual differences and toilet practices is avoided. This policy also generates opportunities for the teacher to supply answers to things young children wonder about, such as explaining why boys urinate standing up whereas girls sit down. The teacher makes simple statements about these matters: "Yes, boys and girls are made differently. Boys have penises, and so they stand up to urinate. Girls have vulvas, and so they sit down." If little girls still want to know why they can't stand up, the teacher can invite them to try it—there's no substitute for learning by experience! Casualness and answering questions actually asked, rather than ones that the teacher is nervously afraid the children will ask, should be the order of the day.

Differences in the mother's and father's functions should be handled the same way—simply, and by answering the child's question. Fathers start the child growing within the mother; mothers have babies and sometimes nurse them from their breasts; then mothers and fathers work together to care for the baby afterwards. It is necessary to think about the child's home situation when discussing such matters. So many children in day care now come from single-parent homes that this has to be gently taken into account so that the child does not feel "different" or peculiar because he has only one parent. And yet, it is these very children who may be least experienced with mother-father roles and who need most help in understanding the mutuality of the parenting relationship. It takes a combination of sensitivity and matter-of-factness without sentimentality or pity to deal with this problem successfully.

Questions about sex at the nursery school level are not likely to be too difficult to answer. They are usually as simple as, "Can I have a baby when I grow up? Where does the baby come out? Doesn't the father get to do anything?" The reader may wish to refer to the references for further readings at the end of this chapter for a list of books that will give detailed advice on how to answer individual queries.

Finally, the use of correct terms and language should be part of teaching about physiological facts. It is just as easy to say *penis* as *wee-wee,* and the use of the correct word takes away the aura of unspeakable secrecy about sexual differences and helps make such knowledge a forthright part of the child's life.

Providing opportunities to try out activities that are traditionally linked to the opposite sex. Are boys really better than girls at solving mechanical problems? Are girls really better than boys at nurturing and comforting others? We don't know; and yet a lot of socialization involves reacting to such possibilities as though they were true and structuring curriculum and behavioral expectations so that, in fact, they become true. Teachers should be wary of limiting children's potential by operating on assumptions that may be inaccurate. Some of the girls are, no doubt, just as clever at inserting a cotter pin in the wagon axle as boys are, and some of the boys may be easily as sensitive to people's feelings as are the girls, if only they are given opportunities to explore and demonstrate these abilities and qualities.

Nursery school teachers should present an open curriculum that provides opportunities for both sexes to participate in all learning activities rather than restricting children to obsolete sex role expectations. Teachers should work to develop wider competence and equal privileges for both sexes rather than seeking to obliterate differences between them. Preschools are often the last chance children have to try out materials and activities that are contemptuously labeled in elementary school as "girl stuff" or "unfeminine." Surely activities such as woodworking should be freely available to girls, just as opportunities to enjoy dressing up or sewing

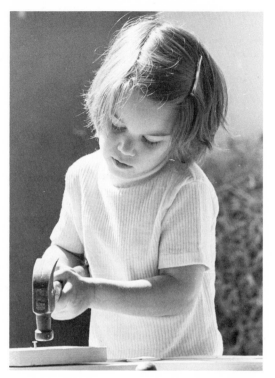

Photo by Jason Lo'Cicero

list of Newberry prizewinners up to 1969.

Encouraging the boys' maleness and meeting their needs for role models. The zest for providing a range of experiences for both girls and boys should not result in emasculating boys. Experience has taught me that it is necessary to remind women teachers to provide young boys with many experiences that fit their needs. At least in our current society, boys are more physically active and aggressive than girls; but women teachers tend to suppress this vigor and energy, since it is contrary to the teacher's own behavior patterns and also makes running a nursery school more difficult. Boys especially need opportunities for vigorous physical activity. They must have room to climb and wrestle. Their play requires large, sturdy equipment, plenty of space, and a teacher who genuinely welcomes such activity rather than regarding it as a threat to her ability to control the children.

Not only must boys be supplied with enough room to move and to let off steam, but they must also have the chance to form relationships with men who can serve as models for them. In an age when divorce is increasing and many unmarried women are electing to raise their children rather than surrender them for adoption, many children in day care centers come from single-parent, mother-centered homes. Since research (Biller, 1969) indicates that the presence of a father does facilitate sex role development (although boys can develop normally without it), nursery schools should do all they can to provide consistent contacts for boys and girls with men who care about children. Low salary schedules often preclude employing family men as teachers, although this picture seems to be improving slightly; but high school and college men can often be employed as aides, and occasionally, warm-hearted fathers will volunteer to come regularly and spend time with the children. All of these contacts, though admittedly not as satisfactory as a father's presence, will help both boys and girls formulate their concepts of what it means to be a man in our society and, hopefully, will help boys to grow up to be sturdy, attractive men themselves.

should be available for boys. The chance to experience a full range of roles enriches the knowledge of each sex, does not produce sexual perverts, and, hopefully, deepens understanding and empathy for the opposite sex.

All teachers should take a closer look at some of the materials they offer for play. A student of mine recently pointed out that a game used at the Center that links people to their occupations had only two females included—one was a housewife, tastefully done up in kerchief and broom, and the other was a ballerina! And only this year were we able to find some accessories for the block corner that had women figures as doctors and policewomen. Children's books are also worthy of inspection for the values they present, which we, in turn, accept unquestioningly. A study by Saario, Jacklin, and Tittle (1973) points out the many undesirable aspects of sex role stereotyping that occur in early readers and testing materials, and Mitchell (1971) mentions that books about boys outnumbered books about girls three to one in the

SUMMARY

Social competence develops at a rapid rate during the years of early childhood. Children become socialized partly as a result of identifying with and emulating models they admire and partly as a consequence of reinforcement that encourages or suppresses various kinds of social behavior.

Although children attain many social skills during this period, seven were selected in this chapter as being particularly important: learning to be generous, developing empathy, understanding that everyone at nursery school has rights that must be respected, learning that it feels good to help other people, discovering the value of cooperation and compromise rather than stressing competition, discovering the joys of friendship, and determining and developing behavior that is appropriate to the sex of the child.

QUESTIONS AND ACTIVITIES

1. *Problem:* You are working as a teacher in a cooperative nursery school. One of the new mothers is supervising the trike area and is firmly telling each child that he can ride his trike around the track three times and then must give a turn to the next child who is standing in line (there are several children standing there already, making plaintive noises about wanting turns). What would you do to handle this situation on both a short- and long-term basis?

2. In this chapter the comment was made that sex roles seem to be changing in the United States. Do you think that, if teachers make a point of offering nursery school children of both sexes equal experiences and equal privileges, this policy is likely to result in the loss of sexual identity for the children?

3. During the next week, watch for situations in which a child could be helped to understand another person's feelings or point of view. Using the situations you observed, discuss possible ways that genuine feeling for another person could have been developed from these situations.

4. Analyze the books in your nursery school: are there ones that present both boys and girls as effective, active people? Are there ones that appear to perpetuate stereotypes of little girl and little boy behavior? Are these necessarily undesirable?

5. *Problem:* You are working in a school that serves many single-parent families where mothers have primary care of the children. Many of the children, therefore, have relatively little experience with men. Suggest some practical plans that would help alleviate this deficit for the children you care for.

REFERENCES FOR FURTHER READING

Overviews

Rosenhan, D. Prosocial behavior in children. In W. W. Hartup (Ed.), *The young child: reviews of research.* Vol. 2. Washington, D.C.: Natio al Association for the Education of Young Children, 1972. This review provides a concise summary of research on prosocial behavior in children. It is a good place to begin for a student who is interested in learning how such research is conducted.

Sutton-Smith, B. *Child psychology.* Englewood Cliffs, N.J.: Prentice-Hall, Inc., 1973. This child development text contains excellent, up-to-date discussions of age-related social behaviors. This book is particularly valuable because it bases conclusions about preschool children on research done with children of that age, a practice that makes generalizing from the studies more tenable.

Sharing and Respecting the Rights of Others

Nicholaysen, M. Dominion in children's play: its meaning and management. In K. R. Baker (Ed.), *Ideas that work with young children.* Washington, D.C.: National Association for the Education of Young Children, 1972. The value of permitting children to establish territories for their own use while playing is discussed, and several practical examples of how individual and group needs may be harmonized are included.

Role Playing

Bender, J. Have you ever thought of a prop box? In K. R. Baker (Ed.), *Ideas that work with young children.* Washington, D.C.: National Association for the Education of Young Children, 1972. This article is brief, but rich in ideas and suggestions for extending role playing to people in the community who are familiar to nursery school children.

Flavell, J. H. Role-taking and communication skills in children. *Young Children,* 1966, **21,** 164-177. This article talks about role taking from a somewhat different point of view, which involves putting oneself more literally in another's place. It reports some ingenious research that attempted to investigate this ability in young children.

Stereotyping of Sex Roles

MacEwan, P. T. *Liberating young children from sex roles: experiences in day care centers, playgroups and free schools.* Boston: New England Press, 1972. This pamphlet makes a good case for more open, nonsexist schools—a good consciousness raiser.

Mitchell, E. The learning of sex roles through toys and books. *Young Children,* 1971, **28**(4), 226-232. This article offers many examples of toys and books that the author feels are sexist.

Saario, T., Jacklin, C. N., and Tittle, C. K. Sex role stereotyping in the public schools. *Harvard Educational Review,* 1973, **43**(3), 386-416. The authors provide an interesting report of a research study on sexist books and testing materials; they also review other findings in this field.

Teaching Children about Sexual Differences

This subject is still such a point of strain for many individuals that I have listed not only books for adults but a few for children, which I hope will be helpful.

Child Study Association of America. *What to tell your children about sex.* New York: Pocket Books, 1968. The Association gives matter-of-fact recommendations for discussing facts about sex for all ages.

Grams, A. *Sex education: a guide for teachers and parents.* Danville, Ill.: The Interstate Printers & Publishers, Inc., 1969. Sex education from preschool through adolescence is reviewed in a very practical, thoughtful discussion. The early childhood teacher should read this to obtain a better feeling for the kind of teachings about sex that is appropriate for each age.

Strain, F. B. *New patterns in sex teaching.* New York: Appleton-Century-Crofts, 1940. This old but invaluable reference is a special help for teachers who are worrying about what to reply to such questions as, "But how does the baby get inside?" and "Why are the dogs fighting?" Chapter 10 gives many examples of exactly what to say.

Some Recommended Books about Sex for Three- to Six-Year-Olds

The following list is provided through the courtesy of the Department of Home Economics, California State University, Long Beach, Calif.

Andry, A. C., and Scheep, S. *How babies are made.* New York: Time-Life Books, 1968.

Evans, E. K. *The beginning of life: how babies are born.* New York: Crowell Collier and Macmillan, Inc., 1969.

Gruenberg, S. M. *The wonderful story of how you were born.* Garden City, N.Y.: Doubleday & Co., Inc., 1970.

Hegeler, S. *Peter and Caroline: a child asks about childbirth and sex.* New York: Abelard-Schuman Limited, 1957. (Translated from the Danish.)

Hodges, B. W. *How babies are born: the story of birth for children.* New York: Essandess Special Editions, 1967.

Scheffield, M., and Bewley, S. *Where do babies come from?* New York: Alfred A. Knopf, Inc., 1972.

Schima, M., and Bolian, P. *The magic of life.* Englewood Cliffs, N.J.: Prentice-Hall, Inc., 1970.

For the Advanced Student

Hoppe, R. A., Milton, G. A., and Simmel, E. C. *Early experiences and the process of socialization.* New York: Academic Press, Inc., 1970. This excellent collection of papers, which discusses the process of socialization from a number of theoretical points of view, has a particularly interesting report of a study by Harvey and Felknor on parent-child relations and their influence on conceptual functioning.

Krebs, D. L. Altruism: an examination of the concept and a review of the literature. *Psychological Bulletin,* 1970, **73**, 258-302. The author gives a comprehensive review of research on altruistic behavior that covers all ages rather than emphasizing early childhood. The numerous charts summarizing research studies of altruistic behavior make this article particularly helpful.

Maccoby, E. E. (Ed.) *The development of sex differences.* Stanford, Calif.: Stanford University Press, 1966. This book is a fascinating summary of what is known about sex-related behavioral differences. It also contains discussions of two theories of how these behaviors are acquired. The annotated bibliography should be very helpful to the student who wishes to pursue this topic further.

Margolin, E. *Sociocultural elements in early childhood education.* New York: The Macmillan Co., 1974. In this thoughtful new book, Margolin attempts to blend what is known of socialization theory with curriculum development for young children.

Parke, R. C. (Ed.) *Recent trends in social learning theory.* New York: Academic Press, Inc., 1972. Chapters written by outstanding scholars who discuss theories of socialization, as well as articles by Gewirtz, Bandura, and Aronfreed, are included; thus a balanced presentation is assured.

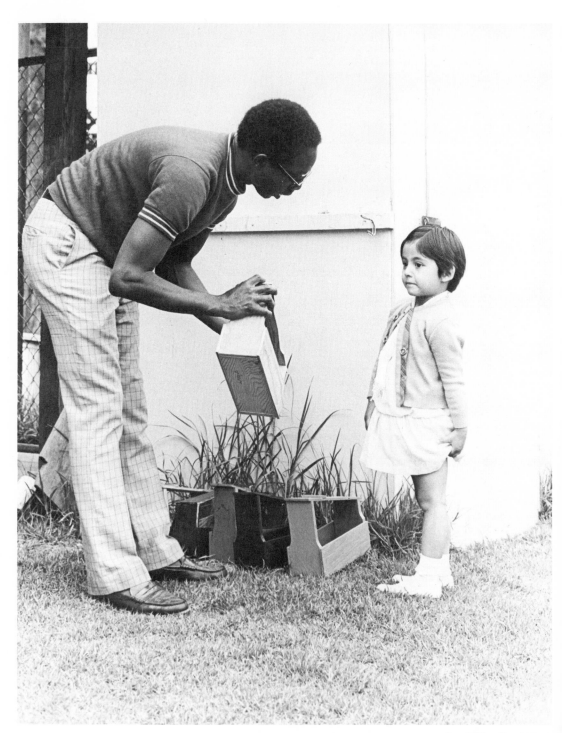

Los Niños Head Start

CHAPTER 10

Cross-cultural education in the nursery school

The problem of educating the culturally different is, then, the problem of educating *all* pupils in such a way that the school is both relevant to the individual and to the *full* heritage of the region and of the nation. True education is always cross-cultural and always cosmopolitan. Perhaps we have now arrived at a stage of sophistication sufficient to allow us to proceed with education and to dispense with a fixation upon conformity and Anglo-American superiority. But if this is the case, it will demand a radical change in the fundamental orientation of most schools, and this in turn will demand intensive analysis, experimentation, demonstration and leadership on the part of innovative educational agencies.*

One of the most exciting possibilities in day care and compensatory programs is the opportunity they present for incorporating cross-cultural education into the curriculum. The broad selection of people served by these centers constitutes a first-rate basis for generating understanding and acceptance of various cultural and ethnic groups if the teacher understands how to achieve these goals.

DO YOUNG CHILDREN NOTICE ETHNIC DIFFERENCES?

Is nursery school too early to begin learning about ethnic differences? Perhaps it would be better to leave well enough alone and not risk making children self-conscious about ethnic differences and similarities when they are so

young. However, research on the perception of differences in skin color shows that children as young as age 3 respond to the skin color of blacks and Mexican Americans (Landreth and Johnson, 1953; Morland, 1972; Werner & Evans, 1971), and the number of these differentiating responses increases markedly from age 3 to 5. Fortunately, the perception of difference at this early age does not necessarily result in rejection. In one nursery school study, Stevenson and Stevenson (1960) found that Southern white children continued to play with black youngsters even though they perceived a color difference between the groups. But perhaps sometime during this period or a little later negative reaction to color begins to form. In their study of white children in elementary school Miel and Kiester (1967) found that out of 237 children, 187 preferred to play with white children, 31 with black, 15 with both, and 2 said they didn't want to play with either. It is evident,

---

*From Forbes, J. *The education of the culturally different: a multicultural approach.* Washington, D.C.: U.S. Government Printing Office, 1968.

then, that in the years of early childhood children are beginning to note ethnic differences just as they are noting sexual differences and differences in occupations. Therefore, if we wish to combat the formation of prejudice, early childhood appears to be the time to start.

TWO APPROACHES TO CROSS-CULTURAL EDUCATION

Two approaches to cross-cultural education, particularly when combined, should prove effective in fighting prejudice. First, the teacher must seek to honor each child for his cultural and ethnic uniqueness. This positive valuing has a profound effect on increasing his self-esteem, which is vital to maintaining good mental health. Such acceptance and honoring of diversity, sometimes termed *teaching cultural pluralism,* helps children learn that different does not mean inferior.

Second, the teacher can fight prejudice by teaching the children that everyone has similar bodily and psychological needs, which can be satisfied if people work together in a cooperative way. This approach is sound because it fosters a feeling of belonging to a group, and belongingness reduces the sense of isolation and alienation that burdens many minority people (Lystad, 1969).

Although an adequate cross-cultural program should be centered around both of these important social learnings, the emphasis in this chapter is primarily on multiethnic pluralistic education, because this appears to be the place where teachers need the most help.

RECOGNIZING AND HONORING CULTURAL DIFFERENCES
Importance of sensitivity

The policy of recognizing cultural differences and honoring them used to be the exception rather than the rule in public schools. The reader may recall the books used in her own elementary school days wherein pink and white children visited Grandpa's farm and pulled their puppy around in a shiny new wagon. Now the trend is in the other direction, and we are finally able to purchase at least a few books and learning materials that have true relevance to family life in a variety of cultures.

Although this trend is good, the student must also realize that teaching about differences must be done with sensitivity. In their extensive study of children's views of foreign peoples, Lambert and Klineberg (1972) question the desirability of teaching that emphasizes that foreign people are different or peculiar. The desirability of emphasizing differences should also be questioned when teaching about friends and neighbors. We do not want young children to deduce from our presentations of varying cultural strengths and values that a child should be set apart because of variation in custom or behavior. It would defeat the entire purpose of cross-cultural education if we generated experiences where people felt that they were being used or as though they were being mounted on the head of a pin and examined.

Instead, the basic learning should be that everyone is worthwhile and that each child brings with him from his family special things that enrich the group and that are fun to share. In other words, we hope to teach that each child is special, not that each child is peculiar.

Relate cross-cultural learnings to the here and now

Just as other learnings are linked to reality, cross-cultural learnings should be linked to present experiences in which the children are actually involved. A study by Estvan (1966) provides support for the value of basing learning experiences on familiar things. He found that children who came from urban environments indicated they generally preferred the pictures that had to do with urban things, since these pertained to items with which they were acquainted. This study reminds us that nursery school teachers should base cultural teachings on real experience with children and families in the nursery school rather than on concepts of "our friends in foreign lands" or "Marie, the little Swiss goatherd." I don't know what leads otherwise sensible teachers to lose their heads and retreat to quaint pictures of little Dutch girls when they begin to talk about people of different cultures. Perhaps it is a way of avoiding coming to grips with the reality of our current life, where a fresh emphasis on the integrity of various minority cultures has, in some cases, frightened the white middle class. But frightened or not, the time is past when white teachers can afford to live with their heads in the sand. It is time to learn how to welcome cultural pluralism in the classroom.

Since it is impossible to discuss each ethnic or cultural group in detail in a single chapter, I have included many references at the end of the chapter for more extended reading and used examples from as many individual cultures as possible in the text. There is, of course, no one set of culture-based learning experiences that is universally appropriate to all nursery school programs, because each group of children has its own ethnically and socially unique composition.

Provide many opportunities for children to participate in cross-cultural experiences

There are a variety of ways to honor cultural differences at nursery school. Some are obvious, others more subtle.

The past 10 years has witnessed the publication of many stories about black, Indian, Mexican-American, and Asian children; resource lists for these are included at the end of this chapter. Records and pictures are also in better supply now, although some schools appear to be unaware of their availability. But it is not necessary to depend on commercial sources. Children often know rhymes and songs from their families, and the teacher can learn these with the parents' coaching and then help youngsters teach them to the group. Most homes have popular records or tape decks, but this is a resource frequently ignored by teachers who deem the music vulgar. However, many of the children's homes are saturated with blues or hard rock, and using such music in school can draw into movement and dance children who spurn less colorful songs about little duckies waddling around the fish pond.

Reaching the child by using his dominant language is even more important. Someone must be available in every nursery school room who can understand what the child has to say and who can make friends with him in his own language. The subject of teaching English as a second language and the use of black English is discussed more fully in Chapter 15. I pause here only to emphasize that a bicultural or multicultural program is a farce if we deny the child the right to speak his native tongue or dialect. To be truly effective, cross-cultural programs must honor language as well as traditions.

Serving familiar food is another excellent way to honor particular backgrounds and to help children feel at home. Sometimes a shy child who appears to be a poor eater is actually just overwhelmed by the strangeness of the food served to him. Food in some day care centers still seems to be planned with the best of nutritional intentions but with total disregard of local food patterns and customs. This situation can be remedied by asking parents for suggestions about appropriate food, by using recipes from ethnic cookbooks (see the references following Chapter 3), and by employing a cook who comes from a culture similar to that of the majority of the children. Children can also be encouraged to bring from home recipes that they can cook at school, or mothers or grandmothers may have time to come and participate in this way. As the children feel more at ease, it can also be fun to branch out and visit local markets and delicatessans that specialize in various ethnic foods. For example, even in a community as small as my own, we have a Chinese market, several Mexican-American tortilla factories, and a German and a Greek delicatessen. (Delicatessens are particularly good to visit because the food is ready, and it smells good and looks attractive.)

Holidays and other special occasions are also good times for children to share various customs. I recall one event in our group when a young boy lit Hanukkah candles and explained their purpose and the custom of gift giving very clearly. (It

Los Niños Head Start

was specially fortunate that he was able to do this because he had recently experienced a severe burn, and the prestige of lighting the candles helped him overcome his fear of fire as well as add enrichment to the life of our group.)

The backgrounds of each child may be savored by the group in many additional ways. Dress-up clothes that reflect the occupations of various parents or national costumes, when they can be spared, contribute much to the life of the school. Stories brought from home, dolls that are both ethnically accurate and attractive, and pictures that are integrated are also good choices. Such cross-cultural materials should be available consistently rather than presented as isolated units. Dolls, pictures, books, and music from many cultures should be deliberately, though apparently casually, woven into the fabric of every nursery school day.

But doing such things as serving appropriate food and valuing cultural traditions only scratches the surface of a true cross-cultural curriculum. Feelings about people are an even more crucial factor in such a program.

Continually work to overcome middle-class prejudices

Extent of teacher prejudice. Nobody wants to be prejudiced, but evidently almost all of us are. Some of the most recent evidence that these feelings show through in relations between teachers and students is provided in a survey of 429 junior and senior high school classrooms. The survey revealed there were substantial disparities in the way teachers behaved toward Anglo-American and Mexican-American students. Teachers gave significantly less praise and encouragement to Mexican Americans, accepted and used their ideas less often, gave them fewer positive responses, asked them fewer questions, and indulged in fewer instances of noncriticizing talk with them (United States Commission on Civil Rights, 1973).

Different people, of course, are prejudiced against different things. Some teachers who are not concerned about skin color or ethnic background may find they have real difficulty accepting the life styles of some families they serve. They may feel ill at ease with long-haired students or uncomfortable with vegetarians, or they may disapprove of how welfare recipients spend their money.

The problem for the teacher is that it is difficult to genuinely accept and not wish to change the attitudes of someone who has different values. Most teachers either consciously or unconsciously intend that families and children will move over to the teacher's side of the value scale and never consider whether they themselves might change and grow in the direction of the families. Thus teachers are likely to use the term culturally deprived to describe children who, though deprived of middle-class Anglo culture, actually possess a rich culture of their own.

A splendid example of this one-direction expectation is shown in an article on educating nonwhites in South Africa (Ireland, 1972). The author quotes the staff as asserting that the purpose of sending Bantu children to nursery school is to teach them to conform to the ways of the white world: "The staffs of the two prototype nursery schools in Johannesburg . . . have developed a dynamic curriculum with the specific aim of making each child completely at home with every facet of white culture" (p. 487).

Shouldn't there be more to nursery school than this? But we do not have to look as far away as Africa to find examples of this approach. It is still quite common, though not as openly expressed, in many American nursery schools.

Suggestions for controlling and overcoming the expression of prejudice. Prejudice and other emotional reactions become deeply ingrained in people. There are no real answers yet about how to overcome these feelings, although prevention is no doubt the soundest long-term solution. But at the very least, the teacher can make sure she practices some mental hygiene rules, such as these suggestions quoted by Kenneth Clark.*

---

*From Clark, K. B. *Prejudice and your child.* (2nd ed.) Boston: Beacon Press, 1963. P. 107.

1. As a beginning, find ways to become acquainted with at least one person or family of each racial and cultural group in your community.
2. Extend common courtesies and titles of address to persons of all groups, regardless of sinful community customs, regardless of their position, and regardless of however strange it may seem at first.
3. Learn the difference between paternalism (that is, loving down, loving in "their place") and true . . . respect of one human being for another.
4. Keep a close check on your thought and feelings. Watch out for any tendency to blame whole groups of people for what individuals do.
5. When you hear rumors that reflect on any group, demand proof. Do not repeat lies.
6. Never use hateful terms that slur any group. Show disapproval when others use them.
7. Do not tell stories, however funny, that reflect on any group. Do not laugh at them.
8. As a present or future employee, welcome new workers without regard to race or creed. Make very sure the boss does not refuse to hire people of some group because he imagines you would resent it. If you are seeking a new job, inquire among organizations where no such distinctions are made.
9. Request a policy of non-discrimination where you spend your money. (Remember, business firms may discriminate in employment and in serving customers because they imagine this pleases you. Make sure they know that it does not.)
10. Where there is a choice, take your patronage where there is the most democracy in every way. And let the proprietor know why.
11. . . . When going with interracial groups to public places, always assume that you will be served. Many places will say "no" if you ask in advance, but will serve you when you come. It is good education for them to know you assume that they will serve you.
12. Watch out for the term "restricted." It generally means discrimination against someone.

Acquisition of knowledge about different ethnic groups and cultures can also foster understanding and acceptance and help the teacher overcome her own cultural deprivation. For example, the teacher who understands that Navajo good manners require children to keep their eyes cast down when speaking with a respected elder does not keep insisting that these youngsters look her in the eye when they have something to say. Nor does the teacher visiting the home of an Italian family refuse the glass of wine often offered as a welcome. It can be extraordinarily instructive to live for even a month on the amount of money allotted by the welfare department. Although some aspects of doing this are admittedly synthetic, finding out the ways people make do and manage to get by can increase the teacher's respect for their ingenuity as well as her understanding of their feelings of rage and helplessness. Finally, learning the language of the families and nerving oneself to use it forms the best cultural bridge of all, since the use of their language says to the families, "I'm really trying to meet you half way."

Some of the new ethnic studies programs offer a wealth of information on particular cultures, and teachers should take such courses whenever they can. It will not only broaden their horizons but may also teach them how to avoid offending those whom they really want to help.

Show respect for people of differing ethnic origins by employing them as teachers

Cross-cultural learning in the nursery school must be based on real experiences with real people. This means, for example, that when we talk about how to emphasize that black people are effective human beings, it is just not satisfactory at the nursery school level to use the historical examples recommended in many black curriculum guides. Historical figures are so remote and intangible that they do not mean much to preschoolers.

Teaching young children that people of all ethnic backgrounds are important can be done if one employs them in positions of power. Many schools have reached the point where they employ black and brown people as aides. But this is far from enough. Children are quick to sense the power structure of the school, and they need to see people of all colors employed in the most respected positions as teachers and directors.

Unfortunately, Asian, Mexican, Indian, and black nursery school teachers are still relatively rare. Nursery school associations can help remedy this deficiency by encouraging their local colleges to recruit heavily among ethnic groups other than Anglo, and they can also help by offering scholarships to sustain such students through college. Even a modest book scholarship may mean the difference for some young people between going to junior college or working in the dime store.

Increase the number and variety of children in the nursery school who come from various ethnic and cultural groups

As I commented earlier, day nurseries and compensatory groups are luckier in the assortment of children who come naturally to their doors than are middle class schools. Such multiethnic contacts can introduce children at an early age to the values of an integrated society. It can teach the basic fact that James's face is not dirty because it is brown and can couple this learning with the fact that James is fun to play with because he's the best block builder in the school.

Suggestions for recruiting children for middle-class nursery schools. In *The Shortchanged Children of Suburbia* Miel and Kiester (1967) comment on the "extraordinary effort [that] was required to bring about any encounter between a child of the suburbs and persons different from himself. . . . He is largely insulated from any chance introduction to a life different from his own" (p. 3). Since this is clearly an undesirable situation, many middle-class schools are trying to achieve a better ethnic balance through recruitment. The teacher should realize, however, that families understandably resent being used as tokens or being included only because of their color or poverty. The slightest trace of condescension or patronage will give offence, and it requires tact and genuine warmth to achieve participation by all.

Middle-class schools may do best when recruiting if they find three or four mothers who can come at the same time and therefore lend each other moral support. The fact that some states now allow their welfare departments to purchase child care from any licensed nursery school also makes recruitment easier. Sometimes the children of foreign students can be sought out and included.

Of course, the closer the school is to the children it serves, the more likely it is that families will participate. Why should a black mother trek her child half way across town for the dubious privilege of placing him in an all white nursery school? It is hardly reasonable to accuse blacks of being standoffish under such circumstances; yet I have heard this conclusion drawn when such an invitation was refused.

Another way to increase ethnic representation is to do tradeabouts. Several nursery schools in our local community who have been unhappy about their ethnic sterility now make a practice of exchanging groups of children with day care centers every week. This provides variety in social contacts and curriculum for all the children and has proved profitable and refreshing for everyone.

Suggestions for recruiting children for schools who serve low-income families. Although most programs that have been operating for a while find they have more children available than they have facilities to serve, new schools may still need to recruit. One way to find children is to contact families whose children are already enrolled in the elementary school or to contact the welfare department for suggestions. In the early days of Head Start we even went door to door, introducing ourselves and making friends and spreading information about the new schools that would be available. In some areas posting invitations and notices in Spanish and English helps get word about the school around and says to the community that their ethnic background is being taken into consideration.

Mothers and children who have had a happy experience are the best recruiters of all. Over a period of time, this word of mouth will make or break the school.

Involve and honor all parents when they visit the nursery school

Successful communication is vital. The teacher who is unafraid of parents and who genuinely likes them will communicate this without saying anything at all; there is really no substitute for this underlying attitude of good will and concern for the children. All parents appreciate the teacher who has the child's welfare genuinely at heart, and this mutual interest in the child is the best base on which to build a solid teacher-parent relationship. Since listening is also more important than talking, the teacher should cultivate this ability in herself.

Other matter-of-fact things about communication can help when speaking with the foreign born. A friend of mine to whom English is a foreign language suggests that teachers speak somewhat slowly when talking with parents who are learning English. It is also very helpful to go to the trouble of having a translator handy when necessary. This may be another adult, but sometimes it can even be a 4- or 5-year-old who is bilingual. Notices sent home stand a much better chance of being read if they are written in the language of the home. Both languages should be printed side by side to avoid the implication that one is first and thus better than the other. Best of all is the teacher who is working to master the second language herself and who attempts to use the language of the family. The reaction to this is not criticism but, typically, an amused, kindly helpfulness from the families, who are obviously pleased at such efforts.

Welcome parent volunteers. The problem with making mothers feel at ease and glad to participate in the nursery school program is that they are always a little out of their element in the beginning. I have often thought that it would be fair to require the teacher to visit and help out in the families' homes on a turnabout basis. If this were possible, it would certainly help the teacher gain a better insight into how it feels to step into a strange situation where the possibility of making a fool of herself is quite likely.

Over and over I have witnessed teachers using mothers only to wipe off tables or to help in the kitchen. Mothers may want to do this in the beginning because it is familiar and not very challenging and because they do not want to make waves or antagonize the teacher. However, keeping them at such tasks is fundamentally denigrating, and it deprives the children of unique contributions such women can make that the teacher cannot otherwise obtain. For example, a mother might be asked to bring a book from her own childhood to share with the children or to bring some photographs of her latest trip to Mexico (particularly if these include pictures of the child) or to share a favorite recipe. Sometimes mothers are willing to bring their baby for a visit; this is always of real interest to the children.

Although it is not fair to put parents on the spot and ask them to control a group of children they don't know, it can be genuine fun and very helpful to have parent volunteers come along on field trips where everyone can be together and where everyone takes some responsibility. Families who are poor may lack such opportunities to get out and do things, and field trips can be a refreshing change for mothers who are homebound otherwise. On trips where toddlers would be a burden, we have, from time to time, worked out arrangements whereby two mothers take over the little ones while others come on the trip, and then switch off childcare for the next trip.

Families can often provide ideas for excursions, too. The children at our Center greatly enjoyed a visit to a communal organic garden one spring, and they also loved a trip to a father's fishing boat.

Make visitors welcome for meals. One of the wisest policies of the Head Start program has been their welcoming, open attitude at meal times. I cannot recall working in a Head Start center where people were not spontaneously invited to share meals with the children, and it is true that breaking bread binds people together in basic friendliness. If possible, this is a good policy for all schools to follow. When finances cannot support this drain, visitors can order lunch a day in advance and pay a nominal fee to defray the cost.

Trust and use parent expertise on the advisory board. All programs receiving federal funds are required to have advisory boards that must have at least 50% parent representation to be legal. But many school use such boards as rubber stamps and present parents with programs and plans literally for approval rather than for consideration and modification—a policy that certainly does not make parents feel welcome or respected. A much better way to make plans is to trust the parents. It is unlikely that they will suggest activities or policies that are detrimental to the children; and when differences arise, they can usually be settled by open discussion, which educates everyone.

The teacher who seeks out parents' suggestions because she values their practical experience with their children will find that this approach reduces the parents' feelings of defensiveness when the teacher happens to be better educated or better paid. If meetings are held during times when child care is available, more board members are likely to attend. Attendance also increases when parent suggestions are actually used and when parents are thanked sincerely for coming.

EMPHASIZING THE SIMILARITIES AS WELL AS VALUING THE UNIQUENESS OF PEOPLE

Children not only need to have their cultural uniqueness welcomed and valued, they also need to learn that all people have many things in common and that they are alike in some fundamental ways.

Teach the commonality of biological and psychological needs

One way to teach the similarities of all people is to emphasize the commonality of biological and psychological needs. Thus, when talking about the children's favorite food or what they traditionally eat for various holidays, the teacher can remind them that no matter what we like to eat best, everyone gets hungry and everyone likes to eat something. Or she can point out at the right moment that it feels good to everybody to stretch and yawn or to snuggle down in something warm and cozy.

The same principle can be taught in relation to emotions: everyone feels mad sometimes, everyone wants to belong to somebody, most people want to have friends, and most children feel a little lost when their mothers leave them at school.

In addition, the teacher can draw the children's attention to the fact that people often use individual, unique ways to reach a goal that most people enjoy. For example, Josie's father plays the guitar, while Heather's mother uses the zither; but they both use these different instruments for the pleasure of making music and singing together with the children.

Help families look beyond various differences to focus on common goods and goals

The effective cross-cultural nursery schools described by Mary Lane and her colleagues (1971) have demonstrated that families of considerable diversity can learn to appreciate differences and at the same time find goals in common that cause them to band together to make a positive impact on their neighborhoods.

Nursery schools of various types can provide opportunities for friendships to form and for people to thrive. Cooperatives are famous for doing this, of course, but it can also be accomplished in other groups. Advisory boards can take the lead in drawing families into projects that focus on the children and benefit everyone. This activity can take the form of a potluck dinner, with slides of what the children have been doing at nursery school; it can be a series of discussions on topics chosen by the parents; it can be a work day combined with a picnic lunch where everyone pitches in to clean and paint and tidy up. (There's nothing like scrubbing a kitchen floor to generate a common bond.) It doesn't matter what is chosen, as long as it results in the realization of a common goal and creates opportunities for everyone to be together in a meaningful, friendly way.

Keep working toward the basic goals of socialization that teach children to consider the rights and needs of everyone

Finally, the teacher should remember that working toward the goals of socialization discussed in Chapter 9 will also help children learn that everyone is respected and treated fairly at nursery school. The social goals that are most important to emphasize in relation to cross-cultural education are developing empathy for how other people feel, learning that everyone has rights that are respected by all, and gaining skill in cooperating rather than achieving satisfaction by competing and winning over others. If these social skills are fostered, living in the group will be a good experience for all the children, and a healthy foundation will be laid for a more truly integrated society in the future.

SUMMARY

Since children as young as the age of 3 differentiate between people of differing skin colors, it is important to begin a program of cross-cultural education at the nursery school level so that they learn that different does not mean inferior. This cross-cultural program should emphasize two main points: (1) each child brings with him a unique ethnic and cultural background that should be honored by the teacher as being a valuable contribution to the life of the group; and (2) everyone has similar bodily and psychological needs that can be satisfied if people work together to meet them in a cooperative way.

Schools who incorporate a cross-cultural emphasis in their programs can help the child learn to value both the differences and similarities of their friends and teachers as being positive strengths; this valuing is the essence of cross-cultural education.

QUESTIONS

1. Have you been with a young child when he commented on differences in skin color or other differences related to ethnic group membership? What did he say, and what would be an effective way to reply to his comments or questions?
2. Do you feel it might be confusing or contradictory to teach children that people are alike and different at the same time?
3. You are a middle-class, white, well-meaning teacher, and you have just gotten a job working with a Head Start group where the children are predominantly first-generation Puerto Ricans. What will you do to make these children feel truly welcome? How can you utilize the rich cultural traditions of this minority group in your classroom? Suppose that you could not serve Puerto Rican food, use their native dances, or read books to the children about Puerto Rican children. What might be other valuable, though more subtle, ways to honor the cultural uniqueness of these youngsters? Are there ways you might change to match the groups you are serving more closely? Would changing yourself mean that you are losing your own cultural heritage?
4. *Problem:* A delegation of parents calls on you and says they want to discuss the racist policies of your school. In particular, they question the fact that all the teachers are white, and all of the aides are minority people. They have called a meeting for this evening and invite you to attend. What would be a desirable way to deal with this situation? Be sure to consider short-term and long-term possibilities.
5. It is the beginning of the year, and there are many new parents in your group whom you hope to involve in participation. List some things you plan to do that will foster this participation. Also list some policies that would subtly discourage parents from wanting to come and be part of the life of the school.

REFERENCES FOR FURTHER READING

General Discussions on Implementing Cultural Pluralism

Forbes, J. *The education of the culturally different: a multicultural approach.* Washington, D. C.: U.S. Government Printing Office, 1968. Jack Forbes questions the usual meanings of "disadvantaged" and "deprivation." He also provides an excellent general discussion of what a multicultural education should include.

King, W. W., and Kerber, A. *The sociology of early childhood education.* New York: American Book Co., 1968. The authors review research related to various aspects of socializing the young child, including multicultural education, and make recommendations about how to develop a curriculum that will implement social goals. Some of the discussion relates to kindergarten and first grade, but many of the ideas can be adapted to younger children if the teacher is aware of the appropriate developmental levels.

Stone, J. C., and DeNevi, D. P. (Eds.) *Teaching multicultural populations: five heritages.* New York: Van Nostrand Reinhold Co., 1971. The editors cover black, Puerto Rican, Mexican-American, Indian, and Asian cultures, discuss various characteristics of each group, and make practical educational recommendations. An extensive bibliography is included.

Zintz, M. V. *Education across cultures.* (2nd ed.) Dubuque, Iowa: Kendall/Hunt Publishing Co., 1969. This lively book, which focusses on Indian and Mexican culture and on associated educational problems, is hard to put down once you start reading it.

Impact of Discrimination and Fear on Children

Coles, R. *Children of crisis: a study of courage and fear.* New York: Dell Publishing Co., Inc., 1967. This thorough, sensitive study by a psychiatrist on the effect of integration on the people of the South is a fascinating account based on interviews with all kinds of people. Dr. Coles seeks to present both sides of the integration question fully and fairly.

Hill, R. B. *The strengths of black families.* New York: Emerson Hall, 1971. In this refreshing reminder that adverse circumstances can sometimes build power and strength as well as destroy, five strengths possessed by many black families are identified: adaptability of family roles, strong kinship bonds, strong work orientation, strong religious orientation, and strong achievement orientation.

Holt, J. *How children fail.* New York: Dell Publishing Co., Inc., 1964. Holt perceptively analyzes what goes on between teacher and student in many classrooms. Although not cast in terms of working with cultural differences, Holt's comments call to mind in a painful way the Civil Rights Commission report on the treatment of Mexican-American students.

Description of Curricula for Various Ethnic Groups

Black children

Spodek, B., Andrews, P., Lee, M., Riley, J., and White, D. *A black curriculum for early childhood education: teaching units.* Urbana, Ill.: University of Illinois, 1971. Although this guide is for elementary school children, it contains numerous resources that would be appropriate to use for nursery school children. The guide is based on educational goals and objectives and also outlines teaching procedures and materials for attaining the goals.

Indian children

Clark, A. N. *Journey to the people.* New York: The Viking Press, Inc., 1969. Mrs. Clark gives an inspiring description of her work among the Indians of the Southwest. There is a good deal of love and no condescension in this account of how she came to understand and accept the culture of the Indian children she spent a lifetime teaching. Nursery school teachers may also recognize Mrs. Clark as the author of "Tia Maria's Garden" and "The Secret of the Andes."

Mexican-American children

Education Service Center, Region XIII. *Information and materials to teach the cultural heritage of the Mexican-American child.* Austin, Tex.: Dissemination Center for Bilingual Bicultural Education, 1972. A wide range of curriculum suggestions, including recipes, poetry, important Mexican historical figures, and arts and crafts, is given in this comprehensive guide. It is suitable for elementary school, but portions can be adapted for young children.

Cross-Cultural Education

Lane, M. B., Elzey, F. F., and Lewis, M. S. *Nurseries in cross-cultural education: final report.* Washington, D. C.: National Institutes of Mental Health, 1971. This report describes the intent of the cross-cultural program that served black, Oriental, and white families in San Francisco. It explains how its humanistic values were implemented in the curriculum and conveys a sense of the struggles and triumphs of the families and staff while the project was in operation. It reads more like a novel than a final report; highly recommended.

Bibliographies of Books and Records

Cross-Cultural Family Center. *A multi-cultural curriculum for today's young children: an outgrowth of a cross-cultural nursery school.* San Francisco: The Center, 1969. This brief summary of the Lane-Elzey-Lewis report listed above identifies the basic purposes of NICE and describes ways they were translated into life in the nursery school. It is valuable to own because it contains an excellent list of cross-cultural records and books ranging from Hebrew to Japanese to African and Indian.

Day Care and Child Development Council of America. *Multi-ethnic reading and audio-visual material for young children: annotated bibliography.* Publication No. 101. Washington, D. C.: The Council, 1972. This is a good resource because it lists references on Indian as well as Mexican and black youngsters, although some of the books are for older children. About fifteen books in each category are listed.

Griffin, L. *Multi-ethnic books for young children: annotated bibliography for parents and teachers.* Washington, D. C.: National Association for the Education of Young Children, no date. This bibliography lists an exceptionally good assortment of books about children ranging from Jewish to Asian and also includes a section on Southern and Appalachian youngsters. Books are identified by age of child and cultural background and are annotated.

King, E. W., and Kerber, A. *The sociology of early childhood education.* New York: American Book Co., 1968. This book contains an extensive bibliography of books and music from many cultures.

Latimer, B. I. (Ed.) *Starting out right: choosing books about black people for young children, pre-school through third grade.* Wisconsin Department of Public Instruction, 1972. Reprinted, Washington, D. C.: Day Care and Child Development Council of America, 1972. The editor first discusses criteria for selecting books for black children and then, in an annotated bibliography, gives a series of frank appraisals of children's books, rating their weaknesses as well as their strengths; very enlightening.

White, D. *Multi-ethnic books for Head Start children. Part I: black and integrated literature.* Urbana, Ill.: ERIC Clearinghouse on Early Childhood Education, 1969. This annotated bibliography deals mostly with books about black children or books that contain integrated illustrations, so it is biethnic rather than multiethnic.

Sources for Ethnic Records

Although space does not allow me to list all the record supplyhouses that make a point of carrying ethnic records, I include two of the best companies for the benefit of the novice teacher.

Bowmar, 622 Rodier Drive, Glendale, Calif. 91201

Folkways Records, 701 Seventh Ave., New York, N. Y. 10036

For the Advanced Student

Bronfenbrenner, U. *Two worlds of childhood: U.S. and U.S.S.R.* New York: Simon & Schuster, Inc., 1970. Dr. Bronfenbrenner compares childrearing practices in the United States and Russia and then formulates suggestions about how our own society could be changed to improve the well-being of children. The book will help the student stand back and objectively assess the society in which we live.

Gordon, I. J. *Parent involvement in compensatory education.* Urbana, Ill.: ERIC Clearinghouse on Early Childhood Education, no date. Research on the effect of family and culture on the developing child is reviewed, and then a variety of research-based programs that have parent involvement as their goal is summarized. A lot of information is packed into a rather small book.

Stent, M. D., Hazard, W. R., and Revlin, H. N. *Cultural pluralism in education: mandate for change.* New York: Appleton-Century-Crofts, 1973. This reference is a series of articles about inculcating the concept and practice of cultural pluralism in the American public school. In their thoughtful discussions the authors often make general recommendations and suggestions that would apply to implementing almost any culture in a classroom.

Los Niños Head Start

CHAPTER **11**

The pleasures of meaningful work *

Mingle your cares with pleasures now and then.

DIONYSIUS CATO

Does the idea of young children performing meaningful work sound ridiculous, impossible, or even repugnant? Apparently it does to many nursery school teachers because it is an area rarely considered in textbooks on early childhood education,† even though we know it is vitally important for adults to have good feelings about their work. In *Childhood and Society* (1963) Erikson quotes Freud, when asked the question, "What should a normal person be able to do well?" as replying, "To love and to work." Maslow also supports the value of work in his comment: "This business of self-actualization via a commitment to an important job and to worthwhile work could also be said, then, to be the path to human happiness" (1965, p. 5).

But is early childhood too soon to begin laying the foundation for enjoying work? Pleasure in work cannot be expected to suddenly appear full blown as the child attains adulthood; at some point in human development it must begin to be nurtured and encouraged. Since work is such a fundamental part of our culture, teachers should start with children as young as age 3 or 4 to establish a wholesome conviction that work is rewarding and that it can be a significant way of giving meaning and satisfaction to life.

TEACHING CHILDREN TO DISLIKE WORK

We all know of people who face the working day as though it were a deadening burden, an oppression to be struggled through; this is nothing short of tragic. What happened to these people that caused them to feel like that? Some of our work-burdened adult friends must have been subjected to very negative training about work as they grew up. Let us picture what such a negative teaching model might be, bearing in mind that this model may exist at home as well as at school.

Suppose we begin by asking, "How do you teach a 3- or 4-year-old child that work is to be loathed, shirked, and put off as long as possible?" For people who have such an aim in mind, the following series of commandments should be followed faithfully to teach children to hate work—and what better time to begin than in the early, formative years?

1. Select the chores you dislike most yourself, such as picking up every one of the small blocks, and insist that each time a child uses such equipment he pick it all up immediately as soon as he has finished.

---

*Adapted from *Young Children,* September 1967, **22**(6), 373-380.
†Montessori is a rare, welcome exception to this statement.

Never offer to help him with such jobs, because this will make him too dependent on you. Bright children catch on to this quickly: "Oh, no! Let's not get those out, we'll just have to put them all away!"

2. Be sure that all work is tedious and drawn out. Also insist that the child finish every task he begins on the grounds that this will teach him to be diligent.

3. Be sure that everyone always works at the same time because this is fair.

4. Provide no variety to the work; keep it dull. Expect each child to repeat the same portion to perfection, over and over, because repetition is valuable habit training and preparation for later life, where a lot of things will be boring anyway.

5. Never allow enough time, and remind the child constantly that he should hurry. This will encourage him to stick to business.

6. Expect a great deal, and be very critical of any work a child attempts. This will teach him that high standards are important.

7. Tell the child exactly how to do the work; be rigid; be demanding; watch closely so that he doesn't make any mistakes, and be quick to call his attention to all errors so that he will learn to do it the "right" way. This will prevent him from forming bad habits.

8. Compare his achievements with the other children's; draw his attention to where he has failed and how he could do better by copying them. This will help him appreciate other children's strong points.

9. If a child does express interest in doing some helpful job, accept his help with condescending indulgence rather than with thanks and respect. After all, he's only a child.

10. Above all, act abused yourself. Talk to the other adults about how tired you are, how much work everything is, and grumble over the unfairness of it all. Be careful to do this in front of the children because it will teach them to appreciate you more and to look forward to becoming a grown-up working person.

TEACHING THE POSITIVE VALUES OF WORK

What if we want the children in our care to relish work, to find deep rewards in accomplishment, and to anticipate each day with at least a mild pleasure because of the interest their jobs hold for them? Then we must not fall into the trap of assuming that work should consist only of doing what we don't like or don't want to do. We must be wary of thinking that work for young children can never be more than helping out in routine tidying up, and we must stop assuming, even tacitly, that the only work children are capable of is the routine, lengthy, repetitive kind of chore usually disliked by both teachers and children.

In place of such negative attitudes we must substitute an appreciation of the potential that meaningful work holds for young children's development and understand the kinds of work that they are likely to find satisfying.

Work allows the child to experience the pleasure of accomplishment linked with helping other people. One of the most important values of work is that it provides children with the opportunity to experience achievement, which possesses obvious social value, since doing a job often results in accomplishing a task and helping other people at the same time. Thus the 4-year-old who has washed the dishes after making cookies or who has sawed off the sharp corners of the woodworking table experiences not only the glow of satisfaction that comes from honest labor but also feels good because he has contributed to the welfare of the group, particularly if the teacher points this out to him and remembers to say "thank you."

Work increases the reality of role playing. Another pleasure inherent in work grows out of young children's passion for imitating adults. When Joel repairs the seat of the rowboat "just the way my daddy would," he gains insight into what it is like to be a man. Perhaps he thinks, "This is the way grown-ups do things. I am just a little boy, but one day I, too, will be doing things like this all the time, and it's good to do them."

Role playing need not stop at the "family" level. In the past few years interest in career education has increased for children of all ages (Budke, Bettis, and Beasley, 1972). Using work as a means of experiencing many careers can be done successfully even with very young children. I am thinking of such possibilities as helping the visiting nurse unpack her tongue depressors and assemble her examination light, lending a hand to polish the fire engine, or raking up leaves for the gardener. This kind of education takes considerable cooperation and briefing of the adults involved but can be very effective from time to time.

In addition, various work roles can be investigated by taking the children on field trips and by having visitors come to the nursery school and show the children what they do, although this approach is inferior to the actual participation suggested above.

Work is an ego strengthener. The experience of success in work can strengthen the ego and build self-esteem. Every time a child accomplishes something tangible and sees the results turn out reasonably well, his image of himself as being a capable person is strengthened. This is particularly valuable for very retiring or very aggressive children.

At school one year our staff had a boy who had been rejected from kindergarten. At the age of 5 he was already convinced that he was helpless, worthless, and a menace, and he expressed this self-despair in the kindergarten room by throwing scissors, destroying other children's achievements, and refusing to try anything himself. When he joined us at nursery school, we all held our breath. Although the teachers worked on the problem from a number of angles, what appeared to do the most direct good for him was the staff's thinking of some specific simple jobs he could do to help them. I recall that the first one of these was smashing, and I mean *smashing,* an old piano

box we no longer needed. It was a real help to us and a genuine relief and achievement for him. His self-image was rebuilt largely through this avenue of productive work. We're still using a beautiful tree in our insect cage that he made for us.

There is something to be said, too, for the value of work in reducing guilt feelings. I would much rather help a child "fix" something he has broken, clean up after a spill, or apply a Band-Aid to someone he has hurt than settle for, "Say you're sorry!" It is valuable not only because a child should experience the actual consequence of his action through repairing the result, but also because it is a good way for him to learn that doing something "wrong" is not the end of the world and that one can often make amends.

INCORPORATING MEANINGFUL WORK INTO THE NURSERY SCHOOL

Now that the reasons have been reviewed why work can be beneficial for nursery school children, the question remains, "Just what kinds of jobs can young children do?" The following list constitutes some of the activities I have seen them participate in that were both productive and pleasureful. Hopefully, most teachers will be able to supply many more examples from their own schools.

Washing dishes after cooking with them
Loading sand in a small wheelbarrow, carting it to the swing area, and shoveling it under the swings after a rainy day
Planting and weeding the garden
Fertilizing and watering the garden
Cutting flowers and arranging them
Cleaning the aquarium
Setting up the rabbit cage for a new baby rabbit
Feeding and cleaning the rabbit (which reminds me of one 3-year-old who looked at the rabbit droppings and informed me, soberly, "Dem's not raisins!")
Mixing paint
Washing the fingerpainting tables
Cutting up fruits and vegetables for snacks
Helping set up the snack baskets

Photo by Jason Lo'Cicero

Fetching juice for the snack table

Doing all kinds of cooking (making butter, uncooked fondant, soup, biscuits, cranberry-orange relish; using a grinder is a special joy because children can carry out the work of assembling it as well as using it)

Carrying simple messages such as, "Mrs. Coffman needs some more clothespins"

Sanding and waxing blocks and then stapling different grades of sandpaper to them to make music blocks for our music corner

Sawing square corners off the tables to make them safer

Puttying up the holes in the much drilled-on woodworking table

Filling the holes in the edges of a new shelf with putty

Dyeing egg shells and crushing them for collage material

Nailing the seat more firmly into the boat when it works loose

Hammering nails back into the benches so that clothing is no longer snagged on them

Mopping the housekeeping corner when the water play runs deep

Oiling tricycles when they begin to squeak

Using the flatbed ride-'em truck to load up and deliver the baskets of sand toys to the sand pile

Washing easel brushes (a favorite)

These chores, which adults regard as rather run-of-the-mill, were all performed with interest and enthusiasm by the children. Their pleasure did not come mainly from satisfaction with the finished job. Children are more fortunate than that in their approach to work. They love the process as much as the product and do not drive relentlessly toward the single-minded attainment of the goal; their satisfaction is spread throughout the experience. It would be ideal if this were also true for more adults in their own working lives.

Handling the experience of failure. It may also be illuminating to talk about some of our failures as well as our successes, because, of course, some work projects do not turn out well.

The second year of the garden was one of these occasions. We gave the children some excellent shovels and talked about seeds, flowers, and worms, and they started to dig with a will—and quit almost as promptly. We couldn't get any enthusiasm going for the garden: the earth was packed too hard. We had assumed that since it had been dug up the previous season that would be sufficient, but it wasn't. The job was too difficult and took too much strength. However, after we spaded it up, the children returned with a gleam in their eyes and dug deeply and well until they pronounced the time ripe for planting.

On another occasion we needed the large hollow blocks sanded lightly before revarnishing them. "Aha!" thought the adults, "This isn't hard work, and it will be a real help." But the children tried it and wandered away. The job was too tedious and dull. We gave up on that one and did it ourselves. The adult goals of saving money and preserving the blocks motivated us, but the children couldn't have cared less.

We had only partial success with another task: the tricycles needed to be painted, and we had to remove the dirt and grease (from all that lubricating by the children) so that fresh paint would stick. The children enjoyed scrubbing with stiff brushes and soapy water, but our standards were pickier than theirs so that we teachers had to really scrub to finish the job to our satisfaction.

Once we tried to bake and decorate cookies all in one day (at least we had the sense not to attempt roll and cut cookies). This was too extensive a task, and working under too much pressure made us all cranky. Now we buy sugar cookies and content ourselves with decorating them at school, or we bake them and eat them plain.

These less successful experiences raise the problem of how to handle failure. In the cases above, where the teachers failed, we admitted honestly to the children that things hadn't worked out as well as we had hoped and promised we would try to work out something better next time. Then we analyzed what was wrong and changed what we could.

Sometimes, too, we ask children why they didn't like a project. They will often go right to the heart of the matter and tell you, "It's no fun," "It's too hard," "I don't want to," or from the more sophisticated 4-year-olds, "My mother doesn't want me to do that today."

When a child tries and fails, there's no point and possibly real harm in pretending he has done something well when he hasn't. Maybe he can't tie that shoelace or get the nail in straight. Honest recognition is still possible, and reassurance is also highly desirable in these situations. The teacher can say, "You're really trying, Nancy. One of these days you're going to get that knack," or "Thank you. I can see you really want to help, and I appreciate it," or "You're working hard. Can I help you?"

Suggestions and conclusions about planning work opportunities so they remain appealing

One basic suggestion for keeping work attractive is that *jobs should be short* or capable of being broken down into short portions. When we made the sand-music blocks, some of the children enjoyed putting the wax on the blocks, but an older crowd was attracted by the use of the stapler and did that part of the job.

Except in the late spring when the teacher may deliberately plan projects that take 2 days to finish (such as painting and shellacking something), tasks should be finished in 1 day. Part of the pleasure of the music blocks was that we made and used them in the music corner the same morning. Young children need the immediate reward and satisfaction of seeing something through promptly.

Reasonable expectations by the teacher are very important. The goal should basically be pleasure in process and accomplishment, not perfection in performance. If a job is too hard or the child must be too meticulous, much of the joy in working that we hope to foster falls by the wayside. Work must be adjusted to the reality of the child's ability and to what he wants to do. A good way to find out what they like to do is to listen for the times children volunteer and take them up on their offers of help. Even if the tub of water is too heavy to carry by themselves, they can turn on the faucet and help carry the tub, with the teacher's hand on the handle, too.

Children need real tools to do work. They should not be given miserable little dime store imitations. Sometimes tools are best if scaled to size. For example, clamming shovels, which are strong but short-handled, are superior to the longer variety. Sometimes regular, adult-sized tools are necessary and suprisingly easy for the children to manipulate. Stout hammers and well-sharpened saws, real C-clamps, and a standard-sized vegetable grinder are all worthwhile investments. Dull, tinny tools build frustration and encourage children to give up in disgust.

In many cases the child should have the privilege of selection and the right of rejection in choosing jobs. In this respect, schools are luckier than families because, with so many children available, chances are good that almost every task will appeal to someone. Since some chores attract particular children and some draw others, a perceptive teacher should try to think of specific things that are likely to be attractive for each individual.

In general, three kinds of materials attract all children and can be successfully incorporated when planning work experiences. These can be stated very simply by the following axioms:

Anything involving food is fun.

Anything involving earth is fun.

Anything involving water is the *most* fun!

Most work requires supervision. Almost all jobs require some supervision by the teacher. This is perhaps one reason children aren't allowed to do more work at home as well as at school (until they are too old to want to do it, of course). Adults often feel it is easier on a short-term basis to do it themselves than to allow the time and exercise the patience it takes to let the child make the effort. The other common reason children aren't allowed to help more is that adults underestimate their abilities. But think what such consistent underestimation does to the child's self-concept!

The teacher's own attitude toward work is significant. The teacher's attitude toward work can influence the way the child feels about it, since children acquire attitudes from models whom they care about. The teacher who willingly lends a hand if the job is onerous (picking up blocks again comes to mind) is setting a pattern for a future young mother who may one day offer her help with equal generosity to her own child. The teacher who enjoys her own job is helping convey the idea that work can be pleasureful as well as challenging. Finally, the teacher who expresses a genuine attitude of respect for the child's work helps him build good attitudes toward it even more directly. If she reveres his power of concentration and refrains from interrupting him while he is working, if she values his suggestions about how to accomplish the task, and if she is quick to acknowledge his achievements, the child's pleasure in this kind of activity will be deepened, and he will be more likely to participate in working again when opportunity arises.

SUMMARY

Although we would never wish to emphasize work in the nursery school to the extent that it minimizes the significance of play, work is a valuable experience to offer young children because it allows them to enjoy the pleasure of accomplishment linked with helping other people, it builds reality into role playing, it strengthens the ego, and it enhances self-esteem.

Many different jobs at nursery school, ranging from preparing the snack to making simple repairs, are both interesting and not too difficult for children to perform. The children's pleasure in these tasks can be increased if the teacher keeps them reasonably short and easy, provides tools that are effective, allows children to select that jobs they prefer to do, and maintains a healthy attitude toward work herself.

QUESTIONS

1. What is it about work that causes many people to think of it as a difficult, tiresome activity to be avoided if possible?
2. In your opinion, would it be practical to rely on children to volunteer to help with work spontaneously when the opportunity comes up, or is it fairer to have a list of jobs that must be done each day and have the children assigned to different ones at different times?
3. If you happen to be someone who feels that work is enjoyable, can you account for how you came to feel this way about it?
4. Why do you think real work is an appetizing activity to young children?
5. Do you feel children should be paid for doing chores around the house, or should they be expected to do them because they are contributing members of the family unit?
6. Watch during this coming week for opportunities for children to participate in new kinds of work experiences that they have not tried before. Be prepared to assess what made these experiences successful or unsuccessful.

REFERENCES FOR FURTHER READING

Overviews

Neff, W. S. *Work and human behavior.* New York: Atherton Press, 1968. In this interesting, readable book Neff discusses the topic of work in terms of its being a human and social problem, in terms of the individual, and in terms of related counseling problems. The chapter titled "The Components of the Work Personality" is particularly helpful because it traces the theoretical development of this part of personality from early childhood to maturity.

White, R. W. *The enterprise of living: growth and organization in personality.* New York: Holt, Rinehart and Winston, Inc., 1972. Although it deals with the adolescent and young adult, White's chapter on "Finding an Occupation" should be read by teachers of young children to fill in their knowledge of early forces that influence the occupational choices of older individuals.

Work in Relation to Young Children

Montessori, M. *The discovery of the child.* Translated by M. J. Costelloe. Notre Dame, Ind.: Fides Publishers, 1967. The *practical life activities* recommended by Dr. Montessori in this and other books describing her curriculum remain one of the rare discussions of work that can be successfully performed by young children.

Teaching Responsibility

Although the subject of work as such is infrequently discussed in relation to children of preschool age, some recommendations concerning "chores" and home tasks can be gleaned under the topic of responsibility. The following references are written with family life in mind, but the principles should also be applied at school.

Foster, C. J. *Developing responsibility in children.* Chicago: Science Research Associates Inc., 1953.

Neisser, E. G. *Your child's sense of responsibility.* New York: Public Affairs Pamphlets, 1956. Pamphlet No. 254.

Young Children and Money

Alexander, A. M. *The money world of your preschooler.* East Lansing, Mich.: Cooperative Extension Science, Michigan State University, 1967. Money as it relates to the preschool child is a rare topic indeed and worth listing here because of money's relationship to work. Alexander gives a sensible, brief discussion of how understanding the uses of money can be part of teaching preschool children to get along in society.

For the Advanced Student

de Grazia, S. *Of time, work, and leisure.* New York: The Twentieth Century Fund, 1962. The author raises the question of what lies beyond the performance of work and discusses problems involved in the use of free time and contrasts it with the productive use of leisure to enhance human existence; excellent reading.

PART **FIVE**

Enhancing creativity

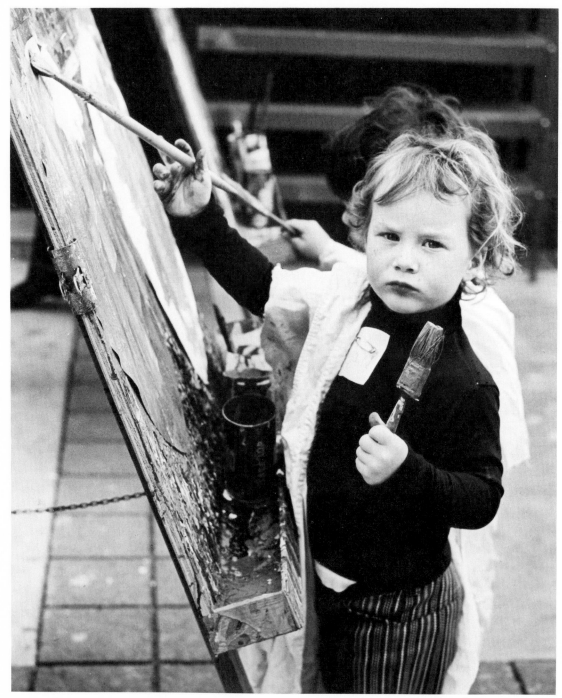

CHAPTER 12

Fostering creativity by means of self-expressive materials

> If a man does not keep pace with his companions, perhaps it is because he hears a different drummer. Let him step to the music which he hears, however measured or far away.
>
> HENRY DAVID THOREAU
> *Walden* (1854)

Nursery school teachers have long valued creativity and sought to enhance it by fostering self-expression in the young children they care for. In the past we teachers have been particularly successful in presenting expressive materials and activities such as paint, clay, and dance in a manner that fosters unique personal responses from the children. But today we are coming to realize that artistic creativeness represents only one facet of creative endeavor and that there are additional aspects of creativity in play and in divergence and originality of thought, which should be encouraged more fully. For this reason, the discussion of creativity in this book does not stop with the presentation of expressive materials but extends, in two additional chapters, to play and to the fostering of originality in thought.

DEFINITION OF CREATIVITY

Defining creativity where young children are concerned is rather difficult, since the commonly accepted definitions include not only the requirement that the idea or product be novel but that it be related to reality and stand the test of being worthwhile, too. However, a definition by Smith suits our needs well, since it fits young children's creative abilities more aptly: creativity is the process of "sinking down taps into our past experiences and putting these selected experiences together into new patterns, new ideas or new products" (1966, p. 43).

This putting prior experience together into something new is a good description of what we hope young children will be able to do when they use self-expressive materials, play imaginatively, solve problems, or generate new ideas. It stresses originality and doesn't emphasize the quality of evaluation, which is less applicable to very young children, although even they can be encouraged to try out ideas, thereby going through reality testing and evaluation in an informal way.

The student should also understand that creativity is not limited to a few gifted Rembrandts and Einsteins; nor is it necessarily associated with high intelligence. The work of Getzels and Jackson (1962),

145

Wallach and Kogan (1965), and Ward (1968) has demonstrated that high scores on creativity tests do not correlate strongly with high scores on academic tests of achievement or with high scores on standard measures of intelligence. In addition, a study by Margolin (1968) indicates that teachers who deliberately foster uniqueness and originality of response in creative activities can actually increase the variety and diversity of such responses in young children.

These findings imply that we do not have to wait for that specially gifted child to come along in order for creative behavior to take place in our groups. The ability to generate original ideas and to produce satisfying, freshly conceived products resides in many children; and since such behavior can be increased by appropriate responses from the teacher, it is worthwhile for her to learn how to do this.

IMPORTANCE OF CREATIVITY

The experience of being involved in creative activity satisfies people in ways that nothing else can, and the ability to be creative appears not only to reflect but to foster emotional health. First, the act of creation enhances the child's feelings of self-esteem and self-worth. (The reader can test the validity of this statement by recalling the last time she produced something original—perhaps something as simple as a Christmas decoration or a variation on a recipe—and then recalling how she felt when it was accomplished.) There is something about creating a unique product or idea that leaves people feeling good about themselves.

Besides enhancing self-esteem, creative experiences offer opportunities to express emotions and to come to terms with them. Since they have this strong affective component, they provide a balance for the emphasis on intellectual development, which may overwhelm the rest of the program unless it is carefully managed.

Finally, creative activities offer an excellent opportunity to individualize teaching. Materials and activities that depend on open-ended replies permit uniqueness and diversity to flourish and allow each child to be himself rather than require him to conform to closed-system, authority-centered learning.

STAGES OF DEVELOPMENT

One of the peak periods for creative self-expression in our culture occurs between the ages of 4 and 6. This stage correlates well with Erikson's developmental stage for this age, which he identifies as the stage of initiative versus guilt (Gowan, 1972). Erikson's stage is characterized by reaching out, exploring, and experimenting and also reflects an increase in creative behavior, which is partially characterized by this same kind of activity.

As is true in other areas, children pass through general stages of development in the use of creative materials (Smart and Smart, 1972). First, *they explore the material itself* and investigate its properties. Two- and three-year-olds, for instance, spend many satisfactory hours in what appears to be mainly manipulation and exploration of paints and brushes or in relishing the mixing of play dough, and they employ all their senses to do this. Who has not seen such a youngster meticulously painting her hands up to the elbow or beheld another squeezing the sponge in the paint bucket or a third looking thoughtfully into the distance as he licks the back of the clay spoon?

Once the qualities of the material have been explored and some skill has been gained in its manipulation, the child is likely to move on to what is called the *nonrepresentational stage.* Paintings at this stage, for example, seem to have more design and intention behind them, but the content is not readily recognizable by anyone but the painter. Since painting at this stage is not always done with the intention of depicting something in particular, the teacher must beware of asking "What is it?" lest such a question unintentionally put the child on a spot.

Ultimately, the youngster reaches the pictorial or *representational stage,* where he quite deliberately sets out to reproduce or create something. He may paint a picture of himself or the sun in the sky or depict a fascinating event such as the toilet overflowing or going trick-or-treating. Some children attain this stage of representational art in nursery school, but many children develop this ability during their year in kindergarten.

Implications for nursery school teachers

One implication to be drawn from these sequential stages of development is that teachers should permit children countless opportunities to experience and explore expressive materials, because this learning is fundamental to the creative experience. The full knowledge gained through such exploration extends the ways a child may use the material, thereby enriching his creative opportunities; and the freedom to explore is also likely to keep alive his interest and openness to the medium.

The second developmental implication is that, when using expressive materials, young children should not be expected to produce a finished product. Some 4-year-olds will do this, of course; but since many will not, the expectation of some sort of recognizable result is not a reasonable creative goal to set for children in their early years.

GENERAL RECOMMENDATIONS ABOUT CREATIVITY

It is hoped that the reader will apply to all three chapters on creativity the general comments made here on fostering the child's creativity with self-expressive materials.

Be aware of the value of nonconforming behavior and of "unattractive" personality characteristics

Paul Torrance (1962) has frequently emphasized that the kind of behavior teachers identify as desirable in children does not always coincide with characteristics associated with the creative personality. For instance, the teacher who thinks she values uniqueness may find, when a youngster has spilled his milk because he tried the original method of holding the cup with his teeth, that she doesn't like creative exploration as much as she thought she did.

Not only can this lack of conformity be inconvenient, but the teacher should also realize that some creative individuals possess character traits that she may not care for. Torrance cites 84 characteristics that differentiate the more creative person from the less creative one (Table 6). Note that some of the less attractive qualities include stubbornness, finding fault with things, appearing haughty and self-satisfied, and being discontented—qualities often disliked by teachers. Yet it is easy to see how stubbornness might be a valuable quality to possess when carrying through a new idea, or how finding fault and being discontented could result in questioning and analyzing a situation before coming up with suggestions for improving it. In all fairness, we must admit that we don't know at present if some of these less attractive attitudes lie at the root of creativity or if some of them are only the result of squelching and mishandling by teachers, peers, and families as the child matures. On the other hand, Torrance also found that creative children possessed many likable qualities, such as determination, being curious, being intuitive, being willing to take risks, preferring complex ideas, and having a sense of humor.

The purpose of pointing out these possible problems of living with creative children is not to discourage the teacher from fostering such behavior but to enlighten her so that she will not subtly reject or discourage creative responses because she fails to recognize the positive side of such apparently undesirable behavior. Hopefully, her understanding will result in increased acceptance and valuing of creative endeavor. Acceptance is vitally important because it will encourage children to develop these abilities further and because it will help balance the rejection and isolation to which people who dare to be different are often subjected. As long as we have creative youngsters in our care, we can help guard against rejection by recognizing and supporting originality in thought and deed.

Cultivate three teaching skills in yourself

Each creative area requires a specific teaching skill for its facilitation. The culti-

Table 6. Contrast of the characteristics of highly creative persons and the values and characteristics of our society*

From studies that were done to distinguish highly creative persons from less creative persons, the following list of characteristics of highly creative persons was compiled.† From what you know about our society and of what most people in our culture value, contrast the characteristics of highly creative persons with the characteristics our society values highly.

Characteristics of highly creative persons†	*Characteristics and values of our society‡*
1. Accepts disorder	1. Disapproves of disorder; demands neatness, tidiness, regularity
2. Adventurous	2. Security
3. Strong affection	3. Indifference; views overt expressions of affection as weaknesses
4. Altruistic	4. Self-centeredness; benevolence thought of as "corny"; any help offered is material rather than moral
5. Awareness of others	5. Noninterference; fears involvement
6. Always baffled by something	6. Unquestioning acceptance
7. Attracted to disorder	7. Rejects disorder
8. Attracted to mysterious	8. Comfortable with and desirous of the known, the concrete facts, the unambiguous
9. Attempts difficult jobs (sometimes too difficult)	9. Desire for the average, the golden mean; undertakes easy, practical, feasible tasks
10. Bashful outwardly	10. Outgoing, extroverted personality
11. Constructive in criticism	11. Criticism interpreted as personal insult; destructive criticism of others to improve one's own status
12. Courageous	12. Spiritlessness, shyness, and timidity viewed as safe personality characteristics
13. Deep and conscientious in convictions	13. Shallow and superficial convictions
14. Defies conventions of courtesy	14. Stresses social etiquette
15. Defies conventions of health	15. Stresses healthy living habits
16. Desires to excel	16. Desires status quo
17. Determination	17. Vacillation, skepticism, distrust
18. Differentiated value-hierarchy	18. Profession of rigid, conventional values
19. Discontented	19. Contentment, satisfaction, tranquility
20. Disturbs organization	20. Adheres to organization
21. Dominant (not in power sense)	21. Dominant (in power sense)
22. Emotional	22. Suppression of emotions
23. Emotionally sensitive	23. Emotionally apathetic, evasion of "involvement"
24. Energetic	24. Passivity, procrastination, lethargy
25. A fault-finder	25. A praise and compliment-giver; flattery
26. Doesn't fear being thought "different"	26. Feels need to be like and do as the crowd
27. Feels whole parade is out of step	27. Falls in and tries to keep in step with parade
28. Full of curiosity	28. Nonchalance, unconcern, "who cares!"

*From Brown, M., and Plihal, J. *Evaluation materials for use in teaching child development.* Minneapolis, Minn.: Burgess Publishing Co., 1966. Pp. 155-158.

†E. Paul Torrance, *Guiding creative talent.* © 1962. Reprinted by permission of Prentice-Hall, Inc., Englewood Cliffs, New Jersey.

‡This is the column students construct. Some examples of society's characteristics and values are here given.

Table 6. Contrast of the characteristics of highly creative persons and the values and characteristics of our society—cont'd

Characteristics of highly creative persons	*Characteristics and values of our society*
29. Appears haughty and self-satisfied at times	29. Appearing to be modest and self-effacing
30. Likes solitude	30. Desires companionship, sociability; lonely and anxious in privacy
31. Independence in judgment	31. Reliance upon other people's opinions
32. Independent in thinking	32. "What will the neighbors think?"
33. Individualistic	33. Conformity
34. Intuitive	34. Rationalization
35. Industrious	35. Leisure, relaxation
36. Introversive	36. Extroversive
37. Keeps unusual hours	37. Follows customary time schedule
38. Lacks business ability	38. Stresses business ability
39. Makes mistakes	39. Correctness without errors; fear of errors
40. Never bored	40. Often experiences monotony, tediousness, boredom
41. Nonconforming	41. Conforming, adapting, agreeing, complying
42. Not hostile or negativistic	42. Annihilation of that which threatens
43. Not popular	43. Popularity, being liked, getting along with others
44. Oddities of habit	44. Stereotyped everyday habits
45. Persistent	45. Change, ease, comfort
46. Becomes preoccupied with a problem	46. Easily distracted from thoughts
47. Preference for complex ideas	47. Preference for simple, single, clear, unmixed ideas
48. Questioning	48. Confidence; make up one's mind quickly
49. Radical	49. Disapproves of extremes, of "drastically" different ideas
50. Receptive to external stimuli	50. Insensitive to many things going on in the world
51. Receptive to ideas of others	51. Intolerant of ideas of others which disturb one's narrow-mindedness
52. Regresses occasionally	52. Regression believed a sign of maladjustment
53. Rejection of suppression as a mechanism of impulse control	53. Use of suppression as an important mechanism of impulse control
54. Rejection of repression	54. Smothers, stifles, curbs, checks ideas and emotions
55. Reserved	55. Outgoing, friendly
56. Resolute	56. Compromise, flexibility
57. Self-assertive	57. Fear of taking a stand; staying on the fence or in the middle of the road
58. Self-starter	58. Requires prodding and support
59. Self-aware	59. A stranger to oneself; not responsible for own behavior
60. Self-confident	60. Uncertainty about oneself; reliance upon others rather than self
61. Self-sufficient	61. Dependence upon others to satisfy needs and wants
62. Senses of destiny	62. Stresses living for the present

Continued.

Table 6. Contrast of the characteristics of highly creative persons and the values and characteristics of our society—cont'd

Characteristics of highly creative persons	Characteristics and values of our society
63. Sense of humor	63. Laughing at someone's hurt, inferiority or authority, or at off-color, smutty jokes
64. Sensitive to beauty	64. Unappreciative of natural and artful beauty
65. Shuns power	65. Seeks power
66. Sincere	66. Imitation, pretense, deception, lip service, hypocrisy, front, evasive, hollow
67. Not interested in small details	67. Involved in trite matters; making mountain out of mole hill
68. Speculative	68. Jumping to rash conclusions; not pondering what might or could or should be
69. Spirited in disagreement	69. Hostile or revengeful in agreement in order not to lose face
70. Strives for distant goals	70. Lacks distant goals or goals focused upon material goods or status
71. Stubborn	71. Unanimity, assention, agreement
72. Temperamental	72. Composure, serenity
73. Tenacious	73. Giving up and in; divorce
74. Tender emotions	74. Soft, kind, loving and delicate emotions as effeminate weaknesses
75. Timid	75. Bravery, heroism
76. Thorough	76. Lax, overlook, inexact
77. Unconcerned about personal power	77. Concerned about personal power
78. Somewhat uncultured, primitive	78. Refinement, polish
79. Unsophisticated, naive	79. Pseudo-sophistication, worldly
80. Unwilling to accept anything on mere say-so	80. "I heard, read that. . . " "That's what the book and the teacher said."
81. Visionary	81. Practicality, realism
82. Versatile	82. Decisive, stable
83. Willing to take risks	83. Cautious
84. Somewhat withdrawn and quiescent	84. Outgoing, exuberant activity

vation of these skills is discussed at greater length in the appropriate chapter, but they are listed here to provide the reader with a quick overview.

In fostering creativity by means of expressive materials, the teacher should make ample materials freely available and cultivate her ability to stand back and let the child explore and utilize them as his impulses and feelings require. When seeking to facilitate play, the teacher needs to be able to move with the children's imaginative ideas and respond to them by providing materials and support that keeps the play ongoing and creative. When developing original thinking, the teacher must reinforce the children's production of ideas by recognizing their value and by learning to ask questions that encourage the development of their thoughts.

Do your best to maintain an emotionally healthy climate in your nursery school room

In the chapters on emotional health, handling routines, and discipline considerable time was spent discussing ways to keep the nursery school environment reasonable, consistent, and secure so that children will feel emotionally at ease. Such a stable, predictable climate is valuable for many reasons, but one of the outstanding ones is that it forms a sound base for the generation of creative activity, which in turn contributes to the development of emotional health. Children who feel secure are more likely to venture forth, try new experiences, and express themselves in creative ways than are children who are using up their energy by worrying or being frightened or anxious.

USE OF SELF-EXPRESSIVE MATERIALS TO FOSTER THE CREATIVE SELF

Expressive materials include such diverse media as painting, collage, dough and clay, woodworking, sewing, and dance. Although the materials themselves are different, some basic principles apply to all of them. (Suggested guidelines for use of specific materials are included later in the chapter.)

Value of using free-form materials

The most valuable quality that expressive materials have in common is that there is no one right thing to do with them or one right way to use them; so, in a real sense, these materials are failure-proof for the child. As long as the child observes a few basic rules, such as keeping the sand down and seeing that the dough stays on the table and off the floor, there is no way he can make a mistake with them. For this reason alone, such materials are an invaluable addition to the curriculum.

There are additional reasons why expressive materials are indispensable. Psychologists and experienced teachers agree that these experiences provide many opportunities for children to express their feelings and come to terms with them. It can be fascinating to watch the development of a shy child who may begin finger-painting by using only the middle of his paper and then see him gradually come to fill his paper with rich colors and swooping strokes of joy as he gains confidence during his months at nursery school.

Since each child is free to do as he wishes, these materials also represent the ultimate in individualized curriculum. The youngster can express who he is and what he is as something within him urges him to do; he is able to suit the material to himself in an intensely personal way.

In addition, many values associated with creative materials lie in the social, sensory, and intellectual spheres. Children who are working side by side often develop a spirit of camaraderie. Using creative materials provides numerous opportunities for rich sensory input in that dough feels sticky and then firm; finger-painting feels cool, gushy, and slippery; dance makes the child aware of his body as he moves in response to the music. Finally, the amount of factual information children acquire about the substances they are using contributes to their intellectual growth: red and yellow mixed together creates orange; some woods are easier to saw through than others; two smaller blocks equal one large one.

Although these social, sensory, and intellectual learnings are worthwhile, I still regard them as being like the frosting on the cake. The primary values of using expressive materials remain in the affective sphere. Expressive materials are fundamentally useful because they foster creativity, build self-esteem, and provide a safe, failure-proof experience. Most important, they can be the source of open-ended opportunities for the child to be himself and for him to express and work through his individual feelings.

Practical ways to encourage the creative aspect of self-expressive materials

Interfere as little as possible. As I mentioned earlier, the most significant skill the teacher can cultivate in presenting self-expressive materials is her ability to stand back and let the child explore them as his impulses and feelings require. This does not mean that children should be allowed to experiment with scissors by cutting the doll's hair off or that they should be permitted to smear clay all over the nursery school chairs to "get their feelings out." It is as true here as in other nursery school situations that the teacher does not allow the child to damage property or to do things that may hurt himself or someone else.

However, although inexperienced teachers occasionally allow destructive things to happen in the name of freedom, experience has taught me that the reverse circumstance is more likely to occur. Many teachers unthinkingly limit and control the use of expressive materials more than is necessary. Thus they may refuse to permit a child to use the indoor blocks on the table "because we always use them on the floor," or they may insist he use only one paint brush at a time despite the fact that using two at once makes such interesting lines and patterns. These ideas are essentially harmless ones and should be encouraged because of their originality.

Never provide a model for the children to copy. A copy is not an original. When I was a little girl in kindergarten, the "creative" experiences that were offered consisted mainly of making things just the way the teacher did. I particularly recall sewing around the edges of paper plates to make letter holders and cutting out paper flowers to glue on sticks. I suppose that what was creative about these activities was that we got to pick which flowers to cut out, and, as I remember, we could choose any color of yarn to sew with. Whatever educational merit such activities possess, creativity is not among them. Yet some nursery schools persist in offering such experiences in the name of creativity. If the teacher really wishes to foster originality and the child's self-expression rather than her own, she will avoid models and will merely set the materials out and let the children go to it for themselves.

Sometimes a child will attempt to lure the teacher into drawing something for him to copy by pleading, "Draw me a house" or "Draw me a man so I can color him." Rather than complying, the wise teacher meets this request by recognizing the child's deeper request, which is for a one-to-one relationship; so she meets this need by talking with him, meanwhile encouraging him to make the picture himself.

Understand that it is the process not the product that matters most to the young child. We live in such a work-oriented, product-centered culture that sometimes we lose sight of the simple pleasure of doing something for its own sake. For young children, however, getting there is more than half the fun. They savor the process and live for the moment. Therefore, it is well not to hurry them toward finishing something or to overstress the final result. They *will* love to take their creations home, of course, and all such items should be carefully labeled and put in their cubbies so that this is possible, but the primary emphasis should remain on doing.

Allow plenty of time and opportunity for the child to use the materials so that his experience is truly satisfying. In the discussion about sharing I made the point that it is important for each child to have enough of an experience in order that he be truly satisfied before he gives his place up to someone else. This is particularly true when using expressive materials. One painting or one collage is just not enough. Children need the chance to work themselves into the experience and to develop their feelings and ideas as they go along. For this reason it is important to schedule long enough time periods to allow for many children to move in and out of the expressive experience as their needs dictate. For real satisfaction this opportunity needs to be available for an hour or an hour and a half at a time.

Learn how to make comments that enhance the child's creative productivity. Making effective comments as the child creates will encourage him to continue and to involve himself ever more deeply in the activity. But it can be risky as well as embarrassing to be trapped into commenting on what the child is making either by trying to guess what it is or by asking him to name it. As mentioned previously, children often do not deliberately set out to represent anything in particular, and, even if they do intend a representation, it may defy recognition by anyone else. An

Los Ninos Head Start

additional drawback to requesting that creations be labeled is that it places emphasis on the product rather than on the creative, dynamic aspect of the experience.

It is more enhancing to comment on the pleasure the child is feeling as he works or to ask him if he would like to tell you about it. These remarks show him that you are interested in and care for him, but they avoid the taint of passing judgment on the quality of what he has made or of emphasizing that the end is better than the means (Sparling and Sparling, 1973).

Grant the child who is dubious the right to refuse. Children benefit from the opportunity to stand and watch before they plunge into an activity more vigorously. Three-year-olds do a lot of this standing around, but older children who are shy or new to school may behave this way, too. This is a valid way to learn, and the teacher should respect the child who copes with new experiences in this manner. Usually, after a few days he will want to try whatever it is he has been watching so intently.

A few children are extraordinarily concerned about getting painty or sticky. These youngsters are usually reassured if the teacher talks with the mother in their hearing and asks the mother to tell them that using paint and glue is all right at school. It can also help if "clean" materials, such as soap painting or snow, are offered as beginning messy activities. It should be made clear to such youngsters that there is water instantly available should they feel the need to wash their hands and that the apron will protect themselves and their clothes from undue contamination.

Some comments on expressive materials themselves. It is important to provide enough of whatever the children are using. There is nothing sadder than children making do with skimpy little fistfuls of dough when they need large, satisfying mounds to punch and squeeze. The same thing holds true for collage materials, woodworking, and painting. Children need plenty of material to work with, as well as the chance to make as many things as they wish.

Providing enough material for the children means that the teacher must develop her scrounging and pack rat instincts to the ultimate degree. Not only must she ferret out sources of free materials, but she must also find time and energy to pick them up regularly and produce a place to store them until they are needed. Parents can be very helpful in collecting materials if the teacher takes the time to show them examples of what she needs. There are many sources of such materials in any community (Appendix C is included to inspire the beginner).

Variety in materials is also crucial. Creative activity should not be limited to easel painting and paper collage. The reader will find numerous examples of variations suggested at the end of each materials outline, and the references included at the end of the chapter list many additional ideas.

Finally, creative materials that will be used together should be selected with an eye to beauty. For instance, rather than simply setting out a hodgepodge, collage materials should be chosen that contrast interestingly and attractively in texture and color. Pieces of orange onion bags could be offered along with bits of dark cork, white Styrofoam, beige burlap, and dry seed pods; a black or bright yellow mat would be a good choice as a collage base for these items. Fingerpainting colors that make a beautiful third color should be selected. For example, magenta and yellow combine to form a gorgeous shade of orange, but purple and yellow turn out dull gray.

PRESENTATION OF SPECIFIC MATERIALS

I have selected only the more common materials for the outlines in the following pages, but the reader can find additional suggestions in the references at the end of the chapter. I hope that these ideas will

not be followed as gospel but will serve to inspire the teacher to develop and carry out her own and the children's creative ideas.

The suggestions for presentation of various materials in this and the following chapter have been written as individual, self-contained units so they may be abstracted and posted in various areas about the school should this be desired. For this reason, I hope the reader will forgive a certain repetition in the descriptions of setting out and cleaning up.

Easel painting*

Easel painting is perhaps the one form of artistic endeavor offered by all nursery schools, and it is an outstanding example of a creative material that is intensely satisfying to young children. In the fall, particularly with younger children and with newcomers, it is wise to begin with the basic experience of a few colors, one size of paint brush, and the standard, *large-sized* paper; but as the year progresses and the children's skills increase, many interesting variations and degrees of complexity can be offered that will sustain interest and enhance the experience of easel painting for the more sophisticated young artists.

When looking at paintings or other expressive products, one can be tempted to play psychologist and read various interpretations into the children's work. Although it is perfectly all right to encourage a child to tell you about what he has painted if he wishes to do so, the interpretation of children's painting should be left to experts. Correct interpretation depends on a knowledge of the order in which the paintings were produced, knowledge of the availability of colors, access to the case history, and a complete record of comments made by the child while the work was in progress. In addition, young children often overpaint, restructuring paintings two or three times as they work; this

---

*I am indebted to the staff and students of the Santa Barbara City College Children's Center for their help in formulating the following outlines.

increases the likelihood of misinterpretation. Since all this information is required for understanding, it is easy to see why even professional psychologists may differ considerably about interpretations of such material, and it makes sense that teachers who have only a modicum of training in such matters should be very circumspect about ascribing psychological meanings to children's art.

A. Preparation

1. Decide where to put the easels for the day. Painting is easiest to clean up if done outside, but in bad weather the easels can and should be moved indoors.

2. Assemble the equipment. This will include easels, easel clips, aprons, paint containers, brushes, large paper, paint, and a felt marker. You will also need clothespins, drying racks or a line, a sink and towels or a bucket and towels, and a sponge.

3. Check the paint to make sure it is rich and bright, not watery and thin. Decide, possibly with the children's help, on what colors to offer.

B. Procedure

1. If time permits, invite one or two children to help you mix the paint. (Sometimes this is done a day in advance, but it is always good to invite a child to help—mixing paint is interesting and educational.) Begin by shaking a generous quantity of powdered paint into the mixing container. Next, add water a little at a time, stirring constantly just as one does when making flour and water thickening for gravy. The paint should look rich and bright; it should not be a thin, watery-looking gruel. If the paint was mixed the day before, be sure it is thoroughly stirred before pouring so that all the pigment is mixed back into the water. A dash of liquid detergent added to each container seems to help paint wash out of clothing more easily.

2. Several pieces of easel paper may be put up at one time—doing this makes getting a new sheet ready for use much faster.

3. Put just a small quantity of paint in each easel container. The paint may have to be replaced more frequently, but frequent replacement means the paint stays brighter and small amounts mean less waste when it is spilled.

4. If necessary, invite children to come and paint, and help them put on the aprons. Use *plastic* aprons to protect clothes, and remember to roll up sleeves firmly.

5. Write the child's name and the date on the back right-hand corner.

6. If it is windy, use additional easel clips.

7. Encourage children to remember to replace brushes in the same color paint and to do their color mixing on the paper.

8. Children may use their hands in the painting as long as they keep them off other children.

9. Hang pictures on drying racks, chain link fence, or clothesline.

10. Children should wash hands *before* removing their aprons. Use an outdoor sink or bucket for hand washing if possible. If children must wash in the bathroom, be sure to alert a nearby teacher to keep track of what is going on. Sometimes children also enjoy sponging off their aprons—if this is the case, rejoice!

C. Cleanup

1. Encourage children to help clean up. Washing paint brushes is usually a richly enjoyed experience.

2. Put clean, unused paint back into the storage bottles, and ruthlessly discard spoiled, discolored paint.

3. Replace all equipment in the correct storage places.

4. Roll and store dry paintings in the children's cubbies; the paintings should go home every day.

Suggested variations. Offer a wide variety

of colors, and ask children to select those they prefer; use a different size or shape of paper or one with a different texture. You may want the children to experiment by learning how to mix a new color from the ones you have presented. Try using the same color paint on the same color paper, or several shades of just one color. Different sizes of brushes in the same color paint make a nice contrast. You might want to try painting to music, painting woodworking, painting the fence with water, using watercolors, having several children paint on one large sheet to make a mural, or painting on a flat surface instead of an easel. Printing and stamping, using paint and sponges, can also be an interesting although not extraordinarily successful experiment to try.

Fingerpainting

Fingerpainting is one of the most tension-relieving and delicious creative experiences available in nursery school. The brilliance of the colors and the general gushiness that characterizes successful participation make it both appealing and relaxing. It is particularly valuable because it is so messy, beautiful, and free, and because it is a direct sensory experience for the children. It should be offered several times a week.

A. Preparation
  1. Decide what kind of fingerpainting you will offer. There are many satisfying variations available.
  2. Fingerpainting should look rich and bright. This means that plenty of paint and starch must be used.
  3. Assemble all equipment before you start. Once begun, this activity is so beloved by children that the teacher will find it difficult to obtain even a moment to fetch something she has forgotten. Needed equipment will include *oil cloth* or *plastic* aprons (paint soaks right through old shirts if a child leans against the table—and most of them do), fingerpaint paper, a felt pen for names, starch, tempera paint (it is possible to buy ready-mixed finger-

paint, but this is likely to cost more), plastic-covered tables, something to hang the paintings on, clothespins, buckets of soapy water, sponges, and towels.
  4. When weather permits, set up outside; cleanup is infinitely easier there.

B. Procedure
  1. Fingerpainting is more successful when children stand up. Standing enables them to use their large arm muscles more freely, reach the entire paper without straining, and really see what they are doing.
  2. Roll up sleeves and take coats or sweaters off. Even liberal mothers may balk at a child coated with fingerpaint from head to toe. Put on aprons.
  3. Allow each child to do as many paintings as he wishes, and let him return for a second time if he desires.
  4. Fingerpaint is usually mixed right on the paper as the child works. Pour about 3 or 4 tablespoons of liquid starch on the paper. Shake powdered paint onto the starch. Ask children to tell you which colors they want, but don't let them shake it themselves; they often waste it.
  5. Offer one, two, or three colors of tempera placed on different paper areas so that the children can combine them. Unless you have some special purpose in mind, pick colors that combine to make an attractive additional color.
  6. Hang up finished paintings. Offer the child a chance to make another one.
  7. Show children how to rub their hands with the sponges in the bucket *before* they remove their aprons. (Many children will spend additional time squeezing the colored soapy bucket water through the sponge—another fine sensory experience.)
  8. If the day is windy or the room drafty, sponging the table lightly

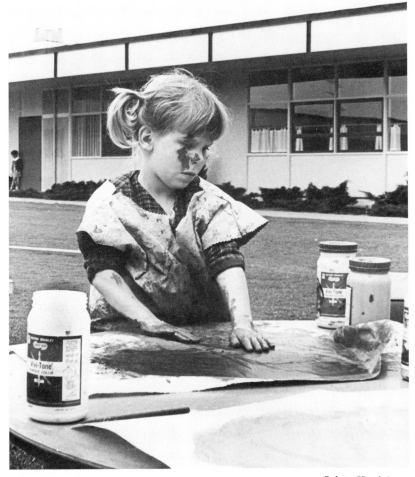

Goleta Head Start

with water before putting the paper down will keep it from blowing away.

C. Cleanup
1. Invite some children to help clean up. (The use of soapy water and sponges will attract helpers.) Wash off table, aprons, and so forth. Be sure to wash the edges of tables.
2. Return all supplies to correct storage places.
3. Roll up dried paintings and place in cubbies; leave remainder to finish drying.

Suggested variations. Children may paint directly on the table, using a whipped soap flake mixture, either white or tinted with food coloring. (For some reason, Lux flakes, not granulated Lux, work best. Remember, the children will enjoy helping beat this up.) They may also fingerpaint directly on the table and take prints of their painting by pressing a piece of newsprint down on it. These prints are often stunning. Painting can be done on textured papers, or different recipes can be used for variation in texture. Using cooked laundry starch in place of the liquid variety is always interesting because different thicknesses can be concocted. Adding a little glycerine or talcum powder makes painting particularly slick. Scents such as oil of cloves may be used to add fragrance. Starch bases can be refrigerated and then offered as a contrast to warmed starch—perhaps one kind for each hand.

Collage

Collage is particularly useful because it fosters an appreciation of the way different materials look when arranged together, thereby emphasizing the elements of design and composition. If offered as recommended below, it also provides opportunities for deliberating over selections and making choices and provides many exposures to a wide variety of materials, which may range from cotton balls to shells and wood shavings. Collage lends itself nicely to carrying out nursery school themes or other matters of interest to the children. Using natural materials in this kind of work adds potential beauty and interest to the activity. For example, shells, seaweed, and sand are nice to use as collage ingredients after a trip to the beach. The teacher should remember that the intent is not to have the child make a picture of where he has been or copy what the teacher has made; the intent is to encourage the appreciation of contrast in texture and color and to foster pleasure in creating a design based on these differences.

  A. Preparation

    1. Plan what materials to use, both background mats and collage substances. Remember that anything may be used as a base; it doesn't have to be paper plates. Cardboard, construction paper, or large pieces of bark are ideal. Select materials for contrast, variety, and beauty. Choose ones that will be esthetically pleasing when used together.

    2. Plan to use two tables for collage: a work table covered with newspaper and a "choosing table" from which the children will make their selections. If you set the materials out on colored paper or in attractive containers, they will be more appealing and also easier to keep sorted and neat.

    3. If the collage items are heavy, use undiluted glue. If light items, such as feathers, fabrics, or paper, are used, dilute the glue with starch or water.

    4. Decide how many children will be able to make collages at one time, and set up accordingly. Four to six children at one time are plenty to keep track of.

    5. Assemble aprons, glue brushes, white glue and containers, felt tip pen, aprons, and collage materials.

  B. Procedure

    1. Give each child an apron. Roll up sleeves.

    2. Encourage the child to take a collage tray and go to the choosing table. Gradually teach children to think about their choices: would that be interesting to use? How would this feel? What would go well with what?

    3. On returning to the work table, give each child a brush and glue container (with very little glue in it at a time; children need to learn that glue is not paint), or allow the child to dip each item lightly in a saucer of glue.

    4. Collage takes patience and perseverance. Many younger children will spend only a little time at it, but most older children will spend 15 to 20 minutes or longer if deeply interested.

    5. Unless monitored carefully, it is easy for the choosing table to become an unsorted mess of rumpled materials. Keep it neat and good looking in order to facilitate judging and selection by the children.

    6. Collages have to dry flat. Glue takes a long time to dry, so select a drying place that will be out of the way.

  C. Cleanup

    1. Children may help wash glue brushes; warm water will make this easier.

2. Return undiluted glue to the bottle and diluted glue to the thinned-glue container.

3. Wipe off furniture that has glue on it.

4. Put dried collages in cubbies.

Suggested variations. Almost anything can be used as collage material. This is one area where the good scrounger is in her element. Carpet scraps, pumpkin seeds, buttons, fur, and textured papers are all attractive ingredients. The experience can be varied by using different mats and bases: large pieces of old bark, heavy cardboard, or pieces of wood too hard to saw make interesting foundations. Food coloring can be used to tint the glue, or tempera can be added if a stronger, brighter-colored glue base is desired.

Dough and clay

Dough and clay are alike because they both offer opportunities to be creative while using a three-dimensional medium. They also provide particularly satisfying opportunities to release aggression harmlessly by hitting, punching, and squeezing. In addition, these materials allow the child to enjoy smearing and general messiness, activities that many psychologists value because they feel it provides a sublimated substitute for handling feces. (Whether or not the reader agrees with this theory or is repelled by it, she will certainly find, if she listens, that children often do talk with relish of "pooh pooh" while they work with this kind of material.) For all these reasons, dough and clay should usually be presented without cookie cutters, rolling pins, or other clutter, since these accessories detract from the more desirable virtues of thumping and whacking as well as from making original creations.

Besides these general benefits, mixing play dough helps the child learn about the transformation of materials and changes in texture. It also provides opportunities to learn facts about measuring and blending.

A. Preparation

1. Cover tables with oil cloth for quick cleanup later on. Keeping a special piece of oil cloth just for clay saves work, since it can be dried, shaken off, and put away for another day without wiping. Masonite boards or plastic-topped boards can also be used very handily.

2. Assemble materials: clay or dough, aprons, oil cloth, clean-up buckets, and towels. (Do not allow children to wash their hands in the sink; this is the quickest way to clog the plumbing.) If mixing dough, assemble ingredients and equipment according to the requirements of the recipe. Offer small pans of water for moistening hands only if children are using clay.

B. Procedure

1. Put on aprons, and help children roll up sleeves.

2. Give each child a *large* lump of clay or dough. It is important to offer plenty.

3. Use the materials to foster children's imagination and creativity: clay and dough often generate a lot of playful talk among the children. Avoid making models, such as ashtrays, for them to copy. Emphasize squeezing, rolling, and patting.

4. Supervise the children's hand washing before removing their aprons.

5. Clay and dough products are usually not saved but are just returned to the storage container.

6. Mixing play dough

   a. Always plan this event so the children can participate in making the dough because this is an additional valuable learning experience and great fun.

   b. Talk about the procedure while it is going on. Ask them, "What's happening? What do you see? How does it taste? How has it changed? How does it feel?"

   c. When mixing dough, make at least two batches at once in two separate dishpans. This avoids overcrowding and jostling among the children.

C. Cleanup
1. Cleanup from these activities takes quite a while, so begin early enough that the children have time to help, too.
2. Sponge off aprons and anything else that needs it.
3. Replace leftover ingredients in containers. Clay goes in tightly sealed containers. Make a depression in each large ball of clay with your thumb, and fill with water— this is an old potter's trick that will keep clay moist until used again. Dough should be stored in the refrigerator.
4. Flush the buckets of water down the toilet to avoid clogging drains.

Suggested variations. Allow the dough or clay objects made by the children to harden, and then paint and shellac them, or dip painted clay objects in melted paraffin. Occasionally use dough and clay with accessories such as dull knives for smoothing or cookie cutters and rolling pins. Offer chilled play dough as a contrast to the room temperature variety. Cookies and bread recipes are also dough experiences. Vary the dough experience by changing the recipe. The following are two of the best.

PLAY DOUGH

5 cups flour	4 tablespoons salad oil
2 cups salt	Add water until right consistency is reached

Powdered tempera may be added in with the flour, or food coloring may be added to finished dough. This dough may be kept in the refrigerator in a plastic bag or covered container for approximately 2 weeks.

CLOUD DOUGH

6 cups flour	1 cup oil

Mix flour and some tempera together; then add oil. Add enough oil to make dough soft and pliable. This dough is very soft and elastic and is different from regular play dough. It can be used with ease by 2-year-olds as well as by 4- and 5-year-olds. Keep in a covered container or plastic bag in the refrigerator. *This dough is greasy and will spot floors and carpets, so it is best used out of doors or supervised very carefully inside.*

Woodworking

Woodworking is a challenging and satisfying experience that should be available to the children at least two or three times every week. It requires unceasing supervision from the teacher, not so much because of possible hammered fingers or minor cuts from the saw, but because an occasional child may impulsively throw a hammer and injure someone. Although rare, this can happen in the twinkling of an eye, and the teacher must be alert so that she steps in before this occurs. In carpentry work *never leave a carpentry table unsupervised.* The teacher can alleviate frustration by assisting children who are having difficulty getting the nail started or the groove made for the saw.

It is essential that the school purchase good-quality tools for the children to use. Tinny little hammers and toy saws are worthless. Adult tools, such as short plumber's saws, regular hammers (not tack hammers, because their heads are too small), and braces and bits can all be used satisfactorily by boys and girls. Two real vises that can be fastened securely at either end of the woodworking table are essential to hold wood while the children saw through it. A sturdy, indestructable table is a necessity.

One of woodworking's best qualities is the opportunity it offers for doing real work. Children can assist in fixing things while using tools or can make a variety of simple items that they have thought up. These often include airplanes, boats, or just pieces of wood hammered together.

I particularly like offering carpentry because it is so easy to increase the challenge and difficulty of the experience as the year moves along. Children can begin with simple hammering, go on to using the saw, and finally enjoy the brace and bit. During the year they can learn many kinds of tool-related skills, and they can learn how to select the right tool for the right job. Carpentry is also an excellent way to develop eye-hand coordination. (But beware of the canny youngster who says, "Now, you hold the nail while I hit it.")

Finally, woodworking is a splendid way to harness intense energy and to sublimate anger. Hammering and sawing in particular are very effective relievers of feelings.

A. Preparation
1. Check the wood supply in advance. You may need to visit a cabinet or frame shop or a construction site to ask for free scraps if your supply is low. Teach yourself to tell hard from soft woods. Plywood and hard woods are good for gluing but are usually too frustrating for children to use in woodworking.
2. Decide whether to use any accessories for added interest.
3. Assemble wood, tools, supplies, and a pencil for labeling products.
4. Arrange tools and materials so that they are easy for children to reach. Make the arrangement attractive. Encourage children to select what they need and to replace what they don't use. Keep rearranging if the area becomes disorganized.

B. Procedure
1. Decide how many children you will be able to supervise at one time. For safety's sake you will probably need to limit yourself to three or four children at once.
2. Help children when necessary; teach them to treat tools with respect and to use them safely.
3. Be alert to interaction between children. Self-control at this age is not highly developed; intervene swiftly when necessary.
4. Be sure to encourage children who persevere in particularly difficult tasks, such as sawing through a large board or making a nail go all the way through two pieces of wood.
5. Remember to label finished products.

C. Cleanup
1. Replace tools and wood scraps in correct storage area.
2. Put each child's work in his cubby.

Suggested variations. Allow the children to take the brace and bit and the vise to pieces to find out how they work. Have a number of various-sized bits available for making different-sized holes, and purchase dowels that will fit these holes. Furnish different accessories for variety: bottle caps and jar lids make nice wheels or decorations. String or roving cotton twisted among the nails is interesting. Unusual wood scraps that come from cabinet shops are nice. Wood gluing in place of nailing appeals to some youngsters and is a quicker form of wood construction. Many children enjoy going on to paint whatever they have made; this works well if done under another teacher's supervision at a separate table. Children will enjoy using a wide array of nails, ranging from flat, broad-headed roofing nails to tiny little finishing nails, which for some reason they often like to hammer in all around the edge of boards. Sandpaper is ocasionally interesting, particularly if there are several grades of it available for comparison. An occasional child will also enjoy measuring and sawing to fit, although this activity is more typical of older children. Very young children will do best if soft plasterboard rather than wood is offered.

Sewing

Sewing is not often offered in nursery school, and yet it is interesting to some children, boys as well as girls. Besides the obvious value of developing eye-hand coordination, it also offers good opportunities to experiment and to be creative. Occasionally it can be an opportunity for accomplishing meaningful work and can also provide a chance to experience the satisfaction of role playing a motherly activity.

A. Preparation
1. Choose a loosely woven fabric as the material for sewing. Thick or heavy fabric will be too difficult for the children to get the needle through.
2. Assemble the equipment: yarn or thick cotton string, fabric, large, dull embroidery needles, scissors,

and embroidery hoops. Offer a choice of different colors of yarn and materials if possible.

3. You might prethread some needles in advance. It helps to knot the thread onto the needle if it constantly slips out or to use double threads knotted together at the ends to prevent them from pulling out of the needle.

B. Procedure

1. Choose a fairly small group of children to work with—four or five children at a time.

2. Be prepared for stuck fingers, some frustration, and a lot of requests for help especially the first few times. Some children are disappointed with their technique; don't end up sewing for them because they want it to look a certain way. Encourage them to do it their own way, and be pleased with their experiments.

3. Embroidery hoops help a lot, although children tend to sew over the edges of them. Rather than constantly criticizing this tendency, you can have them snip the yarn later for an interesting fringed effect. Children will also gradually learn to sew in and out rather then up and over as they become acquainted with the material, but it takes a while to acquire this concept.

4. Safety pin the child's name to his work.

C. Cleanup

1. Put the sewing materials away; never leave needles lying about.

2. Place finished work in cubbies.

Suggested variations. You may want to try sewing on Styrofoam meat trays or sewing through plastic vegetable baskets; these have the advantage of being stiff and light to hold. An occasional very adept 4- or 5-year-old will enjoy sewing top and side seams on simple doll clothes. Sometimes children enjoy sewing very large buttons to material. Children may enjoy appliqueing cutouts loosely to burlap to create wall decorations for home or school. An old

variation to sewing, which is fun but not really creative, is the punched cardboard sewing cards and laces enjoyed by youngsters since the turn of the century.

Dancing and creative movement

Dancing has great potential for self-expression because it stimulates the child's imagination and offers many opportunities for emotional release. Moving to music can involve the child's entire body and draw satisfying expressions of emotion and pleasure from him that other creative experiences cannot tap.

There seem to be two extremes in presenting dance experiences that are not creative. In one, the teacher conceives the dance entirely beforehand and then puts the children through the paces. This is, of course, simply providing a model for the children to copy. In the other extreme, the teacher puts on some music and sits passively by while she expects the children to generate the entire experience for themselves. Children usually require more stimulation than this from the teacher in order to get a dance experience going. Beginning teachers often feel self-conscious about participating, but dancing with the children is essential for success. Taking a couple of modern dance classes at college frequently helps students feel more at ease with this medium.

A. Preparation

1. Reread the student's analysis and recommendations about her dance experience, which are given in Chapter 2.

2. Decide what kind of music to use, and familiarize yourself with its possibilities.

a. It is ideal to have available a pianist who can improvise as the teacher and children request, but this is not essential.

b. Familiarize yourself with records that are available. Choose two or three that offer a good range of rhythms and emotional expression.

c. Don't overlook the possibilities offered by popular music. It has the virtues of being familiar and rhythmic, and it offers a wide variety of emotional moods as well.

3. Clear the largest room available of chairs, tables, and so forth.
4. Arrange to avoid interruptions. It is fatal to the experience for the teacher to answer the phone or to stop and settle a fight on the playground.

B. Procedure
1. Avoid having other activities going on in the room at the same time, although some children will need to putter around the edges, watching before they join in. Accomplished teachers often feel comfortable having children drift in and out of the group, but beginners may find that a more secluded atmosphere where children may leave as they desire but where newcomers may not intrude is helpful. Don't try to have all the children participate at once.
2. The most important skill to develop in dance is the ability to be sensitive to individual responses and ideas as the children generate them and to encourage these as they come along.
3. It is necessary for the teacher to move freely along with the children. Sometimes it helps to ask other adults to stay away while you are leading a dance activity.
4. It is good to have in mind a general plan that contains some ideas about ways to begin and also things to try that will vary the activity. It is essential to offer relaxing experiences and to alternate vigorous with more quiet ones to avoid overstimulation and chaos. Children enjoy showing all the ways they can think of to be kittens or the ways they can get across the floor on their tummies, or, as they become more practiced and at ease, ways of moving as the music makes them feel.

C. Cleanup
1. Warn the children, as the end

nears, that the time is drawing to a close.
2. At the end, involve the group in some kind of quiet response to the music so that they have themselves under reasonable control as they leave the room.
3. Help them put on their shoes and socks if these have been taken off.
4. Return the room to its usual order.

Suggested variations. Accessories add a great deal to dancing and are helpful materials to use to get dance started. Scarves, long streamers, and balloons help focus the child's awareness away from himself and so reduce his self-consciousness at the beginning. Ethnic dance materials offer a rich resource for dance and creative movement. Folk dance records and other rhythmic songs and melodies are delightful resources to draw on. Using percussion instruments can also vary the experience. Dancing outdoors often attracts children who shun this activity in a more enclosed setting. Remember to include dance activities that appeal to boys as well as to girls. Moving like submarines, airplanes, seals, or bears can make this activity genuinely attractive to both sexes.

Using rhythm instruments

There are other ways to respond to music besides dancing, and participating with rhythm instruments is one of them. This activity is both somewhat creative and somewhat an exercise in conformity, since children may respond imaginatively and individually with their instruments while doing something together at the same time. Basically, participating in a musical experience will introduce children to the pleasures and delights of sound, rhythms, and melodies. If well handled it should also teach children to care for instruments as objects of beauty and value and should help them learn to listen to music and respond in a discriminating way.

A. Preparation
1. Familiarize yourself with the music you will present. Listen to the records or practice on the instrument you intend to use yourself.

Los Niños Head Start

2. Select the instruments for the children to use.
3. Plan to start with a small group of children and a small number of instruments at first. You can always add more things later when you know how many children you can comfortably supervise.
B. Procedure
1. Instruments are not toys and to prevent abuse must be supervised when used. It will help if you plan in advance details such as where the children will put them when they are finished and how they will get another instrument. Decide on a reasonable procedure that will allow you to relax and not worry about a child stepping through a tambourine that was left on the floor.
2. Insist on these few basic guidelines: Drums and tambourines are to be hit with the hand only. (Drum heads do not stand up under steady pounding from sticks. Hit the rhythm sticks together if stick hitting is desired.) Allow one maraca to a child. Maracas crack easily when hit together.
3. Be prepared to get right into the music with the children and become involved. Your enthusiasm will communicate itself and make the experience special.
C. Cleanup
1. Warn ahead.
2. Put records back, and return instruments to their area, arranging them so they look attractive and orderly.

Suggested variations. Improvisations with musical instruments are a delight. Children can be encouraged to use them as the music makes them feel—to play soft or loud, fast or slow, together, or a few at a time. They can also make some simple instruments of their own, such as sand blocks and shakers. Moving to music while using instruments (typically, marching) can also be a satisfying way of integrating this experience into a larger activity.

SUMMARY

Nursery school teachers have always valued the creative part of the child's self and have sought to enhance its development by fostering the use of self-expressive materials. Today we also seek to foster creativity in additional ways, which include generating creative play and encouraging originality of thought. In order to accomplish these goals, there are three teaching skills the teacher should cultivate in herself. When presenting self-expressive materials, she must cultivate her ability to stand back and let the child explore and utilize them as his impulses and feelings require. When seeking to facilitate play, she must learn to move with the children's imaginative ideas and support them. When working to develop originality in thought, she must be able to recognize the value of the children's ideas and to ask questions that will encourage further development of ideas.

Creativity is particularly valuable because it increases the child's feelings of self-esteem, facilitates self-expression and the expression of emotion, provides a vital balance for the cognitive part of the program, and helps the nursery school teacher individualize her curriculum.

The teacher can foster creativity by understanding and accepting the creative child and by maintaining in her group an environment that helps children feel secure. When presenting self-expressive materials for the children's use, she should avoid making models for them to copy, emphasize the process rather than the product, allow plenty of time and opportunity for the child to use the material, learn to make enhancing comments, and give reluctant children the right to refuse to participate. But the most important thing for her to do is to make the materials freely available and to stand back and let the child explore them as his impulses dictate.

QUESTIONS

1. If copying a model is really inhibiting to the development of creative self-expression, why do you think so many teachers persist in having children copy projects "just the way the teacher made it"?

2. Do you think of yourself as being artistic, or are you the sort of person who "can't even hold a paint brush right side up"? What attitudes in your previous teachers do you feel contributed to your feelings of confidence or lack of confidence in this area?

3. *Problem:* Chester, who is 3 years old, is still new at school and has been watching the fingerpainting with considerable interest. At last he engages himself in this activity, only to discover to his horror that the purple paint has soaked right through his cotton smock onto his tee shirt. He is very concerned about this, particularly when the teacher is unable to wash all the paint out of the shirt, and his mother is genuinely angry when she picks him up that afternoon. How would you cope with this situation?

4. *Problem:* Irene is painting at the easel and gradually begins to spread paint off the paper onto the easel itself, then to paint her hands and arms up to the elbows, and then to flick drops of paint onto a neighboring child and his painting. Should the teacher intervene and control any or all of this behavior, or should it be allowed to continue?

5. The variations of self-expressive activities listed at the end of the chapter represent only a few of numerous possibilities. What other activities have people in the class witnessed that could be added to these lists?

REFERENCES FOR FURTHER READING

General Subject of Creativity

Bland, J. C. *Art of the young child: 3 to 5 years.* Garden City, N. Y.: Doubleday & Co., Inc., 1957. *Art of the Young Child* contains a sound discussion of developmental trends in children's art and a brief discussion of various art materials and how to present them. The book is outstanding because of its wealth of illustrations of artistic creations all done by children 5 years old or younger.

Jefferson, B. *Teaching art to children: content and viewpoint.* (3rd ed.) Boston: Allyn & Bacon, Inc., 1969. *Teaching Art to Children* is written with elementary school children in mind, but the theory is sound for younger children, too, and the book has won awards for excellence. It makes a strong case for fostering individualism and self-expression through art.

Kellogg, R. *Analyzing children's art.* Palo Alto, Calif.: National Press Books, 1969. The author stresses the universality of certain themes in children's art, sets forth a developmental theory, and provides hundreds of examples of how children use art to express themselves.

Lowenfeld, B. *Your child and his art: a guide for parents.* New York: The Macmillan Co., 1954. In this simply written, practical book, Lowenfeld discusses basic questions that may arise about the creative experience as the child develops from infancy through adolescence.

Maynard, F. *Guiding your child to a more creative life.* Garden City, N. Y.: Doubleday & Co., Inc., 1973. This is an excellent book suitable for parents and teachers. It contains good discussions of play, creativity, and the use of self-expressive materials. It also contains lists of children's books and records tastefully selected.

Torrance, E. P. *Creativity.* Belmont, Calif.: Fearon Publishers, 1969. Almost all books that deal with the general subject of creativity ignore the preschool level. This small volume by Torrance deserves special mention, since it is based on research and theory as they relate to early childhood. Torrance first reviews what research exists and then lists suggestions about how teachers and parents may foster creativity in very young children.

Presentation of Expressive Materials

Pitcher, E. G., Lasher, M. G., Feinburg, S., and Hammond, N. C. *Helping young children learn.* Columbus, Ohio: Charles E. Merrill Publishing Co., 1966. The authors cover the majority of creative experiences and deal with other aspects of curriculum as well. This is primarily a how-to book that is filled with practical, factual information and curriculum ideas based on brief discussions of theory. It has a good bibliography at the end of each chapter.

Woodworking

Moffitt, M. W. *Woodworking for children.* New York: Early Childhood Education Council of New York, no date. There is straight talk here for teachers who may not know much about woodworking. Moffitt actually explains how to use various tools and what to do about such problems as bent nails and splitting wood. The booklet is intensely practical and should be owned and used by every teacher.

Music and Dance

Andrews, G. *Creative rhythmic movement for children.* Englewood Cliffs, N. J.: Prentice-Hall, Inc., 1954. In this well-illustrated book Andrews presents dance in terms of developmental abilities. It has good true-to-life examples of actual teaching episodes with children; very helpful for the beginning student.

Buttolph, E. G. *Music without the piano.* New York: Early Childhood Education Council of New York, 1968. This short pamphlet is filled with suggestions about how to present music using simple instruments and the children's ideas.

Cherry, C. *Creative movement for the developing child: a nursery school handbook for non-musicians.* (Rev. ed.) Belmont, Calif.: Fearon Publishers, 1971. Clare Cherry bases her approach to dance on creative movement. The material is simply presented, and all of the suggested activities can be accompanied by familiar tunes and improvised words, which are included in the text.

Fleming, G. A. (Gladys Andrews) (Ed.) *Children's dance.* Washington, D. C.: American Association For Health, Physical Education & Recreation, 1973. This is a rich, indispensable new resource; highly recommended.

Jones, E. *What is music for young children?* Washington, D. C.: National Association for the Education of Young Children, 1958, 1969. Jones discusses the subject of music rather than only dance. This classic pamphlet is valuable in particular because it includes an anecdotal record of the way a musical experience was developed through a semester in a nursery school class.

Joyce, M. *First steps in teaching creative dance: a handbook for teachers of children, kindergarten through sixth grade.* Palo Alto, Calif.: National Press Books, 1973. The beginning teacher will find this textbook very helpful. It provides general advice followed by a series of explicit lesson plans.

For the Advanced Student

Starkweather, E. K., and Cowling, F. G. The measurement of conforming and nonconforming behavior in preschool children. In R. Mooney and T. Razik (Eds.), *Explorations in creativity.* New York: Harper & Row, Publishers, 1967. Starkweather and Cowling have done some interesting work on measuring creativity in young children, and in this report they discuss a project in which they measured tendencies toward conformity and nonconformity in young children. The instrument the investigators developed not only discriminated between conformity and nonconformity but also between children who were free to use either of these behaviors and those who were compulsive about being either nonconforming or conforming.

Torrance, E. P. *Guiding creative talent.* Englewood Cliffs, N. J.: Prentice-Hall, Inc., 1962.

Dr. Torrance has written many helpful books, but this is one of the best for early childhood teachers because it contains a chapter on development and another on maintaining creativity. In addition, it has a good chapter on sustaining relationships with people who have creative talent.

Los Niños Head Start

CHAPTER 13

Fostering creativity in play

> If life's problems are solved satisfactorily during the years when imagination predominates, then a residue of imaginative activity and a resource of initiative remain, to enliven, sparkle, inspire, and push throughout the rest of life. Such a person will get fresh ideas and will not be afraid to experiment with them. Even though he has attained objectivity, his thinking and feeling will be so flexible that he will be able to take off on flights of his imagination. Both creativity and true recreation have their roots in imaginative play.*

In recent years considerable material has been written on a theoretical level about the value or purpose of play (Almy, 1968; Herron and Sutton-Smith, 1971). Despite the fact that the purposes ascribed to it appear to vary in accordance with the background of the person proposing the theory, we should rejoice that interest is once again increasing in this important subject. It is evident to most people who work with young children that play is serious business to them and that the opportunity to play freely is vital to their healthy development (Curry and Arnaud, 1971; Frank, 1968; Millar, 1968); yet in the past few years, when the emphasis in early childhood has tended to be on developing more structured ways of fostering intellectual gains (Bereiter and Englemann, 1966), the value of play has often been understressed or overlooked. Now, although there is much disagreement about defining basic purposes, at least the subject is once again attracting

interest—a step that is definitely in the right direction.

It is difficult to say why some educators have undervalued play from time to time. Perhaps it goes back to our Puritan ethic, which is suspicious of pleasure and self-enjoyment. Unfortunately, as people advance through our educational system, they seem to conclude that any activity that generates delight cannot result in real learning—in order to learn, one must suffer. But play is a pleasureful, absorbing activity indulged in for its own sake. The live-for-the-moment aspect of it, combined with the fact that play arises spontaneously from within the child and is not teacher determined, lends an air of frivolity to it that may lead work-oriented persons to assume it is not worthwhile. In addition, this uniqueness and spontaneity have made it difficult to categorize and examine in a scientific way. It is only in recent years that work by such people as Sutton-Smith (1967) and Smilansky (1968) has demonstrated the feasibility of more precise investigation of play.

PURPOSES OF PLAY

A variety of reasons why play is valuable for young children are given here be-

---

*From Smart, M. S., and Smart, R. C. *Child development and relationships* (p. 281). (2nd ed.) New York: copyright © 1972, The Macmillan Company.

cause nursery school teachers must be prepared to defend and explain the worthwhile character of this activity to people who still attack it as being a trivial waste of time, which they contend would be better spent "really learning something."

Play fosters physical development

Play fulfills a wide variety of purposes in the life of the child (Hartley, Frank, and Goldenson, 1952). On a very simple level, it promotes the development of sensorimotor skills. Children spend hours perfecting such abilities and increasing the level of difficulty to make the task ever more challenging. Anyone who has lived with a 1-year-old will recall the tireless persistence with which he pursues the acquisition of basic physical skills. In older children we often think of this repetitious physical activity as the central aspect of play, since it is evident on playgrounds where we see children swinging, climbing, or playing ball with fervor; but actually physical motor development represents only one purpose that play fulfills.

Play fosters intellectual development

Piaget (1962) maintains that imaginative play is one of the purest forms of symbolic thought available to the young child, and its use permits the child to assimilate reality in terms of his own interests and prior knowledge of the world. Thus it is evident that imaginative, symbolic play contributes strongly to the child's intellectual development.

Play also offers opportunities for the child to acquire information that lays the foundation for additional learning. For example, through the manipulation of blocks he learns the concept of equivalence (two small blocks equal one larger one), or through playing with water he acquires knowledge of volume, which leads ultimately to developing the concept of reversibility (Moffitt and Omwake, no date).

The work of Smilansky (1968) has offered additional support for the importance of play in relation to mental development. She points out that sociodramatic play develops the child's ability to abstract essen-tial qualities of a social role and also to generalize role concepts to a greater degree.

Play enhances social development

In addition, there is a strong social component to certain kinds of play (Fein and Clarke-Stewart, 1973). Here again, the methodological analysis provided by Smilansky is helpful. She speaks of dramatic and sociodramatic play, differentiating between the two partially on the basis of the number of children involved in the activity. Dramatic play involves imitation and may be carried on alone, but the more advanced sociodramatic play entails verbal communication and interaction with two or more people, as well as imitative role playing, make-believe in regard to objects, actions, and situations, and persistence in the play over a period of time.

Sociodramatic play also helps the child learn to put himself in another's place (El'Konin, 1969; Kohlberg, 1969), thereby fostering the growth of empathy and consideration of others. It helps him define social roles: he learns by experiment what it is like to be the baby or the mother or the doctor or nurse. And it provides countless opportunities for acquiring social skills: how to enter a group and be accepted by them, how to balance power and bargain with other children so that everyone gets satisfaction from the play, and how to work out the social give and take that is the key to successful group interaction.

Play contains rich emotional values

The emotional value of play has been better accepted and understood than the intellectual or social value, since therapists have long employed play as a medium for the expression and relief of feelings (Axline, 1969; Rosecrans, 1968). Children may be observed almost any place in the nursery school expressing their feelings about doctors by administering shots with relish or their jealousy of a new baby by walloping a doll, but play is not necessarily limited to the expression of negative feelings. The same doll that only a moment previously was being punished may next be seen lulled and crooned to sleep in the rocking chair.

Eveline Omwake cites an additional emotional value of play (Moffitt and Omwake, no date). She points out that play offers "relief from the pressure to behave in unchildlike ways." In our society so much is expected of children and the emphasis on arranged learning can be so intense that play becomes indispensable as a balance to pressures to conform to adult standards that may otherwise become intolerable.

Finally, play offers the child an opportunity to achieve mastery of his environment. When he plays, he is in command. He establishes the conditions of the experience by using his imagination, and he exercises his powers of choice and decision as the play progresses. The attendant opportunities for pretended and actual mastery foster the growth of ego strength in young children.

Play develops the creative aspect of the child's personality

Play, which arises from within, expresses the child's personal, unique response to the environment. It is inherently a self-expressive activity that draws richly on the child's powers of imagination. Since imaginative play is also likely to contain elements of novelty, the creative aspect of this activity is readily apparent. In addition, Sutton-Smith points out that play increases the child's repertoire of responses. Divergent thinking is characterized by the ability to produce more than one answer, and it is evident that play provides opportunities to develop alternative ways of reacting to similar situations (Sutton-Smith, 1971). For example, when the children pretend that a fierce dog is breaking into their house, some may respond by screaming in mock terror, others by rushing to shut the door, and still others by attacking the "dog" or throwing water on him. The work of Lieberman (1968) provides added indications that playfulness and divergent thinking are related—though which comes first remains to be determined.

In young children creative play is expressed primarily in two ways: through the unusual use of familiar materials and equipment (Chapter 12) and through role playing and imaginative play.

Conclusion

No matter what value the theoretician perceives in play, the fact remains that it is common to all cultures and that it is the lifeblood of childhood. Thus Russians may offer hollow blocks while reasoning that their size promotes cooperation, whereas Americans may offer them on the grounds that their cumbersome qualities develop feelings of mastery. But the children continue to use blocks with satisfaction regardless of adult rationalizations, just as they continue to play house on the windswept tundra of the North and in the Wendy corners of the British Infant School.

DEVELOPMENTAL STAGES OF PLAY

As is true in many other areas, children's play progresses through a series of developmental stages. Very young children tend to be self-absorbed and to play by themselves. Next they become involved in parallel activities, in which they play side by side with other youngsters, often playing with similar materials but still largely without the social interchange that alters the quality of the play (aside from helping themselves to the other child's things). Finally, children become involved in social play, in which the activity occurs between two or more children and may be quite imaginative in character (McCandless and Evans, 1973).

Some authors, Smilansky (1968) for example, prefer a four-stage outline of play development instead of the simpler one given above. They say play moves from simple, repetitive sensorimotor activities to constructive play (creative use of play materials, which may or may not contain a theme), then to dramatic play, and finally to the stage of games with rules, which is a dominant form of play for the school-age child.

Implications for education

Since children begin with solitary and then go on to parallel play before attaining the more socially oriented form, teachers should allow children to play by themselves or side by side without feeling that such behavior is in some way reprehensible. Also, children do not totally give up the earlier forms of play as the more sophisticated levels develop, although the amount of time spent in solitary and parallel play gradually decreases (Parten and Newhall, 1943). Isolated play and parallel play are natural steps in development as well as a reflection of the temperament of some children. If solitary play continues too long or is the only kind of play indulged in by a 4-year-old who is an old hand at nursery school, it can be cause for concern; but some of this less social play is to be expected from most children attending nursery school.

Nursery school teachers are likely to see large amounts of sensorimotor, constructive, and dramatic play but will rarely come across the final stage, games with rules, because this kind of play is the prerogative of older children. The nursery school teacher should realize that organized games are developmentally inappropriate as well as uncreative for young children. Activities such as relay races, dodge ball, and "Duck, Duck, Goose" are loved by second and third graders but do not belong in nursery school.

Although we hope to foster originality and imagination in young children's play, we must realize that not every idea generated by the children will be new no matter how supportive and encouraging the atmosphere of the school. Children's inspirations will be like flashes—touches here and there, embedded in a foundation of previously played activities. There will always be a lot of "old" mixed in with a little "new."

The teacher should also be prepared for somewhat chaotic play, since it is impossible to organize inspiration before it happens. But this "chaos" can be very productive, and the teacher can maintain reasonable order by picking up unused materials and returning them to their place and by seeing that the play does not deteriorate into aimless running about.

FACTORS LIKELY TO FACILITATE CREATIVE PLAY

There are many things the teacher can do to encourage the creative aspects of play.

The teacher avoids dominating the play

As is true with self-expressive materials, the teacher does her best to avoid dominating the play experience but seeks instead to foster the child's ability to express himself in his own unique way. Such a teacher helps children base their play on their own inspirations because she is convinced they can be trusted to play productively without undue intervention and manipulation by her.

Some teachers are so eager to use play as a medium for teaching that they cannot resist overmanipulating it in order to provide a "good learning experience." For example, I recently visited a teacher who had taken the children to the fire station for a visit. The next day, overwhelmed by the temptation to use play as a teaching device, she set out all the hats, hoses, ladders, and pedal trucks she could muster, and, as the children walked in the door, she pounced on them, announcing, "Boys and girls, I have the most wonderful idea. Remember when we went to the fire station yesterday? Well, why don't we play that here today? Jon, you can be the chief. Now, who wants to hold the hose? . . ."

Children may learn a good deal about fire engines this way, and if this is the real purpose, very well. However, the spontaneous, creative quality of the play will be greatly reduced by the teacher's using this approach. It would be better to wait until the children expressed an interest and then ask them how one can help and what they need.

Smilansky (1968) advocates intervening in sociodramatic play for the purpose of building play techniques. This approach is valuable at times, but it is different from the teacher's telling the children explicitly what to do or how to go about playing. What I am primarily cautioning against is the interfering teacher who deadens creativity by dominating the play with her own ideas and purposes.

The teacher encourages divergence of ideas

As in creative thought, the teacher also seeks to remain open to originality of ideas in the children's play and to do all she can to reinforce their production of imaginative ideas by giving them the satisfaction of trying the ideas out. For this reason, she does not overrestrict the children's use of equipment, and she allows them to use familiar equipment in original and unusual ways. She also makes it

a point to keep play materials accessible so they are instantly available when the children require them.

The teacher casts herself in the role of handmaiden to the child

Fostering creative play demands that the teacher add an additional skill to her repertoire: the ability to move with the child's play and support it as it develops. This does not mean that she plays with the children as their peer, any more than she sits on the sidelines being thankful that the children are busy and not in trouble. Rather, the teacher who is skilled in

Los Niños Head Start

generating creative play senses what will enhance the play, and she thinks constantly of what she might offer to sustain or extend it should this become necessary. This kind of teacher casts herself in the role of handmaiden to the child; she imagines herself inside his skin and sees the child's play from his point of view. This gives her an empathic understanding, which enables her to serve his play needs well. Sometimes she expresses this insight by as simple a thing as going to the shed and getting out a variety of ropes, chains, and hooks for a construction project. Sometimes it is evident on a more subtle level as she quietly decides to delay snack in order that the play may build to a satisfying climax.

Some of this empathic ability may go back to remembering what it was like to be a child oneself, and some of it may be related to opening oneself to sensing the child and taking time to "hear" him. It is a skill well worth cultivating because it makes possible the perception of the child's play in terms of what he intends. This enables the teacher to nurture the play by sensitively offering the right help at the right moment.

Putting the child in command of the play situation is not only valuable because it fosters his creative ability. It is also fundamentally worthwhile because it strengthens his feelings of mastery. When the teacher becomes his assistant and helper and defers to his judgment, the child is freed to determine what will happen next in his play. He exercises his ability to make choices and decisions. As mentioned previously, Erikson maintains that becoming autonomous and taking the initiative are fundamental tasks of early childhood. Creative play presents one of the best opportunities available for developing these strengths.

A rich background of actual life experience is fundamental to developing creative play

Children build on the foundation of real experience in their play. The more solid and rich the background of experience that children accumulate, the more various the play will become. Field trips, holidays, and experiences with many ethnic groups, as well as things brought into the school in the way of science experiments, books, and visitors, will increase the base of experience upon which they can build their play. There is no substitute for this background. In addition, play is thought to serve the function of clarifying and integrating such experiences (Piaget, 1962) as the child gains a greater understanding of reality through his recapitulation of it in make-believe.

Equipment plays an important role in facilitating play

The teacher should buy equipment that encourages the use of imagination. The kinds of equipment the teacher provides has a considerable influence on the play that results. The teacher should be wary of buying equipment that can be used only in specific ways, because it restricts the use of imagination. Boards, blocks, and ladders, for example, lend themselves to a hundred possibilities, but a plywood train tends to be used mostly as a plywood train. The teacher should ask herself, "How many ways could the children use this?" If she can think of three or four rather different possibilities, it is a good indication that the children will use their imaginations to think of many more.

However, there is also a place for more lifelike materials in imaginative play. Dolls, costumes, and little rubber animals generate a lot of very satisfactory "pretend" situations because they induce the child to play through experiences and ideas about life. But, although these projective materials have acknowledged value, the teacher should be wary of the tendency to purchase countless imitations of adult items. There is no need to furnish the doll corner down to the last toaster and fake banana. The children will conjure these up from their imaginations if they are allowed to do so.

The teacher should change equipment frequently. Changing accessories in the basic play areas such as the housekeeping area and the block corner will attract different children, keep life fresh and interesting for them, and encourage them to play creatively. Adding boys' clothes or an old razor or bringing the guinea pig for a visit might break the monotony in the housekeeping corner. Using trains, rubber animals, doll house furniture, or the cubical counting blocks could provide variety in the block area. Moving play equipment to a new location is another fine way to vary play and foster creativity. Boys, for example, are more likely to play house if the stove and refrigerator are out on the grass or if the house is made of hollow blocks for a change. Different locations attract different customers.

The teacher should store equipment in convenient, easy-to-reach places. Besides purchasing equipment that will stimulate imagination and changing it to keep the play fresh and interesting, the teacher must also arrange adequate storage for these materials. This is often the place nursery schools scrimp, but good storage will keep equipment available and save the teacher's sanity as well. Storage can actually make or break a play situation; so it is well worth the time, effort, and money involved to solve this problem adequately. Material should be conveniently arranged so that it can be reached easily, and, of course, it should be returned to the same place after use to expedite locating it the next time it is needed. Labeled shelves, racks, hooks, and storage closets that are large enough all help. In addition, storage should be located close at hand so the teacher may continue to provide supervision while she is getting something out that the children have requested.

Play areas should be attractive

The general appearance and presentation of the play areas will inspire (or discourage) children to play there. All areas should be set up at the beginning of the day in a fresh, appealing way. New touches should be added here and there to spark interest and avoid dull repetition.

Play is also better encouraged if materials are not allowed to degenerate into a shambles during playtime. No one wants to wade through a welter of costumes on the floor or build in a chaos of blocks dumped and abandoned in that corner. Attractiveness fosters attraction, and the teacher is the person who bears the primary responsibility for creating and maintaining appealing play areas.

A final thought

One last reminder: children need plenty of freedom, time, and materials if they are to become maximally involved in imaginative play. They need the freedom to move from one activity to another as their tastes dictate; they need uninterrupted time to build a play situation through to its satisfying completion; and they need enough materials to furnish a challenge and supply a feeling of sufficiency. Making these resources available is a good way to say to a child in tangible terms that there is enough of what he needs in the world and that he need not scheme and plot to get his fair share.

SPECIFIC ACTIVITIES TO ENCOURAGE CREATIVITY IN PLAY
Water play*

Water play is one of the freest, finest play opportunities we can offer children. Although inexperienced teachers often dread it because they fear that the children may become too wild or overstimulated, the opposite of this behavior is usually the case. Water play is absorbing and soothing; children will stay with it a long time and come away refreshed and relaxed if it is well presented. It is also valuable because it offers children many opportunities to work through conflicts resulting from the demands of toilet training (there is no better present for a newly trained 2-year-old than a sprinkling can), it provides relief from pressures and tensions, and it stimulates social play. Sometimes children will play companionably with others while using water, although they remain isolated the rest of the day.

Activities such as pouring and measur-

---

*I am indebted to the staff and students at the Santa Barbara Community College Children's Center for their assistance in developing the outlines on the following pages.

ing help develop eye-hand coordination. Children also acquire intellectual concepts having to do with estimating quantity (how much will the cup really hold?), with conservation (but it looks like more in the tall bottle!), and with physical properties of water (what became of the water when we poured it on the hot sidewalk?). At the end of this chapter a particularly good pamphlet is included in the references: *Water, Sand and Mud as Play Materials,* which makes useful supplementary reading on this subject.

Water play should be offered several times a week to provide maximum satisfaction for the children. In winter, a large indoor bathroom with a drain in the floor is an invaluable asset. Water can be offered in deep dishpans or sinks, but is best offered in larger containers, such as galvanized laundry tubs, concrete-mixing tubs made of plastic, or even wading pools. At the Center we offer it at floor level when we can because this keeps the children's clothes drier.

  A. Preparation
    1. Decide what kind of water play you want to offer and what kind of water you wish to use (soapy, colored, clear, hot or cold).
    2. Assemble additional equipment and accessories for play.
    3. Be sure to include oil cloth or plastic aprons, deep containers for the water, sponges, and towels.
  B. Procedure
    1. Make any rules or guidelines clear to the children before they begin. Children cannot be allowed to run around in soaked shoes or clothes when it is cold. It is better to explain the temperature of the day and also the limits of the experience before someone impulsively gets drenched.
    2. The children will enjoy helping to fill the tubs and setting out the equipment.
    3. Put on aprons and roll sleeves up as far as possible. Remove shoes and do what you can to minimize the problem of getting wet, but be prepared for the fact that considerable dampness is the inevitable accompaniment of water play.
    4. Expect some incidental splashing, but control deliberate splashing unless the weather is warm. You may give a splasher a second chance; but if he or she persists, then the privilege of participating has to be surrendered for a while.
    5. While the children are playing, talk about pouring, measuring, or whatever you have planned as the focus of your activity with the children.
    6. Listen carefully to the children's comments and ideas, and change and provide equipment accordingly.
  C. Cleanup
    1. Children may help bail out water tubs or tip them over on the grass at the end of the play.
    2. If rags are at hand, many children like to help dry buckets and toys.
    3. Replace all equipment in proper storage areas.
    4. Wipe aprons and change wet clothes.

Suggested variations. Too many schools limit this kind of play to hand washing or dabbling in the sink. Although these activities are certainly better than not having water available at all, they stop far short of what children really require for this experience. Many variations can be employed for a change, although basic water play always remains a favorite. Running water from the hose is a fine thing to offer, though it is, of course, a warm weather activity. Water can be used in conjunction with the sandbox or mud pit with real pleasure—apartments and manicured suburban gardens deprive children of the opportunity to play with such concoctions.

In addition, water can be offered to use in sinking, floating, pouring, and quantifying experiments. Unbreakable bottles and containers, as well as various sizes of sieves and funnels, can be saved for this purpose. Ice is a fascinating variation to offer; or washing activities with dolls, doll clothes, nursery school furniture, cars, or tricycles can be presented. Scrubbing vegetables, watering the garden, and washing dishes should not be overlooked as additional variations, which have the added appeal of participating in meaningful work. Adding sponges, soap, or a little color will also change the appeal of the water and create additional interest.

Mud and sand

Mud and sand have wonderful messy, unstructured qualities that make them among the most popular creative play materials in nursery school. They offer rich tactile sensory experiences and provide emotional relief as well: messing and slopping through water and sand or mud is relaxing and is thought by some psychologists to provide relief from the stringent toilet training demands of our society. These materials also facilitate a lot of social interaction. Older children play imaginatively and cooperatively with each other while digging tunnels, constructing roads, and carrying on "bake-offs"; but sand and mud are also very rewarding for younger children to use, and they often settle down to this activity in a particularly absorbed and satisfied way. In short, the chance to mix, stir, pour, measure, mold, and squish sand and mud are indispensable components of the nursery school curriculum.

Since this experience is often restricted at home, it is particularly important to offer it consistently at nursery school, where it can be planned in advance and where it is relatively easy to clean up. It is good planning to locate the sandbox as far from the nursery school door as possible, in the hope that some of the sand will shake off clothes on the way inside, and it is also sound to check pants cuffs when the play has been especially vigorous, to reduce the likelihood of dumping the whole sandbox on the carpet. The sandbox should have a wide border around it so that children may sit on it and stay warm and dry when the weather is chilly. A waterproof chest beside it will make storage of commonly used equipment easier; plastic laundry baskets also make good equipment containers because they allow the sand to fall through.

Mud is different from sand, and the nursery school should provide chances for the children to play in both these materials. A mud hole and the opportunity to dig deep pits and trudge around in mud is very interesting to children, so a place in the yard should be set aside for this purpose. (If the holes are very deep, it will be necessary to fence them off for safety's sake.) Children will dig astonishingly deep pits if given room, good tools, time and opportunity, and the satisfaction of doing this work is plain to see on their faces.

A. Preparation
1. Consider various possibilities for sand and mud play in terms of the weather and time available. If the day is warm, water is a valuable addition to this experience.
2. Make sure the sand is at least damp so that it holds its form well when patted and molded. It may be necessary to sprinkle it a little.
3. In hot weather, if the area is not shaded, set up paper beach parasols to provide cool oases for the play.
4. In cold weather, encourage the children to sit on the edge of the sandbox to keep knees and seats of pants warm and dry.
5. Have some sandbox accessories set out as the children arrive, but be alert to special requests and ideas from the children; it is excellent policy to change equipment according to their expressed needs.

B. Procedure
1. Stay nearby and keep a careful eye on what is happening. Children will occasionally throw sand and will need to be controlled from time to time. Shovel users need lots of space and must learn to be careful of other people's toes and noses.
2. Think of additional ideas you might suggest to continue the play if the children's interest lags.
3. If the day is warm and water is

being used freely, have the children roll up their pants and take their shoes off.

4. Encourage children to keep the sand in the box and mud in the pit so it will be there for play next time.

5. If sturdy shovels are being used for digging, make sure there is plenty of space between children and that they have shoes on so that shovel edges will not cut their feet.

6. Foster the use of imagination and language whenever possible by playfully chatting with the children about what they are doing.

C. Cleanup

1. Warn the children that it will soon be time to finish their play.

2. Solicit their help in gathering up the play equipment and putting it away.

3. If the day is warm, hose off the area to get rid of the sand and mud, or sweep up the extra sand and return it to the box.

4. Help the children brush each other off, and shake out cuffs of pants and sweaters.

5. Put away accessories that will not be used during the next play period.

Suggested variations. It's a shame to leave the same old buckets and shovels in the sandbox day after day when there are so many interesting variations that may be employed. All kinds of baking and cooking utensils make excellent substitutes and may be readily and cheaply acquired at rummage sales. Toy trucks and cars are nice to add, too, particularly if they are wood or very sturdy plastic, since metal ones rust and deteriorate alarmingly fast if used outside. Sturdy tools of various kinds are also good to use. (Remember that, when digging large holes, children need real shovels or entrenching tools— often sold in "surplus" or sporting goods stores—just as they need real hammers and saws at the woodworking table.)

Adding water to sand and mud is the best accessory of all. It can be offered in deep galvanized washtubs or buckets or as running water from hoses (having two hoses available at once will considerably reduce fighting and competition). Many children will enjoy having temporary low tables, constructed from sawhorses and planks, added to the sandbox. Such tables are particularly helpful to provide when the weather is cold and children shouldn't get chilled.

Some substitutes for sand and water may be offered when the real thing is unavailable. Cornmeal is good for pouring and measuring, and may be presented in deep tubs or a sand table indoors, but the reader should realize that cornmeal makes floors slippery. Some schools also use rice or dried peas as a substitute.

Gardening is another useful variation of digging and working with mud pits. Since digging is the best, most involving part of gardening from the children's point of view, several weeks of this experience should be offered to the children before seeds are planted.

Creative dramatic play

Creative dramatic play such as dress-up and housekeeping is usually very social and imaginative in nature. It almost always involves more than one child at a time and contains a lot of role assigning and role assuming ("Now, you be the mother and I'll be . . . "). Three-year-olds tend to play a simple version of "house," but four-year-olds love to embellish the premises with dogs, milkmen, naughty boys, and interesting domestic catastrophes. All of these activities develop the use of language, since the children will discuss and describe among themselves what is happening ("Let's get the babies and pretend they've been in that mud again!"). Teachers should encourage this use of imaginative language whenever possible.

Costumes can enhance the play, but having unstructured materials available that may be used in many ways is even more desirable because it helps the children be inventive and use their imaginations. Thus a scarf may become a hat, an

apron, a blanket, or even a child's wished-
for long hair.

A. Preparation

1. Be attuned to the interests of the
children. Has something happened in the life of the group that
could be played through? Perhaps
a child has had her tonsils out or
the children went to see a car
being lubricated. Have a few
props available that may enhance
this play if it develops.

2. Think back to yesterday's play:
could it be drawn over and continued with satisfaction today? Is
there a little something extra that
might be added to sustain interest?

3. Arrange materials attractively. If
costumes are offered, hang them
neatly in view, or set out play accessories in an appealing way.
Make sure the clothing is clean
and not torn and that buttons and
fastenings are in place.

4. Hold one or two possibilities in reserve to offer in case play begins
to lag (perhaps an old piece of
rope to hitch the wagon to the
trike in case the boys decide to lu-
bricate a trailer truck).

B. Procedure

1. Sit quietly nearby, or, while working in the general area, keep an
eye on the role-playing activity.

2. Stay alert; step in with a facilitating suggestion before the play de-
teriorates into a hassle, but be
prepared for the children to refuse
your idea if they wish.

3. The teacher's role is facilitation of
the play, but not participation as
a peer. However, sometimes it is
necesssary to be more involved at
first and then withdraw gradually.

4. Be sensitive to the children's
needs as they materialize. It is
better to supply helpful equipment on the spot as requested
rather than tell the children you
will "get it tomorrow; it's put
away now."

5. Remember that too obvious an interest in the play or amused comments to other adults will make
the children ill at ease and self-
conscious, thereby destroying
some of their pleasure in the activity.

6. Tidy up unobtrusively whenever
possible in order to keep the area
attractive. (This advice should not
be construed as advocating compulsive neatness but is intended
to encourage the student to pick
costumes up off the floor and return unused, scattered equipment
to the appropriate play area.)

C. Cleanup

1. Warn the children in advance that
it is almost time for the play to
draw to a close.

2. Encourage them to restore order
and to take satisfaction in arranging the materials for the next time.
This is also a good time to chat
with them about what they did
and what fun they had.

3. Remove any torn, soiled, or broken materials for repair, or discard them.

4. Put away accessories you do not
intend to use during the next play
period.

Suggested variations. Some teachers
enjoy assembling play kits for the children. This is all right as long as the teacher resists the tendency to supply every little thing or to offer such specific equipment that there is no room left for developing a creative use for a familiar material. It is well to vary dress-up clothes and
housekeeping accessories regularly. Using
different hats and costumes, different
pans, empty food packages, or a milk bottle holder and bottles can kindle new interest. Dress-up clothes for both sexes
should be provided. Hats, vests, and old
firemen's jackets and boots will find favor
with boys, but both sexes should be encouraged to try all kinds of garments. Ethnic costumes are a nice variation, too, and
often enhance the image of the child who
lends them; but be sure these are not
valuable, treasured mementoes. Doctor

play is always popular, partly because it represents thinly veiled concerns about sexual differences and partly because it offers invaluable chances for children to play out their fear of doctors, shots, and being hurt. The teacher should be available for interpretation and control when such play takes place.

Blocks

Blocks are one of the timeless, classic play materials that have withstood the many comings and goings of ideologies and theories of early childhood education ranging from Froebel's "gifts" to the big hollow blocks designed by Patty Hill. No matter what theory of learning is espoused by which educator, children have continued to play with blocks with concentrated devotion.

Infants begin to stack objects (a very primitive block-building skill) almost as soon as they are able to sit up, and children continue to use blocks with satisfaction throughout elementary school years if given this opportunity. Blocks provide endless opportunities for the development of emerging perceptual-motor skills. Stacking, reaching, grasping, lifting, shoving, carrying, and balancing are only a few of the countless motor skills practiced in block play.

Possibilities for emotional satisfactions abound as well. What teacher has not seen a shy child build himself a corral and seek safety within it, or a pent-up child send blocks toppling down, or two little girls construct block houses and establish families firmly within their confines?

Blocks lend themselves readily to achieving large effects quickly, thereby building ego-expanding structures of considerable height and large dimensions, which help the child feel strong and masterful, as well as providing opportunities for him to be creative.

Blocks are also strong in their contribution to learning the intellectual operations basic to Piagetian theory. They offer many opportunities for the child to grasp the principle that operations are reversible (when a tower falls, it returns to a prior form). They may be used to demonstrate

conservation (four blocks can be piled into a variety of shapes and yet retain their quality of "fourness"), and they provide additional opportunities to demonstrate the principle of transitivity (four short blocks equal two longer ones, which in turn equal one very long one).

Finally, blocks foster the development of creative play. By nature, they are unstructured and may be used to build anything that suits the child's fancy. Older children enjoy planning such structures in advance, but younger ones will content themselves with the experience of stacking and balancing for its own sake and perhaps assign a useful function to the construction at a later point in the building.

A. Preparation
1. Make sure the blocks are well sorted and neatly arranged.
2. Try to include accessories that are related to current curriculum interests; for example, it may stimulate play to offer some boats after a visit to the harbor.
3. Recall what the children were interested in the previous day when they played with blocks, and be sure to have these materials (and a possible embellishment) readily available should they be called for again.
4. Be sensitive to the expressed interests and requests of the children as they draw near the blocks: *the best accessory is the one they request.*
5. Children may be attracted if the teacher builds some small, interesting structure to begin with (the old principle of the nest egg under the chicken); but this creation should be offered as a stimulus, not as a model intended for emulation.
6. Avoid setting out every accessory the school owns. This usually results in a clutter, which ultimately discourages participation.
7. Out of doors, a good supply of large hollow blocks should be set out to begin with. Children should

Los Niños Head Start

be encouraged to get out the rest as needed. There is no point in owning a beautiful supply of outdoor blocks if they remain unused in the shed.

B. Procedure

1. Settle yourself nearby on a low chair. The teacher's presence is one of the best incentives to block play.
2. Teach the children to select blocks and carry them somewhat

away from the shelves or storage shed so that everyone can easily reach more of them as building continues.

3. Be an interested observer of the children's block play, but be ready to redirect children or offer suggestions to extend the activity according to their interests should the need arise. Avoid taking over the play; make sure it remains the children's activity.

4. Remember that children need time to play with their block structures after they have built them. Children appreciate having the privilege of leaving such things up during nap or overnight if it is possible to arrange this.

5. Remember to stress that block buildings belong to the children who did the work. Children may knock down their own structures but may not destroy the work of other children unless they have the owner's consent. Dumping all the blocks onto the floor and running off or throwing blocks should be prevented. Children who sweep blocks off the shelves need to stay and help pick them up.

6. Drawing diagrams of the children's constructions from time to time increases the child's interest and satisfaction in this activity. If a carbon copy is made, one copy can go home and the other be retained in the child's folder as part of his developmental record. Be sure to date it and note the child's companions and comments.

7. Mathematical relationships such as equality and seriated relationships should be casually drawn to the children's attention as the occasion warrants.

8. Tidy up as needed to keep the play area attractive and to make room for further building.

C. Cleanup
   1. Some teachers discourage the use of blocks because they dislike picking them up, but this problem can be somewhat alleviated by encouraging children to help, too. However, it is not desirable to enforce the rule, "You have to put away every block you got out before you leave the block corner." Since many children won't participate under these conditions, enforcement of this rule can spoil play. The teacher will obtain the best cooperation from the children if she pitches in with them and everyone puts the blocks away together at the end of the morning.

   2. Always neatly categorize blocks when putting them away, and shelve them with the long side in view so their size is readily apparent. Never store blocks by dumping them into a bin or tub; it is impossible for children to find needed sizes in such a welter, and it knocks corners off the blocks as well.

   3. Return extra accessories to the block closet, and arrange the remaining ones so they make attractive, colorful accents in the room.

Suggested variations. Accessories that may be offered to stimulate block play are legion. Since blocks are usually neutral in tone, the touches of color lent by accessories add beauty as well as stimulation to the play. Doll house furniture and rug samples, small rubber animals, and miniature people are all successful accoutrements. Variations in blocks themselves, such as gothic arches, flat "roofing" blocks, spools, and cubical counting blocks, add embellishment. Not all of the blocks should be offered all the time: it is sound to save the arches, switches, or triangular blocks and ramps and offer them as interesting variations when the more common varieties begin to pall. The Skaneateles train is an incomparable block accessory; tracks and additional cars should be purchased every year, since it seems to be impossible to own enough of these materials. It is also fun to build pens for the rats and guinea pigs with blocks, although

Los Ninos Head Start

this requires careful supervision from the teacher for the animal's protection. Cars, trucks, derricks, boats, and airplanes are also delightful to use with block materials.

Outside, the addition of boards, sawhorses, ladders, and old bedspreads and parachutes will extend large block play in a very satisfactory way. Large, sturdy boxes and cement pipes are additional accessories that make good combination units with blocks, and wagons and wheelbarrows are handy for carting blocks about and delivering them to many locations in the yard.

It is also fascinating to combine large and small blocks indoors. Older children often enjoy using the small blocks as trimming on large block constructions, and some very creative and interesting structures can result from this merging of materials.

SUMMARY

Play serves many valuable purposes in the life of the child. It provides occasions for intense practice of sensorimotor skills; the symbolic nature of imaginative play fosters development of the intellect and generates increased understanding of events; play facilitates role playing and develops social skills; it furnishes opportunities to work through emotional problems and to experience the relief of acting like a child instead of an adult; and it provides many occasions for the child to be creative by using his imagination and his ability to think in divergent ways.

The teacher who wishes to foster the creative aspects of play will avoid dominating it and will encourage children to make original use of materials. She will purchase, plan, and arrange equipment so that creativity will be enhanced. But above all, the teacher who wishes to foster creativity in play will cast herself in the role of assistant to the child, seeking to move with and support his play as it develops and to serve his play needs to the best of her ability.

QUESTIONS AND ACTIVITIES

1. *Problem:* Suppose a parent comes to you, after touring the school, and says dubiously, "Well, it looks nice enough here, and I can see the children are happy; but don't they

ever learn anything? Don't they ever do anything but play around here?" How would you reply?

2. Take time to make a brief record of the play of several children during the coming week. Can you find evidence in these observations that play is used symbolically by children to translate experience into a deeper understanding of events? Did you find evidence that children employ play to express emotions and work these through? Did you observe any instances where the children generated new, divergent solutions to problems by trying them out in play?

3. What is the difference between overcontrolling play and acting in a supportive, fostering role that encourages it to develop in greater depth? Role play the same play situation, demonstrating differences between these two approaches.

4. *Problem:* It is winter time, and you live in an eastern city. The children play outdoors at your school, but water play cannot be offered outside for most of the year, because it is too cold. Identify several ways it could be offered on a regular basis indoors.

5. Survey the play yard of your school. List the different play units around which activity occurs. Are there some that appear to generate more imaginative activities than others? Identify what properties these units possess in common. How are they alike?

6. Put all the housekeeping equipment away for a change, and offer only hollow blocks in its place and some props, such as pots and pans and dolls. Observe what happens to the children's play under these circumstances.

REFERENCES FOR FURTHER READING

General References

Almy, M. Spontaneous play: an avenue for intellectal development. *Young Children,* 1967, **22,** 265-277. Almy discusses the place of structured and spontaneous play in the nursery school and makes a very good case for the significance and value of fostering spontaneity.

Curry, N. E. and Arnaud, S. (Eds.) *Play: the child strives toward self-realization.* Washington, D. C.: National Association for the Education of Young Children, 1971. This is a good, basic pamphlet that contains several papers on the value of play—its use in dealing with stress, the role of the adult in facilitating the activity, and a discussion of current issues related to this subject.

Millar, S. *The psychology of play.* Baltimore, Md., Penguin Books Inc., 1968. Millar begins his thoughtful discussion of play with a review of historical theories, next discusses the play of animals, and then covers the functions of play. He draws interesting comparisons of play between a variety of cultures and presents a good, though brief, discussion of the uses of play therapy.

Smart, M. S., and Smart, R. C. *Children: development and relationships.* (2nd ed.) New York: The Macmillan Co., 1972. Chapter 7 has a solid discussion of play and imagination that is well worth reading. The authors also talk about other creative activities, such as expressive materials and creative storytelling.

Specific Values of Play

Axline, V. *Play therapy.* (Rev. ed.) New York: Ballantine Books, Inc., 1969. In this thoughtfully written, practical text, Axline describes how play is used as a therapeutic technique.

Hartley, R. E., Frank, L. K., and Goldenson, R. M. *Understanding children's play.* New York: Columbia University Press, 1952. This old but invaluable book discusses the virtues of specific play materials and what each contributes to the healthy development of young children. Of particular interest here are the chapters on dramatic play; but blocks, water play, clay, and graphic materials are also discussed in detail.

Moffitt, M., and Omwake, E. *The intellectual content of play.* New York: New York State Association for the Education of Young Children, no date. These two articles contain a sound analysis and defense of play as it relates to the intellectual development of young children; worth reading.

Rosecrans, C. J. Play—the language of children. *Mental Hygiene,* 1968, **52,** 367-373. Rosecrans presents a good discussion of the emotionally therapeutic value of play.

Practical Advice on Generating Play

Wittes, G., and Radin, N. *Ypsilanti home and school handbooks: helping your child to learn: the learning through play approach.* San Rafael, Calif. Dimensions Publishing Co., 1969. Wittes and Radin present a series of lessons, designed for a parent group but applicable also to nursery school, which are intended to teach mothers how to foster and generate play at home. The authors are particularly strong on discussing the purpose of offering play activities and in making practical suggestions about what to do—very down-to-earth. They advocate a strong leadership role for the adult.

Specific Activities and How to Present Them

Johnson, H. M. *The art of block building.* New York: Bank Street College of Education, 1933. Johnson gives an excellent description of block play, which includes a list of suggested blocks, and a description of developmental stages of block building, accompanied by many illustrations of the children's constructions. This is the classic publication in the field and, although first published in 1933, remains in print because of its excellence.

Matterson, E. M. *Play and playthings for the preschool child.* Baltimore, Md.: Penguin Books Inc., 1965. This is a first-rate, but unpretentious little paperback from England, which is filled with practical suggestions, pictures, and discussions of various play materials and how to present them; has a nice emphasis on how to make things yourself.

Publications Committee, National Association for the Education of Young Children. *Water, sand and mud as play materials.* Washington, D. C.: The Association, 1959. My favorite pamphlet! The Committee discusses the values of these indispensable materials for young children and ends up with practical suggestions about how these experiences can be effectively integrated into the curriculum.

Starks, E. B. *Blockbuilding, blockbuilding, blockbuilding.* Washington, D.C.: Elementary-Kindergarten-Nursery School Educators, 1960. Starks approaches the subject in terms of what blocks can teach children. She uses examples drawn from kindergarten, so the pictured structures are quite advanced, but her comments on what children can learn from using this material are sound and helpful.

For the Advanced Student

Almy, M. *Early childhood play: selected readings related to cognition and motivation.* New York: Simon and Schuster, Inc., 1968. This collection of papers includes materials by Erikson, Frank, Almy, and Sutton-Smith. The article by Lawrence Frank, "Play in Personality Development," is particularly valuable and hard to find elsewhere.

Corrado, J., and Reed, J. *Play—with a difference.* New York: The Play Schools Association, 1970. This is a report of the staff training program carried out by the Play Schools Association, 1970 at Letchworth Village. It is a heartening and fascinating description of how profoundly retarded individuals were encouraged to involve themselves with simple play materials and of the difference this made to their happiness and personal growth.

Ebbick, F. N. Learning from play in other cultures. *Childhood Education,* 1971, **48**, 2. Ebbick provides an interesting cross-cultural discussion of play and the way it is viewed by people of differing cultural backgrounds.

Herron, R. E. and Sutton-Smith, B. *Child's play.* New York: John Wiley & Sons, Inc., 1971. This is the most comprehensive book on the theory of play thus far available. *Child's Play* analyzes theoretical approaches having to do with play in terms of its normative, ecological, psychoanalytic, comparative, cognitive, and developmental aspects.

Piaget, J. *Play, dreams and imitation in childhood.* New York: W. W. Norton & Co., Inc., 1962. In his classic description Piaget discusses how children assimilate knowledge of the world around them by means of imitation and the use of symbolic play; rather difficult but interesting reading.

Smilansky, S. *The effects of sociodramatic play on disadvantaged children.* New York: John Wiley & Sons, Inc., 1968. This book represents a breakthrough in methods of studying play. Smilansky describes the way she and the project teachers sought to increase the ability of the children to play on the sociodramatic level by improving the play techniques of the children; interesting work.

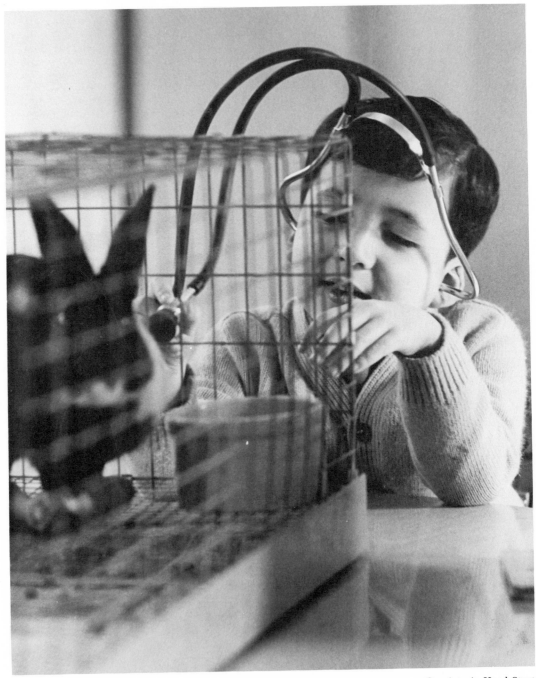

Carpinteria Head Start

CHAPTER 14

Fostering creativity in thought

No matter how unstable and shaky the mental life of the preschool child may seem to us (especially during the first five years of his existence), we must not forget that the child "from two to five" is the most inquisitive creature on earth and that the majority of the questions he asks are evoked by the daily need of his tireless mind to comprehend his surroundings.*

Smith's definition of creativity as "the process of sinking down taps into our past experiences and putting these selected experiences together into new patterns, new ideas or new products" (1966, p. 4) applies to thought as well as to play and the use of expressive materials. The ability to put prior experiences together to form new ideas is crucial in developing creative thinking. Young children can learn to produce more than one answer to a question, to conceive new uses for familiar materials, or to generate uniquely descriptive language and self-expressive stories. But in order to do these things they need a wealth of experience to draw upon, and they need the help and expertise of the teacher.

Although nursery school teachers have long maintained that the development of creative thinking in children is desirable, in recent years the work of J. P. Guilford has drawn fresh attention to the value of thinking that emphasizes a many-answers approach. Guilford terms this ability *di-*

vergent thinking and contrasts it with *convergent thinking.* He maintains that the critical difference between these mental operations is that in convergent thinking the kind of response is completely specified (that is, there is only one correct answer), whereas in divergent thinking more than one solution or answer is possible (1967).

Convergent thinking is elicited by such questions as, "What color is this? Can you tell me the name of this shape? What must we always do before we cross the street?" There is nothing wrong with this kind of mental activity; children need to have a variety of commonly known facts at their fingertips. But teaching that stops at the fact-asking level fails to develop the creative aspect of the child's mental ability. Children who are trained like robots to produce facts when the right button is pushed are unlikely to grow up to produce the new ideas desperately needed in science, medicine, and human relationships.

Unfortunately, most teaching is still geared to convergent, one-answer learning. Zimmerman and Bergan (1971) found that even as early as first grade there was what they termed "an inordinate emphasis placed on factual knowl-

---

*From Chukovsky, K. *From two to five.* Translated by M. Morton. Originally published by the University of California Press; reprinted by permission of the Regents of the University of California, 1968.

edge questions." They reported that only about 2% of the questions asked by first-grade teachers were structured to draw forth divergent replies. But just because this has been true of teaching in the past does not mean it must continue. The following examples of ways to generate creativity in thought may encourage teachers to produce more divergent thinking in the children in their groups. Doing this is fun; it is interesting; and it can be exciting for both children and teachers when it is presented in the right manner.

THINGS TO REMEMBER ABOUT CREATIVE THINKING
Number of original ideas can be increased if the teacher recognizes their value and responds to them in a positive way

It is easy to go on doing things the same old way or to establish a set of procedures that have become so sanctified by custom that no one considers deviating from the established formula. But an open-minded teacher who keeps on the lookout for spontaneous ideas and suggestions will find she can frequently go along with variations in approach and changes in procedure when they are suggested by the children. The teacher who is willing to let the children put their ideas into practice offers strong positive reinforcement for this behavior, which will nourish creative talent in the children, and she will find herself blessed with ever more interesting, fresh contributions from the youngsters in her group.

For example, I remember the time we offered a cooking project that involved slicing bananas for Jell-O. The inexperienced young student in charge felt she could watch only two children working with paring knives at once and therefore sensibly limited the activity to two children at a time. A third little boy hung around and watched, badly wanting to have a chance with the bananas; but the student truthfully explained she was so new that she felt she just couldn't supervise more than two knives at once. Then he said to her, "I tell you what—I could use one of the scissors for the bananas. I know how to do that. I *never* cut myself

with scissors." She immediately saw the value of his suggestion and let him snip up as many pieces as he liked.

Another independently minded $2^1/_2$-year-old was going through a streak of wanting to get into the swing by herself. Since she was short and the swing was high, she struggled and wriggled, doggedly refusing assistance. Finally, she rushed away and returned with a large hollow block, which she put under the swing and used successfully as a mounting block.

Asking thought-provoking questions will help children generate creative ideas

Although a few youngsters may continue to solve problems and create interesting stories without outside help, the teacher generally needs to take an active role in stimulating creative thought. The most effective way to do this is by asking the child questions that help him think up his own answers.

Sorting out fact and thought questions. We have already noted that all questions are not alike. Some simply require the child to tell the teacher something he has learned. These questions can usually be spotted because they (1) request information ("Do you make cookies in the oven or in the broiler?"), or (2) request labeling or naming ("Let's see, I have some things in this bag, and I wonder if you can tell me what they are."), or (3) request the child to recall something from memory ("How about telling us what happened when you went to the pet store? Did you buy rabbit food?"). All of these questions are "closed," or convergent, questions since they anticipate simple, correct-answer replies.

Questions that are likely to draw forth creative, divergent ideas are phrased like these: "What could you do about it? How could we fix it? I wonder if there's another way. How else could you do that? What else could we use?" These kinds of questions place the burden of thinking up possibilities and solutions on the child. They emphasize process and problem solving and leave room for many suggestions and answers.

Waiting for answers and asking only a few

questions. Even when the question is well phrased, something additional is required. After asking the child a question, the teacher needs to pause and wait, looking at the child in an expectant but relaxed way. Many teachers ask excellent questions but then plunge right ahead and answer them themselves; perhaps they are afraid of silence or of the child's failing. But children, like adults, need time to collect their thoughts and formulate their replies. Pausing allows them to do this.

Another thing to beware of is asking too many questions. Most young children are not highly verbal, and they do not enjoy long, drawn-out intellectual dialogues. It is best to weave questions into general discussions while the actual experience is going on, as well as to provide all possible opportunities for children to promptly put their suggestions into practice.

Stimulating the inquiry process by helping children answer their own questions. To develop creative thinking the teacher must also learn to deal sensitively with questions the children ask. And, of course, they ask questions endlessly. Children are entitled to information when they cannot figure things out for themselves, but often a child can satisfy his curiosity by providing his own answer if the teacher does not rush in and furnish the fact immediately. This is another instance where she needs to pause and think before replying.

Thus when a child asks, "What do rabbits eat," the teacher does not immediately reply, "Oh, rabbits eat lots of things —carrots, alfalfa pellets, lettuce, and clover." Instead, the teacher who wishes the child to investigate for himself and generate his own answers might say, "Well, I guess they eat a lot of things. What do *you* think they eat?" One of our Center children replied to this by saying, "Well, they eat those green things in the bowl, I know that! And I think maybe they eat those little black things in the cage, too." The student refrained from explaining what those little black things were, but asked, instead, if he could think of anything else the bunny might also eat. He listed pellets (both green and black), meat, oranges, and lettuce. Then she

asked him if he could think of some way to find out if the rabbit really would eat them all. They decided to put the things he suggested in the cage and watch and see which ones the rabbit ate—an experiment that proved to be quite interesting to all the children. When the "black things" remained untouched in their bowl, this led to further speculations and experiments.

The moral of this tale is that it is always better to answer a question with a question, if possible. Answering a child's questions by supplying a fact deadens his ability to produce his own answer. It deprives him of the chance to think for himself.

Ideas that turn out to be unsuccessful are also a valuable learning experience

Of course, creative ideas and experiments don't always work; and adults, who have a much better grasp of cause and effect as well as more experience than children have, can often foresee problems and difficulties associated with ideas produced by young thinkers. But, if the situation is reasonably safe, the children should be allowed to try out their ideas even if the adult knows they won't work. Children are entitled to the right to fail as well as to the right to succeed. The sensitive teacher will be very matter-of-fact and low keyed about such ineffective trials. She might say, "I'm sorry that didn't work out just right, but I'm proud of you for trying it," or, simply, "I can see you're really disgusted. Is there some way I can help? Can you think of something else we could do to make it work?"

Children can learn a lot from experiencing failures, just as they learn from successes. Sometimes they can modify the idea and make success more likely next time. More important than that, they can learn to cope with the experience of failure if they undergo it in a generous, noncritical atmosphere.

Language should be used along with more tangible means of trying out ideas

Although there are perils in overintellectualizing the role of question asking, language is of genuine importance in the development of ideas. Language is a great facilitator of thought, and language and cognition are closely linked (Lewis, 1963). Therefore, it is vital to couple talk with experience and to discuss what the children learned when the experience is completed; but conversation must not be allowed to take the place of actual involvement with real things.

EXAMPLES OF CREATIVE MENTAL ACTIVITIES AND SUGGESTIONS ABOUT HOW TO ENHANCE THEM
Encourage the child or the group to produce more than one answer

In divergent thinking, as opposed to convergent thinking, more than one correct answer is possible. Teachers need to learn how to encourage children to propose more than one possible solution to a problem.

Making sure the child's ideas are not criticized will help generate many answers, whereas negative reinforcement will make sensitive children clam up and refuse to take the risk of confiding a second thought. If the goal is to encourage children to mention their ideas, it makes simple good sense to welcome the suggestions and ask for more rather than to submit each one to instant critical appraisal.

In addition, as mentioned before, questions such as, "What else could you do?" or "Is there another way?" will stimulate many suggestions from the children. For example, Aline and Franklin, both 4-year-olds, are trying to get the rat cage open to feed him. As they work, the teacher jokes with them a little and asks them, "I wonder what we'd do if the gate were really stuck and we *couldn't* get it open. How could we feed rat then?" "We could poke it through the lines [bars]," says Franklin. "Sure we could—that's a good idea, Franklin—but let's suppose we couldn't get it through the bars; what then?" "We could teach him to reach out," says Franklin. "Yes, he likes to reach; but if he couldn't do that, what then?" There is a long silence while the children consider. "But he *can*," answers practical Franklin. "But let's imagine, just pretend for fun, that he can't. Could we feed him another way, or would he just get hungry?" Sud-

denly Aline brightens visibly and says, "We could slide the tray out and feed him from the cellar!" (She means from underneath.) "Yes, we could," says the teacher. "My goodness, Franklin, you and Aline sure have a lot of ideas. I guess we'll be able to feed rat after all," and the children laugh with her.

This kind of elementary brainstorming can be done quite successfuly with preschool children in a playful way. It encourages them to see that questions can have a number of right answers and to develop the habit of looking for more than one solution to a problem.

Sometimes with older 4- and 5-year-olds this approach can be presented as a guessing game during lunch or group time. A problem can be postulated such as, "What if we didn't have any blankets at nap; how could we keep warm?" Then all kinds of possibilities can be suggested. (One of our little boys said, "Grow fur.") Four-year-olds often delight in thinking up nonsense solutions whose funniness adds delight to this process and exercises their sense of humor as well.

Permit the child to explore new ways to use equipment, and provide opportunities to try out unconventional ideas

Dealing with questions for which there is more than one right answer is just one example of creative thinking. Children can also be encouraged to develop creative thought by allowing them to use equipment in fresh and unconventional ways. When they do this, they are carrying out what Guilford terms *transformations*. They are looking at a familiar thing in a new way and perceiving new possibilities in it. This is a fine way to develop originality.

Sometimes such uses can be quite ingenious. An acquaintance told me an interesting instance of such an unconventional idea. His little boy was going through the stage of flipping light switches on, something he could just manage to do by standing on tiptoe and shoving up on the switch. The trouble was that he was too short to pull the switch down again, so his father always had to

Los Niños Head Start

walk over and turn the light off for him. This went on for several days; and finally, as he said, "I reached my limit—I'd had it. He flipped the switch, and I was just too tired to get up and turn it off. I was really mad. So I said to him, 'All right Joey, I've warned you, and you did it anyway. Now *you* think up some way to turn it off, and you do it before I count to ten. No! you can't drag that chair over there; that scratches the floor.' And so," he continued, "I began to count: one, two, three, four. Well, he just stood there for a minute

and looked at the light and looked at me. Then he ran over to me and took my steel measuring tape out of my pocket and hurried over to the switch. He extended the tape up to reach it, hooked the little metal lip over the switch, and pulled it down. I gotta hand it to that kid! Don't you think that was smart? After all, he's only 3!"

The incident above is a particularly felicitous example of using familiar equipment in an original way, but teachers can have this kind of original thinking happen at nursery school, too, if they do not overrestrict children and equipment. Many things children want to try out are unconventional but not seriously dangerous. I have seen various children try the following things, which, though unusual, were reasonably safe.

1. A child turned a dump truck upside down and pushed it along, making train noises.
2. Another one extended the slide by hooking a board to the end of it. Then, finding that it slid off and dumped him on his bottom, he talked his crony into bracing it at the end to keep it from slipping.
3. Another youngster used the half-moon plywood blocks to make a cradle for her doll.
4. Someone else first experimented with riding his trike backwards and then, since that didn't work to his satisfaction, spent the remainder of the morning sitting on the back step of the bike, laboriously straining to reach the pedals to push them around.
5. A fifth youngster needed a pillow for the doll bed and thought of the beanbags, which she used very satisfactorily for this purpose.

None of these ideas worked perfectly or were world shakingly different, but all of them had two cardinal advantages: they were original ideas that came from within the children, and they required a generous amount of imagination to make them be completely satisfactory.

Foster the development of imaginative, self-expressive storytelling

As we saw in the chapter on creative play, children often play out situations that are developed from their past experience but that are not literal representations of events as they actually occurred. This part fact/part fantasy condition is also true when young children are encouraged to tell stories. In order for the teacher to know what to expect in the stories of children of various ages, it is helpful if she understands their developmental trends.

Pitcher and Prelinger (1963) have stud-ied over 300 stories told by children aged 2 to about 6 years. They found that as the children matured, their stories included an increasing utilization and mastery of space, a less clear differentiation of main characters from other characters but an increasing complexity of such characters, more happenings that affect the characters, and a significant increase in the use of fantasy and imagination. Therefore, when pursuing creative stories with nursery school children, the teacher should be prepared for considerable literalness in stories by younger children and a greater use of fantasy and imagination by older ones. But, since the stories are personal descriptions and reflections of the children's feelings and perceptions, they may also be considered self-expressive and hence creative.

The following two examples of dictated stories are both factual and quite expressive of feelings.

The Doctor and the Nurse

MARICE

When I got the cast off we used an electric saw, and I had something on my ears. The saw was very sharp and looked just like the sun.

The thing I had on my ears was round. I couldn't hear the electric saw, but the other doctors could. It played music very loud, as loud as the saw.

The doctor held my hand because he didn't think I could walk by myself. He's not a very good doctor, and I don't like him, either—the first doctor I'm talking about.

The nurse clipped the cast off. She went out after that. I needed my privacy anyways.

My House Story

ANGELIQUE

This first page will be about my dog. His name is Toulouse. Sometimes I can't play with him, because he goes to dog school. At dog school somebody makes him fetch sticks and makes him beg. Then he comes home, and he shows me what he has learned. I also have a cat. His name is

Goya, named after a painter. We always name our animals after painters.

Now about my grandmother and grandfather. My grandmother goes to Weight Watchers. They weigh her there without her shoes on.

Now about my grandfather. He drives a car. It's a red Datsun wagon pickup.

My house is white with a white picket fence. My grandma, grandpa, mommy, and me all live in the house.

My grandfather went to the hospital the day before yesterday. He had his operation yesterday. I don't like to have him in the hospital. He's not here to read me a bedtime story.

I miss him.

These stories mattered a lot to the children who wrote them. At that time, the teachers were using little handmade books for recording the stories so that the children were free to illustrate them if they wished. This provided an additional way to work off their feelings and be creative. But it is not necessary to make storytelling that elaborate an occasion. Taking the story down as the child dictates it often provides sufficient encouragement for the young storyteller. Evelyn Pitcher collected her stories by waiting until a child was either sitting quietly by himself or playing alone and then by saying, "Tell me a story. What would your story be about?" This is a good way to get started. Of course, children sometimes don't want to participate. In this case the teacher just says, "Well, I expect you'll want to do it another time. I'll ask you then."

As with other creative materials, the teacher should scrupulously avoid suggesting what the story should be about or what might happen next. But it does encourage the creator to ask, "Then what happened? Then what did she do?" or "Do you want to tell me anything else?" These questions will help sweep the child along into the narrative.

Creative stories can also be stimulated by providing hand puppets or flannel board materials, which can be set out for the children to use as they feel the need. Rubber dolls and animals that can be bent offer another medium for imaginative stories and play. Creative stories can also be stimulated by providing pictures, which may be used as starting points for discussion.

SUMMARY

Creativity does not have to be limited to the use of self-expressive materials such as paint and clay or to creative play. It also includes the realm of creative thought.

The teacher can do three specific things to enhance creative mental ability in young children: she can (1) encourage the child to produce more than one solution to a problem, (2) permit him to explore new ways to use equipment and try out unconventional ideas, and (3) foster his ability to create imaginative, self-expressive stories.

It is particularly important that the teacher reinforce such activities by responding to them positively and that she form the habit of asking questions that encourage original and various replies.

QUESTIONS AND ACTIVITIES

1. The next time you have to solve some sort of problem, take a few minutes and just for fun list all the ways, both silly and practical, that the problem might be solved. Try not to evaluate the merit of the ideas as you produce them, but just play around with many possibilities. Then evaluate them. Is there a fresh one included that might be a good, new, though perhaps unconventional way to solve the situation?
2. *Problem:* You have in your room a little boy about 3 years old who asks a lot of questions. For example, he may ask, "Why are we going in now?" When dutifully provided with the reasons, he then asks, "But why do we have to do that?" When answered, he asks, "But why?" If you were his teacher, do you think this type of inquiry should be encouraged? How would you handle it?
3. Select a learning experience based on a scientific subject (ants, for instance), and make up a list of questions on this subject that will require convergent answers. Now modify the questions so they will encourage creative thought and divergent replies instead. Can you determine the basic differences between the way these kinds of questions are phrased?

4. Isn't it a waste of time to let children try things out that obviously won't work? Might it not be better just to lead a discussion with them about the proposed solutions rather than going to all the trouble of actually trying something out, only to experience failure?

5. Observe the children during the next week, and report back to the class the unconventional ways you saw them using equipment. What role did imagination play in their activities? How practical were their substitutions and solutions? How satisfying?

6. Make up blank paper "books," and invite the children to dictate stories to you on any relevant subject. Many youngsters will relish adding illustrations to these tales if encouraged to do so.

REFERENCES FOR FURTHER READING

Learning to Ask Productive Questions

Estvan, F. J. Teaching the very young: procedures for developing inquiry skills. In R. H. Anderson and H. G. Shane (Eds.), *As the twig is bent: readings in early childhood education.* New York: Houghton Mifflin Co., 1971. In my research, I came across only one discussion of inquiry training that was suitable for very young children. It is this brief article by Estvan, which discusses how the teacher should go about asking questions to guide the child through the inquiry process.

Further Information about Guilford's Ideas

Meeker, M. N. *The Structure of Intellect: its interpretation and uses.* Columbus, Ohio: Charles E. Merrill Publishing Co., 1969. Although the advanced student should read the original source, the newcomer may prefer to read a book written for teachers in which Guilford's Structure of Intellect is discussed in simple terms and in which many examples of how this material may be applied to teaching are provided.

Examples of Children's Creativity in Thought

De Bono, E. *The dog exercising machine.* New York: Simon & Schuster, Inc., 1970. This is one of my favorites. Replete with illustrations of a great many dog-exercising machines conceived by children of various ages, this amusing book provides a good example of divergent solutions to a single problem.

Chukovsky, K. *From two to five.* Translated by M. Morton. Berkeley: University of California Press, 1968. This classic work by the well-known Russian author Chukovsky captures the excitement and genius of children as they learn to use language. The chapter "The Tireless Explorer" is rich with examples of the way children use language to question and reason.

For the Advanced Student

De Bono, E. *Lateral thinking: creativity step by step.* New York: Harper & Row, Publishers, 1970. This perceptive, leisurely book written for teachers is intended to assist them in fostering creative thinking in the classroom.

Guilford, J. P. *The nature of human intelligence.* New York: McGraw-Hill Book Co., 1967. This is the basic reference in the field, in which Guilford describes all 180 components of the Structure of Intellect. It is technical and somewhat difficult, but also quite interesting to read.

Pitcher, E. G., and Prelinger, E. *Children tell stories: an analysis of fantasy.* New York: International Universities Press, 1963. The authors make an interesting attempt to analyze the content of young children's stories and to interpret their fantasies in terms of Erikson's theory of psychological development. The book abounds with examples of stories by children ages 2.3 to 5.10 years.

Watson, J. D. *The double helix: being a personal account of the discovery of the structure of DNA.* New York: Atheneum Publishers, 1968. This is a readable account of how two young men solved the riddle of the chemical construction of deoxyribonucleic acid. All the excitement, disappointments, satisfaction, intuition, and tenacity associated with this supremely difficult kind of creative effort comes through clearly in this book. Watson and Crick were about 25 years old when they won the Nobel Prize for their discovery.

PART SIX

Developing language skills and mental ability

CHAPTER **15**

Fostering the development
of language skills

Language is knowledge in our heads; speech is the realization of that knowledge in behavior. Language consists of all the words in a person's mental dictionary, and all the rules at his (usually nonconscious) command for combining those words into an infinite number of novel sentences and for interpreting the equally novel sentences that he hears. Speech, by contrast, consists of his actual utterance spoken to particular people in particular situations. Language exists even in moments of silence and sleep; speech exists only in moments of actual speaking or listening, including the silent activation of language in thought.

It is easy for us as teachers to admit that we need to know more about mathematics. But, because we all talk, we assume that we're experts on language. The trouble is that the knowledge about language we require as teachers is one level beyond using it ourselves, no matter how richly we may do so. We need to know about language. And then we have to plan how to use that knowledge in the classroom.*

In the past few years we have become increasingly aware of the value of developing language skills in early childhood, and almost without exception the newer, research-based schools have included a language component in their curriculum. This emphasis is the result of research findings that indicate that a close relationship exists between language competence and cognitive development (Lichtenberg and Norton, 1970), that differences exist between the speech of middle- and lower-class children (Bernstein, 1960; Deutsch, Katz, and Jensen, 1968; Labov, 1970;

Shriner, 1971), and that children acquire most of their language skills, though not most of their vocabulary, by age 4 or 5 at the latest (McCarthy, 1954; Menyuk, 1963).

Whether one sees language as being separate from thought, as does Piaget (1969), or as ineluctably bound together, as theorized by Luria (Beiswenger, 1968), there is still general agreement that the development of language abilities goes hand in hand with the development of mental ability (Lewis, 1963). For this reason, we devote considerable attention to methods of fostering language development as we study the child's intellectual self.

Petty and Starkey (1967) have defined language as a learned, arbitrary, struc-

---

*From Cazden, C. B. *Child language and education* (pp. 2 and 3). New York: Holt, Rinehart and Winston, Inc., 1972.

tured system of sounds and sequences of sounds that includes a system of socially shared meanings. But this is a bare-boned definition indeed to the preschool teacher, who must come to grips with the problem of how to foster language development to maximize the child's potential for both comprehension and expression. In order to bring this about she must understand how the ability to use language is acquired and how it develops; above all, she must determine what she can do in the nursery school to foster its growth.

HOW LANGUAGE IS ACQUIRED

Knowledge about language acquisition is increasing rapidly, and it behooves nursery school teachers to know as much as possible about the process so they may apply this knowledge when teaching language skills. At the present time, we have considerable information on what happens and when it happens. But since we still do not understand completely how it happens, it is necessary to employ several theories that are, at best, only partial explanations of the process.

Role of imitation

Brown and Bellugi (1964) present a clear-cut discussion of some processes by which children acquire speech. According to them, imitation is one primary means of speech acquisition. In their study of two children nicknamed Adam and Eve, they present evidence that some of the very early sentences used by the children were obviously imitations of the mother's speech. But imitation works in two directions. The investigators also found that much of the maternal speech consisted of imitation and expansion of the infant's speech—the mother preserving the infant's word order but adding auxiliary words. For example, when Eve said, "Mommy sandwich," the mother replied, "Mommy'll have a sandwich." This building directly on what the child knows is enough to gladden the heart of any educator.

Role of reinforcement

But the question remains: What causes children to imitate their mothers or to imi-

tate other people who are important to them? Perhaps the most satisfactory explanation can be found in learning theory, the principle that people tend to repeat acts from which they gain satisfaction. Children probably imitate because their imitation is rewarded with maternal pleasure and warmth as well as with getting other things they want.

Thus language acquisition begins with imitation, perhaps first by the mother, who stimulates the infant to repeat his random vocalizations. When his repetition is reinforced in turn by maternal pleasure, the baby persists in the behavior: this process finally results in verbal labels becoming attached to important things in the environment, such as "mama," "bye-bye," and "baw" (bottle). After a number of these labels have been acquired, the child gradually pairs them together (Braine, 1963) and then begins to place them in sequences.

Contributions of linguistics

The new science of linguistics is proving helpful in furnishing a map of how children construct language. Although linguistic theory is too advanced and complicated a subject to be presented in detail here, two examples of the kinds of information this science is producing may help the beginning student gain an appreciation of the importance of this approach.

Paula Menyuk (1963) has been using the grammatical theory developed by Noam Chomsky, a linguistic theorist in transformational grammer, to study the language of young children. She studied 3- and 6-year-olds and found that there were very few examples of restricted children's grammer at this level. Surprisingly, most of the children's speech was similar to that of adults, and the children had gained a remarkable proficiency in structuring language correctly even by age 3. This is important information for the nursery school teacher to possess, since it implies that we need to stress the development of language function skills earlier than age 4—the point at which many preschool compensatory programs now begin. Obviously, if grammatical structure has been largely acquired by this time, we should be building language skills in children between 18 months and 3½ years old to be maximally effective.

In another recent study, Courtney Cazden (1970) has also used transformational grammar to study the way children learn to pose questions. Briefly, she found that children first form questions by using inflection. Following that, questions become the "yes-no" kind, which depend on interchanging only two phrases. For example, "The boy can drive a car" would change to "Can the boy drive a car?" Next, children learn to perform a more difficult transformation, the "wh" question—"When can the boy drive a car?"—which involves two transformations. The next step involves forming negative questions: "Won't he be able to drive the car?" Finally comes the use of tag questions: "It's all right if he drives the car, isn't it?"

As more of these studies become available, it will become possible to outline sequential steps for many forms of grammatical structures. Then, following an analysis of a child's present level of ability, the teacher will be able to refer to it and know what next step should be selected for him and to plan her teaching accordingly.

Conclusion

Do these processes offer sufficient explanation of how language is acquired? The foregoing explanations are sensible and useful as far as they go, but the fact remains that, although we are in the process of acquiring linguistic maps of the order in which the forms of language develop and although we are fairly certain that imitation and reinforcement play an important role in the acquisition of these forms, we still cannot explain what happens in the child's mind that enables him to generate original sentences he has never heard before. Herein lies one of the mysteries and unexplained abilities of the human mind.

ADDITIONAL FACTS ABOUT LANGUAGE DEVELOPMENT

In addition to understanding that grammatical structure develops according to predictable rules, the teacher should become acquainted with additional developmental milestones so that she can identify children who show marked developmental lags and also so that she may have a clear idea of what is reasonable to aim for when establishing goals for language development. The teacher may find Table 7, developed by Mary Wooton Masland for the National Institute of Neurological Diseases and Stroke (1969), quite helpful; but she should remember that the checkpoints represent averages, and children who are developing well may often be either above or behind the suggested time listed. The lag should be considered serious enough to warrant concern if the child is more than a year behind on a particular measure.

Another quick rule of thumb for checking language development is sentence length, still thought to be one of the best indicators of verbal maturity. In general, sentence length increases as the child grows older. McCarthy (1954) lists the following pattern.

Sentence of 1 word	18 months
Sentences of 2 to 3 words	30 months
Complete sentences averaging about 4 words	40 months
Sentences averaging 5 words	78 months

When assessing language competence, the teachers in our Center have also found it helpful to determine whether English or some other language, typically Spanish, is the child's dominant language and also to determine whether he appears to possess what I term "the habit of verbalness." For whatever reason, be it temperament, age, level of intelligence, cultural pattern, or socioeconomic status, it is evident to our Center teachers that some children use language to meet their needs more frequently than others do. We always try to note this behavior and to use the techniques described in the following section to encourage less verbally oriented children to increase their language abilities while attending the Center.

Table 7. Milestones in the development of language ability in young children*

Average age	Question	Average behavior
3–6 months	What does he do when you talk to him?	He awakens or quiets to the sound of his mother's voice.
	Does he react to your voice even when he cannot see you?	He typically turns eyes and head in the direction of the source of sound.
7–10 months	When he can't *see* what is happening, what does he do when he hears familiar footsteps . . . the dog barking . . . the telephone ringing . . . candy paper rattling . . . someone's voice . . . his own name?	He turns his head and shoulders toward familiar sounds, even when he cannot see what is happening. Such sounds do not have to be loud to cause him to respond.
11–15 months	Can he point to or find familiar objects or people when he is asked to? *Example:* "Where is Jimmy?" "Find the ball."	He shows his understanding of some words by appropriate behavior; for example, he points to or looks at familiar objects or people, on request.
	Does he respond differently to different sounds?	He jabbers in response to a human voice, is apt to cry when there is thunder, or may frown when he is scolded.
	Does he enjoy listening to some sounds and imitating them?	Imitation indicates that he can hear the sounds and match them with his own sound production.
1½ years	Can he point to parts of his body when you ask him to? *Example:* "Show me your eyes." "Show me your nose."	Some children begin to identify parts of the body. He should be able to show his nose or eyes.
	How many understandable words does he use—words you are sure *really* mean something?	He should be using a few single words. They are not complete or pronounced perfectly but are clearly meaningful.
2 years	Can he follow simple verbal commands when you are careful not to give him any help, such as looking at the object or pointing in the right direction? *Example:* "Johnny, get your hat and give it to Daddy." "Debby, bring me your ball."	He should be able to follow a few simple commands without visual clues.
	Does he enjoy being read to? Does he point out pictures of familiar objects in a book when asked to? *Example:* "Show me the baby." "Where's the rabbit?"	Most two-year-olds enjoy being "read to" and shown simple pictures in a book or magazine, and will point out pictures when you ask them to.
	Does he use the names of familiar people and things such as *Mommy, milk, ball,* and *hat?*	He should be using a variety of everyday words heard in his home and neighborhood.
	What does he call himself?	He refers to himself by name.

*From National Institute of Neurological Diseases and Stroke. *Learning to talk: speech, hearing and language problems in the pre-school child.* Washington, D. C.: U. S. Department of Health, Education, and Welfare, 1969.

Table 7. Milestones in the development of language ability in young children—cont'd

Average age	Question	Average behavior
2 years—cont'd	Is he beginning to show interest in the sound of radio or TV commercials?	Many two-year-olds do show such interest, by word or action.
	Is he putting a few words together to make little "sentences"?	These "sentences" are not usually complete or grammatically correct.
	Example: "Go bye-bye car."	
	"Milk all gone."	
2½ years	Does he know a few rhymes or songs? Does he enjoy hearing them?	Many children can say or sing short rhymes or songs and enjoy listening to records or to mother singing.
	What does he do when the ice cream man's bell rings, out of his sight, or when a car door or house door closes at a time when someone in the family usually comes home?	If a child has good hearing, and these are events that bring him pleasure, he usually reacts to the sound by running to look or telling someone what he hears.
3 years	Can he show that he understands the meaning of some words besides the names of things?	He should be able to understand and use some simple verbs, pronouns, prepositions, and adjectives, such as *go, me, in,* and *big.*
	Example: "Make the car go."	
	"Give me your ball."	
	"Put the block in your pocket."	
	"Find the big doll."	
	Can he find you when you call him from another room?	He should be able to locate the source of a sound.
	Does he sometimes use complete sentences?	He should be using complete sentences some of the time.
4 years	Can he tell about events that have happened recently?	He should be able to give a connected account of some recent experiences.
	Can he carry out two directions, one after the other?	He should be able to carry out a sequence of two simple directions.
	Example: "Bobby, find Susie and tell her dinner's ready."	
5 years	Do neighbors and others outside the family understand most of what he says?	His speech should be intelligible, although some sounds may still be mispronounced.
	Can he carry on a conversation with other children or familiar grown-ups?	Most children of this age can carry on a conversation if the vocabulary is within their experience.
	Does he begin a sentence with "I" instead of "me"; "he" instead of "him"?	He should use some pronouns correctly.
	Is his grammar almost as good as his parents'?	Most of the time, it should match the patterns of grammar used by the adults of his family and neighborhood.

METHODS USED FOR INCREASING LANGUAGE COMPETENCE IN YOUNG CHILDREN

As one might expect, methods of teaching language skills are closely linked to the philosophy of the teachers involved, and at present there is much controversy about how nursery school teachers should teach language. Approaches range from Moore and Anderson's talking typewriter (1968) and Bereiter's (1969) emphasis on drill and rote learning to using finger plays that stress the development of English sounds for Mexican-American children (Forrester, 1969). The works by Bereiter (1969), Carter (1969), Forrester (1969), Hodges, McCandless, Spicker, and Craig (1971), Karnes (1968), and Kraft, Fuschillo, and Herzog (1968) provide examples of kinds of nursery school programs that present a wide variety of approaches to the teaching of language.

It is not within the scope of this book to go into detail about these individual programs. In summary, all of the programs of the authors listed above had the effect of significantly increasing I.Q. scores and scores on the Illinois Test of Psycholinguistic Abilities or the Peabody Picture Vocabulary Test. The great diversity of these programs makes it evident that a variety of approaches can succeed in teaching language to children.

I prefer an approach that seeks to develop fluency and the child's ability to use language to verbalize concepts and express thought. This approach, characterized by Bartlett (1972) as being based on instructional dialogue, is illustrated by curricula developed by Lavatelli (1970ab), Bank Street College (1968), Weikart (1971), and many others. These programs have the advantage of providing a framework for the teacher so that she knows what she should teach next; yet they also allow enough scope that the child, as well as the adult, is free to initiate conversation.

There are some basic principles that the beginning teacher should seek to apply, however, no matter what program she decides to espouse. They are fundamental to the success of any more particularized

language program the school may elect to use.

SEVEN BASIC WAYS TO FOSTER LANGUAGE DEVELOPMENT
I. Listen to the children

Many adults, particularly women and most particularly nervous women teachers, are so busy talking themselves that they drown the children out. But children learn to talk by being heard. Paying attention to what they say and listening both to the surface content and to the message underneath offer the most valuable inducements to children to continue making the effort to communicate.

Of course, it isn't always easy to understand what they have to say. If a comment is unintelligible, it is all right to ask a child to repeat it; and, if the message is still unclear, it may be necessary to admit this and say, "I'm sorry, I just can't tell what you're saying. Could you show me what you mean?" At least this is honest communication and shows children that the teacher is really interested and is trying.

II. Give the children something real to talk about

Children's talk should be based on solid, real, lived-through experience. Sometimes inexperienced teachers want to begin at the other end and set up group experiences wherein the children are supposed to discuss planting seeds or thinking about what will sink and float before they have been exposed to the experience itself. This means they are expected to use words that have few actual associations for them and to talk about something vague and relatively meaningless. No wonder their attention wanders! It is much more satisfactory to provide the opportunity to live through the experience and to talk about what is happening while it is going on as well as after it has been completed. At this point the child can really associate "sink" with "things that go down" and "sprout" with the pale green tip that poked its nose out of the bean.

Note, also, that talk and questioning are

advocated as an accompaniment to experience. In former years, some nursery school teachers seemed to assume that mere exposure to interesting materials in the presence of a warm adult would automatically produce growth in language and mental ability. The work of Blank and Solomon (1968, 1969) has shown that unfocussed attention in a rich environment is *not* enough. Children develop language best when required to use words to express concepts and thoughts about what is happening, has happened, or will happen; it is this kind of activity that produces the greatest gains.

III. Encourage conversation and dialogue

There is much more to language development than teaching the child to name colors or objects on demand, although learning the names of things and building vocabulary is of value, too. More important than the acquisition of words is using them to express ideas, and building conversational skills is fundamental to this ability.

In order to develop such interchanges the teacher has to relax and stop seeing her role as one of instructor and admonisher. Always supplying a fact or rendering an opinion in reply to a child's comment kills conversation very quickly. Cazden quotes a perfect example of this. As she points out, the more frequent the prohibition in an adult's talk, the less the children reply.

Tape plays
Teacher: Oh, you tease, Tom, what are you telling Winston?
Tom: I tellin' him my brother Gary a bad bad boy.
Teacher: Oh, now that ain't nice.

After an analysis and discussion on this tape recording, the same teacher returns to the child, and the following conversation ensues.

Teacher: Tom, what was you tellin' Winston this mornin' when you playin' with the ball?
Tom: I tole him Gary my brother.
Teacher: You like Gary?
Tom: Yeah, I lahk him, but he bad.
Teacher: Why's dat?
Tom: 'Cus he walked up and set with his friend when they was singin' 'bout Jesus and the preacher was preachin'.
Teacher: Who whipped him?
Tom: Daddy—he tuk him outside and whupped him with a red belt.
Teacher: Did Gary cry?
Tom: Oh, yeah, he got tears in his eyes. Mama wiped his eyes with a rag when he come back in. Then he popped his fingers. That boy can't *never* be quiet.*

The example brings out another important point to remember when building conversation. The teacher should seek to prolong the interchange whenever she can. Tossing the conversational ball back and forth is a very sound way to build fluency and also to establish the habit of verbalness.

The value of the one-to-one situation cannot be overestimated in this regard. It isn't necessary to put this off and wait for a special moment; indeed, this is impossible to do if the teacher wants to talk specially with every child every day. Instead of waiting, the teacher can seize many little interludes to generate friendly talk between her and a child or between two children. One of the teachers in our Center maintains that some of her best opportunities for such chatting occur while she is helping children go to the toilet; another capitalizes on brief moments while putting on shoes and greeting children as they arrive at school.

The teacher should monitor herself regularly to make certain that she is not talking mainly to the most verbal children. Some youngsters have a knack for striking up conversations with adults, whereas others do not. It is the children who lack this ability who are often overlooked and who, therefore, receive the least practice in an area where they need it the most. If the teacher will make a checklist of the children's names and review it faithfully, she will be able to recall which youngsters she has talked with and which she has not and then make a particular effort to include the ones who have been passed over in conversation.

---

*Adapted from Greenberg, P. *The Devil has slippery shoes.* New York: The Macmillan Co. Copyright © 1969 by Polly Greenberg.

Besides these one-to-one conversations, there are two classic larger group opportunities that occur each day in the nursery school where it is particularly possible to generate conversation: at the snack or lunch table and during story time.

Developing conversation at mealtimes

Gone are the days when children were expected to be seen and not heard at meals or when they had to clear their plates before they were allowed to talk. There are several practical ways the teacher can encourage conversation during meals.

Keep lunch and snack groups as small as possible. It is worthwhile to keep the mealtime groups down to five or six children if possible. Anyone who has ever sat at a banquet table knows how difficult it is to get conversation going under such circumstances, and yet an occasional nursery school persists in seating twelve or fifteen children all around one table. This kills interchange (as well as making supervision difficult).

It is also wise to avoid putting two adults together at one table. The temptation to carry on a grown-up conversation over the heads of the children is too great when two adults eat lunch together. It is better to add more tables when more adults are present, thereby seizing this golden opportunity to reduce group size and making it more likely that individual children will join in the talk.

Think of good conversation starters. Such questions as, "Did you see anything good on TV last night?" "What would you like for Christmas?" or, "How's that kitty of yours?" will lead the children into talking about things that really interest them and that they can all share together. It is also fun to talk about brothers and sisters, or birthdays, or what they did over the weekend. In addition, their memories can be developed by asking them if they can remember what they had for lunch yesterday or what they saw on the way to school.

It takes tact to ensure that one ardent talker doesn't monopolize the conversation under these circumstances, and the teacher may need to make a deliberate ef-fort to draw all the children into the discussion lest someone be consistently drowned out; but in the space of the half hour or so that lunch requires there is really ample opportunity for everyone to converse.

It is also desirable to generate talk between children rather than solely between teacher and child.

Don't let the children get by with pointing to food they wish to have passed or with saying "I want that!" Conversation as such is highly desirable to develop at the lunch table, but mealtime also provides many opportunities to build the children's vocabulary and concepts. All too often teachers permit pointing and saying "give me" to pass for language. This is just not enough. Children, particularly children from low income families, need to acquire commonly used vocabulary, and mealtime is a very effective place to teach this. It is easy for the teacher to make sure that the child says the real name of the food he is requesting and then give it to him promptly—there's no quicker way to teach him that talking pays off!

If the child doesn't know the word, the teacher can say, "This red stuff is called Jell-O. Now you can tell *me*." When he does, she should give it to him right away and tell him, "Good for you! You said the real name." Sometimes, however, the child refuses to reply. It is best to pass over such a response lightly without making a major issue of it, perhaps saying, "Well, maybe you'll be old enough to tell me it's Jell-O next time."

Mealtimes are also good opportunities to teach certain concepts. For example, the teacher might start by talking about the food: "What are we having today? Did any of you look in the kitchen to see what dessert is?" She might then go on to ask, "What does this meat taste like? Is it hard or soft? Hot or cold? Tough or tender? Can you think of anything else that's like that?"

A word of warning is in order here. Mealtimes should remain basically social occasions where verbal fluency and fun are the keynote. Vocabulary and concept building should not be allowed to dominate the occasion, and such a delightful event as lunch should never be permitted to degenerate into a mechanical drill where the talk centers on naming each food and discussing where it came from.

Developing conversation during story time

We know that reading aloud to children can be a very effective way to encourage verbalization. In his classic study Irwin (1967) reported that when mothers of lower-class children read aloud to their youngsters (aged 17 to 30 months) 15 minutes a day, the children's vocalization rate increased phenomenally.

In order to obtain maximum benefit from the story time, children should not be lumped together all in one large group any more than they should sit banquet fashion at lunch. Such large groups almost always produce behavior problems because of lack of involvement and inattention, which means that the assistant teacher spends her time admonishing some children, patting others on the back, and holding still another restless nonparticipant on her lap. It is much better to split the group in half so that each staff member reads to a small number of children. Under these circumstances there can be a better balance between reading and conversation, and the children will pay closer attention and develop their language skills more quickly and richly.

It helps a lot to select books that the children genuinely enjoy. Unfortunately, the world abounds in dull books designed to improve children's minds but not lift their spirits. These can spoil a story hour. However, there are also some interesting books, such as *Curious George* (Rey, 1941), *The Circus Baby* (Petersham and Petersham, 1950), *Whistle for Willie* (Keats, 1964), and *Dear Garbage Man* (Zion, 1957). The teacher who selects stories like these will enjoy them right along with the children, and they will arouse much comment and discussion from everyone. When a book is dull and the children are not interested, it is not necessary to read grimly through to its end; it is better to simply set it aside and go on to a more attractive choice.

IV. Use questions to generate and develop language

Ask questions that require more than one-word answers. In Chapter 14 I mentioned the desirability of asking questions that are open ended so that more than one reply is possible. It is also desirable for the teacher to avoid asking questions that require only single-word answers, such as, "How many bunnies are there on this page?" or "What color is this?" If the teacher wants to lead the children into discussion, it is more productive for her to frame questions so the children will need to use several sentences in reply. For example, when reading she might ask before turning the page, "Gosh! What do you think will happen next?" or, "Well, he certainly *is* in trouble now. If you were George, what would *you* do?"

When replying to a child's question or statement, elaborate. After the work of Brown and Bellugi (1964) revealed that parents spend a good deal of their time reconstructing and expanding the restricted sentences used by their small children, some teachers concluded that this technique of expansion would naturally be the most effective way to teach enriched language to all young children. Thus when a child commented, "Train, bye-bye," the teacher would dutifully reply, "Yes, the train is going bye-bye." It now appears that this technique may be most effective with children about 18 months to 3 years old, but Cazden's work (1965) with developing vocabulary seems to indicate that expansion is not as effective as providing enriching replies when working with 4-year-olds. This would mean that rather than replying "Yes, the train goes bye-bye," the teacher would respond to an "older" child by saying, "Yes, the engine is pulling the train out of the station. Goodbye, train. Goodbye, people." This kind of enrichment is superior to simple expansion in fostering language progress.

V. Provide auditory training for the children

Sometimes teachers forget that children have to be able to hear differences in sounds and words before they can produce them accurately. In addition to building fluency, conversation, vocabulary, and concepts, the teacher must plan daily opportunities for the children to develop their ability to listen carefully and discriminate between sounds.

In general, the nursery school curriculum has been very weak in this area. Perhaps this is because teachers shun drill and practice exercises for preschool children and do not realize that such activities don't have to be presented as drill. There are many simple activities, such as matching the sounds of shakers, some of which have been filled with sand, some with beans, and some with rice; shutting eyes and opening them when a particular sound is heard; listening for words left out of familiar nursery rhymes; or having the children signal when they hear sentences that don't make sense, such as "When I went to the market, I bought a camelope," a game that appeals strongly to 4-year-olds.

Most speech correction texts (Van Riper, 1972, for example) contain many suggestions for such activities that may be adapted for nursery school age children. Auditory discrimination skills are important, and practice on them should be consistently incorporated into the curriculum at the preschool level. For a list of suggested activities, the reader may refer to Appendix D.

VI. When necessary, seek professional assistance promptly

Every once in a while, a teacher will come across a child who speaks rarely, if at all, or one who has a pronounced speech problem of some description. I discuss such disabilities in more detail at the end of this chapter, but I want to emphasize here, as a basic principle, that it is important to seek professional help for these children promptly. Too often, both teacher and parent let the year pass by, hoping the child will somehow outgrow his difficulty. Although this does happen occasionally, it is generally wiser to refer such youngsters for professional help after 2 or 3 months at most. Children who have pronounced developmental lags or other speech disorders and who do not

show signs of improvement by that time generally need consultation from a qualified speech therapist or psychologist, and a gentle referral is definitely in order.

VII. Become acquainted with research-based language development programs, and draw on these for resource materials

The need for utilizing packaged programs varies a good deal in relation to the requirements of the children in the school and the sophistication, philosophy, and background of the staff who teach there. There is nothing reprehensible in taking the advice of experts on such an important matter as language development, but it is worthwhile to take a close look at the philosophy and coverage of such programs rather than just buying the glossiest one that is advertised by mail. We are fortunate that a summary of many different language development programs is now available (Bartlett, 1972); the teacher should read it over carefully before making up her mind about which program to choose.

LANGUAGE AND DIALECTICAL DIFFERENCES
Which language should the teacher encourage?

In the chapter on cross-cultural education a good deal of time was spent discussing ways to honor the cultural background that the child brings with him from his home. Although there is no finer way to do this than by welcoming and encouraging him to use his native language or dialect at nursery school, teachers are often torn in two directions on this question. On one hand, they want to make the child welcome and facilitate his learning in every possible way. This makes the use of his dominant language essential. On the other hand, the teacher can't help but look ahead and know that, as schools function today, each youngster will soon move on to elementary school, where he will have to speak standard English, the dominant language of the middle-class world.

It is quite a dilemma. Somehow, the teacher who provides the first school experience for such children must stand with a foot on either side of the stream. To be truly effective, she should be bilingual herself, as well as knowledgeable about dialectical differences that exist between herself and the children in her care. Failing this, she should at least see that the assistant teacher possesses these strengths.

It is also vital for the teacher who forms this bridge to acquaint herself with recent research which indicates that black children who come from city ghettoes speak a form of nonstandard English, whose value, prior to the work of Labov (1970), went largely unassessed and unappreciated. For example, white teachers often bemoan the lack of language skills of their black students and yet are in total ignorance of verbal games such as "the dozens," which are played on street corners and depend on the ability to concoct elaborate and very funny insults—obviously a language-based skill of a very high order. Moreover, middle-class teachers are often unable to use even the commonest form of argot that is used by the black families they serve (Cazden, 1966). This ignorance causes them to look down on the verbal abilities of the children. However, there is now a rapidly growing body of literature on the subject of black English; and as our understanding about this dialect grows, it is becoming evident that its grammar has definite rules and that there is real sophistication to its structure (Bambara, 1972; Labov, 1970; Smith, 1973a, 1973b). Indeed, some theorists are already asserting that the variation in language that exists between social classes or ethnic groups may ultimately turn out to be more a question of difference than defect (Cole and Bruner, 1972).

The best recommendation appears to be that the teacher should respect the black child's dialect just as she respects the Mexican or Puerto Rican child's Spanish, yet, while doing this, also make it possible for him to learn standard English because it is such a valuable tool for the child to possess. It is to be hoped that the child has the opportunity to learn this English in an atmosphere that values and appreciates his already present linguistic strengths rather than in one that smacks of condescension and noblesse oblige.

At present, the effects of learning two languages at once remain difficult to assess, since most research studies about bilingualism are confounded by the presence of additional variables such as poverty. Therefore, we don't know whether bilingual children who lag behind their monolingual peers do so because they are bilingual, because they come from families of the poor, or because of other reasons yet to be identified.

Common sense, however, argues in favor of not insisting that children try to learn important new concepts in a language they are only beginning to acquire. Imagine having to learn geometry by means of first year French, which you are learning simultaneously—that's the stuff nightmares are made of. Yet we are, in essence, often expecting this degree of expertise from a young bilingual child when we teach him "all the important things" only in his second language.

Probably the best we can do at present, since children are expected to speak English in grade school, is follow the bilingual model wherein children are taught concepts first in their dominant language and then in English. This approach has been shown to be successful in a number of studies involving concept training or learning to read (Macnamara, 1966; Nedler and Sebera, 1971; Orata, 1953) and has been effective with children speaking a variety of languages and ranging in cultural background from Mexican American to Irish. Children who are coming to school for the first time are undergoing a complicated enough set of adjustments without the teacher's expecting them to function entirely in a new language at the same time.

Make it clear to the families that you value the child's native language and cultural background

In the following discussion I use Spanish for the sake of brevity, but Navajo, French, Japanese, or any other language could be used to make the same points.

The most important thing for children to learn about school is that it is a place where they feel welcome and comfortable. Including songs and stories in Spanish, multiethnic pictures, and observing Mexican customs honors the family by using the language and customs of the home at school. Asking children for the Spanish equivalents of English words will help clarify that there are two languages and, if done with respect and enthusiasm, points up the fact that the Spanish-speaking child has a special ability and skill.

It is also valuable to form close bonds of mutual concern with the parents of the children. Not all parents want their children to continue to learn in Spanish. This attitude varies a good deal from family to family, and the teacher should discuss this subject with them, help them weigh the pros and cons, and respect their preferences in every way she can. Most families are realistic about the value of learning English and are almost too eager to have their children gain this skill. It may even be necessary to explain why Spanish is being included as a major component in the curriculum. Other families, more rare in number, will welcome the bicultural emphasis to such an extent that they may be reluctant to include English at all.

Sometimes school values in language development run counter to deep-seated cultural values in the home. For example, it may be necessary to explain to parents the positive relationship between language competence and the maximum development of intelligence. Such explanations may encourage families to overcome their traditional view that children should be seen and not heard, and the parents may make greater efforts to encourage their children to talk more at home.

Sometimes, of course, it is the teacher rather than the family who needs to make the cultural adjustment. Some teachers, for instance, in their eagerness to promote verbalness in the children fall into the habit of allowing them to interrupt adult conversations whenever they please. This is frowned on in Mexican-American homes, and in such cases the teacher would do well to change her policy and encourage participation by the children while seeing to it that they continue to observe the basic good manners taught by their own culture.

When teaching bilingual children, do not attribute all verbal, expressive, and comprehension difficulties to bilingualism

Many children who come to nursery school speaking only a little English are quite fluent in their mother tongue, and for them the transition to English is not too difficult. *It is very important to distinguish between these youngsters and those who do not talk very much in either language.* These nontalkers are the ones who need all the help they can get in developing the habit of verbalness. For such youngsters the goal is to increase fluency and participation in whichever language they feel more at ease; teaching English to them is of secondary importance to gaining fluency and the habit of talking.

Further suggestions about teaching English

As I have said before, at the present time children need to learn English while in nursery school to help prepare them for the later grades. The following suggestions are intended to guide the teacher in this task. However, basic concept learning should take place first in the dominant language to facilitate the acquisition of ideas.

Speak simply and use both languages. In the beginning it works best to speak in Spanish and then repeat the message in English. After a time, as the children become more at ease and familiar with hearing the language, it will gradually be possible to speak the English sentence first, pause to give the child a chance to grasp what is being said, and then repeat it in Spanish if necessary. For the sake of clarity and good usage of both languages, it is wise to avoid a polyglot approach where words from both languages are used and mixed up in the same sentence.

Demonstrate what you mean in order to increase comprehension and retention. As in any other subject area, young children learn best when they are involved in real experiences. For this reason, it is better to build vocabulary about rabbits while playing with them or to pick up a paint brush and demonstrate what you have in mind while asking, "Would you like to paint?"

Reinforce and encourage the use of English. Be alert and respond quickly to the child's attempts to use the newer language. He is bound to feel self-conscious about using it at first, and responding to him promptly without making a big fuss about it will encourage him to continue. It is also helpful to try to have all the children talk and play together. In some schools English and Spanish speakers divide themselves along language lines; this deprives both groups of valuable learning opportunities.

It is particularly important, when working with bilingual children, to keep track of each youngster and make certain he is being talked with each day. All too often the shyly smiling, well-mannered minority child is passed over in discussions at lunch and story time to avoid embarrassing him by putting him on the spot; so the child remains shy and ill at ease in the second language. Of course, it is vital not to humiliate shy children in front of the group, but they must not be left out, either. The solution is to use a checklist to assure coverage and to generate daily, quiet chats on a one-to-one basis to ensure that every child is learning English as the year moves along.

Remember to continue using Spanish throughout the year. Finally, be sure that, just because the children are gaining facility in English, Spanish is not abandoned at school. It is always a temptation to let this happen, particularly if the teacher is not a native Spanish speaker; but a teacher who truly honors both cultures will continue to make use of both languages throughout the year.

CHILDREN WHO HAVE SPECIAL DISABILITIES OF SPEECH AND HEARING

Children with several kinds of speech and hearing disabilities are seen quite commonly in the nursery school classroom. Indeed, the teacher may find that she is the first person to be aware that the child has a speech problem, since the mother may be too accustomed to it to notice or too inexperienced to identify it as deviating markedly from normal speech. The four problems the teacher is most likely to come across in nursery school are articulation disorders, delayed speech, children who are hard of hearing, and children who stutter.

With all of these conditions, if the difficulty is pronounced or continues without positive change for 2 or 3 months after the child enters nursery school, the teacher should talk the problem over with the parents and refer them to the most appropriate resource in their community. Colleges and universities often maintain speech and hearing clinics that are free to the public because they are used to train speech clinicians. Children's hospitals often have speech clinicians on their staffs, and public schools almost always have a speech therapist available who will be glad to suggest appropriate referrals for speech therapy if the teacher and family are unacquainted with these resources.

Children with disorders of articulation

The teacher's problem with articulation disorders is deciding which ones are serious and which should be overlooked. In order to make this decision, the most important thing the teacher must know is that children do not acquire accuracy in pronouncing certain sounds until they are in the first or second grade. At the nursery school level, therefore, there will be many distortions, substitutions, and omissions that can be treated with a combination of auditory training and benign neglect. However, referral is warranted when the child's speech is generally unintelligible and the child is older than 3 or $3\frac{1}{2}$, since it is likely that he will need special help from a professionally trained clinician to learn to speak more plainly. The only unfortunate outcome of such a referral is that the therapist might decide the child does not need special help after all, and this can be mildly embarrassing to the teacher. However, it is better that she take this risk if the child's speech seems seriously impaired than let him continue

AGE LEVEL

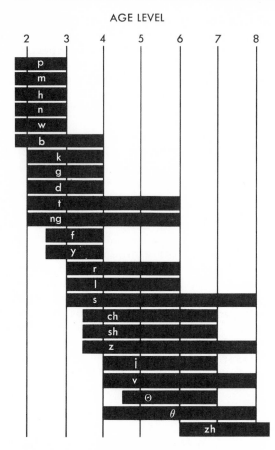

Average age estimates and upper age limits of customary consonant production. The solid bar corresponding to each sound starts at the median age of customary articulation; it stops at an age level at which 90% of all children are customarily producing the sound. (From Sander, E. K. When are speech sounds learned? *Journal of Speech and Hearing Disorders,* Feb. 1972, **37**(1):62.)

to practice poor speech habits until he reaches kindergarten.

Besides knowing when to refer and when to overlook the articulation disorder, the teacher should realize that there is a lot more to correcting an articulation problem than just reminding the child, "Don't say 'wed' say 'red'." Speech therapists usually proceed by (1) working with the child to help him hear the error and tell it apart from other sounds, (2) eliminating the cause of the disorder if possible (for

example, encouraging the mother to raise her speech standards at home so that the child no longer gets by with infantile speech patterns), (3) teaching him to make the correct sound by itself, and (4) finally incorporating it into familiar words (Van Riper, 1972). The nursery school teacher can assist this process by providing regular auditory training and by avoiding spot corrections of the "Don't say 'wed'" variety; this kind of nagging is rarely successful.

Children with delayed speech

Although articulation disorders are encountered with greater frequency, the teacher is more likely to notice the child who does not talk or who talks very little. Such youngsters are often referred to nursery schools by pediatricians and in certain cases can be helped very effectively by the nursery school teacher.

Causes of delayed speech. Causes of delayed speech are myriad and range from the child's being hard of hearing to having a neuromuscular disorder such as cerebral palsy. Low intelligence is another common cause of delayed speech, and negativism or extreme shyness also takes its toll. Lack of sufficient environmental stimulation or low parental expectations may also mean that a child has not developed to his full verbal potential.

In such cases the teacher needs to take a keen, continuing look at the child to try and determine what lies behind the lack of speech. Making a home visit can help ascertain whether he just does not talk at school or whether his nonverbal behavior is consistent in all situations.

It is often difficult or impossible to spot the cause of lags in speech development. Contrary to general opinion, children who are slow to learn do not necessarily look different from their peers. I have known several instances where mildly or even moderately retarded youngsters were denied help and appropriate teaching because the cardinal symptom of delayed speech went unquestioned by an inexperienced teacher because the child "looked normal." The services of a competent psychologist can be enlisted to identify the slow learner if the child is referred to him. Neuromuscular disorders do not always manifest themselves in obvious ways, either; so when such a condition appears to be a likely possibility, a referral to the child's pediatrician is a sound approach to take.

Children who restrict themselves from talking because they are overwhelmed by the newness of school or who do not talk because they appear to have been deprived of sufficient speech stimulation at home are the ones with the brightest prognosis. In these cases, the teacher can gently draw them forth and elicit more speech by responding positively to their venturings. Many of these children will make a heartening gain in fluency during the year or two they spend at nursery school if the methods described in the previous section on developing language skills are applied to them.

Children with disorders of hearing

Another useful way the teacher can help the children in her care is to be on the lookout for those who do not hear well. This is a surprisingly common disorder, and yet it often goes by unnoticed. One year, for example, the teachers in our Center discovered that three children out of a group of forty-five showed a significant hearing loss when tested by the school nurse. Fortunately, the hearing of all three improved greatly following tonsillectomies and adenoidectomies.

A child with the following behaviors or conditions should alert the teacher to the possibility that he may be hard of hearing. The teacher should be on the lookout for:

1. The child who does not talk
2. The child who does not respond or turn around when the teacher speaks to him in a normal tone of voice from behind him
3. The child who consistently pays little attention during the story hour or who always wants to sit right up in front of the teacher
4. The child whose speech is indistinct and difficult to understand—most particularly if high-frequency sounds such as "f" and "s" are missing from his speech
5. The child who talks more softly or loudly than most of the children
6. The child whose attention you have to catch by touching him on the shoulder
7. The child who often asks you to repeat sentences for him
8. The child who has a perpetual cold, runny nose, frequent earaches, or who usually breathes through his mouth
9. The child who consistently ignores you unless you get right down and look him in the eye as you talk to him
10. Any child who has recently recovered from measles, meningitis, scarlet fever, or from a severe head injury

Such youngsters are prime candidates for audiometric testing. Of course, it is also true that children talk indistinctly, want to sit close to the teacher, or fail to pay attention, for reasons other than hearing loss; but particularly if more than one of these symptoms describes his usual behavior, the possibility of a hearing deficit would be worth investigating. Referrals may be made to an otolaryngologist (a doctor who treats ear and throat disorders) or to the child's pediatrician, who will send him to the best place to receive help.

Hearing losses can result from many causes. Sometimes the loss can be remedied through surgery; but if the loss is permanent, continued professional guidance will be necessary. Although hearing aids do not alleviate all forms of deafness, they can be effective in many cases, and hearing aids combined with speech therapy and auditory training are helpful for many children suffering from loss of hearing.

Children who stutter

Although we do know that an easy, unselfconscious form of repetitive speech is often observed in children of nursery school age, we do not yet understand why this should be the case. This first stage of repetitive speech differs markedly from the strained, emotion-laden hesitancies and repetitions of the confirmed stutterer and is more than likely liable to vanish if teachers and family don't react to it with concern and tension.

The nursery school teacher can play a very effective role in helping parents deal with their concern over this potential problem. First, she should encourage them to relax and not to direct attention to the behavior. This includes *not* saying to the child, "Now, just slow down; I'll wait 'til you're ready," or "Don't talk so fast," or "Your ideas just get ahead of your tongue; take it easy." The teacher should also reassure the family by explaining that this behavior is common in young children who are undergoing the stress of learning to talk. The goal here is to encourage parents to relax so that the child will not become concerned about his speech.

Since stuttering seems to increase when the child is undergoing stress, it is also wise to find out if something is currently making life harder for him and to mitigate the situation whenever possible. Examples of stressful events could include a visit from a critical grandparent, parents taking final examinations, moving to a new home, the arrival of a new baby, holding the child to unreasonably high standards of behavior, a death or divorce in the family, or generally weakening situations, such as continued poor health or consistently late bedtimes (Travis, 1971). Tension-relieving activities can be provided at school to tide a child over these rough spots. Dramatic play, water play, and various forms of sublimated aggressive activities may help him feel easier and reduce his tensions and attendant stuttering.

As with other speech disorders, it is also necessary to have some rule of thumb for referral when working with a child who stutters. At the nursery school level, it seems wise to refer the family for further help if they appear to be reacting very strongly to the behavior and are unable to control their signs of concern or if they seem incapable of reducing the tension-generating situations without outside help. Sometimes psychological counseling is the answer, and sometimes the matter is best handled by a speech clinician.

SUMMARY

The development of language skills in preschool children has become of cardinal interest to nursery school teachers as evidence mounts that linguistic competence and mental ability go hand in hand.

Children appear to acquire language in part through the process of imitation and in part by means of reinforcement. The science of linguistics is also providing the teacher with valuable maps of the order in which linguistic structures are acquired. At the present time, however, we still cannot provide an adequate explanation of how children learn to form novel sentences. This remains one of the tantalizing mysteries of human development. But we do know that the growth of language occurs in a predictable, orderly sequence.

The nursery school teacher can do many things to facilitate children's language acquisition: (1) she listens carefully to what children have to say; (2) she provides a meaningful base of experience to talk about; (3) she fosters the growth of language by using one-to-one encounters and lunch and story times to develop conversation; (4) she uses questions to generate and develop language; (5) she extends rather than just expands her replies to the children's questions; (6) she provides consistent practice in auditory training; (7) she seeks professional help for children who require it; and (8) she acquaints herself with research-based speech development programs and draws on these resources when they match her philosophy and educational goals.

In this chapter the question of bilingualism in the nursery school was also discussed, and some suggestions were included about teaching English as a second language. Finally, four common disorders of speech and hearing were identified: disorders of articulation, delayed speech, deficient hearing, and stuttering. Recommendations were made for classroom treatment and remediation of these disorders, and suggestions for referral were included.

QUESTIONS AND ACTIVITIES

1. Identify some factors in the school where you teach that encourage the development of conversation between children and adults: What are some things that discourage conversation between them?
2. List some additional conversation starters you have found useful in getting young children involved in talking with the teacher or with other children.
3. Role play a story hour where the teacher seems to do everything possible to prevent the children from talking.
4. *Problem:* A mother calls and says her pediatrician has suggested that she place Silas in nursery school because he has been a little slow in learning to talk. As you become acquainted with Silas, it does appear to you that his speech is slow to develop. He is 3 years old and still communicates mainly by grunting, nodding his head, or pointing when he wants something. List some possible reasons why his speech might be developing so slowly. How would you go about determining which cause is the most likely one? Propose a course of action that would be most appropriate for each probable cause.
5. Do you feel that teachers have the right to change something as personal to the child as his dialect or dominant language? Under what circumstances do you think doing this is warranted or unwarranted?
6. Do you advocate setting up schools that use only the child's native tongue or dialect? What would be the strong point of doing this? What might be the drawbacks to doing this?

REFERENCES FOR FURTHER READING

Overviews

Cazden, C. B. *Language in early childhood education.* Washington, D. C.: National Association for the Education of Young Children, 1972. This book contains a series of valuable articles that provide an overview of oral language education in the nursery school. Although scholarly and based on research studies, it is both readable and practical in tone and is the best book in the field, an excellent place to begin a more detailed study of language as used by young children.

Lavatelli, C. S. (Ed.) *Language training in early childhood education.* Urbana, Ill.: ERIC Clearinghouse on Early Childhood Education, 1971. The book contains a review of research, a discussion of the language of the disadvantaged child, and descriptions of several language programs. It concludes with an article on testing and one on psycholinguistics.

Development of Language

National Institute of Neurological Diseases and Stroke. *Learning to talk: speech, hearing and language problems in the pre-school child.* Washington, D. C.: U. S. Department of Health, Education, and Welfare, 1969. This is an elementary but sound pamphlet written primarily for parents to help them identify children who may have hearing or communication problems. It has clear explanations of the basic mechanisms of speech, gives standards of appropriate expectations of speech behavior for young children, and then goes on to discuss hearing and speech problems in nontechnical language. The pamphlet contains one of the best informal discussions of the development of speech presently available.

Sutton-Smith, B. *Child psychology.* Englewood Cliffs, N. J.: Prentice-Hall, Inc., 1973. Chapter 8 contains a clear, concise, up-to-date summary of language development. In this chapter Sutton-Smith not only discusses the development of oral language but also covers variables that affect its development and discusses the relationship of language to cognition.

Specific Recommendations

Bartlett, E. J. Selecting preschool language programs. In C. B. Cazden (Ed.), *Language in early childhood education.* Washington, D. C.: National Association for the Education of Young Children, 1972. Bartlett surveys and summarizes various language development programs and creates order out of a welter of information; an indispensable reference.

Engel, R. C. *Language motivating experiences for young children.* Van Nuys, Calif.: DFA Publishers, 1968. Engel offers many suggestions for activities, ranging from shining shoes to taking walks around the school. Since suggestions of what to talk about are always included, this book would be helpful for beginning teachers who may feel at a loss for conversational topics.

Karnes, M. B. *Helping young children develop language skills: a book of activities.* Washington, D. C.: Council for Exceptional Children, 1968. This is another book of activities that employ language to develop thought. Activities are classified under such headings as

"Verbal Expressive Abilities," "Verbal Associations," and "Auditory Memory." The book is strongly teacher centered.

Weikart, D. P., Rogers, L., Adcock, C., and McClelland, D. *The cognitively oriented curriculum: a framework for preschool teachers.* Washington, D. C.: National Association for the Education of Young Children, 1971. This is a very explicit and useful guide for developing motor and verbal activities based on sequential learning. This guide moves from simpler to more complex activities and is cast in term of Piagetian theory. It contains many illustrations of the way verbal learning should accompany participation and real experience.

Bilingual and Multidialectical Education

Hughes, M. M., and Sanchez, G. I. *Learning a new language.* Washington, D. C.: Association For Childhood Education International, 1957. This pamphlet was published far ahead of its time; its statements about bilingual children still ring true—a classic worth reading.

John, V. P., and Horner, V. M. *Early childhood bilingual education.* New York: Modern Languages Association of America, 1971. Since it is impossible to list all the resources available on this subject, I limit myself to listing this overview, which in turn contains many additional references. John and Horner describe many programs and list many sources of curriculum materials for children who speak Spanish or native American languages. The book concludes with an article on research in bilingual education.

Labov, W. The logic of nonstandard English. In F. Williams (Ed.), *Language and poverty,* Chicago: Markham Publishing Co., 1970. Labov provides a spirited analysis and defense of the strengths and values of the language used by children from urban ghetto areas. He makes a strong, documented attack on the theory that such youngsters are suffering from verbal deprivation. He attacks Bereiter and Jensen in particular. This chapter should be read by every person who works with children who come from families of the poor.

Smith, H. Standard or nonstandard: is there an answer? *Elementary English,* Feb. 1973, 225–234.

Smith, H. Black English: considerations and approaches. *The English Journal,* Feb. 1973, 311–318. In both of these publications Smith presents brief reviews of black English and then gives useful summaries of other research on this subject.

Disorders of Speech

Travis, L. E. *Handbook of speech pathology and audiology.* New York: Appleton-Century-Crofts, 1971. This hefty compendium of articles by many authoritative authors covers the entire field of speech and hearing disorders; it includes discussions of etiology and therapy—a comprehensive reference.

Van Riper, C. *Speech correction: principles and methods.* (5th ed.) Englewood Cliffs, N. J.: Prentice-Hall, Inc., 1972. This classic text is filled with countless suggestions of activities that may be used to correct a wide variety of speech problems. It is a practical book written with the beginning speech clinician in mind, but it is one that would also make a useful reference for teachers who wish to build language skills in children.

For the Advanced Student

Bernbaum, M. *Early language development: an abstract bibliography.* Urbana, Ill.: ERIC Clearinghouse on Early Childhood Education, 1971. Bernbaum briefly describes the subject content of research studies having to do with early language development; a good starting point for future research.

Bernbaum, M. *Early childhood programs for non–English speaking children.* Urbana, Ill.: ERIC Clearinghouse for Early Childhood Education, 1971. In this useful topical paper Bernbaum reviews research on bilingualism in question-and-answer form and then describes many different bilingual programs (for both Spanish and native Americans) and lists addresses for contacting these programs. The paper concludes with a description of various handbooks and bibliography.

Brown, R. *A first language: the early stages.* Cambridge, Mass.: Harvard University Press, 1973. Brown gives a highly technical description of the way very young children acquire speech using the principles of transformational grammar.

Cazden, C. B. *Child language and education.* New York: Holt, Rinehart and Winston, Inc., 1972. The student who wishes to learn more about the theoretical structure of language and how it develops would profit from reading this book. It presents research in clear, readable form; a valuable reference.

Cole, M., and Bruner, J. S. Preliminaries to a theory of cultural differences. In I. J. Gordon (Ed.), *Early childhood education: the seventy-first yearbook of the National Society for the Study of Education. Part II.* Chicago: University of Chicago Press, 1972. Cole and Bruner present a thoughtful analysis of the "deficit" hypothesis as compared with the "difference" hypothesis discussed in relation to mental and linguistic ability. They examine the question of what constitutes genuine competence in terms of the individual's own culture.

Ervin-Tripp, S. Language development. In L. W. Hoffman and M. L. Hoffman (Eds.), *Child development research.* Vol. 2. New York: Russell Sage Foundation, 1966. This careful review of research relating to the language development of children is technical but readable.

Los Niños Head Start

CHAPTER 16

Developing the cognitive aspects of the child's self

I sincerely believe that for the child . . . it is not half so important to *know* as to *feel*. If facts are the seeds that later produce knowledge and wisdom, then the emotions and the impressions of the senses are the fertile soil in which the seeds must grow. The years of early childhood are the time to prepare the soil. Once the emotions have been aroused—a sense of the beautiful, the excitement of the new and the unknown, a feeling of sympathy, pity, admiration or love—then we wish for knowledge about the object of our emotional response. Once found, it has lasting meaning. It is more important to pave the way for the child to want to know than to put him on a diet of facts he is not ready to assimilate.*

I have left the thinking and knowing aspect of the child's self until last for two reasons. First, cognitive learning prospers best when the child is physically healthy, emotionally stable, and socially competent; so it is logical to discuss these aspects first. In addition, cognition is so intertwined with creativity that it is obvious that these topics should be discussed together.

Second, working with the cognitive aspect of the child's self seems to bring out the worst in some teachers, and by putting this chapter toward the end of the book I hope that the reader may have absorbed enough of its basic philosophy to be armed against the tendency to reduce intellectual learning to a series of isolated activities and drills or to assume that the fundamental intent in developing cogni-

tive ability should be acceleration of the child to the point of precocity.

Rather than focussing intellectual learning on academic exercises or struggling to push adequately developing children beyond their peers, the student should realize that the real goal of cognitive development is giving each youngster ample opportunity to achieve performance standards that are reasonable and typical for his age. Such opportunities are helpful for all children, but they are vital for children from our lower socioeconomic groups, who tend to lag behind in this area. These youngsters need knowledgeable assistance so they can realize their true potential. In order for a child to achieve his full development, cognitive learning must be based on experience-centered, language-enhanced activities that add depth and richness to his thinking.

The subject is a complex one containing many aspects that must be considered. The first one discussed in this chapter is

---

*From Carson, R. *The sense of wonder.* New York: Harper & Row, Publishers, 1956.

the question of values and priorities—what the most important things are that the child should learn about learning. Next, three steps in constructing a cognitive curriculum are outlined. Then the special area of vertical curriculum is amplified in greater detail, first by a review of the contributions of Jean Piaget and J. P. Guilford to our understanding of mental ability and then by an analysis of six concept formation skills that are of particular importance to the developing child. The chapter concludes with a sample outline exemplifying a unit of a cognitive curriculum.

VALUES AND PRIORITIES OF COGNITIVE GOALS

The question of how to foster cognitive learning in the nursery school may be thought of as a question of determining priorities: it is often helpful to stop and compare the significance of various goals before deciding how to proceed. For example, is it more important that the child experience joy and verve when learning or that he be able to sit quietly and not interrupt the teacher? Is it more significant that he speak fluently and spontaneously, or is it more important that he speak

standard English sentences of a certain length?

It is not that any of the values listed above is reprehensible or should not receive attention when the teacher plans her cognitive curriculum; it is a question of deciding which goals should receive primary emphasis, because the teacher who elects to foster joy and verve is likely to employ a different teaching style from one who feels that quietly paying attention is vital to classroom success.

Thus we must begin by asking ourselves what are the most important things we want children to learn in the cognitive sphere; which goals should have first priority? Then we can go on to consider some additional points that are significant but secondary in value to those discussed below.

Priority I: Maintain the child's sense of wonder and curiosity

As nursery school teachers know, most children come to school wondering about many things. They want to know where the water goes when the toilet flushes, what it is like to go out in the rain, and when their mothers are coming to get them. The age of 4 is particularly appeal-

Los Niños Head Start

ing in this respect. Four-year-olds are able to look beyond the horizons of their close personal relationships and are ready to inquire about the larger world. As anyone who has read the Lois Lenski books to them will attest, 4-year-olds are avid gatherers of facts and are interested in everything. For this reason it is a delight to build a cognitive curriculum for them. But 3-year-olds are seeking and questioning also. They are more concerned with the manipulation of materials and with finding out what everyday things and people close to them are like. This kind of investigation, although different in focus from that of the 4-year-olds, may also be utilized to make a rich contribution to mental development.

The most obvious way to maintain the children's sense of curiosity is by encouraging them to continue to ask questions and helping them find out the answers. But underlying the teacher's willingness to encourage investigation lies something deeper: her ability to support the child's drive toward venturing and independence —to capitalize, in other words, on their passing through the stage of autonomy described by Erikson (1963). Autonomy and the willingness to venture flourishes best in a climate where there is a balance of reasonableness, choice, protection, spontaneity, moderate control, and challenge. Given both security and encouragement, the child feels he has a firm base from which to explore when the impulse moves him to do so.

Sometimes rather than sustaining and encouraging curiosity, the teacher finds it necessary to awaken it. This is best done gently by presenting materials that are fascinating and by modelling curiosity and wonder as well. Asking simple questions about cause and effect or wondering together what will happen next often captures the interest of unawakened children and starts them observing, wondering, and thinking for themselves. Thus the teacher might discuss with the children whether the mother rat will do anything to get ready for her babies now that she is growing so fat and full of them, or she might ask the children whether they think

it would be better to keep the ice in the sun or shade until time to make the ice cream. Given this kind of encouragement, children who have not done so will soon begin to question and wonder for themselves, and then the teacher can encourage them and lead them on to further investigation and thinking.

Priority II: Let cognitive learning be a source of genuine pleasure

If we agree with the behaviorists that people tend to repeat activity that is rewarded in some way, it follows that we should do everything in our power to attach pleasure to cognitive learning. We want children to want to think and learn, and they are more likely to continue do so if they experience pleasure while they are involved in learning (Wilson, Robeck, and Michael, 1969). Therefore, the second most important priority that we should consider when planning a cognitive curriculum is presenting it so that it is a genuine source of pleasure to the child. This can be accomplished in a number of ways.

Sustain interest by making curriculum content relevant. In these days of "relevant curriculum" it has become almost a truism to say that a good curriculum for any age is based on the student's interests and that it teaches him what he wants to know. A curriculum that does not accomplish this goal breeds disinterested, disatisfied learners, no matter how old they are. Yet even nursery school teachers often lay out a year's curriculum in advance formulated, at best, on knowledge of what other children in previous years have cared about. Thus a schedule will show that in September the school will be building experiences around the family, in December on holidays, and in the spring on baby animals. Although this approach has a certain value, the danger of such extremely long-range planning is that the teacher may become so tied to it that she is unable to respond to the interests of the children who are now in her nursery school room, thereby deadening some of their pleasure and motivation for learning. This does not mean that the curriculum will be completely unpredictable; it does mean that the subject matter should be drawn from the current interests of the group.

The teacher's responsibility is to use the children's interest in two ways: she supplies the children with information and vocabulary about subjects that matter to them, and she also employs the material as a medium for teaching a number of basic skills she feels they need to acquire. For example, almost any topic of interest to children, whether it be animal homes or changes in the weather, can be used to provide interesting facts, to foster proficiency in language, and supply opportunities to learn the concepts of grouping, arranging items in appropriate order, or learning about simple cause-and-effect relationships.

Keep it challenging. Although keeping the curriculum relevant to the child's expressed and discovered interests is the best way to help sustain his pleasure in learning, there are other ways to keep the experience satisfying and pleasureful for him. One way is by creating learning opportunities that are challenging but not so difficult that they are beyond the child's grasp. This does not mean that the child should be continually confronted with a fresh array of facts about fire engines as soon as he has finished investigating how animals eat. Rather, it means that the teacher understands how to move the curriculum from easy to more difficult as the year progresses so that the bright little 4-year-olds in her class are not bored by too much repetition at the same ability level all year. It also means that the teacher knows what level of learning can reasonably be expected at various developmental stages so that she expects neither too much nor too little.

Keep it real. Cognitive learning should be based on actual experience (Piaget and Inhelder, 1969), a point I shall not belabor further, since I have discussed it a number of times in earlier chapters.

Keep it brief and unstressful. The episodes should be brief enough that the children do not feel strained from working too long. It is always better to stop before stress and boredom set in, since stopping at the right moment makes it more likely that the child will want to return the next time.

The teacher must learn to recognize common signs of stress in children because these behaviors are an indication that it is past time to stop or that the activity needs to be modified to a more attractive and appropriate level. Common signs of stress include thumb sucking, wiggling, inattention, restlessness, hair twisting, constantly trying to change the subject, asking to leave or just departing, picking fights, and creating disturbances.

Enjoy the experience with the children. The final way to sustain the child's pleasure in learning is to enjoy it with him. Cognitive learning does not have to be a sober-sided, no-nonsense business. It is a fine place for one-to-one experiences that include humor and fun when the teacher enjoys the activity along with the children. The teacher who is able to share her joy in learning with the youngsters in her care makes a valuable contribution to their satisfaction.

Priority III: Bind cognitive learning to affective experience whenever possible

Other emotions in addition to pleasure are bound to be involved in cognitive learning, since such learning does not take place in an emotional vacuum. For this reason the curriculum outline at the end of this chapter begins with suggestions for developing affective components because feelings and social experience should be a fundamental part of cognitive learning. Good education recognizes, accepts, and deals with feelings as they arise; it does not ignore them or push them aside until later because now it is time to learn about baby animals or study the weather. The same principle holds true for social skills. Many opportunities for understanding and getting along with others will arise during experiences that are primarily intellectual—these moments should be capitalized on as they occur.

Priority IV: Accompany cognitive learning with language whenever possible

The word *accompany* is crucial here because language should be part of rather than precede cognitive learning. One of the commonest errors of beginning teachers seems to be that they forget this principle when they approach cognitive development, and the first thing they do is begin a new experience with a formal discussion. As noted in the chapter on creative thought, a discussion about growing things is largely worthless for children who need to have experience with real beans and earth and water and sunlight before they can talk meaningfully about how plants develop.

On the other hand, mere experience has also been shown to be insufficient (Blank and Solomon, 1968, 1969). The teacher plays a vital role in concept and mental development because it is she who blends language with experience, adding a word that the children cannot supply themselves or asking a thought-provoking question that leads them to think something through more clearly. It is this deliberate interweaving that enriches the meaning of both experience and language for young children and increases the likelihood of mental activity and development.

Priority V: Develop concept formation abilities in addition to teaching facts and names for things

As a study of the questions asked by teachers substantiates (Zimmerman and Bergan, 1971), even in the early grades many teachers still see their role as that of fact provider and extractor. But with factual knowledge increasing at a phenomenal rate, it appears that learning time is better spent on developing underlying concept formation abilities and processes for dealing with facts rather than emphasizing mainly facts themselves.

In the past the problem with developing these abilities in children was that teachers felt unsure of what the processes involved. Since they were uncertain, they tended to teach colors and names of shapes because they knew that at least children could pass certain tests if they possessed this particular information. Thanks to such men as Piaget and Guilford, however, we are now beginning to

have a more adequate grasp of what some of these concept formation skills are; therefore, the task of building a cognitive curriculum is not as difficult or mysterious as we once surmised.

CONSTRUCTION OF A COGNITIVE CURRICULUM

Developing a cognitive curriculum that meets the priorities discussed above requires a great deal of flexibility and open-mindedness on the part of the teacher. Because of this, inexperienced teachers sometimes assume that flexibility also means that planning is either unnecessary or undesirable. Actually, the reverse is true. Implementing these priorities requires that the teacher have a clear idea not only of her goals but of how to reach them as well. Planning, then, is crucial to success. The remainder of this chapter provides an explanation of how to plan a good cognitive curriculum.

Three steps in the construction of a cognitive curriculum have to be considered and included if the model is to be maximally effective. The first is the utilization of spontaneous contributions and interest that come from the children. The second is the horizontal expansion of their interest through the provision of additional information and experience, and the third is the development of a vertical curriculum that provides opportunities for the practice of certain concept formation abilities that we believe underlie later intellectual competence.

Spontaneous curriculum

When developing a spontaneous curriculum, the teacher takes whatever comes to hand and builds experiences around it. Thus if a child brings a grasshopper to school, the teacher may draw on her picture file, poetry box, and book shelf to provide learning supplements based on this fortuitous circumstance. If one of the children digs a rusty cup out of the sandbox, the teacher may help the children plan a series of experiments to find out what rusts and what doesn't.

The advantages of building curriculum this way are numerous: the curriculum

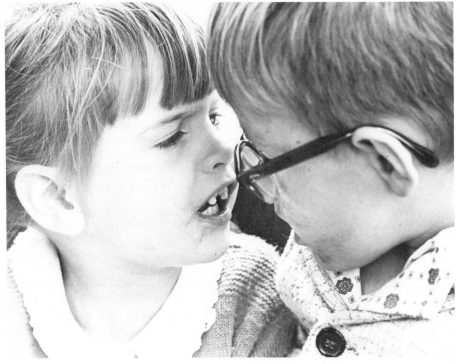

Photo by Gene Garrett
Los Niños Head Start

will certainly be relevant, since it stems from the children's interests; using the children's ideas enhances individual children's feelings of being valued and important; it often includes the home in school activities; and its spontaneity adds desirable freshness and interest to the day.

The danger is that excessive reliance on a spur-of-the-moment curriculum may result in the children's gaining only small pepperings of factual knowledge on a multitude of subjects but lacking an overall sense of integration and direction in what they learn. In addition, it may mean that some valuable opportunities for practice of more specific conceptual abilities are not provided, since the fortuitous nature of these curriculum "happenings" makes advance planning impossible and since improvisation in vertical curriculum development is difficult for all but the most experienced teacher.

Despite these dangers, there remains a definite and important place for welcoming spontaneous interests as they well up from the children, although a spontaneous curriculum is insufficient to use by itself.

Horizontal curriculum

Many teachers do go beyond the hunt-and-peck method of curriculum building and also seek to develop a thread of continuity. They usually accomplish this by selecting a topic and gradually enriching it by offering more and more experiences related to it, like dropping a stone into water and having concentric rings of experience radiate from the center.

Thus if the children are studying birds, many different experiences involving every avenue of the senses are provided. These might include hatching out a chicken, making suet bird feeders, bringing in old nests to examine, eating hard-boiled eggs, raising a baby duck, keeping parakeets, or visiting an aviary—the list of possibilities is endless. These experiences are typically accompanied by language that identifies and labels different aspects of the experience. For example, the children may learn a number of words, such as *feathers, wings, hatch, droppings, sea gulls,* and *robins.* Many schools also add books, songs, pictures, and poetry, which widens the experience and, happily, encourages the use of symbolic representation as well.

This horizontal curriculum, therefore, provides the children with an excellent opportunity for reality-based experiences about what birds are actually like. This kind of learning is indispensable, as anyone who has ever felt the underside of a setting hen knows. Words alone can never equal the adventure of slipping a hand between the eggs and the warm softness of that irritable chicken.

Additional advantages to this broadening development of subject matter include the fact that the teacher can select the next experience in accordance with the children's interest as it develops from the previous one. For example, she might go on to investigate things that fly by visiting the airport, building kites, and blowing up balloons with some youngsters or by visiting the mynah bird at the zoo and inviting a parrot to school for other children who have become interested in how birds talk. Thus a horizontal curriculum is relevant to the real interests of the children (unless the teacher becomes carried away with her own interests and enthusiasm and loses sight of their concerns), is based on actual experience, results in the acquisition of facts and information, can be used to develop language ability, and is also satisfying to the teacher because it draws on her own creative powers to present experiences that are attractive, integrated, and various.

With all these strong values, it is easy to understand why many nursery school teachers stop at this point and do not go on to the third step of curriculum construction, which has to do with fostering more esoteric conceptual abilities. But children need more than the opportunity to acquire the rich experience and vocabulary that a horizontal curriculum provides; they also need the chance to do some thinking. For this reason, the third

aspect of curriculum development should not be overlooked.

Vertical curriculum

The third step in curriculum development is termed *vertical* because it builds on the experience provided by horizontal development and uses its factual content as a medium for practicing thinking skills. For instance, while learning about birds the teacher could develop the concept of grouping by providing opportunities for sorting pictures or models of birds into various categories as well as by asking the children, "How do we know these things are birds? Are airplanes birds? Are kites birds? Are robins birds?" She might use the hatching of baby chickens to develop the children's ability to arrange events according to their occurence in time, or she could help the children understand cause and effect by comparing a raw egg with one they have boiled.

The inclusion of this kind of learning opportunity requires careful planning by the teacher, and this rests in turn on a clear knowledge of what she is doing and what conceptual skills she is seeking to enhance. It also requires that she participate actively with the children, since it is not only necessary to develop learning materials but also essential to talk with the children while they are using the materials and to ask them questions that encourage them to think. Children of nursery school age need this assistance in order to focus clearly on the task at hand.

Summary

There are, then, three steps in building a cognitive curriculum for preschool children. The first, which is most *spontaneous,* depends on what happens from day to day in the school and capitalizes on these teachable moments in a valuable way. The second, which seeks to link these related experiences together and expand them in a *horizontal* way, increases the richness of background and adds information to the child's repertoire. The third, *vertical* curriculum, employs the horizontal content as the medium for developing and generalizing important concepts that underlie later, more advanced thinking abilities. A well-rounded cognitive curriculum requires that the teacher appreciate and include all three of these aspects of curriculum development when she plans her educational program.

FURTHER COMMENTS ON THE DEVELOPMENT OF A VERTICAL CURRICULUM

Since the vertical step in curriculum construction is the most poorly understood of the three, the remainder of this chapter concentrates on this aspect. However, the reader should bear in mind that, although important, the following material is only one of three steps in such planning.

Contributions of Jean Piaget

Although it is not within the scope of this book to attempt a comprehensive summary of his work, any discussion of the thought processes of young children must begin with at least a brief review of the work of Jean Piaget, since he has devoted a lifetime to studying the mental development and characteristics of young children (Piaget, 1926, 1930, 1950, 1962, 1963, 1965; Piaget and Inhelder, 1967, 1969).

Although Piaget has been criticized on such grounds as inconsistency of theory, obscure terminology, and poor scientific rigor, there is little doubt that despite these weaknesses he has made many significant contributions to our understanding of the growth of children's mental abilities. Among these contributions is the idea that mental development is a dynamic process that results from the interaction of the child with his environment and that it is also the product of interaction among maturation, experience, socialization, and equilibration. Although his own areas of investigation have been primarily in the cognitive area, Piaget maintains that af-

Table 8. Summary of the Piaget model

Basic stages	Behavior commonly associated with the stage
Sensorimotor stage (0-2 years)	Composed of six substages that move from reflex to intentional activity involving cause-effect behavior
Understanding the present and real	Involves direct interactions with the environment
Preoperational stage (2-7 years)	Child uses signifiers: mental images, imitation, symbolic play, drawing, language
Symbolic representation of the present and real	Understands verbal communication
Preparation for understanding concrete operations	Believes what he sees—is "locked into" the perceptual world
	Sees things from his own point of view and only one way at a time ("centering")
	Thinking is *not* reversible
	Busy laying foundations for understanding concrete operations stage, which involves grasping concepts of conservation, transitivity, classification, seriation, and reversibility
Concrete operations (7-11 years) Organization of concrete operations	Has probably acquired the following concepts: conservation, reversibility, transitivity, seriation, and classification; that is, now believes that length, mass, weight, and number remain constant; understands relational terms such as "larger than" and "smaller than"; is able to arrange items in order from greatest amount to least amount; can group things according to more than one principle
Formal operations (11-15 years)	Age of abstract thinking
Hypothesis making	Able to consider alternative possibilities and solutions
Testing the possible	Can consider "fanciful," hypothetical possibilities as a basis for theoretical problem solving

fective, social, and cognitive components go hand in hand (Piaget and Inhelder, 1969). Since these components are interdependent, it is evident that a school where good mental health policies are practiced and where sound social learning is encouraged will also be one where mental growth is more likely to occur (Kamii, 1972).

Piaget sees growth as progressing in an orderly manner through a series of predictable, observable stages. He has demonstrated that children's thought processes differ in kind from those of adults in certain characteristic ways at particular points. For example, in the preoperational stage, which is typical of most children attending nursery school, youngsters are likely to be deceived by appearance and believe that a taller jar contains more water than a squat jar does, even though they have previously seen that the quantity of water in both containers is equal. At this stage, also, children may have difficulty shifting objects into more than one kind of category (sorting according to size and then to color, for example), taking two attributes into account at once (sorting pink circles and pink squares, blue circles and blue squares into separate categories), or arranging a long series of graduated cylinders in regularly ascending order. Adults, however, no longer have difficulty grasping these concepts.

Piaget also believes that certain mental abilities underlie the logical thought processes characteristic of older children and adults. According to Kamii (1972) these primary abilities include classification (which I refer to as *grouping,* since true Piagetian classification applies to children of elementary school age), seriation (ordering things according to their relative dimensions), structuring of time and space (which is, in part, a form of temporal ordering), social knowledge (knowledge of accepted conventional ways to behave), and representation (using a symbol to represent an actual object or activity). He maintains that children use language and play to represent reality. For this reason he emphasizes the value of play and extolls it as a basic ave-

nue through which children learn. Finally, he stresses the importance of actual manipulation of materials and concrete experience as a medium of learning, particularly for preschool children (Piaget, 1962).

Many of Piaget's ideas are bound to sound both familiar and comfortable to the contemporary student, since a good deal of what he has been saying for 50 years has been practiced in nursery schools during the same period and is similar in part to the philosophy of John Dewey and Maria Montessori. For a variety of reasons, however, his work passed largely unnoticed in the United States until the 1960's, and it is only in the past few years that it has been deliberately implemented in the classroom by such investigators as Almy (Almy, Chittenden, and Miller, 1966), Kamii (1972), Lavatelli (1970), and Weikart (Weikart, Rogers, Adcock, and McClelland, 1971).

At present, it appears that in addition to his general theoretical ideas, his identification of significant cognitive concepts and the steps by which they develop may be the most helpful contribution he has made to our understanding of the cognitive self. It is this understanding that makes possible the generation of a curriculum for stimulating the growth of cognitive abilities.

Contributions of J. P. Guilford

Another classification of mental abilities is less well known to nursery school teachers but is also helpful to use when building curriculum, since it includes descriptions of additional mental abilities. This is the Structure of Intellect developed by J. P. Guilford (1967). It can be visualized as a three-dimensional cube that represents 180 abilities divided into three primary categories: operations, contents, and products. Each ability consists of one item taken from each of these categories. (See Appendix E for a more detailed explanation.)

Although the language that describes the mental abilities is somewhat difficult for a novice to grasp, the serious student should make the effort to become ac-

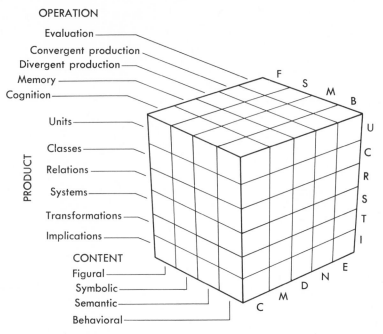

Model of the Structure of Intellect. (From Guilford, J. P. *The nature of human intelligence.* New York, © 1967, McGraw-Hill, Inc. Used with permission of McGraw-Hill, Inc.)

quainted with the Structure of Intellect (SOI) model in addition to Piagetian theory because the SOI enumerates and defines many more abilities than Piaget's theories do. For example, one large area of the SOI is concerned with divergent thinking and with transformations—concepts that were discussed at length in the chapter on fostering creativity in thought. Another emphasis of the SOI lies in the area of memory, which plays a significant role in the thinking processes expected of children in elementary and high school.

Since Guilford's work on mental ability is based primarily on research carried out with young adults, evidence is not always available that similar abilities exist in very young children. Nor does Guilford discuss the steps by which such abilities develop. However, the particular SOI abilities selected for discussion in the following pages have been shown to be present in tests that were carried out with preschool children and analyzed in terms of Guilford's theory (Orpet and Meyers, 1966; Sitkei and Meyers, 1969; Stott and

Ball, 1965); so we are on fairly firm ground as far as these particular conceptual skills are concerned.

Selection of concept formation abilities

Although there are numerous differences between the theoretical approaches of Guilford and Piaget, which need not concern us here, an examination of their work reveals the existence of some conceptual abilities identified by them both. These include *grouping* (Piaget, grouping and classification; Guilford, cognition and evaluation of semantic and figural classes), *ordering* (Piaget, seriation; Guilford, cognition and evaluation of semantic and figural systems), *perception of common relationships between items* (Piaget, one-to-one correspondence; Guilford, cognition and evaluation of figural and semantic relations), and *cause and effect* (Piaget, causality; Guilford, cognition and evaluation of figural and semantic implications). In addition to these concepts, the following sections also include a discussion of how to provide opportunities for children to understand the Piagetian principle of *conservation* and *matching of identical items* (Guilford, cognition and evaluation of figural and semantic units). These abilities are included because it appears likely that they will be useful to the child when he enters elementary school.

Concept formation abilities that should be included in a vertical curriculum

Grouping. I use the word *grouping* here in place of *classification* to remind the reader that we are discussing an elementary form of the more sophisticated skill described by Piaget (1965) wherein older children can form hierarchical classes and/or classify items according to a number of properties at the same time. Preschool children perform at a simpler level than classification, but 4- and 5-year-olds in particular are able to sort objects or pictures into categories that are meaningful to them. Such activities range from placing doll house furniture into rooms according to their function (kitchen equipment in the kitchen, for example) to sorting shells according to whether they are clams or mussels or pectins, rough or smooth, large or small. Teachers encourage categorizing every time they ask children "Are airplanes birds? Why not?" or say "Show me all the buttons that belong together." In these instances the child is being asked to determine what it is that various items have in common—to determine the common property that defines the class—and then he is usually expected to decide whether an additional item also possesses this property and can be included.

In essence, there are three ways to present such material. First, the child can be confronted with an assembled group and asked to choose additional things to add to it (perhaps it is pictures of clothing such as a sweater, dress, and shirt, and the additional pictures might be a doll, a pair of pants, and an ice cream cone). Second, he can be presented with an assembled group and asked to remove items that do not belong ("Everyone who isn't wearing a plaid shirt, sit down."). Finally, he

Photo by Jason Lo'Cicero
Santa Barbara City College Children's Center

can be given a melange of articles or pictures and asked to sort them according to whatever criteria he establishes. This third kind of presentation permits more divergent thinking than the first two do and has the additional advantage of making regrouping according to different criteria more feasible.

Four-year-olds are rarely able to put their reasons for forming such groups into words at the beginning of the learning experience, although they can indicate by the sorting activity itself that they do perceive common properties. At our Center we have found that many of them gradually learn to explain why particular items go together as they practice throughout the year (Hendrick, 1973). Thus a child who is inarticulate in the fall may by spring put a toy frog, turtle, and salamander together and be able to tell us that he did this because they all like water.

Although many children will at first be unable to put the reason for grouping particular things together into words, the category may be obvious to the onlooker. If a child is unable to formulate a reply after he has assembled a group, the teacher can help by saying, "Hmmm, it looks to me as though you are putting all of the red ones here and the blue ones here. Is that what you're doing?" This assists the child in translating his actions into words.

It is wise to encourage the child to determine the categories for himself whenever possible. If the teacher hands him a box of little animals and tells the child to "pick out all the red ones" or to "pick out all the ones we saw at the zoo," she has done most of the thinking for him before he goes to work. But if she says, "Show me which ones you think belong together," and follows this with, "Why do they go together," he must do more of the thinking for himself.

Piaget has noted that younger children will change categories as they sort. This is a natural phenomenon and does not mean they are unintelligent. Maturation combined with opportunities to practice and talk about grouping will help the children learn to maintain consistent criteria.

Occasionally teachers become confused and attempt to teach grouping by using identical items for this purpose. Although being able to pick out things that are exactly the same and to tell them apart from those that are different is a useful prereading skill, it is not grouping; it is simple matching. In order to teach grouping it is necessary to use materials that possess common properties but are not identical.

The easiest form of grouping is sorting that requires simple responses to a prominent sensory quality such as color (Lavatelli, 1970ab). Some children at nursery school will need to begin at this level, but this is only the beginning. The task may be made more difficult by asking the children to think of a way the materials can be regrouped, by using more complex materials, by increasing the emphasis on verbalization, or by asking them to group materials according to several properties at the same time. There are several examples of grouping activities included in the curriculum outline at the end of this chapter, and the reader may wish to refer to

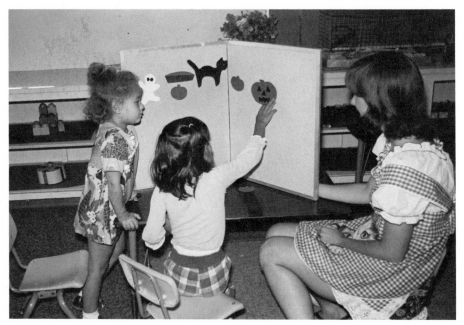

Photo by Jason Lo'Cicero
Santa Barbara City College Children's Center

them in order to see how such experiences may be worked into the ongoing nursery school curriculum.

Ordering. Ordering means arranging objects or events in logical order. The two kinds of ordering that appear to be most useful are arranging a variety of items according to a graduated scale (Piaget's *seriation*) and arranging events as they occur in time. The basic question that the child must be able to answer when dealing with either of these concepts is "What comes next?"

There are many interesting activities that require a child to answer this question and to infer the logical order of either a spatial or temporal series. For example, almost any kind of item that comes in graduated sizes may be used for the purpose of teaching spatial, or seriated, ordering: various sizes of bolts and nuts, measuring cups, measuring spoons, nested mixing bowls, and empty tin cans of assorted sizes. There are also many commercial materials made for the purpose of practicing seriation. Montessori cylinders are excellent for this purpose, and an examination of equipment catalogs will reveal many additional possibilities, ranging from nesting blocks to flannel board materials. Hardwood blocks, of course, present classic opportunities for becoming acquainted with the relationship between their varying lengths as well as for studying the regular relationships of equivalency that occur in block construction, since blocks may vary in length but have the same width and depth.

I also favor including variations on seriation that teach gradations in quality. Grades of sandpaper can be provided so that children have opportunities to arrange them in order from rough to smooth; flavors can be provided that range from sweet to sour; and tone bells can be arranged from high to low.

The easiest kinds of seriation problems are ones where the youngster is asked to choose which items should be added to a chain of two or three in order to continue an upward or downward trend (Siegel, 1972). Very young children often grasp this principle well if it is presented in terms of, "This is the daddy, and this is the mother, and now show me what comes next." The activity may be made more difficult by increasing the number of objects to be arranged, and even more difficult by asking the child to arrange a series and then giving him one or two items that must be inserted somewhere in the middle to make the series more complete. Finally, the challenge can be increased even more by asking the child to arrange two sets of objects in corresponding order or, more difficult yet, in contrasting order. Nuts and bolts make particularly nice items to use for this purpose, as do padlocks with various sized keys and paper dolls with appropriately sized clothing.

Recalling or anticipating the order of events as they occur in time is called temporal ordering. A child can be asked to recount the order in which he got up that morning: "First you got up, and then you went to the bathroom, and then . . ." Flannel board stories are another fine way to help children visualize the order in which things happen, and some social occasions also make excellent topics for discussion and pictures. Birthday parties, for example, often run quite true to form: first the guests arrive, then the birthday child opens his presents, and so forth. Recipes, also, can be set out with the ingredients arranged in the order in which they will be needed. Many of these orderly events can be played through as well as discussed—recapitulation through play is a most valuable way to rehearse the order in which events take place. Growth sequences based on human, plant, and animal development fit in here very naturally as a topic for study, as does the excellent series of sequenced puzzles that are generally available.

Although even 2-year-olds are keenly aware of the order in which daily events occur and are sticklers for maintaining that order, as many a mother will attest, older preschoolers need continuing practice with this concept. The level of difficulty for these more sophisticated children can be increased by adding more episodes to each event, asking the child to arrange a series of pictures and then to interpolate additional ones after the series has been formulated, asking him to arrange the events in reverse, or asking a child to consider what might happen if something occurred out of order ("What if you got in the bathtub and then took your clothes off?" To which one child replied, "Nothing—as long as I don't turn the water on!")

Conserving. Perhaps no mental ability has come under more investigation in recent years than the ability to conserve quantity (Reese and Lipsitt, 1970). When a child possesses this ability, he is able to recognize that the amount of the substance remains the same despite changes in its appearance. When he is too young to be able to conserve (typically before age 6 or 7), the child is deceived by appearances into reasoning that the quantity has increased or decreased because a change in shape has made the material look like more or less. For instance, two glasses of water that have been judged equivalent will then be judged unequal when one is poured into a squat, low dish and another into a tall, thin cylinder, and the two are compared again; or two balls of clay previously demonstrated to be the same amount will be judged different in quantity when one has been mashed flat or divided into many little balls.

Considerable interest has centered on the question of whether children can be taught this skill before the time they would typically acquire it, but the findings have been mixed and appear to be affected by a number of factors. For example, Inhelder (1968) reports that the amount children improve in their ability to conserve is always related to their prior level of development, and Bruner (1966) reports that modifying the way materials are presented affects the children's answers to conservation problems. Following a review of the literature, Reese and Lipsitt (1970) conclude that it is still too early to make any general statements about how teachable this Piagetian task may be. Generally, it appears that children who are on the verge of comprehending conservation may be pushed on to the

next step in this process if they receive adequate instruction.

Acceleration, however, is less important than making sure the child has ample opportunity to develop richly and fully at every level as he passes through it. This opportunity is particularly significant for children who come from lower socioeconomic levels, since evidence is mounting that such youngsters often lag behind their middle-class peers in developing such abilities (Almy, Chittenden, and Miller, 1966; Sigel and McBane, 1967) and that additional experience and opportunities to practice may help them catch up.

Therefore, the nursery school teacher should see to it that the children in her group have many occasions to try out and experiment with the results of pouring liquids back and forth into various-shaped containers in order to learn that shape does not alter quantity. Blocks present outstanding opportunities to demonstrate conservation of mass, since it is relatively simple to see that a tower of four contains the same number of units as does a two-by-two stack. Clay and dough also lend themselves well to teaching this concept. In short, any material, whether liquid or solid, that can be divided and put together again may be used to investigate the principle of conservation.

It is also worthwhile to provide opportunities for measuring in order to demonstrate equality or inequality. Scales are useful in this regard, and yardsticks and measuring tapes are also valuable. However, the teacher must realize that despite these aids, children who are unable to grasp the principle of conservation will continue to insist that what their eyes tell them to be true *is* true.

The teacher's role in this area lies in providing many opportunities for the children to manipulate materials and experiment with changing their forms and with returning them to their prior state (reversing the reaction). In addition to supplying experiences, she should make a point of talking with the children and drawing their attention to the unchanging nature of quantity as they manipulate the materials. This is also an excellent time to build related vocabulary, such as *more than, less than,* and *equal to.* Finally, besides talking with the children herself, the teacher should foster discussion and "argument" among the children about the nature of conservation, since research (Murray, 1972; Smedslund, 1966) supports Piaget's (1926) contention that such interaction between children will help them decenter and also help them reach correct conclusions.

It is unlikely that children of prekindergarten age will do more than begin to grasp the principle of conservation, but it may be of interest to know how problems could be increased in difficulty should they do so. Conservation problems can be made more difficult by making the contrasts in form more extreme; that is, by making the cylinder taller and thinner or the balls of clay more numerous. (This principle is easy to remember if the reader recalls that even adults can be seduced into believing that tall, thin cereal boxes are a better buy than thick, squat ones of the same weight.) The more pronounced the apparent contrast is between the two quantities, the more likely it is that the child will be misled by appearance and forget that the quantity is actually equal.

Perceiving common relations. The basic skill required in developing this concept is the ability to identify and pair items that are usually associated together. The activity of perceiving common relations is similar to grouping because it depends on the identification of a common property or bond; it differs from grouping because it involves pairing such items rather than working with larger numbers of them. It is useful to cultivate because it probably forms the basis for the later understanding and formulation of analogies (ring is to finger as belt is to—waist, buckle, or sash?). Since these combinations are usually culturally based (salt and pepper, shoes and socks, hat and head), it is very important to know the home backgrounds of the children in order to develop pairs that are likely to be familiar to them.

Opposites can also be included in this activity, since there is also a true relationship between them. Thus, hot can be contrasted with cold, up with down, and thick with thin.

We have found that 3- and 4-year-olds enjoy practicing this conceptual task a great deal. It has the kind of appeal that riddles generally have, and the children relish pairing up an assortment of items that are either presented all together in a box or in more gamelike form where several items are set out and their related members are drawn out of a bag one by one. There are some commercial materials on the market that are useful, such as two-piece puzzles linking animals with their homes or occupations with appropriate tools. It is also helpful to acquire many pairs of real objects or models of them that belong together and to keep a reserve of these handy to be brought out from time to time for the fun of it.

When the teacher is working with these combinations, it is usually effective for her to ask the child to pick out the thing that *goes most closely* with a selected item or that *belongs best* with it. This is language that the children understand and that is clear enough for them to be able to follow the direction.

Perceiving common relations may be made more difficult by including less familiar combinations, by increasing the number of choices, or by setting up true analogies in which the child has to ascertain the quality common to both pairs of items.

Matching. Matching is the ability to perceive that two items are identical, and it depends on the child's grasping the concept of sameness and differentness. At our Center we have found that this is one of the easier concepts for young children to acquire. Even 2- and 3-year-olds will work at this occupation with interest and diligence if the materials are attractive and not too detailed.

Many commercial materials are available that may be used to provide practice in matching. These range from simple, obvious pictures with few details to quite elaborate discrimination tasks that contain a great deal of detail and very subtle differences. Lotto and Bingo games are

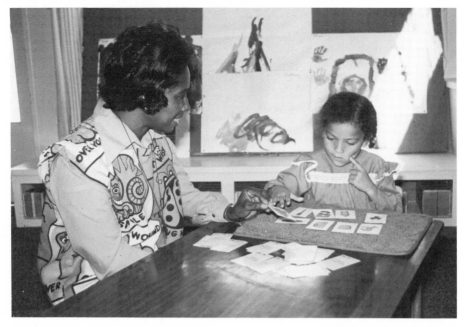

Photo by Jason Lo'Cicero
Santa Barbara City College Children's Center

probably the most prevalent examples of such materials. But matching should not be limited to these kinds of activities. Younger children can grasp this concept by matching buttons (a perennial favorite), matching animal stamps or Christmas stickers, or playing simple picture dominoes. Fabric swatches and wallpaper samples are fun to use for this purpose, too, and can be surprisingly difficult.

Matching experiences need not be limited to the sense of vision, of course. Children will also enjoy matching by touch (for texture and thickness), by hearing (duplicating simple sounds, rhythms, or melodies), or by taste and smell (it is interesting to cut up a variety of white fruits and vegetables, for instance, and ask the children to taste bits of them and find the ones that are the same). Imitation can also be thought of as an attempt to match actions; shadow or mirror dancing, follow-the-leader, and Simon-says may be employed for this purpose.

When asking children to complete a match, the teacher should use sentences such as "Show me the one that matches" or "Find me one that's just the same"

rather than, "Show me two that are just alike," since an occasional child is misled by the term *alike* and will blithely select something to show the teacher, saying, "Here, I like this one best!" Once he has acquired this verbal misconception of what the teacher means, it can be difficult to get him to change his mind; so talking about *same* rather than *alike* is the more effective choice of language.

As the child becomes more skilled, matching tasks may be increased in difficulty by making the matches more complex and difficult to analyze. This is usually accomplished by increasing the number of details that must be inspected in each picture and also by increasing the number of items to be compared. Ultimately, the material shifts from depending on pictorially meaningful content to more symbolic form; this leads, finally, to using the symbols of the alphabet and numbers.

Understanding the relationship between simple cause and effect. Although it takes children a long time to develop clear ideas of physical causality (Piaget, 1930), they can begin to acquire this concept while attending nursery school. Indeed, good discipline often depends on teaching exactly this kind of relationship between action and outcome, since letting the punishment fit the crime usually results in allowing the child to experience the logical consequence of his behavior. Thus the child who pulls all the blocks off the shelf is expected to help restack them, and the youngster who dumps his milk on the table must get the sponge and wipe it up himself.

In addition to understanding cause and effect in social consequences, 4-year-olds can often handle cause-related questions that are phrased, "What would happen if . . . ?" (Kamii, 1972) or "What do you think made [something happen]?" These questions are sound to use because they do not require the child to apply or explain scientific principles that lie beyond his ken, but depend instead on what he can see happen with his own eyes or on what he can deduce from his own experience. Some examples of successful questions are:

1. What will happen if we add some sugar to the dough?
2. What will happen to your shoes if you go out in the rain without your boots on?
3. How come John dropped the hot pan so quickly?
4. What made the kittens mew when mama cat got up?
5. What made the egg get hard?

Finding the answer to these questions can be accomplished by setting up simple experiments to identify the most probable cause. These experiments enable the children to try out suggested causes, compare results, and then draw conclusions about the most likely reason for something's happening, thereby introducing them to the scientific method. For example, in order to determine if it is boiling water or just water itself that makes the egg hard, the children can test both possibilities by poaching one egg in water and the other in water heated on the stove. Four-year-olds in particular enjoy carrying out this kind of investigation, although they will need help figuring out how to set up the experiment.

Teaching about simple cause-and-effect relations presents one of the most interesting educational opportunities available to the nursery school teacher, and both natural history and physical science offer rich possibilities that can be used for this purpose. For this reason, several references on science for young children are listed at the end of this chapter.

Provision of opportunities for practicing concept formation skills

Develop needed materials. There are two ways to obtain materials to use for teaching these concept formation tasks. The easiest, most expensive, and most obvious way is to rely on commercially developed tabletop activities. There are many such materials available, particularly in the area of matching and seriation. The trouble with them is that they often do not relate closely to curriculum topics, and they generally use only pictures as the medium of instruction. (Montessori materials are a welcome exception to this trend.)

The second way to introduce opportunities for this kind of concept development is to embed them directly in the curriculum. This is likely to be more work for the teacher, who will have to develop materials for the children's use, but it is also more satisfying because it gives her a chance to be creative and to utilize a much wider variety of materials and activities. Best of all, teacher-developed experiences mean that vertical activities can be directly related to and coordinated with the subjects that have interested the children. It is not very difficult to generate such ideas; the outline that follows this section provides an example of how this can be done using the subject of baby animals. Interested readers would also gain a good deal from studying *The Cognitively Oriented Curriculum* (Weikart, Rogers, Adcock and McClelland, 1971).

Although the curriculum-embedded approach is generally to be preferred, the more specifically designed tabletop activities have the advantage of being readily available and convenient and can be self-selected and monitored by the children. The danger that must be guarded against is offering only boxed activities for concept development. This results in too narrow and dull a presentation to be fully effective.

Provide consistent opportunities for practice. It is necessary to provide repeated opportunities for experience and practice (Hendrick, 1973). One or two chances to practice grouping, matching, or ordering are not sufficient. To understand these concepts fully, children need to practice them consistently, using many materials and moving from simpler to more difficult activities as their skills increase.

SAMPLE OUTLINE FOR DEVELOPING A UNIT OF COGNITIVE CURRICULUM

The difficulty with offering an outline of curriculum is that it may give the impression that the teacher planned it all before-hand and then simply dished it out to the children. This should never be the case. A curriculum must stem from the children's interests as these develop. The teacher capitalizes on these interests to provide (1) opportunities for emotional and social learnings, (2) information and vocabulary that she feels would be valuable for the child to possess, and (3) opportunities to practice various concept formation tasks. In addition, the reader should not conclude that all the activities listed below would be included in one curriculum. They are simply listed here to suggest a variety of approaches that might be utilized. The examples are suitable for children to use early in the year. Older children who have had considerable practice would be able to go on to more challenging activities.

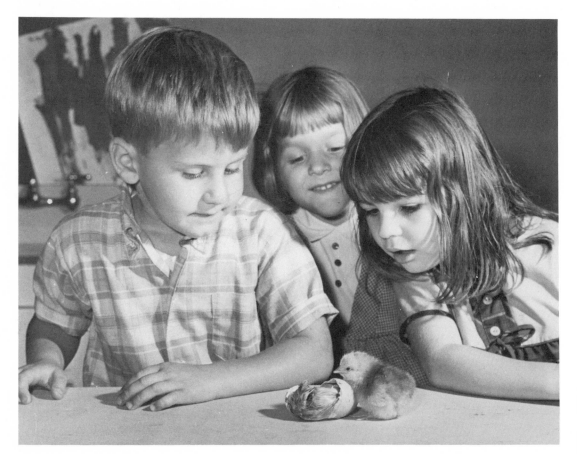

St. Andrew's Nursery School

A Curriculum Based on Baby Animals*

I. Affective components
  A. Possibilities related to the subject of baby animals that could be used to foster emotional health
    1. Child can relive own infancy by playing babies (either human or animal) and reliving and clarifying the relationship with the mother—dependency, weaning, and so forth; could use puppets, storytelling, and flannel boards for same purpose
    2. Play out feelings he has about arrival of a new baby in the family
    3. Overcome apprehension of certain animals by exposure to them during the study
    4. Experience feeling love for animals and witness love and caretaking by mother animals for their young
    5. Experience the satisfactions and burdens of responsibility, since caged animals must depend on the child for nourishment and care and since eggs will die if not turned regularly in the incubator
    6. Gain increased feelings of competence as a result of acquiring knowledge and skills related to this subject
    7. Learn self-control and restraint in handling delicate babies, perhaps will learn to decenter a little, imagine how it feels to the animals to have incautious humans handling such little beasts
    8. Experience with animals may offer opportunity to come to a better understanding of death, since often one or more of a litter dies
  B. Possibilities that could be used to encourage socialization
    1. Rich opportunities for social interaction among the children during field trips, animal care, and discussions; might include apportioning responsibilities for care, being considerate of mother animals and their babies by not creating undue disturbances, learning not to argue over an animal by pulling on him
    2. Child can learn basic elements of family relationships and social roles
    3. Can learn cooperation by helping other people and animals during caretaking experiences
    4. Share experiences with other children about animals they know outside of school and contribute to life of the group by bringing such animals from home for a visit
    5. Four-year-olds might contribute to animal's well-being and experience pleasure in meaningful work by constructing a simple cage; three-year-olds by preparing nesting materials; all by helping clean, feed, and perhaps exercise animals

II. Horizontal components dealing primarily with facts and information (The following items are stated in the form of educational objectives. Only a few have been selected for documentation here; the possibilities are numberless.)
  A. Child will be able to identify two ways babies are born: either live or hatched from eggs
    1. Breed animals at school and follow entire developmental process; rats, rabbits, pigeons, and guinea pigs ideal subjects
    2. Raise pigeons at school and also incubate chicken eggs
    3. Field trips to visit a sanguine mother cat and kittens, a mare and foal, and the bird sanctuary during hatching season
    4. Supplement actual experience with books, pictures, and poetry (Two good examples: Stevens,

---

*I am indebted to Virginia Tirado and Vilja Williams for many suggestions included in this outline.

C. *The birth of Sunset's kittens.* New York: Young Scott, 1969; McClosky, R. *Make way for ducklings.* New York: Viking Press, 1941)

B. Child will be able to explain role of mother animal in feeding, protecting, and cleaning her babies

1. Watch the mother cat nursing kittens and licking them, and discuss how the mother protects the kittens by hiding them from other animals and people; see how she replaces kitten if he is removed from box

2. Watch frog eggs develop and hatch; see if the mother takes care of them

3. Compare incubator-bred chickens and nursery school hens and chicks; see if chickens can get along without their mother

4. Observe and discuss ways these and other baby animals are fed; see whether all animals nurse

5. Use dramatic play and dance to express how it feels to be a baby animal or how it feels to be the mother

6. Analyze nesting materials of birds, mother rabbit, and compare substances they are made of; try building such nests ourselves

7. Supplement actual experience with books, pictures, stories, and poems

C. Child will be able to explain that human babies are also baby animals

1. Visit maternity ward (our city has one that is open to children) and observe how new babies act; compare with behavior of other animals to determine similarities

2. Have a mother come and nurse baby for children, also give baby bath, change diapers; compare with ways mother cat and dog care for their babies

3. Compare stages of pregnancy of human mothers and animals at school, using pictures and actual living resources where available

D. Additional possible horizontal goals

1. Child would become aware of likenesses and differences in the development and growth of baby animals after birth, and be able to discuss these processes

2. Child would be able to explain the basic facts of reproduction

3. Child would learn differences between mammals and other living things in a more formal way

III. Vertical components to provide practice in forming various mental concepts

A. Grouping (child will be able to identify the common properties that define a group and to discriminate between things that belong and things that do not belong)

1. Have pictures or models of baby animals, and ask children to sort them into those that are born live and those that are hatched from eggs

2. Ask children if these could be sorted in additional ways (they may think of such categories as large and small, mothers and babies, self-sufficient or dependent at birth); encourage them to talk about categories they have selected

3. Teacher may sort pictures into groups or pin up on the bulletin board pictures that belong to a particular group and ask children to guess and explain why some are in one group and some in another

4. Ask children if they can tell how younger babies are different from older babies, how they are the same; ask them to explain how human babies are the same and different from kittens and puppies

5. Talk about the names for groups of animals, such as litter of kit-

tens, nest of fledglings, and so forth

6. Set up groups that have an incorrect member and ask child to remove one that does not belong

B. Ordering (child is able to arrange a temporal series in logical order or to indicate what should come next in a series)

1. Ask children to retell the sequence of how the mother rat had her babies and how they changed as they developed

2. Start with an empty chart for each animal being raised or visited regularly by the children; take pictures or draw animals and develop a set that the children can arrange in order and talk about

3. Measure animals as they grow, record on same sheet of paper to indicate development

4. Collect baby pictures of the children; ask them how they acted as babies and how they behave now they are older; draw comparisons with behavior at present age

5. Use commercial sequence puzzles that illustrate hatching from an egg, developing from a cocoon, a baby growing up

6. Ask children to pretend with their own bodies how it feels to hatch from an egg or develop from being a baby to growing up and being a parent

7. Ask children to list order for animal care each day—what should be done first, what next, and so forth

C. Conserving (child will use materials that illustrate principle that quantity remains the same although appearance may change) (Experiences in conservation of quantity should be regularly available, but there seems to be no apropos way to link these to the study of baby animals. One might discuss whether living creatures can turn back into babies.)

D. Perceiving common relationships (child can indicate which objects are most closely related; that is, which belong together as a pair)

1. Offer mother-baby match-up pictures so that children can link babies with appropriate mothers

2. Associate correct adult name and baby name, such as duck-duckling, dog-puppy, cat-kitten

3. Play animal sounds and ask children to act out the animals that go with the sounds; then go on to talking about baby noises and adult noises, such as the cat's meow and kitten's mew

4. Stress that each animal reproduces its own kind—mother guinea pigs always have baby guinea pigs

E. Matching (child can identify two items that are identical)

1. Make a set of cards from rubber animal stamps, or duplicate clear line drawings of animals and glue them to felt backings for flannel board match-up games

2. Have two identical pictures of the same baby animal and cut one picture up as a puzzle, leaving the other whole; child can then match cut picture to whole picture

3. Use homemade lotto game of baby animals made from sets of animal stickers

4. Collect set of twin baby pictures and ask children to match pictures that are alike; compare identical and nonidentical twins at school

F. Learning cause and effect (child can identify probable cause of an event) (Reproduction, though not included as a goal here, is of course a classic example of cause and effect.)

1. Place some fertile eggs in incubator and leave others out of incubator for the same period of time; ask the children what they

think will happen to both sets of eggs; later, open eggs that did not hatch and ask if they changed; compare with incubator eggs and ask what caused the changes

    2. Talk over with the children what might happen if mother animals didn't lick their babies

    3. If any of the children has had a mother cat who moved her kittens, help the children think about what happened before she moved them; ask what caused her to move the kittens

    4. Talk about what happens if babies get hungry; experiment in a mild way with this, observing behavior of baby rats when mother is removed for half an hour; ask children if they know how human babies behave when they get hungry, what makes babies cry, why does the mother return

  G. Possibilities for divergent learning

    1. Provide many opportunities for the children to experience and express their individual impressions of what they are learning by means of dramatic play, self-expressive materials, storytelling, and so forth

    2. Rely whenever possible on the children to select the animals for study that are of particular interest to them

    3. Begin a story about a mother and baby and ask various children to finish it; ask if they can think of more than one way it might turn out

    4. Individualize curriculum so that children can pursue own questions and activities as they express an interest in them; for example, some children may especially want to work on building a bigger rabbit hutch, while others may be more interested in playing babies in the housekeeping corner

IV. Possibilities to continue as determined by the interests of the children

  A. Continue with learning about reproduction; ask where the babies came from in the first place

  B. Pursue the study of any particular animal that has caught the children's interest

  C. Learn about wild versus domesticated animals

  D. Learn about animals as compared with plants and move on to learn more about plants

  E. Investigate in greater depth the relationship between humans and other animals in terms of sequential growth, biological needs, stressing similarities and differences

  F. Visit the humane society, veterinary, and pet store and find out how animals obtain new homes

QUESTIONS AND ACTIVITIES

1. What are some of the pros and cons of stressing intellectual development at the preschool level? Can you suggest a model for such learning that you feel would have undesirable side effects?

2. Do you agree that pleasure should be the inevitable accompaniment to learning? Can you think of occasions where this has been true of your own educational experience and cases where it has not been true? Analyze the circumstances that made the learning pleasureful or burdensome.

3. Might it be possible that nursery school teachers are depriving children of the right to learn the things that would help them succeed best in elementary school when we stress play, creativity, and mental health rather than emphasizing prereading skills such as learning the alphabet and counting? What might be the case for placing greater emphasis on academic learning at the preschool level?

4. After viewing the Stendler-Karplus films on classification and conservation, try out some of the Piagetian tasks demonstrated in the films with children ranging in age from 3 to 8. Do your experiments bear out Piaget's contention that children pass through various stages of development in thinking?

5. Pick up on a current interest of the children in your group, and make an outline, based on the examples at the end of the chapter, that utilizes affective and cognitive learning

and incorporates both horizontal and vertical curriculum.

6. Concoct activities that fit the various mental abilities, such as ordering and grouping, and try them out with the children. Then add variations to the activities that make them easier or more difficult in order to suit the needs of individual children in the group. Set aside some shelves in your school where these materials can be accumulated.

7. Once you have acquired a fundamental understanding of these mental abilities, keep a record of ways you have been able to add spontaneous practice of them to your curriculum as the day develops, and discuss these activities with your curriculum class.

REFERENCES FOR FURTHER READING

Building Desirable Attitudes toward Learning

Ashton-Warner, S. *Teacher.* New York: Bantam Books, Inc., 1965. Sylvia Ashton-Warner gives an exciting description of the way she approached teaching and learning and made these activities truly relevant to the lives of her young Maori students.

Carson, R. *The sense of wonder.* New York: Harper & Row, Publishers, 1956. This is a beautifully written account concerned with generating a sense of wonder in young children. The outstanding illustrations in this volume, combined with the excellent text, make it a classic of natural history.

Understanding Piaget and Guilford

Since both Piaget and Guilford can be difficult reading for the uninitiated, it is best to begin with descriptive overviews of their work.

Beard, R. *An outline of Piaget's developmental psychology for students and teachers.* New York: The New American Library Inc., 1972. This is a brief, well-written summary of Piaget's major concepts presented in chronological order from infancy through adolescence; excellent, clear, unpretentious handling of potentially obscure material.

Brearley, M., and Hitchfield, E. *A guide to reading Piaget.* New York: Schocken Books Inc., 1966. Brearley and Hitchfield present Piagetian concepts according to topics such as moral development, number, and measurement. They include many samples of quotations from Piaget's own writing, which convey the flavor and style of his investigations.

Lavatelli, C. S. *Piaget's theory applied to an early childhood curriculum.* Boston: American Science and Engineering, Inc., 1970. Lavatelli demonstrates how Piaget's findings can be translated into classroom policies and curriculum. She reviews the steps by which important concepts such as classification and seriation develop and provides examples of curricula that would be appropriate for working with these concepts.

Meeker, M. N. *The Structure of Intellect: its interpretation and uses.* Columbus, Ohio: Charles E. Merrill Publishing Co., 1969. This book is written with teachers in mind, and in it Meeker defines and explains the various Structure of Intellect categories, identifies tests for each cell, and gives many suggestions for a curriculum intended to fit the categories. Although written for use with older children, it is possible to modify some of the suggestions and use them with preschool children.

Relationship of Language and Thought

Lewis, M. M. *Language, thought, and personality.* New York: Basic Books, Inc., Publishers, 1963. Chapter 10, "Language and Concrete Thinking," contains a good analysis of the relation of language to cognitive development cast in terms of Piagetian theory. It is nice to read because it describes the Piagetian concepts and discusses research on language related to these concepts.

Suggestions for Curriculum and Activities for Developing Various Mental Concepts

Cratty, B. J. *Intelligence in action: Physical activities for enhancing intellectual abilities.* Englewood Cliffs, N. J. Prentice-Hall, Inc., 1973. The suggestions included in this book are helpful because they remind us that cognitive learning can and should be implemented by use of large muscle skills as well as by means of more typically intellectual activities.

Marzollo, J., and Lloyd, J. *Learning through play.* New York: Harper & Row, Publishers, 1972. Written in nontechnical language, *Learning through play* suggests many activities intended to provide practice in various abilities. It is notable because the activities are interesting, and each one is accompanied by a specific explanation of its intended purpose; delightfully illustrated; suitable for teachers and parents.

Meeker, M. N., Sexton, K., and Richardson, M. O. *SOI abilities workbook.* Los Angeles: Loyola-Marymount University, 1970. This workbook lists innumerable activities fitting the Guilford cells. It is primarily appropriate for older children but still useful because it suggests ideas that could be translated into activities suitable for younger children.

Sharp, E. *Thinking is child's play.* New York:

E. P. Dutton & Co., Inc., 1969. This simple, yet well-done book begins with a brief outline of Piaget's philosophy and then describes various games to be used for the purpose of providing experience in classifying, seriating, and so forth; contains many useful ideas.

Weikart, D., Rogers, L., Adcock, C., and Mc-Clelland, D. *The cognitively oriented curriculum: a framework for preschool teachers.* Washington, D.C.: National Association for the Education of Young Children, 1971. The authors describe a model of a Piagetian nursery school, discuss the philosophy and management of the school as a whole, and then provide sample days that illustrate the way Piagetian concepts can be integrated into ongoing curriculum—an invaluable resource for nursery school teachers.

Specific Resources for Teaching Science

Carmichael, V. *Science experiences for young children.* Los Angeles: Southern California Association for the Education of Young Children, 1969. This book contains a wealth of suggestions for teaching science to very young children. Exceptionally good lists of additional references, including books and movies, follow each chapter.

Neuman, D. Sciencing for young children. In K. R. Baker (Ed.), *Ideas that work with young children.* Washington, D.C.: National Association for the Education of Young Children, 1972. This is a clear-cut discussion of how to plan a curriculum that is based on science. It provides some good examples of suitable materials, but the article is most helpful because of the theoretical framework that it describes. Neuman stresses the importance of process rather than fact learning.

Seefeldt, C. *A curriculum for child care centers.* Columbus, Ohio: Charles E. Merrill Publishing Co., 1973. The chapter entitled "Science for Young Children" is rich in suggestions and ideas related to science and shows how Craig's key scientific concepts can be used to develop a curriculum appropriate for preschoolers.

For the Advanced Student

Refer also to the references at the end of the book for a list of publications by Piaget and Guilford.

Evans, E. *Contemporary influences in early childhood education.* New York: Holt, Rinehart and Winston, Inc., 1971. Evans presents a solid review of the pros and cons of Piagetian theory. This work should be read with attention, since it discusses weaknesses and raises issues as well as describing the theory itself.

Flavell, J. H. *The developmental psychology of Jean Piaget.* Princeton, N. J. Van Nostrand Reinhold Co., 1963. In this classic work Flavell reviews and interprets the bulk of Piaget's writing; still an important reference for any serious student of Piaget.

Sigel, I. E. The Piagetian system and the world of education. In D. Elkind & J. H. Flavell (Eds.), *Studies in cognitive development.* New York: Oxford University Press, 1969. Sigel provides a thoughtful discussion of the implications of Piagetian theory for teachers and raises a nice point about the often unappreciated value of using divergent thought in relation to developing classification skills.

Sigel, I. E., and Hooper, F. H. (Eds.) *Logical thinking in children: research based on Piaget's theory.* New York: Holt, Rinehart and Winston, Inc., 1968. Research that explores various aspects of Piaget's theory can make almost as interesting reading as Piaget's original ingenious investigations. Sigel and Hooper present the findings from many such projects conveniently gathered together in one place for the benefit of the student; an important, basic reference for the serious student.

PART SEVEN

Working with special situations

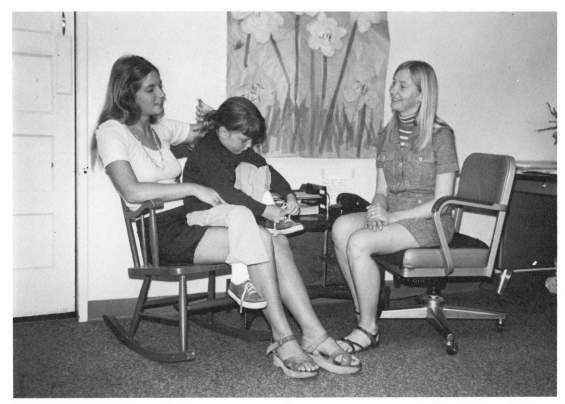

Photo by Jason Lo'Cicero

CHAPTER 17

What mothers need*

Before this enlightened point of view came into practice, parents were usually treated as people to be endured or to be taught. In those days, parents' meetings were strictly "telling" occasions. Parents were either told what they should do or not do, or were told what the teachers did and why it was right. The implication was "if you did the same, you would have no problems." They were told what toys to buy, what books to read. It seems quite likely that such practices succeeded admirably in increasing their sense of inadequacy.†

No matter how dedicated and meticulous we are about establishing a good life for the child at school, nursery school teachers must never forget that the most significant part of the environment of the young child lies outside the school. Quite wholesomely and rightly, there is a much more profound influence in the child's life —his home, his family, and, most particularly, his mother. Because this is true, it makes good sense, if we hope to establish the best total environment for the child, to include his mother and family as being an important part of the nursery school experience.

This is a desirable policy to follow because the child's anxiety over leaving his home will be lessened if he senses that there is a strong bond between his home and the school. It is also desirable because the teacher may be able to offer the mother meaningful help about everyday problems of child rearing as well as gain the opportunity to learn much from the mother about her youngster and how to get along with him.

PROBLEMS THAT INTERFERE WITH GOOD COMMUNICATION

Despite these important advantages in keeping communication open, many mothers and teachers do not get along comfortably together.

The teacher may dread the mother's criticisms ("Why does Harry have paint on his shirt again?") or feel financially at her mercy because a displeased parent may yank her child out of nursery school. Moreover, the teacher may blame the mother for the child's shortcomings; this is bound to interfere with a good relationship between them.

The mother also feels vulnerable to criticism. After all, her child, who is an extension of herself, is on view. First-time mothers particularly can be quite frightened of the teacher's opinion, and all mothers yearn to know that the teacher likes their child and that he is doing well. The relationship is doubly touchy because the mother may be seeking validation of

---

*Adapted from *Young Children,* 1970, **25,** 109-114.

†From *Teaching young children* (p. 160), by Evelyn Beyer, copyright © 1968, by Western Publishing Company, Inc., reprinted by permission of The Bobbs-Merrill Company, Inc.

her own worth as a person by ascertaining that the teacher approves of her offspring. She is ready to believe the teacher (and also to feel threatened and angry) if blame is implied.

The mother may also fear that if she speaks frankly and mentions something she doesn't like about the school or about what her child is doing there, that she will antagonize the teacher. She worries about the possibility of reprisals on the child when she is not there. This is comparable to the parent who fears complaining to hospital personnel lest they discriminate against her child. The fact that most professional people are more mature than this may not affect the parent's innate caution in this matter.

Besides being vulnerable to criticism and wishing to protect her child, the mother may dread being displaced by the teacher in the child's affections. Separation involves mixed feelings for her. On one hand, she deeply wants to wean her child: she is tired of changing his pants and tying his shoes and never going anywhere alone. But, at the same time, something inside her resents having the teacher take over. To add to her confusion, the mother may also be struggling with guilty feelings over the relief she feels at being able to parcel Agatha out for a few days a week. Surely, if she were a "good mother," she wouldn't feel so elated at the thought of going shopping by herself! So she worries about what the teacher would think of her if the teacher only knew.

For both mother and teacher there remain all the past experiences and previous relationships with other teachers and mothers that set the tone of what each expects of the other. In addition to pleasant memories, there are emotionally powerful ones of the principal's office, staying after school, authoritarian teachers and militant, unreasonable parents that lie at the back of consciousness and plague parents and teachers during their initial contacts. It's no wonder then, with all these things conspiring to build walls between families and teachers, that we must invest some effort and understanding if we wish to establish a more rewarding relationship between the adults who are so important in the life of the young child.

SUGGESTIONS FOR ESTABLISHING A GOOD RELATIONSHIP BETWEEN MOTHER AND TEACHER

Surely there must be some way to establish a bond that leads to problem solving rather than to defense building. The question is, how can the teacher go about doing this?

Probably the most essential ingredient in a more satisfactory relationship between teacher and mother is that the teacher have the child's welfare truly at heart and that she be genuinely concerned about him. My experience has been that when the mother believes this to be true—which means, of course, that it has to *be* true and not just something the teacher *wishes* were true— when the mother really senses the teacher's good will, she will forgive the teacher her inadvertent transgressions, and the relationship will warm up as trust develops.

Genuine concern and caring can be expressed in a variety of ways. Faithful caretaking is one way. The teacher takes pains to see that everything the child has made is valued by being put in his cubby for him to take home, his belongings are kept track of, his nose is wiped when it needs it, and, although he may not be the pristinely clean youngster at the end of the day that he was upon arrival, he is tidied up and has had his face washed before his mother picks him up. The teacher also shows that she cares by carefully enforcing the health and safety regulations and by planning a curriculum that is interesting, various, and suited to the needs of individual children.

Another way for the teacher to show concern is by expressing genuine interest in each child to his parent. For example, it is always sound practice to comment to the mother on something her youngster has enjoyed that day. It may be the friendly statement that "Helen really loves our new bunny; she fed him and watched him half the morning," or it might be, "I think Jerry is making friends with our new boy, Todd; they spent a lot of time with the trains in the block corner today." These comments assure the parent that the child has had attention from the teacher and that she is aware of him as an individual rather than as just one of the troop.

Still another kind of caring can be indicated on a more subtle level by letting the mother know that the teacher is on the child's side *but not on the child's side as opposed to the mother's*. Occasionally, teachers fall into the fantasy of thinking, "If only I could take that child home with me for a week and give him a steady, loving environment . . ." Sometimes a child will say in a rush of affection, "Oh, I wish *you* were my mother!" In order to avoid an emotionally confusing and difficult situation for the child, it is important that the teacher clarify her role. She can handle this by gently replying, "We *are* having fun, and I like you, too; but, of course, you already have a mother—I'm not your mother, I'm your *teacher*. I take care of you at school, and your mother takes care of you at home." This avoids rivalry and makes a friendly alliance between mother and teacher more likely.

It is also difficult to be on the mother's side if the teacher blames the parent for all the child's problems. This disapproval, even if unspoken, cannot help but be sensed by the mother. In any situation where I feel critical of a parent, I have found it helpful to remember what Beth Leonhard recommends: "Ask youself, if *I* were that mother, with that set of problems and that background, could I do any better with that child?"[*]

Another thing to remember is that, as any mother of more than one child knows, children are born with different temperaments. No matter what parents do, children are different to start with and remain so, no matter what the environment. Therefore, it is ridiculous to hold the parent accountable for all of the child's shortcomings.

Thus we see that the teacher can put the mother at ease by letting her know that she is concerned about the child, that

*Leonhard, B. Keynote address. Paper presented at the TAEYC Workshop, September 1963, Santa Barbara, California.

she is on both the child's and mother's side, and that she does not feel that everything the child does is the mother's fault. After all, mothers are not ogres—they also want what is best for their children. A sense of common, shared concern is worth working for, because once the mother feels its existence, she is freer to work with the teacher in the child's behalf.

Working with mothers in a positive way requires that the teacher be accessible in two senses of the word. First, she must be accessible because she cares about the child; second, she must be physically available when the mother is around the school. In some schools, availability can be hard to come by. The teacher may be occupied with setting up as the children arrive and able to give the parent only a passing word, or at the end of the day she may be so harrassed that she hasn't time or energy to talk.

It is possible, however, to arrange the schedule so that whoever handles counseling does gate duty the first and last 15 minutes of the day or during peak arrival and departure times. If she is free from other responsibilities at that time, she can see each parent for countless casual meetings and can build relationships of friendliness and trust more easily. The sheer informality of this encounter robs it of a good deal of threat. Chatting right by the gate, the mother knows that she can hasten away if the conversation takes too threatening a turn. In addition, she is likely to see the teacher in a variety of moods and predicaments, which will increase the teacher's humanity.

This repeated, consistent contact is far superior to relying solely on the more formal and frightening "conference" which may occur once or twice a semester. After a comfortable, everyday relationship is well established, then an occasional conference with a longer uninterrupted opportunity to talk can be used to better advantage.

COUNSELING WITH PARENTS

Once lines of communication are open, the question remains, what do we do then?

When people talk together, many levels of relating can exist between them. During the year all these levels can be used by nursery school teachers, depending on the situation.

The simplest level is a rather impersonal one where the teacher may say to the parent, "This is what we did in school today," or "He's coming along very well." On this level, at least the mother knows that the teacher wants her to know what's happening at school. Most new relationships have to start about here.

On another level the teacher acts as the supportive information provider and general comforter. In this guise she interprets the child's behavior to the mother on the basis of her extensive experience with other children. For example, the simple information that many 4-year-olds relish "disgraceful" language can be a great relief to a mother who is secretly tormented by the worry that she suddenly has a pervert on her hands.

At yet another level the mother-teacher relationship has more of a counseling flavor to it. This is guidance, but not guidance in the sense that the teacher tells the mother what to do. Guidance means that the teacher works with the mother in terms of conscious motivation and behavior to help her discover what may be causing various behavior problems in the child and to help her figure out how to cope with them.

My impression is that teachers who have had special training are more likely to have the aplomb to attempt this third level. However, all teachers could increase their skills, do no harm and probably considerable good, by offering themselves in a guidance role to parents in need of help—especially if they concentrate on listening rather than prescribing. The truth is that even when parents ask for help, they usually know the answer already. They are simply having difficulty applying it.

Excluding the occasional special situation where more professional help is required, what mothers need in order to work out a difficulty is the chance to talk out how they feel and evaluate whether a tentative solution is right for them and their unique child. Tremendous comfort comes to a distressed mother when she is given the opportunity to air a problem with someone who can listen attentively and who is not too shaken by the confession that Ethel and Mary have been sitting behind the back fence doing you know what! Allowing her to express her feelings of shame, or occasionally even anguish, over her child's behavior is a positive good to offer a mother in a counseling situation.

It is also true that teachers who have known literally hundreds of youngsters do have a broader background of experience than most parents. It seems only right to pool this knowledge with the mother's, as long as the teacher's alternatives are offered in such a way that the mother feels free to accept or reject them. The parent will be able to use the teacher's range of knowledge most easily if the teacher points out to her that no matter how much she knows in general about children, she will *never* know as much about the individual child as the mother does.

Instead of providing instant answers to all problems posed by parents, the teacher will find it more useful to ask questions instead, such as "Why don't you tell me what you've tried already?" or, "What are your thoughts about what to do next?" When a mother comes to say that her child has begun "misbehaving" in some new way (perhaps he is fighting a great deal with his sister or has begun having nightmares), the best question to ask is, "I wonder if you could tell me what else happened about the same time?" The typical response is, "Well, nothing much. Let me see, now, I guess that was about the time my in-laws came to visit, and, oh yes, his little dog was run over, and . . ." By this means the mother gains useful insight into what has upset her child and usually can formulate a plan about what she might do to help him get on an even keel again.

Another cornerstone of good counseling is patience. It seems to be human nature that we want instant results, but change often takes a very long time. I used to despair when I made a suggestion that the parent ignored. I was most concerned on the occasions when I referred the family to a specialist, and the parent declined to act on the referral. My implicit assumption was that if the family didn't do it then, they never would. Happily, I have found this to be a false assumption. To be sure, parents may not be ready this year to face the problem of Jeffrey's temper tantrums and hyperactivity, but they have at least heard that the possibility of a problem exists, and the next professional person who approaches them may have greater success because the ground has been prepared.

Nowadays I am more wary of the mother who agrees completely and instantly with my suggestions. Usually there isn't very much movement in these cases. The chance to think out, backtrack, consider various solutions, and take time to get used to an idea is indispensable in a guidance situation.

LIMITS TO GUIDANCE WORK

We must also recognize that there are some behavior and developmental problems that are beyond the teacher's ability to handle. It is vital to be clear about where to draw the line and how far to go in guidance work. My rule of thumb is, "When in doubt, refer." If the situation looks serious or does not respond to matter-of-fact remedies, it is time to suggest a specialist. In general, it is too risky and takes more advanced training than a typical nursery school teacher possesses to draw implications and offer interpretations to mothers about deeper, more complex reasons for behavior. Fortunately, there are highly trained, skilled specialists on whom we can rely to solve serious problems, so let's leave Oedipus and his troublesome kin to our psychiatric cohorts.

SUMMARY

Sensible caution and referral to an expert is advisable under some circumstances, but teachers can offer a lot of help and work in many ways with parents to bring about a happier life for their chil-

dren. In order to do this, it is first necessary to overcome various problems that make communication between parents and teachers difficult. One of the most effective things a teacher can do is make it plain to the parent that she has the welfare of the child at heart and that she wants to join with the mother to help the child. She can also take care to be available when the mother wants to talk, and she can provide the opportunity for many easy-going, casual contacts.

Once the lines of communication are open, the teacher can offer help by serving as a friendly listener who assists the parent in assessing the nature of the difficulty and in proposing alternatives until she finds the one best suited for her and her child. Teachers who assume this guidance function offer mothers what they need the most—an accepting attitude, an open ear, and a warm heart.

QUESTIONS AND ACTIVITIES

1. Have the class split into groups of two. One person in each pair should select a problem or difficulty to discuss while the other person listens. The only restriction on the listener is that, before making any other reply, she must first restate in her own words what she hears the speaker saying; that is, her primary task is to be open to the feelings and import of the communication. Then shift roles and have the speaker practice this sort of listening and responding.

2. Select children in your group who appear to require special diagnostic help of some description. List the reasons for your conclusion that they need help. With another student, practice how you might broach the subject of referral with the family. It is helpful to practice this with a "parent" who is resistant, one who is overly aggreeable, and one who is obviously upset about your suggestion.

3. If you have children of your own, have you ever been summoned to school to discuss a problem? How did you feel about being asked to come in and do this?

4. *Problem:* A child comes to school acting listless and looking pale and washed out. At nap time, when he undresses, you find he has several bruises on his chest and around his arms, and he complains that his neck hurts. There has been a previous occasion where he arrived with a bump on his head and a

black eye, which his mother said was due to his falling down a flight of steps. Under these circumstances, do you think it wisest to approach the parent with your concern, or are there other, alternative solutions that should be explored?

REFERENCES FOR FURTHER READING

Beyer, E. *Teaching young children.* New York: The Bobbs-Merrill Co., Inc., 1968. Beyer's chapter on working with parents traces the development of the concept of mutuality of concern as it has replaced the older idea of the teacher as a didactic parent instructor. It does a good job of describing the overall climate that should be established between teacher and parent and includes matter-of-fact suggestions for achieving it.

Bromberg, S. L. A beginning teacher works with parents. In K. R. Baker (Ed.), *Ideas that work with young children.* Washington D.C.: National Association for the Education of Young Children, 1972. Bromberg presents a candid, comforting, and informative discussion of the sucesses and failures of an inexperienced teacher learning to work with parents.

D'Evelyn, K. E. *Individual parent-teacher conferences.* New York: Teachers College Press, 1963. This is down-to-earth material on conferencing and how to manage it successfully.

Gotkin, L. G. The telephone call: the direct line from teacher to family. In K. R. Baker (Ed.), *Ideas that work with young children.* Wash-

ington, D.C.: National Association for the Education of Young Children, 1972. Gotkin advocates use of the telephone as an additional way to reach parents quickly and directly.

Hildebrand, V. *Introduction to early childhood education.* New York: The Macmillan Co., 1971. Hildebrand provides an overview that contains many practical suggestions of different ways to link family and school together more effectively.

Markun, P. M. *Parenting.* Washington, D.C.: Association for Childhood Education International, 1973. This excellent pamphlet considers parenting in its many guises. It contains several strong articles in it; among the best are the one on Mexican-American parents and the one on the problems of the parent who is divorced.

Read, K. H. *The nursery school: a human relationships laboratory.* (5th ed.) Philadelphia: W. B. Saunders Co., 1971. The chapter entitled "Teachers and Parents Work Together" has a good discussion of the feelings parents may bring with them to the nursery school experience.

Taylor, K. W. *Parent cooperative nursery schools.* New York: Teachers College Press, 1954. This classic discussion of teacher-parent interaction remains one of the best in the field. Taylor talks about real life problems the teacher may experience when working with parents and proposes helpful ways to work these through in the framework of a cooperative nursery school.

Photo by Jason Lo'Cicero

CHAPTER 18

Working with exceptional children

A handicapped child reacts to pity and solicitude either by withdrawing into himself or by just giving up the struggle for independence. The child needs support, warmth, interest, concern, appreciation of his achievements, and respect for his personality. Feeling for the child must be combined with knowledge of the child.*

Although all children have special educational needs at one point or another in their lives, some children require specialized attention more consistently. This group includes a wide assortment of youngsters ranging from those who are physically handicapped to those who are emotionally disturbed or who are experiencing intellectual development that lags behind or is markedly ahead of their peers. In short, the category of exceptionality covers children who deviate in at least one respect far enough from the typical that they are noticeable in the group because of this deviation.

The first part of this chapter is intended to increase the ability of the nursery school teacher to spot children who may have special problems and to develop her sensitivity and skills in bringing this problem to the attention of the parents and in carrying out a successful referral to a specialist. In the second portion of the chapter some basic educational recommendations are given for including exceptional children in the ordinary nursery

school. An extensive bibliography is provided at the end of the chapter.

NURSERY SCHOOL TEACHER AS A SCREENING AGENT

One of the most important services the nursery school teacher can provide is screening the children in her care for physical emotional, and mental behavior that may indicate a serious underlying difficulty. It is a mistaken notion that such difficulties are always first noticed in the physician's office. Doctors see children for brief periods of time often under conditions that can be quite stressful to the child. In addition, they can be hampered by mothers who either raise questions about symptoms that are insignificant or who resist being told anything about their youngsters that may be upsetting. When physicians are caught in this kind of situation, it is only to be expected that occasional difficulties slip past without notice. These comments are not intended to imply that a highly trained medical specialist knows less than the nursery school teacher does; rather, it means that the teacher should keep her eyes open because she has the advantage of seeing the child in a natural setting for extended periods of time, and she has seen many youngsters

---

*From Schattner, R. *An early childhood curriculum for multiply handicapped children* (p. 36). New York: copyright © 1971, Intext Press.

of similar age and background. Thus it is possible that she may become aware of difficulties that should be drawn to the attention of the physician or psychologist.

The sooner such potential handicaps are identified, the sooner they may be ameliorated and further formation of undesirable habit patterns and emotional reactions reduced (Caldwell, 1973). Sometimes early diagnosis means that a condition can be cleared up entirely (as when a child's hearing is restored following a tonsillectomy-adenoidectomy), and sometimes the effect of the condition can only be mitigated (as is often the case with mentally retarded youngsters); but *nothing* can be done until the child is identified as needing assistance and a referral has been successfully carried out. These are points at which the nursery school teacher's help is crucial.

Some physical conditions and symptoms of which the teacher should be aware

Speech and hearing problems. Various speech difficulties and symptoms of possible hearing impairment have already been reviewed in the chapter on language, so it will only be noted here that speech and hearing problems are among the physical disorders that occur most frequently in childhood. Speech difficulties are likely to be noticed, but hearing loss may be overlooked as a possible cause of misbehavior, inattention, or lack of responsiveness. However, once hearing loss is suspected, it is a relatively simple matter to refer the child to an otolaryngologist for examination. Since such losses may be due to infection, they can and should be treated promptly.

Difficulties of vision. Another physical disability that may pass unnoticed but that occurs frequently is an inability to see clearly. The incidence of visual defects may run as high as one in four or five children of elementary school age (Dalton, 1943). This means that in a nursery school group of fifteen children there may be three or four youngsters who have some kind of difficulty with their eyes.

The presence of the following symp-toms* should alert the teacher to the possibility that the child needs to have his eyes examined.

1. Strabismus (crossed eyes); nystagmus (involuntary, rapid movement of the eyeball)
2. How the child uses his eyes; tilting his head, holding objects close to his eyes, rubbing his eyes, squinting, displaying sensitivity to bright lights and rolling his eyes
3. Inattention to visual objects or visual tasks such as looking at pictures or reading
4. Awkwardness in games requiring eye-hand coordination
5. Avoidance of tasks that require close eye work
6. Affinity to tasks that require distance vision
7. Any complaints about inability to see
8. Lack of normal curiosity in regard to visually appealing objects

One defect of vision in particular requires treatment during early childhood, since later attempts at correction are not as effective. This is *amblyopia,* sometimes called *lazy eye,* a condition in which one eye is weaker than the other because of a muscle imbalance (Harley, 1973). Common signs of this condition include squinting with one eye or tilting the head to one side in order to see better. Since early treatment of this condition is important, if there is any possible way to incorporate visual screening tests into the nursery school program it should be done. Sometimes local opthalmological societies will sponsor this service; sometimes a public health nurse can be prevailed upon or an interested civic group will employ a trained nurse to visit the nursery schools and conduct such tests.

Screening is best done at school rather than at a central clinic because coverage of children attending the school is likely to be more complete and the environment in which testing takes place is familiar to the children, so they will be more at ease. Giving the children practice before the actual examination day in holding the "E"

---

*From Kirk, S. A. *Educating exceptional children.* (2nd ed.) Boston: Houghton Mifflin Co., 1972. P. 295.

according to instructions will facilitate testing and help save the examiner's sanity. Central clinics should also be offered as a service to children who do not attend nursery school.

Following identification of a possible problem by means of the screening test, the youngster should be referred to an opthalmologist for diagnosis and follow-up.

Hyperactivity. The term hyperactive tends to be abused by some parents and teachers who use it to describe every active, vigorous child (Grinspoon and Singer, 1973). For this reason, it is helpful to apply the following criteria developed by Paul Wender, a psychiatrist who specializes in this condition, when trying to determine whether a child should be referred for medical evaluation and possible treatment (1973).

The following behavior* characterizes this condition in young children; additional learning problems may arise during the elementary school years.

1. Restlessness—the child appears to be a bundle of energy. The mother may come to feel that she can't take her eyes off him for a minute without his climbing on the refrigerator or running into the street. At nursery school, the child may be incessantly in motion except that he seems able to settle down when given one-to-one attention.

2. The child is easily distracted and has a short attention span. In nursery school he may rush from activity to activity and then seem at a loss for what to do. He may do as the teacher asks but forget quickly and revert to his former behavior.

3. The child demands attention insatiably—monopolizes conversations, teases, badgers, repeats annoying activities. May be emotionally unresponsive or undemonstrative.

4. Shows a weaker than average ability to control his impulses. Hard for him to wait, he may become upset rapidly, has many temper tantrums, acts on the spur of the moment—often with poor judgment.

---

*From *The hyperactive child. A handbook for parents* by Paul H. Wender, M. D. © 1973 by Paul H. Wender. Used by permission of Crown Publishers, Inc.

Parents may complain that the child is incontinent.

5. About half of these children exhibit difficulties in the coordination of fine muscle activities such as using scissors, coloring and so forth, or with problems of balance.

6. The child may have various kinds of interpersonal problems including resistance to social demands from parents and teachers, excessive independence, and a troublesome tendency to dominate the children he plays with, which makes him unlikable.

7. He may have various emotional problems including swings of mood, becoming excessively excited over pleasant activities, sometimes appearing to be insensitive to pain, demonstrating a low tolerance to frustration and overreaction to it when frustrated, low self-esteem.

8. Some of these children have real difficulty tolerating change.

Of course, most young children exhibit these kinds of behaviors from time to time. What sets the truly hyperactive child apart is the intensity and consistency of the behavior. Most youngsters seem to "outgrow" it as they reach adolescence, but the years of stress and the unhappy side effects of this condition have usually taken a painful toll by then. Dr. Wender suggests that the most adequate referral is one made to a child psychiatrist or a pediatrician conversant with behavior problems, since medication can be a factor in successful management of this condition. A child psychologist or social worker can also make a helpful contribution, but they are unable to prescribe medication should that prove necessary.

Convulsive seizures. Another condition that responds well to medication is epilepsy. Indeed, *grand mal* attacks, in which the individual loses consciousness, are now rarely witnessed in nursery schools. Unless a major convulsive seizure occurs for the first time at school, the teacher usually need not worry about referring such children, since it is almost certain that they are already under treatment by their physician. She should, however, report seizures to the family. She will need to allow the child to rest and probably sleep following an attack, and she will also need to explain to the other children, who may be either curious or distressed, what happened. The explanation should be simple and matter of fact to make it as easy as possible for the child to return to the group with little comment.

The teacher needs to be more alert to the much milder form of convulsion, *petit mal,* because this lighter seizure sometimes escapes the notice of the family, to whom it may seem to be a case of daydreaming or inattention.

According to Robb (1965) these attacks are short (only a few seconds), and the child may indicate their presence only by a blank stare and immobility but does not fall to the ground. A second type of petit mal seizure is characterized by the eyes blinking or deviating, the head turning a little, lip smacking, and stereotyped movements of the hands. It is worthwhile to identify this behavior and refer the child for treatment to a pediatrician or neurologist because the probability of successful control by means of drugs is high: Robb estimates that probably 75% to 80% of all patients afflicted with convulsive seizures experience good control when given medication.

Excessive awkwardness. The teacher should also be aware of children who are exceptionally clumsy, who run on their toes consistently, or who run with their toes markedly turned out or in, who are knock-kneed, or whose legs are exceptionally bowed. All of these conditions should be drawn to the attention of the parent and referral to the pediatrian suggested, since there are a variety of causes for these symptoms and since many of them are amenable to treatment if caught in time.

Other physical problems. In general, the teacher should watch for pronounced changes in the physical appearance of the child and, in particular, should take notice of children who are excessively pale or who convey a general air of exhaustion or lassitude. These conditions often develop so gradually that parents are unaware of the change. It is especially important to watch a child with care during the week or two after he has returned from a serious illness, such as measles, scarlet fever, or meningitis, since occasional problems develop following such infections.

Signs of emotional disturbance that indicate a referral is needed

Deciding when referral for emotional disturbance is warranted and when it is unnecessary can be a difficult problem because symptoms of emotional upset are common during early childhood (Buckle and Lebovici, 1960). One study, for example, found that the average child of nursery school age manifested between four and six "behavior" problems and that they seemed to appear and disappear over a period of time (Macfarlane, 1943). A good nursery school environment can accomplish wonders with children who are emotionally upset, and many physicians routinely refer children who are having emotional difficulties to nursery school because they have witnessed many happy results from such referrals.

There comes a time, however, when the staff begins to question whether the nursery school environment, no matter how therapeutic, can offer sufficient help to a particular youngster. Perhaps after a reasonable period for adjustment and learning, he persists in "blowing his stack" over relatively inconsequential matters, or perhaps he insists on spending most of each morning hidden within the housekeeping corner or even crouched beneath a table. These behaviors, to name only two of a much wider list of possibilities, should arouse feelings of concern in the staff, since they are examples of behavior that (1) is too extreme, (2) happens too often, and (3) persists too long. When these criteria describe a child's behavior, it is time for the staff to admit their limitations of time and training and to encourage the family to seek the advice of a qualified psychologist or psychiatrist.

The teacher should also apply a fourth criterion when considering the necessity of a referral: whether the number of symptoms manifested by the child at any one period is excessive. We have seen that signs of upset are common and often disappear either spontaneously or as a result of adequate handling by parents and teachers. Occasionally, though, a child will exhibit a number of reactions at the same time. He may begin to wet his bed again, be unable to fall asleep easily, insist on always having his blanket with him, and refuse to play. If such habits are so numerous and so intense that they interfere with the child's enjoyment of life and are a burden to him and his family, the possibility of a referral should be explored.

Early infantile autism: a special case. Another psychological condition is seen occasionally in nursery schools, particularly in less sophisticated areas where medical and psychological advice is not readily available. A family may enroll a youngster who can generally be described in the following terms: he pays scant attention to other children or adults and seems emotionally distant and uninvolved; it is difficult or impossible to get him to look the person who is speaking to him in the eye; he may become very distressed when asked to change from one activity to another (for example, he may fly into a panic when asked to stop swinging and go inside for snack); his speech may be minimal or nonexistent; and he may show a marked interest in things that spin or twirl, such as a tricycle wheel, which he may sit by and spin absorbedly, or a spoon, which he will twirl with great skill (Kanner, 1944; Rutter, 1966; Shaw, 1966). When several of these symptoms occur together, the youngster may be suffering from infantile autism. This condition is rare, but my experience indicates that the nursery school teacher will come across such children from time to time. Treatment is difficult, and these youngsters need highly professional help as soon as they can get it. Therefore, the family should be urged to seek help from a child psychiatrist promptly.

Problems related to mental ability

Children with developmental lags. All nursery school teachers need to know enough about developmental sequences and the ages at which behavioral milestones can be anticipated that they can tell when a child is developing normally or when he is lagging markedly behind his peers or is quite advanced for his age. Lists of developmental standards have been included in many chapters in this book, not with the intention of urging developmental conformity, but in the hope that they will help the teacher be tolerant of behaviors characteristic of various ages and also alert to children who are developing so far out of phase that they require special help.

Many nursery school teachers do not recognize retardation when they see it. Being unaware of retardation can be an advantage in a way, since it means that a child is not stuck with a stereotyped reaction to his condition or burdened with an undesirable label. On the other hand, it may also mean that an undiagnosed, slow-learning 4-year-old who is actually operating at a $2^1/_2$-year-old level may be expected to sit with the other 4-year-olds for long stories he does not comprehend or may be criticized and disciplined for refusing to share equipment when actually he is behaving in a way typical of his developmental but not chronological age. An adequate diagnosis would enable the teacher to match her expectations to the child's real level of ability.

Behavior that should be cause for concern includes a widespread pattern of development that is a year or more behind the typical in physical, social, and intellectual areas. Such lags are usually accompanied by speech that is obviously immature for the child's chronological age.

Causes of slow development are numerous, ranging from chromosomal disorders to pseudoretardation induced by an insufficiently stimulating environment, and it is often impossible even for specialists to determine why the child is developing slowly (Bakwin and Bakwin, 1972; Kessler, 1966).

The simplicity and adaptability of the nursery school curriculum mean that many mildly or moderately retarded children can fit comfortably into the nursery school environment. Some, of course, require more special educational services. Since truly retarded children do not outgrow their condition or ultimately catch up with their more fortunate peers, it is necessary for teachers and parents to come to a realistic understanding of what can be expected of them. Knowledgeable, humane specialists can provide many helpful suggestions about how to maximize learning for these youngsters.

Pseudoretarded children. Although heredity appears to control the range of intelligence of each individual, environment has been shown also to have an effect on how well individuals develop (Lichtenberg and Norton, 1970), and there is general agreement that cognitive development can be depressed by the adverse environmental circumstances often associated with poverty. However, the extent of this pseudoretardation and the ability of education to remedy it are still the subject of debate.

Since the middle 1960s preschool education has been characterized by the development of many programs intended to overcome retardation due to environmental insult. Some results of these attempts have been disappointing (Cicerelli, Evans, and Schiller, 1969), but some programs have reported heartening successes in achieving this goal (Evans, 1971; Weber, 1970).

CHARACTERISTICS OF PSEUDORETARDED CHILDREN. Children who come from the lower socioeconomic class have many characteristics and needs that are common to all children, but many of them also have some characteristics that reduce the likelihood of their succeeding in a middle-class school. Teachers who wish to work with them need to take these characteristics into account when planning educational programs in order to help the children develop maximally.

Many of the children will have poorer health than middle-class children do, since they receive little medical care after they stop attending well-baby clinics around the age of 2 years. Poor diet (both prenatally and postnatally) also contributes to less than optimum conditions for fostering growth (Sunderlin and Wills, 1969; Thomas, 1972). Many poor children are behind in their ability to use standard English, although they may be fluent in a

dialect such as black English or another language such as Spanish; and some lack verbalness in any language. Children from families of the poor characteristically score lower on verbal tests than middle-class children (Bruner, 1970; Deutsch, 1971; Sutton-Smith, 1973). They may lack experiences that are common among middle-class children. (For example, in my own community we found that many of the children had never been to the beach or to a supermarket, even though they lived within walking distance of both.) These youngsters often appear more action oriented than given to reflective thought. When confronted with standard measures of intelligence, such as the Stanford-Binet or the Peabody Picture Vocabulary Test, they usually score, for many reasons, below the average performance of their middle-class peers (Reese and Lipsitt, 1970).

Unfortunately, these kinds of reports may cause the teacher to overlook the positive strengths of such children, strengths that middle-class children may not possess. For example, children from poor families may be able to cope with various human failings, make money stretch, or get along with intrusive adults from welfare or law enforcement agencies with an aplomb that a middle-class child could not manage. There can also be a self-reliance, sense of humor, and a kind of wise cynicism expressed even by 4-year-olds, which may make a sentimental teacher's heart ache, but which should also arouse her admiration if she realizes how effective such attitudes are as coping mechanisms.

Unfortunately, most of the literature on working with children from the lower socioeconomic class makes it sound very difficult and possibly frightening to the beginning teacher, but there are cogent reasons why many teachers who become involved in a Head Start or day care program vow never to return to teaching middle-class children. This decision may partly be due to ego-gratification related to noblesse oblige, but some of it is also due to the pleasure of seeing children flourish and go on to a better school experience as a result of their years in preschool care.

It takes considerable energy, perseverance, and skill to help young "disadvantaged" children supplement their home educations with material that will enable them to fit into the middle-class school. A number of successful programs are at present demonstrating that this can be done (Gray and Klaus, 1970; Weikart and Lambie, 1968), and it behooves the teacher who works with such youngsters to acquaint herself with a variety of these programs, select a model that fits her own tastes and predilections, make a consistent plan based on the model, and carry it out with determination.

Intellectually gifted children. Although the child who is slow to learn and the child who is pseudoretarded have been receiving increased attention and service in the past few years, intellectually gifted preschoolers have been virtually ignored—unless the child is so precocious that he is singled out as a piece of curiosa. Why such promising children should be overlooked is difficult to say. Surely they deserve the interest and support of their teachers. Perhaps they are overlooked because many of them fit smoothly into the nursery school curriculum (although it may present insufficient challenges for them), or perhaps most preschool teachers are uncertain about what kinds of behavior indicate outstanding mental ability and thus fail to identify the children.

A child with exceptional mental ability usually exhibits a general pattern of advanced skills; his language is more elaborate and extended than that of other children of the same age, and his vocabulary is likely to be large; his attention span may be longer if his interest is aroused; he grasps ideas easily; he probably possesses an exceptional amount of general information, which is characterized not only by more variety but also by greater detail. Gifted preschoolers like to pursue reasons for things and talk about cause-and-effect relationships. They are often almost insatiably interested in special subjects that appeal to them. Some of them already know how to read. Teachers who do not build their curriculum and increase its complexity sufficiently during the year may find that these children become increasingly restless and gradually get into difficulties because they have lost interest in what is happening at school.

The teacher can deal satisfactorily with this kind of exceptionality by modifying the curriculum so that it meets the needs of these youngsters through the addition of challenges. Some suggestions are offered later in the chapter about how to accomplish this.

Summary

The nursery school teacher must be aware of many different symptoms and behaviors as she works with her group of children so that she can determine when a child needs special help. These symptoms range from signs of physical disabilities to indications of pronounced emotional upset and deviations in intellectual development.

The teacher who has learned to recognize these signs has achieved the first step in working with children who have special needs. The next step is understanding how to go about making a referral so the youngster can obtain whatever special help he requires.

REFERRING CHILDREN FOR SPECIAL HELP
Calling the difficulty to the parent's attention

Calling a parent's attention to a special problem requires delicacy and tact on the part of the teacher, since it is all too easy for the mother to feel that she is being attacked or criticized and that she has failed to be a good parent. This is particularly true if the teacher must raise the issue of a pronounced behavior problem. However, the teacher can do several things to reduce the strength of this understandable defensive reaction.

If the teacher listens carefully while in general conversation with the parent, she may find that the parent herself is raising the problem very tentatively. For example, the mother may ask nervously, "How did she do today?" or comment, "He's just like his older brother. Doesn't he ever sit still?" Many a teacher responds to such questions by just as nervously reassuring the mother, saying brightly, "Oh, he did just fine!" (while thinking wryly to herself, "Just fine, that is, if you don't count biting Henry, destroying Emily's block tower, and refusing to come to story time.") Rather than being falsely reassuring, the teacher could use the opening the parent has provided by responding, "I'm glad you asked. He *is* having some difficulties at school. I'm beginning to think it's time to put our heads together and come up with some special ways to help him."

It takes time to bring about a referral. It is best to raise problems gradually with parents over a period of time because it takes a while for families to accustom themselves to the fact their child may need special help. Even such an apparently simple thing as having an eye examination may loom as either a financial or emotional threat to particular families, and the teacher should not expect acceptance and compliance with her recommendation just because she has finally worked her courage up the point of mentioning a difficulty.

The teacher should have the reasons why the child needs special help clearly in mind before raising the issue with the parent. This recommendation is not intended to mean that the teacher should confront the parent with a long, unhappy list of grievances against the child, but that she should be prepared to provide examples of the problem while explaining gently and clearly to the family the reason for her concern.

It is not the teacher's place to diagnose. A particular behavior can have many different causes. For example, failure to pay attention in story hour may be the consequence of a hearing loss, inappropriate reading material, borderline intelligence, fatigue, poor eyesight, or simply needing to go to the toilet. The teacher's role is to recognize that a difficulty exists, do all she can to mitigate it in the nursery school group, inform the parent, and suggest a referral to an expert professional person for diagnosis and treatment when necessary.

Therefore, when she confers with the parent, she should discuss the symptoms and express her concern but avoid giving the impression that she knows for certain what the real cause of the problem may be. Instead, she should ally herself with the parent in a joint quest to find the answer together.

Finding the appropriate referral source

The teacher needs to acquaint herself with referral sources available in her community, since it is both senseless and cruel to raise a problem with a parent and have no suggestions about where she can go for help. Some communities publish a directory that lists such services, but the teacher will often find she must locate them by calling the public health nurse, asking friendly pediatricians, checking with local children's hospitals, county medical societies, and mental health clinics, and by generally keeping her ears open and getting to know people in her community who have contacts in these areas. If possible, it is always desirable to list three referral possibilities so that the family has the opportunity to select the one they feel suits them best.

Observing professional ethics

I have already pointed out that the teacher should not assume the role of diagnostician. However, she often possesses information that is of value to the specialist to whom the child is referred. It can be a temptation to pick up the telephone and call this person without pausing to ask the parent's permission, but this is against professional ethics. The teacher must obtain the parent's consent before she talks to the specialist. Some professional people even require that this permission be in writing before any information is exchanged. After permission is obtained, exchanges of information and suggestions from the specialist can be extraordinarily helpful and should be utilized whenever the opportunity presents itself.

Also, when dealing with a special case, the teacher may be tempted to discuss it with people who are not entitled to know about it, because it is so interesting and it makes the teacher feel important. This gossiping is an unforgivable violation of the family's privacy, and the desire to do this must never be indulged in.

LIVING AND WORKING WITH EXCEPTIONAL CHILDREN IN THE NURSERY SCHOOL
Including exceptional children

Since special education programs for handicapped preschool children remain the exception rather than the rule, the following material concentrates on effective ways to integrate children with special needs into the ordinary nursery school.

Admission to regular nursery school has the advantages of keeping the child with his normal peers, helping normal and exceptional children become accustomed to and feel comfortable with each other, emphasizing the typical aspects of the youngster's abilities and personality rather than focussing on the atypical aspects, and providing the child with the benefits of a good nursery school experience. Another advantage is that, since the trend is to place the great majority of handicapped children into regular classrooms in elementary school (Kirk, 1972; Shaffer, 1973), nursery school placement can gradually prepare the child for this experience. Head Start is now taking the lead by mandating that 10% of the children it serves shall fall in the handicapped category (Jordon, 1973). Placement in nursery school also aids the child's family by providing some relief for the mother from constant care of the youngster, perhaps by helping her see how similar his behavior is in many respects to that of all children, and by helping her feel a part of the educational community.

Determining which children should be admitted

Many nursery schools have long made it a point to welcome exceptional children into their groups (Moor, 1960; Northcott, 1970), and their inclusion usually works out quite satisfactorily. The individualized curriculum characteristic of nursery schools in this country makes it relatively easy for children with special needs to participate in activities appropriate to their abilities, although the school may be weak in meeting the special educational requirements of exceptional children.

It must also be admitted, however, that occasional exceptional children will not be able to fit into the nursery school environment; thus the staff needs to handle potential placements carefully in order to maximize the possibility of success and provide emotional protection for the family, the child, and themselves in case the placement is not successful.

It is important to make it clear to the family that the staff has great goodwill but also has certain limitations and will not be able to work miracles. Very few nursery school teachers have much training in working with exceptional children. In addition, it is not likely that during the year they will be able to devote a large amount of extra time to studying this subject. On the other hand, they do know a great deal about working with children in general and will bring to this particular child the benefit of these insights and practical, matter-of-fact treatment that emphasizes the normal rather than the exceptional.

The staff will have to come to terms with how much extra effort the child will require them to expend every day. It is one thing to accept a mentally retarded child in a flush of helpfulness and sympathy, but it may turn out to be quite another when his pants have to be changed three or four times a morning. Some emotionally disturbed children may also require an inordinate amount of time and attention. The difficulty is that the staff has obligations to all the children, and the time required to work with an exceptional child may eventually deprive the other youngsters of their due share of energy and concern.

Fortunately, the examples given above are the exception rather than the rule, but the possibility of overtaxing the staff must be taken into consideration. However, experience has taught me that most exceptional children can and should be gathered in. Usually the amount of special care is considerable during the first few weeks but gradually declines as the child and staff make the adjustment.

It will be necessary for the staff to examine

their feelings about why they wish to accept the child. It is all too easy to succumb to a rescue fantasy and decide that what the handicapped youngster really needs is plenty of love, and he will be all right. This is, of course, untrue. Children, whether exceptional or ordinary, require a great many other talents from their teachers besides the ability to express affection, and teachers should not delude themselves that affection can overcome all problems. If they intend to work with the child effectively, they must plan on learning the best ways to help him.

Recommended admission procedures

Once these potential hazards have been thought through and a positive decision to accept the youngster has been reached, then the staff and family should embark on a trial period that is as flexible and open minded as possible.

Many seemingly insurmountable problems can be solved during the trial period if the staff and family are creatively minded. For example, a child who cannot negotiate a flight of stairs and who is too heavy to be lifted can come to nursery school if his father builds a ramp over the stairs, or a child who requires a good deal of extra physical care may be able to attend if she is accompanied in the beginning by her mother or, if the parent needs relief, by a companion who tends to the extra chores until the child becomes more self-sufficient.

There are several ways to ease entry pangs. The regular practice of asking the mother to stay with the child until he has made friends should be followed when welcoming handicapped children into the group. Research has shown that this policy is of special importance for young retarded children (Kessler, Gridth, and Smith, 1968).

A chat with the child's physician may also reassure the teacher and provide any special guidelines that may be necessary for handling the youngster. Children with heart conditions, for instance, occasionally require special treatment, but sometimes arrive with firm instructions to let the child alone so he can pace himself.

Sometimes it also helps to begin with a short day and gradually extend the time the child attends as his skills and toleration of the group increases The shorter day means that he can go home while he is still experiencing success and has not been overwhelmed with fatigue. It may be easiest if the child arrives in the middle of the morning and leaves when the other children do, since this means he does not have to depart when everyone else is still having a good time.

Many disabilities will pass unnoticed by the other children in the group, but some will require explanation. The explanations need not be elaborate. They should avoid the condescension of pity and should stress matter-of-fact suggestions about how to get along with the child who is being asked about. It may be necessary, for example, to help the children understand that a particular child uses her ears and hands in place of her eyes, since she cannot see, to coach them to stand in front of a child who is hard of hearing and catch his attention before speaking to him, or to explain that another youngster has to stay outside the sandbox because the grit gets in his braces.

GENERAL RECOMMENDATIONS FOR WORKING WITH EXCEPTIONAL CHILDREN
See through the exceptional to the typical in every child

It can be easy to become so caught up in the differences of an exceptional child that the teacher loses sight of the fact that he is largely like the other children in her group and should be treated as much like them as possible. Feeling sorry for a child weakens his character and ultimately does him a terrible disservice. Many exceptional children have too many allowances made for them out of pity, misguided good intentions, and inexperience—and sometimes, where parents are concerned, as a consequence of guilt. The outcome is that the child may become a demanding and rather unpleasant person to have around. In other words, he becomes just plain spoiled.

Consistency, reasonable expectations, and sound policies are, if anything, *more important* to employ when dealing with handicapped children than when dealing with ordinary children. The teacher should feel comfortable about drawing on her common sense and considerable experience, but she should also be able to turn freely to experts for consultation when she feels puzzled and uncertain about how to proceed.

Try to steer a middle course, neither overprotecting nor overexpecting

The commonest pitfall in working with an exceptional child is becoming so concerned for his safety and well-being that the child is stifled and deprived of the opportunity to be as normal as he might be were he not overprotected. In general, the teacher should proceed on the assumption that the child should be encouraged to participate in every activity, with modifications provided only when necessary to ensure success. Thus a child who is behind his peers in intellectual development should be expected to participate in story hour but may enjoy it most if he sits with the youngest group.

On the other hand, some parents and teachers set their expectations unreasonably high and are unwilling to make any exceptions for the child with a handicap. This causes unnecessary strain and even despair for the child. Teachers can be helpful here by pointing out what is reasonable to expect of 3- or 4-year-old children in general and helping the parent understand what a reasonable expectation would be for her particular youngster. It is often helpful with such families to note each step as the child attains it and discuss what the next stage of development will be so that the parent can see progress coming bit by bit. This may reduce the feeling of desperate driving toward a difficult distant goal.

Be realistic. It is important to see the child as he is and to avoid false promises and unrealistic reassurances when talking with parents or the child himself. Everyone yearns for an exceptional child to "make it," and sometimes this yearning leads to unwitting self-deceptions, which can do the family and child a disservice by delaying acceptance of the disability or

by encouraging them to make inadequate future plans. I once watched as a blind preschooler said to her teacher, "I can tell by feeling things with my hands what they are like; but when I grow up, then I will be able to see the colors, too, won't I?" The teacher replied, with tears in her eyes, "Yes, my darling, then everything will be all right."

Acceptance of the child's limitations as well as capitalization on his strengths is the balance to strive for and to model for the family. Some children will in time overcome a disability entirely, but others will not be able to do this. Helping the parents and the child accept this fact, as well as accepting it oneself, is difficult to do but valuable.

Keep regular records of the child's development. Since progress with all children, including exceptional ones, occurs a little at a time, it is easy to feel discouraged from time to time and lose sight of how far the youngster has come. If the teacher keeps regular written records, however brief, a review of them will encourage her.

It is particularly important to keep records on an exceptional youngster so that they may be summarized and added to his medical record or given to his next teacher to acquaint her with his interests and progress. The records should cover whatever incidents seem particularly important to the child, indications of growth or slipping backward, special interests and tastes, and significant information contributed by the parents and physician.

Occasionally, the teacher may be asked to participate in an in-depth study of an emotionally disturbed younster, and so she will want to make more detailed written observations to be used in discussion and consultation. Although time consuming, this kind of study can be helpful and revealing. The reader can refer to references at the end of the chapter for models and suggestions about how to carry out such observations successfully.

GUIDELINES FOR WORKING WITH PHYSICALLY HANDICAPPED CHILDREN

Since physical disabilities range from blindness to cerebral palsy, it is, of course, impossible to discuss each condition in detail here. The references at the end of the chapter provide further information on particular problems.

In general, the suggestions already listed apply to these children. A physically handicapped youngster should be treated as typically as possible, and he should be neither overprotected nor underprotected. A conference with his physician or physical therapist can help the staff ascertain the degree of protection that is necessary.

The teacher who bears these guidelines in mind and who approaches each situation pragmatically will find it relatively simple to deal with children who have physical handicaps. Also, parents are often gold mines of practical advice about how to help the child effectively, and their information, combined with the fresh point of view provided by the nursery school staff, can usually solve problems if they arise.

GUIDELINES FOR WORKING WITH EMOTIONALLY DISTURBED CHILDREN

Even though the teacher may not have a chronically disturbed youngster in her nursery school, it is certain she will have to deal with children who are at least temporarily upset from time to time. These upsets may be as minor as occasional emotional outbursts or as major as a child who weeps frantically when he comes to school, refuses to eat anything, and is unable to lose himself in play.

Adults often discount the effect of important family crises on young children, either assuming that the children do not understand or that they simply aren't aware of what is going on; but this is far from the real truth. Children are very sensitive to the emotional climate of the home; and although they may draw incorrect conclusions about the reasons for the unhappiness, they are almost always aware that something is going on and are likely to respond with a variety of coping mechanisms.

There are many causes of such disturbances, including hospitalization of the child or of a family member, desertion by one of the parents, a death in the family, divorce, the birth of a sibling, moving from one home to another, a mother going to work, a father losing his job, chronic alcoholism, or involvment with drugs (Varma, 1973). Even something as relatively innocuous as a long visit from a grandparent can be upsetting to the child if it becomes an occasion for disturbances in routine or for dissention.

The teacher should watch for any pronounced change in the child's behavior as well as for signs of withdrawal, inability to give or receive affection, reduced ability to play either by himself or with other children, reduced interest in conversation, aggressive acting out, marked preoccupations with a particular activity or topic, and extreme emotional responses, such as bursting into tears or temper tantrums. She should also notice the usual signs of tension commonly seen in young children who are upset: whining, bed-wetting, increased fretfulness and irritability, hair twisting, thumb-sucking, stuttering, an increased dependence on security symbols such as blankets or toy animals, and so forth.

The teacher should realize that these behaviors are not reprehensible and that it is not desirable for her to concentrate her energy on removing them from the child's repertoire. They *are* signs that the child is suffering from some kind of stress either at home or nursery school and that this should be looked into and mitigated.

Short-term techniques

First, a note of caution is in order. When a child who has been getting along well at nursery school suddenly falls apart, it is always best to consider whether the upset could be due to physical illness. Many an inexperienced teacher has spent a sleepless night over such a child only to have his mother call and report an illness the next morning.

Make a special point of offering tension-relieving activities to the youngster who is upset. The best of these is water play in a relaxed atmosphere where the child can have his clothing well protected or can change afterwards into something dry. Mud, dough, and soft clay can also be helpful, as are the sublimated activities listed in the chapter on aggression (Chapter 7).

Relax standards somewhat in order to take stress off the child. This does not mean that anything goes; it does mean that the teacher should ease the child's way through the day with only the more important demands enforced. In other words, she should take the pressure off where she can without creating additional insecurity by letting the child get away with murder.

Talk things over with the family and work with them to identify what may be generating the upset in the child. Discussing a child's emotional problems requires a delicate touch to avoid the impression that the teacher is prying into personal matters that are none of her business, but the insight gained from such discussions can provide valuable information that can enable the teacher to draw the child out and express in play or words what is troubling him. Increased understanding of the cause will help the teacher be more tolerant of the child's behavior. She may also be able to offer some helpful counseling resources for the family to explore or may sometimes offer help herself by listening and assisting the parents in clarifying alternative ways to solve the difficulty.

Help the child work through his feelings by furnishing opportunities to use dolls, puppets, and dramatic play to express his concern. For example, a child who has been through a term of hospitalization may delight in using a doctor's kit and administering shots to dolls or other children with spirited malevolence. When such play is combined with the teacher's perceptive comments that recognize how frightened and angry the child is, this activity can do a world of good.

Long-term techniques

There are a few fortunate communities that offer special nursery school experiences for children categorized as chronically disturbed. However, because such opportunities are still quite rare and because many disturbed children profit from inclusion in regular nursery school, it is desirable for nursery school teachers to offer this special service whenever they feel they can manage it. Apart from treating psychotic children, who usually require a specialized environment that allows more one-to-one contact combined with special expertise, there is nothing particularly mysterious about providing care for emotionally disturbed youngsters. What it really takes to make such a placement turn out successfully is common sense, patience, determination, faith in oneself, and faith that the child and his family will be able to change.

Treat the chronically disturbed child as much like the other children as possible, and utilize his strengths to bring him into the life of the group. In my school one youngster who was unable to talk with either children or adults loved using the large push broom and spent many hours sweeping sand off the tricycle track. The first words he ever used at school grew out of this participation when, after weeks of sweeping, he yelled at one of the children who had bumped into his broom, "You just stay outta my way or I'll pop you one!" Once the sound barrier was broken, this youngster became increasingly verbal and was able to move on to kindergarten with reasonable success.

Anticipate that progress will be uneven. Chronically disturbed children may move ahead in an encouraging way and then suddenly backslide. This should not be cause for despair. If he progressed once, he will do it again, and probably faster the second time. It is, of course, desirable to identify and ameliorate the reason for the regression if this can be discerned.

Draw on the advice of specialists and encourage the family to continue to do this. A disturbed child often comes to school because he has been referred by a specialist. A regular arrangement for calling and reporting progress to the expert, invitations to him to come and visit the school, and perhaps some written reports during the year should be part of the teacher's professional obligation when she agrees to enroll a chronically disturbed youngster. Needless to say, the specialist who makes the referral should be willing to discharge his responsibility by guiding the teacher when she requires his help.

GUIDELINES FOR WORKING WITH MENTALLY RETARDED CHILDREN

Mental retardation is defined as "subaverage intellectual functioning which originates during the developmental period and is associated with impairment of adaptive behavior" (Heber, 1961). The severity of the condition varies widely: mildly or moderately retarded children are the best prospects for inclusion in nursery school. The mildly retarded child will probably fit so easily into a nursery school curriculum serving a heterogeneous age group that no special recommendations are necessary other than reminding the teacher to see the child in terms of his actual developmental level rather than his chronological age.

The moderately retarded child will also often fit comfortably into the heterogeneous nursery school, but many teachers find it helpful to have a clear understanding of the most worthwhile educational goals for these children and also to understand some simple principles for teaching them most effectively.

Basic learning goals for a moderately retarded preschool youngster should center on (1) helping him to be as independent as possible, which includes learning simple self-help skills as well as learning to help other people by doing simple tasks, (2) helping the child develop language skills, and (3) helping him learn to get along with other children in an acceptable way.

These goals are really no different from ones that are part of the regular nursery school curriculum. The only differences are that the retarded child will be farther behind other children of his age and that he will need a simpler manner of instruction. Children who learn slowly should not be confused with a lot of talk and shadings of meaning. They need concrete examples, definite rules, and consistent reinforcement of desired behavior. In general, the bywords with these children are: keep it concrete, keep it simple, and keep it fun.

Some specific suggestions may also help the teacher:

1. As much as possible, treat the child as you would treat all children in the group, but exercise common sense so that you expect neither too much nor too little.
2. Know the developmental steps so that you understand what he should learn next as he progresses.
3. Remember that retarded children learn best what they repeat frequently. Be prepared to go over a simple rule or task many times until the child has it firmly in mind. (This need for patient repetition is one of the things inexperienced teachers may find most irritating, particularly when the child has appeared to grasp the idea just the day before. Don't give up hope: if the teaching is simple and concrete enough, he will eventually learn.)
4. Pick out behavior to teach that the child can use all his life; that is, try to teach ways of behaving that will be appropriate for an older as well as a younger child to use. For example, don't let him run and kiss everyone he meets, since this will not be acceptable when he is just a little older. He has enough to do without having to unlearn old behavior.
5. Allow sufficient time for him to accomplish a selected task. Complex things take longer; simpler things take less time.
6. Encourage the child to be persistent by keeping tasks simple and satisfying. This will encourage him to finish what he starts.
7. Remember that independence is an important goal. Make sure the child is not being overprotected.
8. Teach one thing at a time. For instance, teach him to feed himself, then to use a napkin, then to pour his milk.
9. Don't rely on talking as the primary means of instruction. Show the child what you mean whenever possible.
10. Encourage the development of speech. Wait for at least some form of verbal reply whenever possible. Gently increase the demand for a

"quality" response as his skills increase.

11. Remember that retarded children are just as sensitive to the emotional climate around them as ordinary children are. Therefore, *never* talk about a child in front of him. It is likely that he will at least pick up the feeling of what you are saying, and this may hurt his feelings badly.

12. Show the child you are pleased with him and that you like him.

13. After a fair trial at learning something new, if he cannot seem to learn it, drop the activity without recrimination. Try it again in a few months; he may be ready to learn it by then.

TEACHING MENTALLY GIFTED PRESCHOOL CHILDREN

Although there have been interesting investigations of intellectual giftedness in older children and adults (Marland, 1972; Terman, Baldwin and Bronson, 1925), the possibility of educating intellectually gifted children has been largely ignored on the preschool level. Yet it is obvious that children of exceptional mental ability must be present in this portion of the population. (Martinson [1973] estimates that 3% of the older school population is intellectually gifted.) However, when I raise the question of making special provision for such youngsters in the nursery school curriculum, my students and teaching colleagues appear bewildered at this possibility.

Perhaps this is because we have fought a battle against undue intellectual pressure in the nursery school for so long that we forget that gifted children thrive when provided with additional intellectual stimulation and that we may be cheating them when we deprive them of it. Of course, gifted children should not be treated as precocious little adults or worshipped because of their special talent, but they should be provided with stimulating things to learn while at the same time keeping their social and emotional life as natural and easy as possible.

The provision of an enriched curriculum does not necessarily mean that the teacher must teach the child to read, although many gifted children already know how to read before they enter kindergarten (Martinson, 1961). I will never forget my surprise when one of the bright lights in my school wandered into my office, picked up a plain bound book from my desk and commented, "Hmmmmm, this looks interesting—*All about Dinosaurs.* Can I borrow this?" (I let him.)

What the teacher *can* do is make sure such children have plenty of opportunities to pursue subjects that interest them in as much depth as they desire. It is important to avoid the trap of thinking to oneself, "Oh, well, *they* wouldn't be able to do *that!*" It is astonishing what gifted children can do if they are provided with encouragement and materials. For example, I once had two young students, a boy and a girl, who were interested in the weather. They went from this to an interest in temperature and how heat makes thermometers work. Of course, all the children were interested in this subject to an extent, but these two youngsters, who later proved to be gifted, were truly absorbed. Their investigations included breaking open a thermometer to discover what it was made of, collecting different kinds of thermometers to see if they all worked the same way and if they all measured the same kinds of things, and even working out a number scale with drawings to show the range of temperatures measured by different instruments.

Intellectually gifted preschool children often love discussion that focusses on "What would happen if . . ." or "How could we . . ." These questions require creative reasoning as well as transforming old information into new solutions. These children will also relish the more difficult activities suggested in the chapter on mental development, since these activities can be adjusted to their level of ability and thus sustain their interest.

Gifted children at our Center have also enjoyed the investigation of how simple machines work and the determination of cause-and-effect relationships in these machines. I am indebted to students in my classes for the following suggestions, all of which the children enjoyed: investigation of can openers, pencil sharpeners, eggbeaters, auto jacks, old gum ball machines that can be opened, flashlights, vacuum cleaners, fishing reels, meat grinders, small juice presses, a hand-cranked ice cream freezer, coffee percolators, a Christmas tree stand, coffee grinders, cookie presses, old music boxes, and food mills.

Language activities are also particularly dear to mentally gifted preschoolers. They enjoy more advanced stories than average children do and also can put their superior ability to work by concocting tales of their own which are almost invariably complex, detailed, and advanced in vocabulary. Discussion and conversation should be employed at every opportunity to allow these children to put their ideas into words and to test them out against the ideas of other people.

CONCLUSION

The teacher who works with an exceptional preschool child must seek all the information she can on the condition if she really wants to be an effective teacher. This chapter can do no more than scratch the surface.

There are increasing numbers of courses in exceptionality being offered by schools of education, as inservice training, and by university extension units as the general trend toward including exceptional children in regular public school classes gains ground. In addition to these courses, books are also available, and many are listed in the references at the end of this chapter. Unfortunately, the education of very young exceptional children is still only sparsely covered in the literature, but with the Head Start mandate on exceptionality this situation is likely to change for the better in the next few years.

SUMMARY

The nursery school teacher has two primary responsibilities to exceptional children. First, she must serve as a screening agent and help identify possible problems, whether they are physical, emotional, or mental, that have escaped the attention of the physician. Following identification of a difficulty, the teacher should attempt to effect a referral to the appropriate specialist.

Second, she must do all she can to integrate children with special problems into her nursery school group. This requires careful assessment before admission and flexibility of adjustment following entrance to school. It is vital that she treat the exceptional child as typically as possible and encourage his independence without demanding skills that lie beyond his ability. Following the recommendations for working with physically handicapped, emotionally disturbed, mentally retarded, and intellectually gifted preschool children included in this chapter will also assist her in working with exceptional children.

QUESTIONS AND ACTIVITIES

1. *Problem:* After viewing the film *One of Them Is Brett,* which describes children who were malformed as a result of thalidomide poisoning of the mother during pregnancy, discuss how you could integrate a youngster without arms into your nursery school. Be sure to consider not only practical ways he could participate in activities, but also how you will explain the nature of his handicap to other children and parents. What would be the most constructive attitude to take in relation to this youngster?

2. Many people are confused about the difference between children who are termed mentally ill and those termed mentally retarded. Explain the similarities and differences between these conditions.

3. Do you feel that it is generally wise to suggest medication as a means of controlling hyperactivity in children? Why or why not?

4. This chapter makes a strong case for the early identification of potentially handicapping disorders. What are the real disadvantages of labeling children as being different? What are some ways to obtain help for such youngsters without stigmatizing them at the same time?

5. What do you feel accounts for the fact that very intelligent children are often overlooked at the preschool level? Might the provision of a special curriculum for them result in

precocity and overintellectualization, thereby spoiling their childhood?

6. *Problem:* Your staff has carefully interviewed and evaluated a severely handicapped youngster whose family has requested admission to school and has reluctantly decided that he cannot be accepted. How could this decision be relayed most effectively and humanely to the family?

REFERENCES FOR FURTHER READING

Overviews

Bowley, A. H., and Gardner, L. *The young handicapped child: educational guidance for the young cerebral palsied, deaf, blind and autistic child.* (2nd ed.) Edinburgh: E. & S. Livingstone, 1969. This small book is filled with practical advice about living with and educating exceptional children; very helpful.

Dunn, L. M. (Ed.) *Exceptional children in the schools: special education in transition.* (2nd ed.) New York: Holt, Rinehart and Winston, Inc., 1973. This excellent collection of articles is written by specialists in the fields of various kinds of exceptionality ranging from mental retardation to physical disabilities.

Jordan, J. B., and Darley, R. F. *Not all little red wagons are red: the exceptional child's early years.* Arlington, Va.: The Council for Exceptional Children, 1973. In this indispensable reference from the Invisible College Conference on Early Childhood Education and the Exceptional Child, Jordan and Darley emphasize the importance of beginning education early, discuss training of parents and teachers, and include a valuable list of resources for day care and for working with young handicapped children.

Kirk, S. A. *Educating exceptional children.* (2nd ed.) Boston: Houghton Mifflin Co., 1972. Kirk, a famous authority in the field, discusses many kinds of exceptionality, as well as general practices that are used to educate exceptional youngsters.

Kliman, G. *Psychological emergencies of childhood.* New York: Grune & Stratton, Inc., 1968. Based on studies of emotionally healthy children's reactions to crisis situations, the book recommends directness and honesty when dealing with life's catastrophes. It has a particularly extensive section on illness and death.

Spock, B., and Lerrigo, M. O. *Caring for your disabled child.* New York: The Macmillan Co., 1965. (Also available in paperback.) This is a good book for parents and teachers to read because it is filled with practical, frank information about child care and also anticipates problems the child may encounter as he reaches adulthood; highly recommended.

Varma, V. P. *Stresses in children.* New York: Crane, Russak & Co., 1973. This English book is a useful reference because it covers some special problems, such as bereavement and immigration, as well as the more frequently discussed problems of blindness, deafness, and physical disability.

Identification of Disorders

For additional references on testing, also refer to the references following Chapter 20.

Gallagher, J. J., and Bradley, R. H. Early identification of developmental difficulties. In I. J. Gordon (Ed.), *Early childhood education: the seventy-first yearbook of the National Society for the Study of Education, part II.* Chicago: University of Chicago Press, 1972. The authors present an excellent discussion of the purposes and problems associated with diagnostic testing and with the early identification of disability. They also cite a selection of tests used for identifying difficulties of various kinds.

Teaching Exceptional Children in the Nursery School

Conner, F. P., and Talbot, M. E. *An experimental curriculum for young mentally retarded children.* New York: Teachers College Press, 1970. In their extraordinarily helpful book, Conner and Talbot list five levels of difficulty for each curriculum item, describe behavior that would reflect each level, and outline teaching procedures that can be used to develop the skill in question. The book also contains a narrative description of the 5-year project for preschool educable mentally retarded children as it was developed by Teachers College of Columbia University and the U. S. Office of Education. This book should be in the library of every teacher who is interested in the development of a sequential curriculum whether or not she is working with retarded children.

Dashe, M. *Children with special problems: a manual for day care centers.* Washington, D. C.: Day Care and Child Development Council of America, 1972. Dashe's short pamphlet contains criteria for determining the eligibility of the exceptional youngster for day care. It also includes a discussion of special problems that may be encountered with a variety of difficulties and a few recommendations for coping with these difficulties.

Engel, R., and Gold, B. The early childhood unit—a lot of room for children to grow. *Teaching Exceptional Children,* 1974, **6**(2), 59-67. Engel and Gold describe the early childhood unit of the Sophia Slavin school, a public school that serves orthopedically handicapped, trainable mentally retarded, and educable handicapped children. They outline the daily program and include a floor plan of the early childhood unit.

Furman, R. A., and Katan, A. K. *The therapeutic nursery school.* New York: International Universities Press, 1969. An account of a nursery school that was established primarily to study and relieve emotional problems in young children, this book would be of particular interest to students concerned with the application of psychoanalytic theory to early childhood education.

Glockner, M. *Integrating handicapped children into regular classrooms.* Urbana, Ill.: University of Illinois and ERIC Clearinghouse on Early Childhood Education, 1973. Glockner reports an interview with Jenny Klein which offers practical suggestions about including handicapped children in a normal group. An annotated bibliography is included.

Granato, S., and Krone, E. *8—Serving children with special needs.* Washington, D. C.: U. S. Department of Health, Education, and Welfare, Office of Child Development, 1972. In this practical, information-filled pamphlet, Granato and Krone discuss admission policies and working with parents, and give useful suggestions for working with several kinds of exceptional children. The pamphlet has an outstanding list of community resources, associations dealing with special problems, and addresses of special educational programs and funding sources. It also has a good annotated bibliography. These additional resources make this pamphlet the best brief reference in the field.

Lawrence, T. M. (Ed.) *Teaching Exceptional Children,* 1971, **3**(3). An entire issue of this journal is devoted to the subject of precision teaching, emphasizing the value of charting and reinforcement to promote learning in exceptional children.

Lindsay, Z. *Art and the handicapped child.* New York: Van Nostrand Reinhold Co., 1972. Lindsay suggests many kinds of creative materials that can be used successfully with children who have special needs. Many of these could be refreshing variations to use with ordinary preschoolers also.

Michal-Smith, H. *The exceptional child in the normal nursery.* New York: Early Childhood Education Council of New York, 1966. This is the best general article on the pros and cons of admitting exceptional children to nursery school that has been written; it is forthright, clear, and sensible.

Murphy, L. B., and Leeper, E. M. *The vulnerable child.* Washington D. C.: U. S. Department of Health, Education, and Welfare, Office of Child Development, 1970. Murphy and Leeper identify several kinds of vulnerabilities in general terms and discuss how to handle stress effectively. Simply written, this is a useful introduction to the subject.

Schattner, R. *An early childhood curriculum for multiply handicapped children.* New York: Intext Press, 1971. This is a rare book because it discusses the education of preschool-aged multiply handicapped children—a subject just beginning to receive the attention it deserves.

Webb, L. *Children with special needs in the infants' school.* London: Collins Fontana Book, 1969. Webb presents a series of case studies describing problems of children 5 years old or older attending a British infant school. Brief analyses are given at the end of each section; interesting reading.

Overviews of Mental and Emotional Disorders

Bakwin, H., and Bakwin, R. M. *Behavior disorders in children.* (4th ed.) Philadelphia: W. B. Saunders Co., 1972.

Kessler, J. W. *Psychopathology of childhood.* Englewood Cliffs, N. J.: Prentice-Hall, Inc., 1966.

Shaw, C. R. *The psychiatric disorders of childhood.* New York: Appleton-Century-Crofts, 1966. The Bakwins', Kessler's, and Shaw's books all offer competent discussions of a great many kinds of exceptionality and overviews of treatment procedures.

Mental Retardation

Adams, M. *Mental retardation and its social dimensions.* New York: Columbia University Press, 1971. *Mental Retardation* focusses on the problems of families with retarded children. The teacher who anticipates counseling such families would find the chapters on casework and on the dependent client and his family enlightening.

Dittman, L. L. *The mentally retarded child at home: a manual for parents.* Washington, D. C.: U. S. Department of Health, Education, and Welfare, The Children's Bureau, 1964. This inexpensive, helpful booklet is packed with practical suggestions about how to help the young retarded child learn what he needs to know.

Hunter, M., Schucman, H., and Friedlander, G.

The retarded child from birth to five: a multidisciplinary program for child and family. New York: The John Day Co., Inc., 1972. This excellent overview of the kinds of services that should be available to assist the retarded child has a helpful emphasis on working with the entire family. It also contains recommendations and suggestions for working with children who have developmental lags.

Kirk, S. A., Karnes, M. B., and Kirk, W. D. *You and your retarded child: a manual for parents of retarded children.* (2nd ed.) Palo Alto, Calif.: Pacific Books, Publishers, 1968. Simply written and full of useful information, this manual is particularly good because of the developmental standards that are provided in one of the chapters. It also has an unusual chapter on teaching the retarded child through play.

Mycue, E. de los S. *Young children with handicaps: part III. Educable and trainable mentally handicapped: an abstract bibliography.* Urbana, Ill.: University of Illinois and ERIC Clearinghouse for Early Childhood Education, 1973. Many aspects of retardation are covered in this good reference resource.

Pseudoretardation

Hellmuth, J. (Ed.) *Disadvantaged child: Head Start and early intervention.* Vol. 2. New York: Brunner/Mazel, Inc., 1968.

Hellmuth, J. (Ed.) *Disadvantaged child: compensatory education, a national debate. Vol. 3.* New York: Brunner/Mazel, Inc., 1970. Volumes 2 and 3 are good places to begin a study of the disadvantaged child because the articles cover many aspects of this problem.

The Gifted Learner

DeNevi, D. The education of a genius: analyzing major influences in the life of America's greatest architect. *Young Children,* 1968, **23**(4), 233-239. Denevi gives a fascinating account of the influence of Froebelian early education on the development of Frank Lloyd Wright, relating his interest in architecture to early experiences with block play. Diagrams are included.

Grost, A. *Genius in residence.* Englewood Cliffs, N. J.: Prentice-Hall, Inc., 1970. This is a good book for the reader who is looking for a chatty, informal account of what it can be like to bring up an extremely intelligent child. Mrs. Grost describes her trials with the school system and how her family managed to accommodate to her son's needs and yet keep him as natural and unaffected as possible.

Martinson, R. Children with superior cognitive abilities. In L. M. Dunn (Ed.), *Exceptional children in the schools: special education in transition.* New York: Holt, Rinehart and Winston, Inc., 1973. Martinson provides a competent up-to-date review of issues and research in the field of giftedness.

Teaching Emotionally Disturbed Preschoolers

Braun, S. J., and Lasher, M. G. *Preparing teachers to work with disturbed preschoolers.* Cambridge, Mass.: Nimrod Press, 1972. Braun and Lasher give an interesting description of a training project for teachers who were learning to serve as resource people and as teachers of disturbed young children. The book is valuable because of the case histories and descriptions of how disturbed preschool youngsters were handled in the nursery school environment.

Cohen, S. How to alleviate the first-year shock of teaching emotionally disturbed children. In M. S. Auleta (Ed.), *Foundations of early childhood education: readings.* New York: Random House, Inc., 1969. Cohen presents an understanding discussion of what the teacher of disturbed children needs to realize to help her survive her first difficult months with disturbed children.

Kanner, L. Early infantile autism. *Journal of Pediatrics,* 1944, **25**, 211-217. In this unassuming, classic paper Kanner identified the psychosis called early childhood autism.

Menninger Clinic Children's Division. *Disturbed children.* Jossey-Bass, Inc., Publishers, 1969. The process of outpatient diagnosis of disturbed children is described. How the abilities of different specialists can work together to provide a comprehensive diagnosis is shown; interesting reading.

Mycue, E. de los S. *Young children with handicaps, part I. Emotional disturbance and specific learning disabilities.* Urbana, Ill,: College of Education Curriculum Laboratory, 1973. This is a good beginning place for those who wish to pursue further research by means of a bibliography.

Shaffer, H. B. *Emotionally disturbed children.* Washington, D. C.: Educational Research Reports, 1973. Shaffer outlines the history of litigation concerned with the rights of emotionally disturbed children to education and briefly discusses other problems, including diagnosis and cost of care.

Wing, J. K. (Ed.) *Early childhood autism: clinical, educational and social aspects.* Oxford: Pergamon Press, 1966. This is a balanced, sensible book about a puzzling condition.

Information about Specific Disabilities

Brooks, M. Helping the child amputee. *Newsletter, Association For The Care Of Children In Hospitals,* 1973, **1**(1), 1-4. Brooks illustrates how play therapy can be an effective help in bringing about a sound adjustment in young children who must cope with an amputation.

Buchanan, R. and Mullins, J. B. Integration of a spina bifida child in a kindergarten for normal children. *Young Children,* 1968, **23**(6), 339-344. Buchanan and Mullins give an account of the successful inclusion of a severely handicapped youngster into a normal kindergarten.

Gearheart, B. R. *Learning disabilities: educational strategies.* St. Louis: The C. V. Mosby Co., 1973. Although learning disability does not commonly become evident until the child is in kindergarten or the later grades, knowledge of this subject is increasing, and it may be that earlier identification at the preschool level will result in increased effectiveness of treatment. Therefore, it is a subject early childhood teachers need to know more about, and this book reviews many approaches to educating the child with this problem.

Goodman, W. When you meet a blind person. In S. A. Kirk and F. E. Lord (Eds.), *Exceptional children: educational resources and perspectives.* Boston: Houghton Mifflin Co., 1974. Goodman gives valuable advice about what to do and not to do when accompanying a blind person; stresses ways to encourage independence.

Grinspoon. L., and Singer, S. L. Amphetamines in the treatment of hyperkinetic children. *Harvard Educational Review,* 1973, **43**(4), 515-555. The authors present a thoughtful analysis of the possible adverse effects of using medication on hyperkinetic children and urge restraint and moderation.

Halliday, C. *The visually impaired child: growth, learning and development: infancy to school age.* Louisville, Ky.: American Printing House for the Blind, 1971. Halliday gives an interesting factual description of general developmental patterns combined with comments and suggestions about how to help the blind child achieve these developmental steps.

Lowenfeld, B. *The visually handicapped child in school.* New York: The John Day Co., Inc., 1973. This wide-ranging book is filled with practical information about the management of blind children as they grow and develop. The history of the education of the blind and teacher preparation are also discussed.

Moor, P. What teachers are saying—about the young blind child. *Journal of Nursery Education,* 1960, **15**, 2. Moor gives sensible suggestions about how to include a blind child in a sighted nursery school group.

Mycue, E. de los S. *Young children with handicaps, part II. Physically handicapped.* Urbana, Ill.: University of Illinois and ERIC Clearinghouse for Early childhood Education, 1973. This helpful reference for further reading in this field covers many physical disabilities.

Northcott, W. H. Candidate for integration: a hearing-impaired child in a regular nursery school. *Young Children,* 1971, **25**(6), 367-380. Northcott discusses placement of such children in the typical nursery school and briefly discusses ways to facilitate their learning once they have been admitted.

O'Connell, D. *Multiply handicapped children: a bibliography.* Urbana, Ill.: University of Illinois and ERIC Clearinghouse on Early Childhood Education, 1973. This annotated bibliography dealing with youngsters who have a combination of problems lists topics covered by articles but makes no attempt to report actual content.

Robb, P. *Epilepsy: a review of basic and clinical research.* Washington, D. C.: U. S. Department of Health, Education, and Welfare, National Institute of Neurological Diseases and Blindness, 1965. This inexpensive government publication contains a gold mine of information about epilepsy, although it does not discuss handling this condition in the classroom.

Wender, P. H. *The hyperactive child: a handbook for parents.* New York: Crown Publishers, Inc., 1973. Wender discusses possible causes, symptoms, and treatment of hyperactivity; the book is highly recommended.

Using Observations for Child Study

Cohen, D. H., and Stern, V. S. *Observing and recording the behavior of young children.* New York: Teachers College Press, 1958. In this classic reference, Cohen and Stern suggest many different aspects of the child's behavior that may be observed and recorded to deepen the teacher's insight into the child's personality.

Rowan, B. *The children we see.* New York: Holt, Rinehart and Winston, Inc., 1973. Rowan approaches child study by means of observation and uses these observations to illustrate basic principles of child development. A good section on characteristics of children at different developmental levels, as well as many examples, is included.

Referral and Information Resources

Ellingson, C., and Cass, J. *Directory of facilities for the learning-disabled and handicapped.* New York: Harper & Row, Publishers, 1972. This invaluable referral resource contains succinct information on the type of service offered by facilities throughout the United States, listed by state.

Glassman, L., and Erickson, D. *A selected guide to government agencies concerned with exceptional children.* Arlington, Va.: IMC/RMC Network, 1972. A broad spectrum of programs concerned with activities for the handicapped is listed—a good way to get an overview of government-sponsored centers and resources.

Mycue, E. de los S. *Young children with handicaps: part IV. Resources: directories, newsletters, bibliographies and general information: an abstract bibliography.* Urbana, Ill.: University of Illinois and the ERIC Clearinghouse for Early Childhood Education, 1973. The title is self-explanatory.

PART EIGHT

Setting goals and evaluating results

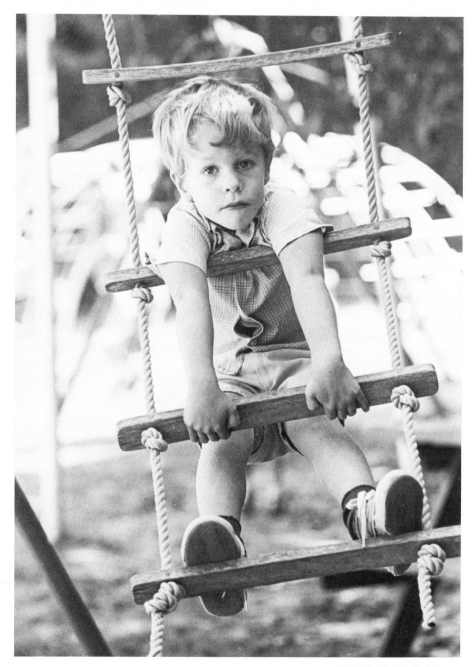

Photo by Jason Lo'Cicero

CHAPTER **19**

Using educational objectives in the preschool

> Once upon a time the animals had a school. The curriculum consisted of running, climbing, flying, and swimming, and all the animals took part in all the subjects.
>
> The Duck was good in swimming, better, in fact, than his instructor, and he made passing grades in flying, but he was practically hopeless in running. Because he was low in this subject, he was made to stay in after school and drop his swimming class in order to practice running. He kept this up until he was only average in swimming. But average is acceptable, so nobody worried about that except the Duck.
>
> The Eagle was considered a problem pupil and was disciplined severely. He beat all the others to the top of the tree in the climbing class, but he used his own way of getting there.
>
> The Rabbit started out at the top of the class in running, but he had a nervous breakdown and had to drop out of school on account of so much makeup work in swimming.
>
> The Squirrel led the climbing class, but his flying teacher made him start his flying lessons from the ground instead of the top of the tree down, and he developed charley horses from overexertion at the takeoff and began getting C's in climbing and D's in running.
>
> The practical Prairie Dogs apprenticed their offspring to a Badger when the school authorities refused to add digging to the curriculum.
>
> At the end of the year, the abnormal Eel that could swim well, run, climb, and fly a little was made valedictorian.
>
> ANONYMOUS

PROS AND CONS OF BEHAVIORAL OBJECTIVES

The use of behavioral objectives to identify curriculum goals is coming into vogue in some preschool programs, and the growing popularity of this approach is borne out by the fact that some states now require programs they support to furnish such objectives in order to retain their funding.

Nonetheless, reaction to using this technique in early childhood education is mixed. The cardinal disadvantage is that there is little research-backed evidence that the use of objectives in preschool or in the upper grades produces a more effective program (Eisner, 1969), although common sense argues strongly that clear identification of values and goals should make planning and implementation of

273

the curriculum easier and more definite.

It is also true that poorly used objectives may stultify and narrow an educational program. They can absorb great quantities of the teacher's time in composing and then never be looked at again, or they can be written to specify such tiny points of behavior that they miss the broader goals that are the real substance upon which education should be built (Combs, 1972; Ebel, 1970; Moskovitz, 1973).

Although these undesirable outcomes are a real possibility, the use of behavioral objectives does not have to be a restricted, time-wasting, nit-picking occupation. Objectives can be used to help the teacher think seriously about which goals have the greatest value as well as define clearly how she will be able to tell when the child has reached these goals. This clear-sightedness can be a worthwhile antidote to the high-minded pronouncements that abound in education and that give the reader a pleasant glow but don't actually mean much when one begins to think about them. Consider the following excerpt, paraphrased from a nursery school brochure:

Our little school, nestled amid the rustic pines and hills of . . . , has as its goal the development of the whole child—we want him to be mentally healthy, physically able, authentically creative, and socially sensitive.

There is nothing wrong with this statement as a long-range, extremely general foundation for an educational program. But many teachers never bother to ask themselves seriously what practical things they will do to translate these lofty phrases into the nitty-gritty reality of the nursery school day. Behavioral objectives can help the teacher bridge this gap between broad purposes and actuality.

DEFINITION

Behavioral objectives are not as appalling as they sound. An objective is simply a clear statement that identifies a goal the teacher deems to be important. It usually consists of a sentence or two that describes how the child will behave when he has reached the goal. Although sometimes called *educational* or *instructional objec-*

tives, the term *behavioral objective* is used in this chapter to remind the student that the objective must be based on behavior she can see.

Objectives can and should cover many areas of learning rather than be restricted to only the cognitive domain. Thus a teacher who feels originality of ideas is important might write, "When presented with a problem that requires a solution, the child will be able to think of and try out a variety of solutions until he has found one that works. For example, when unable to get into a swing that is too high, he will be able to think of and try out several ways to reach the seat until he achieves success." Another teacher, who feels physical development is valuable, might specify, "Given one or two trials, the child will be able to catch a large ball at a distance of 5 feet."

SELECTING BROAD-RANGE BEHAVIORAL OBJECTIVES

It appears that the worst pitfall for the beginning teacher is a tendency to select picayune behaviors to document. This is probably because behavior such as finger snapping or color naming is easy to see and count. The student should realize that it is equally possible to write behavioral objectives in the affective or cognitive domain that identify richer, more significant behaviors (Lee and Merrill, 1972). The examples used throughout this chapter illustrate the truth of this assertion.

One approach that will help broaden the scope of the objectives and also reduce the feeling of being overwhelmed by the tremendous assortment of possibilities is to acquire an outline of the areas that education usually covers or to draw up such an outline oneself. These outlines are often called *taxonomies;* several of them are listed at the end of this chapter (Bloom, Engelhart, Furst, Hill, and Krathwohl, 1956; Hoepfner, Stern, and Nummedal, 1971; Krathwohl, Bloom, and Masia, 1964).

Following a perusal of the taxonomy, the teacher should select portions from it that she thinks are valuable and that she wishes to include as curriculum goals for the children in her group. From then on, writing objectives becomes a process of defining what behavior represents the attainment of the goal and of deciding how often and under what circumstances the behavior is expected to occur.

WRITING A BEHAVIORAL OBJECTIVE

The steps in writing a behavioral objective are as follows: (1) select the general goal the teacher feels is significant; (2) brainstorm a list of many behaviors that would reflect the accomplishment of the goal, and write objectives for the best of these; (3) state the conditions and performance levels for these objectives; and (4) add a list of suggested activities if desired.

Defining the general goals

Let us suppose that the teacher has consulted various taxonomies to help assure breadth of coverage and has decided that she wishes to cover five general areas when identifying her primary goals for education. The next step is for the teacher to state these goals in writing. For example, among many that might be selected, she could choose the following ones as meeting the needs of the children in her school.

Physical development
1. The child will be able to demonstrate or acquire physical skills appropriate to his age.
2. He will develop a sense of himself as being physically competent both in relation to his personal aspirations and in comparison with his peers.

Emotional stability and mental health
1. The child will remain in touch with a wide range of feelings, both positive and negative, within himself and will be encouraged to recognize and acknowledge their presence and express them in appropriate ways.
2. As he matures, the child will begin to achieve empathy and insight into the feelings and concerns of other children and members of the staff.
3. The development of self-esteem, which is basic to mental health, will be fostered through the development

of a variety of skills and competence in activities that the child sees as valuable.
4. The child will develop a sense of identity by learning who he is in relation to the space about him, in relation to other members of his family and their cultural background, and in relation to the children and staff in the school.

Creative self-expression
1. The child will express his own ideas and feelings through the use of self-expressive materials.
2. Creativity in ideas and in problem solving will be deliberately fostered in the children by the staff.

Social competence
1. The child will gain the ability to care about the rights and needs of other people. This is related to the mental health goal of feeling empathy for the feelings and needs of other people.
2. He will develop the ability to tolerate separation from his parents.
3. He will develop the ability to share staff attention with other children part of the time.
4. He will develop the ability to experience pleasure in working for the good of the group.
5. He will develop the ability to play with other children, accepting leadership from others from time to time and also contributing his own ideas when desirable.

Language and cognitive development
1. The child will be able to express himself verbally by using an increasingly wide range of vocabulary and by gradually extending the length and complexity of his syntax.
2. He will increase his communication skills by learning to listen to other people and grasp what they mean.
3. The child will develop his intellectual ability by performing a variety of tasks intended to provide practice in particular mental abilities that are relevant to later success in school. These abilities include:
   a. The ability to group and classify items.

b. The ability to arrange items in logical order and tell what comes next (using both spatial and temporal sequences).

c. The ability to formulate common associations.

d. The ability to identify objects that are identical and match these together.

e. The ability also to identify items that are different and label them as such.

f. The ability to grasp elementary principles of cause and effect.

g. The ability to transfer learning in order to facilitate the solving of problems.

Developing a list of behaviors that reflect the goals and writing behavioral objectives that describe the desired behavior

After identifying the broad goals, the teacher next needs to decide what behaviors could be used to indicate that the child has reached the goal. For example, in the first goal from the area of social competence ("The child will gain the ability to care about the rights and needs of other people"), the teacher would decide what some situations might be that would require the child to take the rights and needs of other people into consideration. One such occasion might be lunchtime, where everyone is entitled to a fair amount of food, or perhaps it would be respecting the privacy of other children's cubbies, being quiet at nap time so that all may sleep, not breaking other children's toys, or refraining from constantly demanding to be the center of attention.

Let us suppose the teacher has winnowed through this list and has picked sharing food at lunchtime as one of the situations to use when assessing whether the behavioral objective of caring about the rights of others is being attained.

Writing the objective. Now, after considerable trial and error, she writes an objective to fit lunchtime. "Given a bowl of a favorite food, the child will show that he cares about the rights of others by serving himself a portion and leaving enough food to serve others" (Peterson, Gonzalez, Hen-

drick, Johnson, Miller, Rhodes, Statucki, and Wilson, 1973).

Note that this teacher avoided a frequent pitfall in writing an objective by picking behavior she could *see* as the activity she was going to record. Notice she did not write, "The child will think of others and will be aware that everyone is hungry at lunchtime." The action described by such verbs as *think, be aware, understand,* or *appreciate* is impossible to observe, and their use should be avoided when writing objectives. Gerlach and Sullivan (1967) list several verbs gleaned from the American Association for the Advancement of Science behavioral classification system that are sound ones to use: *identify, name, describe* (tell about), *construct, order* (arrange in order, show what comes next), and *demonstrate* (show). (The words in parentheses are paraphrases of the verbs that seem more suitable to use with preschool youngsters.)

Note, also, that the objective given above does not explain how the child is going to learn to take some and leave some. Since teachers are likely to be teachers before they become objective writers, they often fall into the trap of trying to explain in the objective how the goal will be reached. For example, an inexperienced writer might produce the following objective: "The child will learn to share food at lunch by having to wait until last when he grabs out of turn." Aside from whether this is a sound teaching technique, note that it explains how the teacher intends to reach the goal of teaching social concern. This is incorrect. An objective should state only the desired outcome, not the means by which the goal is to be attained.

Occasionally, teachers like to list a specific example along with the more generally stated objective. This was done in the first objective given in this chapter, where the example of getting into the swing was added to the general objective having to do with creative thought in order to clarify what the teacher had in mind.

Writing objectives for individual children. Of course, it is also possible to write objectives for specific children. Many beginning objective writers will find this the easiest level at which to start. Here is an objective written by a hard-pressed preschool aide with a particular little boy in mind: "At snack time, Henry will wait until the basket of fruit is passed to him. He is not to grab or yell, 'Give me!' If he can usually wait until the basket has been passed to two other children before him, the goal is accomplished." Note how specific her goal is. Note also that she does not describe how she intends to teach him "not to grab or yell 'Give me!' " Note particularly the very last sentence of the objective because it brings us to the final item that must be included to make an objective complete.

Stating the conditions and performance level of the objective

The final things that must be added are the conditions and levels of performance the child is expected to reach in order to accomplish the objective. In the case above, the condition is that he can "wait until the basket has been passed to two other children before him," and the level, or frequency, of performance is "usually."

The portion of the objective that stipulates when and how consistently a child must carry out the behavior can be one of the most valuable parts of writing objectives, because statements of expectancy force one to examine underlying values as well as standards of performance. Consider an objective that states, "The child will provide evidence that he likes to eat by eating everything on his plate at each meal." Another example, written for a group of 3-year-olds, might be, "The children will sit quietly during story time. They will not interrupt the reader or talk to their neighbor while the story is being read." But are "eating everything on his plate" and "sitting quietly during story time" truly desirable educational goals? Are there other, more desirable ones that could be selected in place of these? What are the most fundamental values it would be desirable to stress?

Note also the level of expectation in the examples above. Should anyone be expected to be 100% perfect? Is it reasonable to demand that a youngster always clear his plate or that a group of 3-year-olds always sit quietly during story hour? Unless these objectives are modified, they imply an expectation of perfection. It is necessary to take the developmental level of the children into account and not set too high a standard of performance for them when writing objectives.

IMPLEMENTING THE OBJECTIVES

Sometimes a teacher finds it helpful to list some sample activities with each objective to clarify her thinking about how she will achieve the goal. The following activities might be included as means of implementing the objective about sharing food ("Given a bowl of a favorite food, the child will show that he feels concern for the other children by serving himself a portion and leaving enough food to serve the others"):

1. The teacher will check the kitchen and make sure the amount of food supplied will be plentiful.
2. She may delegate the child as the one to return to the kitchen for seconds to show him there is plenty.
3. When food is passed, she will remind the inexperienced child to take some and leave some, showing him what she means if this is necessary.
4. She will make sure the child has a second helping when he wants one.
5. She will commend his behavior when he does help himself and remember to leave enough for the other children.

CARRYING THROUGH THE OBJECTIVES

It is very well to make out a yearly plan and compose a list of objectives to fit it, but these objectives will have little effect on the actual program unless they are reviewed from time to time to make sure that the program is focussing on the objectives that were selected. If the objectives turn out not to fit what is really happening in the nursery school, then either they should be rewritten in terms of the real goals or the program should be modified to return to the stated standards.

ASCERTAINING WHETHER THE OBJECTIVES ARE BEING REACHED

The final step in using objectives is to evaluate not only whether they are being pursued but to find out whether the children are reaching them. The following chapter provides suggestions for building criterion-referenced measures that make evaluation possible.

SUMMARY

The application of educational objectives to curriculum planning is coming into vogue in some preschools. Properly developed objectives can help the teacher examine her value system, select goals she deems significant, and translate lofty ideals into practical behavioral expectations for the children in her group.

A well-written objective confines itself to specifying behavior that is readily apparent and to stating the frequency and conditions under which the behavior is expected to take place.

However, it is not sufficient only to write objectives. Checks must be made during the year to ascertain whether the objectives are being implemented in the actual curriculum, and evaluations should be carried out to determine whether the teaching has been effective.

QUESTIONS AND ACTIVITIES

1. What kinds of educational values do you think would be most likely overlooked when writing a set of behavioral objectives for a nursery school?
2. What might be some important educational values that are so intangible that you feel it might not be feasible to write objectives that could cover them?
3. Identify the differences between the general goals listed in the first part of the chapter and the behavioral objectives discussed later.
4. Select one of the general goals and practice identifying activities that would represent the goal in action; then write objectives based upon the satisfactory performance of these activities.
5. For negative practice, write the very worst objective you can think of. Be sure to make it an objective that is difficult to observe and that represents a value you feel would be in-consequential. Share these morsels with the class.

REFERENCES FOR FURTHER READING

Taxonomies and Discussions of Educational Values

Bloom, B. S., Engelhart, M. D., Furst, E. J., Hill, W. H., and Krathwohl, D. R. *Taxonomy of educational objectives: handbook I, the cognitive domain.* New York: David McKay Co., Inc., 1956; Krathwohl, D. R., Bloom, B. S., and Masia, B. B. *Taxonomy of educational objectives: handbook II, the affective domain.* New York: David McKay Co., Inc., 1964. The Bloom and Krathwohl taxonomies are listed here because they are so frequently referred to in the literature having to do with behavioral objectives. However, these particular taxonomies do not specify overt behavioral outcomes, and it may be difficult to translate the sophisticated skills listed in them into behavior that is characteristic of preschool children.

Chittenden, G. E., Murphy, M. N., and Williams, B. *Essentials of nursery education.* Washington, D. C.: National Association for the Education of Young Children, no date. This pamphlet lists basic purposes of early childhood education and helpfully provides descriptions of curricular provisions and teacher activities that would implement these purposes and goals.

Committee for Early Childhood. The fundamental learning needs of today's young children. *Young Children,* 1970, **25**(6), 326-335. This statement by the Ad Hoc Committee of the National Association for the Education of Young Children sets forth standards for educational policies intended to meet the fundamental needs of young children.

Hoepfner, R., Stern, C., and Nummedal, S. G. *CSE-ECRC preschool/kindergarten test evaluations.* Los Angeles: School Evaluation Project, Center for the Study of Evaluation and the Early Childhood Research Center, 1971. This applicable and useful taxonomy was developed following consultation with teachers, supervisors, early childhood specialists, and a perusal of the literature in the early childhood field. The goals identified by these sources were then translated into operational definitions. The outline covers the affective, intellectual, psychomotor, and subject achievement domains.

The Case against Behavioral Objectives

Combs, A. W. *Educational accountability:*

beyond behavioral objectives. Washington, D. C.: Association for Supervision and Curriculum Development, 1972. For a strong statement of the case against behavioristic psychology and behavioral objectives, the student should read this excellent article by Combs.

Construction of Objectives

Dillman, C. M., and Rahmlow, H. F. *Writing instructional objectives.* Belmont, Calif.: Fearon Publishers, 1972. This detailed, explicit, step-by-step manual for the construction of objectives contains many examples and suggestions. The authors also explain how to develop test items to evaluate whether an objective is being achieved.

Instructional Objectives Exchange. *Early childhood education.* Los Angeles: The Exchange, no date. This book contains a great many behavioral objectives purported to be on the early childhood level. It is necessary to be selective in using this list, but it makes a good starting point for developing objectives. Since it also supplies criterion behaviors, it could be used to build checklists for evaluation as well.

Lee, B. N., and Merrill, M. D. *Writing complete affective objectives: a short course.* Belmont, Calif.: Wadsworth Publishing Co. Inc., 1972. Lee and Merrill present convincing evidence that objectives need not be limited to the cognitive and psychomotor domain.

For the Advanced Student

Popham, W. J., Eisner, E. W., Sullivan, H. J., and Tyler, L. L. *Instructional objectives.* Chicago: Rand McNally & Co., 1969. Published under the auspices of the American Educational Research Association, this book contains discussions of the values of using educational objectives. Comments and appraisals of each paper follow each chapter; readable and interesting.

Tyler, R. W. *Basic principles of curriculum and instruction.* Chicago: University of Chicago Press, 1950. Tyler's work is a famous exemplar of the behavioral objectives movement.

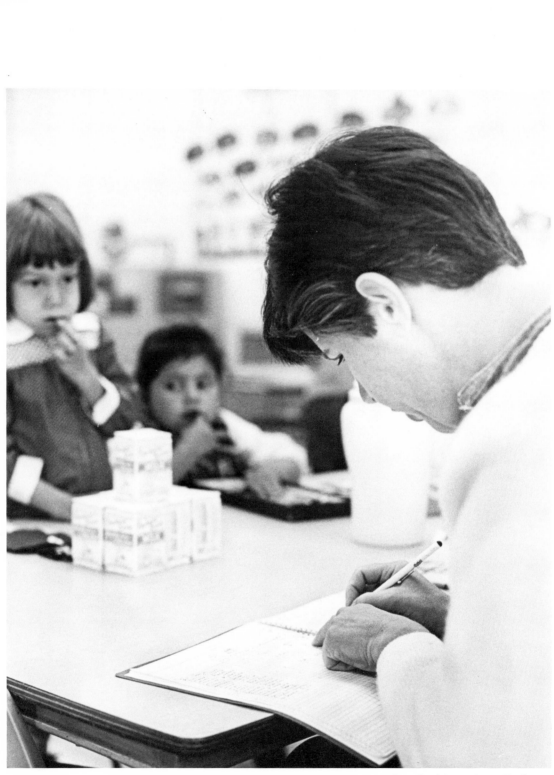

Goleta Head Start, Santa Barbara

CHAPTER 20

Practical methods of recording and evaluating behavior

The subje̱
ment of the
as 2, 3, and
over in begi
education. I
tion has bee
of the begir
because eva
been used
schools in t

However,
makes it ir
teachers gai
Recent dis
Evans, and
sell, 1970) o
sure effectiv
vant to the
ers to the im
using evaluat

(handwritten note overlaid: small serial boxes / purple lug paper bags 12"by18" / cardboard – large / large darning needle or tapestry needle / Oct 18 / Palmer)

priate to the programs in their schools. In addition, there is a growing trend toward requiring schools, even schools for very young children, to be *accountable:* schools are being expected more and more frequently to furnish proof that what they are doing with children makes a difference to the children's learning and behavior.

For both these pressing reasons, as well as for other educational ones, which are considered later in the chapter, it behooves teachers to understand methods for measuring and evaluating the behavior of young children.

In this chapter additional educational advantages of carrying out an adequate

rogram and the basic princi-
 to all four kinds of evalua-
are discussed. Following
ed methods of evaluation
detail. The methods in-
rent interview, the use of
s, the use of anecdotal
the use of criterion-
klists and rating scales.
es with a discussion about
mation after it has been
e purposes of planning in-
urriculum, reporting to
eparing reports for boards

) ADVANTAGES OF USING ROCEDURES

serves several basic pur-
be used to describe the current behavior of a child and what he knows, and, if repeated, it can show ways the child has changed over a period of time. When data on a number of children are combined, the results give a picture of the current status of the group as well as identify changes that have occurred since the previous evaluation was carried out.

The student should not picture this process as requiring the services of a psychologist who comes in and administers a series of commercially developed tests. Although such formal measures have a definite place in sophisticated research programs, useful information can also be obtained by means of simpler, less costly procedures, which the teacher can carry out herself as part of her ordinary routine. The drawback to developing one's own procedures is that it takes time and effort; but if the advantages of assessing children are fully understood, the teacher may be better motivated to include this process in her busy schedule.

Educational advantages

No matter what method the teacher settles on for recording behavior, its use will result in her gaining increased knowledge and awareness of every child in her group. Simply having to consider the same questions for each child helps assure that no one has been overlooked.

Evaluation can increase the quality and specificity of the curriculum. Once the degree of the children's skills is known and their strengths and weaknesses are identified, the planning of a curriculum becomes easier and more focussed. For example, the majority of the children in a Head Start group might be evaluated in September as "usually show interest in field trips." However, the majority might also place in the "hardly ever" category on "able to tell a connected story." A curriculum that uses the group's strength (shows interest in field trips) to help clear up the weakness (inability to tell a connected story) could be planned in which the teacher takes the children to visit the car wash and then asks them to tell what happened when the car went through the wash and she forgot to roll the windows up.

Moreover, evaluation permits specific inabilities of particular children to be noted, and plans then can be developed to work on these difficulties. For instance, a staff member at our Center noted in her running observation record that one of her lively little boys had a difficult time sitting through lunch. Rather than criticizing him and restraining him constantly, she resolved to ask him to be the kitchen messenger. This individualized prescriptive activity helped him contribute to the well-being of the group, made him feel genuinely important, and gave him an escape hatch as well. This did help him eventually become less restless and more able to settle down to his meals.

Evaluation can improve teacher morale. It is surprising how easy it is to forget in May what a child was like in September. Many a nursery school teacher has been left at the end of the year with only a hazy impression that the children have changed a lot and with the memory of a few more specific cases where Leroy no longer bites or Elizabeth no longer screams a protest when her mother leaves, but with nothing more tangible than these memories to point to. It was not until I participated in a research project that measured certain abilities in the fall and again in the spring that I realized how much tangible records of progress can raise teacher morale by providing concrete evidence of progress.

Evaluation aids the compilation of reports to parents. Since more detailed suggestions about consulting with parents are included in Chapter 17, I shall only point out here that there is an obvious advantage to having written data on which to base parent conferences. Parents appreciate the information and are favorably impressed when shown evidence that the teacher has cared enough to make this special effort to know about their child.

Evaluation is an invaluable resource to draw on when compiling reports to boards and funding agencies. The trend that requires preschools to be accountable in order to qualify for continued public support means it is important that teachers in such schools use sound, relevant evaluation procedures to measure change and growth. The following methods may serve not only the attractive purpose of directly benefiting children in the group, but also be used to furnish evidence that progress has taken place and that further financial support of the facility is justified.

BASIC PRINCIPLES OF EVALUATION

Before reviewing the actual methods of evaluation, the teacher needs to understand some general principles that apply to all forms of evaluation.

Observe confidentiality and professional discretion at all times. All records concerned with children and their families must be regarded as confidential. This means that they must never be left lying around for someone to pick up and read even while the teacher is working on them. The competence of individual children should never be discussed with people outside the school who do not have a right to know about it. Above all, results of evaluations should be interpreted with caution and mercy, since it is possible that the teacher may have reached an incorrect conclusion about the child's abilities or that the test is a faulty one.

Select evaluation measures that match the educational goals of the school. Perhaps the staff has selected the development of self-esteem as one of the most important educational goals. In order to find out if the children are developing good self-esteem, it is vital that the teacher use either a school-developed measure or a commercial test that evaluates this specific trait. General measures of "socialization" or "personality" or "intelligence" should be avoided, since they are unlikely to reveal progress in specific areas.

Be sure to carry out more than one evaluation. Sometimes teachers employ measures of evaluation only at the end of the year. This provides a summing up for the family and for the next teacher (who may or may not read it) but is of little value to the teacher who has done the work. It is more useful to employ evaluative measures shortly after the youngster enters nursery school and again later on. Early assessment helps the teacher quickly become acquainted with the child and begin to plan around the child's needs and interests. It also provides a pretest to be used as a comparison at the middle and end of the year. Without this measurement at the beginning, there is no way to show how much the child has learned during his stay at school.

Be careful to present checklist material to each child in the same way. Sometimes it can be a temptation to change the way a checklist item is presented in accord with the personality or skills of a particular child. For instance, a teacher might unconsciously take a few steps forward to

shorten the distance when throwing a ball to a younger child; or she might be recording balance beam walking and allow more accomplished children to walk on the narrow beam but use the wider side for a less able child, and yet she will mark all the children as successful on the checklist. Such inconsistencies make comparison between children impossible and spoil the accuracy of the group report. Hard hearted as it may seem at first, if a specific measure of accomplishment is included, it is essential to measure all the children against the same standard. The only way this can be adjusted for less skilled children is to provide two measures: one that, in the case given above, measures performance on the broad beam and a second that measures performance on the narrower one.

Sometimes, also, the teacher gradually changes her method of presenting a checklist item as she becomes more experienced using it and figures out a "better" way to do it. Doing this is also forbidden. Every item must be presented in the same manner from the first test to the last if comparisons are to be drawn between subjects or even if comparisons are to be made between early and later performances of the same child. In order to draw valid conclusions, the teacher must compare the same behaviors, not different ones.

Beware of the getting-better-and-better syndrome. Although it is a happy fact that many children will make progress, it is also true that some children will not, at least not in all areas. In order to avoid tester bias, which sees every child getting better all the time, the teacher must discipline herself to observe behavior objectively so that she sees it as it *is* rather than as she wishes it to be. The development of explicit descriptions of behavior as checklist items will help the teacher be objective in her judgment. It is also helpful to have another teacher participate in the evaluation when possible.

A different kind of tester bias that must also be guarded against is the tendency of many teachers to check the same level of accomplishment for most items on a child's checklist. This is sometimes termed the "halo" effect. Again, the teacher must discipline herself to consider each item on the list on its own merits in order to resist the influence of the halo effect as much as possible.

EVALUATION IN THE PRESCHOOL

It is easy to become carried away when talking about evaluation and to advocate methods that, though excellent in many respects, are simply not practical for day by day use. If the method of record keeping requires too much time or effort, it is almost certain to be dropped by the wayside as the year progresses and the teacher puts it off in favor of preparing for the parent pot luck night or Valentine's Day. Very occasionally, schools have access to extra help (parent cooperatives and laboratory schools are particularly fortunate in this regard) and are able to employ a more elaborate system of recording behavior, but this is not the case in most working situations. For this reason, elaborate case studies, long written observations, and even the suggestion that the teacher carry a little notebook in her pocket in which to jot down bright sayings and astonishing incidents are not advocated here as practical methods of evaluating children in the nursery school. There is a valuable place for such activities in teacher training and for occasional studies of children who have special needs (Rowan, 1973), but I do not believe it is realistic to suggest that such lengthy methods be utilized as primary ways to gather information on the majority of the children.

However, there are at least four briefer kinds of evaluation that have proved useful and feasible: the parent interview, the use of commercial tests, the maintenance of brief anecdotal records, and checklists.

Parent interview as a source of information

The parent interview remains one of the outstanding means of collecting information about the child. Some information may be obtained in written form, but some is best gathered by means of personal interviews. Effective methods of talking with parents are discussed in Chapter 17, but the interview must be mentioned here once again to remind the teacher that it is a very good way to find out about a child's skills. Children's behavior is sometimes quite different at school and at home. For instance, a child who is silent as the sphinx at school may be quite talkative at home. This is an important fact for the teacher to know when evaluating his language development as well as when making recommendations for a prescriptive curriculum.

Use of commercial tests

The advantages to using published tests for preschoolers should not be overlooked. If the teacher selects a test that has been normed on many other children, it is possible for her to compare the performance of her group or of individual children in her group with the larger, national sample. Standardized tests, if sold by a reputable company, are likely *(but not necessarily)* to have been developed by experts. When carefully administered and correctly interpreted, well-constructed tests can be valuable diagnostic aids.

The drawbacks to using commercial tests must also be considered. An inspection of test information compiled by Hoepfner, Stern, and Nummedal (1971) reveals the following weaknesses. The majority of such tests require one-to-one administration, which can be time consuming and inconvenient to arrange even for a class of fifteen children. Many tests have professional restrictions that require that they be administered by a psychologist, a service rarely available to nursery schools. It can also be difficult to find a test that measures what the nursery school teacher wishes to measure.

An even more serious problem is the question of quality. Oscar Buros, editor of the *Mental Measurements Yearbook,* has recently cautioned:

Test publishers continue to market tests which do not begin to meet the standards of the rank and file of *Mental Measurements Yearbook* and journal reviewers. At least half of the tests currently on the market should never have been published. Exaggerated, false or unsubstantiated claims are the rule rather than the exception (1972, p. xxviii).

This finding is substantiated by the Hoepfner study (1971), which concentrates on preschool and kindergarten tests and which rates only a handful of the tests as good. All the rest were rated as fair or poor.

Finally, there is the disadvantage that many tests appear to favor the white, middle-class child and are inappropriate to use with children who come from families of the poor, who are bilingual, or who come from different ethnic backgrounds (Reese and Lipsitt, 1970).

For all the foregoing reasons, it is evident that selection of commercial preschool tests remains a difficult problem for teachers not specifically trained in measurement and evaluation. Nevertheless, standardized, commercial preschool tests are potentially helpful. The teachers who wish to explore more thoroughly the possiblity of using them will find the references at the end of this chapter helpful.

It is hoped that future work in preschool test development will result in more easily administered, relevant tests, whose norms are developed from a variety of populations. These improvements would considerably enhance the value of the tests for the early childhood teacher.

Use of observations as records

In addition to information gathered from parents or from commercially developed tests, the teacher draws upon observations she has made in order to learn about the child. The observations should be recorded either as brief anecdotal records or, more briefly yet, on checklists. (See the references following Chapter 18 for suggestions about the compilation of more detailed case studies.)

Suggestions for maintaining anecdotal records

A simple method of keeping anecdotal records straight is to use large index cards, one for each child, with the child's name, birth date, and date of entering school written at the top of the card. Then, on alternate weeks, the teacher may leaf through half the cards, enter the date, and write a sentence or two about

significant happenings or learnings that took place for half the children during the past 2 weeks. At this time, also, she may add anything to the remaining cards that seems vital to record.

Here are two examples of records kept by a teaching intern at our Center. The records state only the child's behavior, not the measures taken to alleviate the condition.

Roy W. aged 2 years 9 months
Recorder: Judy Whitefoot

The following record describes a very young boy who had considerable difficulty learning to swallow. . . .

Sept. 20   Roy is now swallowing his food under special circumstances. He takes a bite, hands me his plate, swallows, then takes his plate back. Still very insistent about sitting next to his brother. He is still wetting his pants every day.

Oct.   2   Now he refuses to swallow, but just keeps stuffing his food in his mouth without waiting to swallow. The psychologist suggests that we should not force Roy to swallow and let him spit it out. His mother claims it is due to his teeth, but the doctor does not confirm this opinion.

Oct. 12   Spent 15 minutes working on a puzzle.

Oct. 23   Is fascinated by trucks. Today during snack the children heard the garbage truck and immediately raced to the window. Both youngsters imitated the sound of a truck.

Oct. 25   Is now better at swallowing his food. When given smaller portions he does not have enough to stuff his mouth full.

Oct. 29   Still gets upset if he can't sit next to his brother. Today he did swallow his food—hooray!

Nov. 14   Was reprimanded today. Quite upset. Is still having trouble with his swallowing. Today he had trouble and ended up spitting it out in the trash can.

Nov. 28   Had a real good day today—he swallowed all his food and asked to get dessert. Formerly, he was unable to tell the cook what he wanted, but today he walked right in and said, "Russ—dessert, now!"

Dec.   5   He called another little boy by his

last name and pleaded with him to sit by him today at lunch. When he refused, Roy threw a tantrum and had to be asked to leave the table.

Dec. 12 Has had trouble once again this past week in swallowing certain foods. He has his "up" days and his "down" days. He seems to stuff his mouth so full that even when he tries to swallow, he can't, because there is just too much food in his mouth. He saved a chair for his friend, who agreed to sit there. Roy was elated.

Jan. 2 (After Christmas vacation) Roy was real bashful today. It was his turn to get the dessert, but he couldn't do it, so one of the other children had to go. He was shy with the other children, also.

Jan. 9 Has been doing very well this past week. He has a good appetite and, more important, he has been swallowing his food. Both he and his brother are now taking naps at the Center and both have adjusted well. Also, Roy has been going "poddy" in the toilet more than before.

Angeline aged 2 years 3 months
Recorder: Judy Whitefoot

This is a tiny little girl, who, for all her lack of size and her tender years, has fit in easily at nursery school.

Sept. 16 When asked to get the trash can, she went right down, got it, and climbed back up the stairs with it.

Oct. 15 Has a real liking for Russ, the cook. He plays with the children after lunch.

Nov. 14 Seems to be competing with R. and W. for any adult attention. Today she and W. had "episodes" four times. Right after he went home, Angeline seemed happier.

Nov. 28 Today when W. started to squeeze her, she pushed him and said "No, W., I don't like it!" She is now beginning to defend herself rather than just start crying.

Dec. 5 Has a new favorite word, "No!" She uses it all the time and with force. She isn't eating very much at snack or lunch time. Her mother says she doesn't eat at home very much either. Perhaps she isn't growing at present.

Dec. 12 Played with R. this morning, and they got each other all wound up.

She still gets very upset when her brother won't let her have her way—all she does is scream until he gives in to her. He's afraid he'll get in trouble for making her scream.

Jan. 2 Seems very happy and relaxed after a long Christmas vacation. She ate a real good lunch and was very cooperative. She played with a friend this morning, and the two of them got along real well.

Jan. 9 Is really becoming "obnoxious" in her 2-year-old way. I think she is becoming more courageous and feels more at ease. When W. squeezed her yesterday, she looked at him ferociously and said, "You make me mad!" He stopped. She is doing fine.

A variation of this brief recording technique, which is refreshing and which may help clarify impressions, is to jot down three or four adjectives that seem to best define each child at a particular time. Thus one youngster was described by a student as "curious, often furious, affectionate, and lively"; another was pictured as "determined, thoughtful, sturdy, and gregarious."

Another variation on this observation theme is listing the activities the child has participated in with greatest pleasure during that week. Still another variation is to list something that might be especially appealing to him and to include it in plans for the coming days.

Sometimes the teacher will be dismayed to find that she is unable to record anything on a few of the cards. This should not be the point at which she gives up; rather, it should alert her so that she may become more sensitive to the children and aware of those whom she has overlooked.

Construction and use of checklists and rating scales

For sheer usefulness and potential comprehensiveness of coverage in the preschool, nothing beats the checklist–rating scale. Checklists may be developed on almost any conceivable aspect of child development or behavior.

Since they are criterion referenced, which means that they are designed to match specific objectives, checklists are congruent with what is going on in the teacher's own classroom. They offer an excellent means of assessing whether educational objectives have been accomplished, and they can be filled out at the teacher's leisure and need not be completed in one sitting.

Possible ways to use and develop a checklist. A checklist is merely a convenient way to take an inventory of behavior. It may be a list of anything that the teacher deems important and that she wishes to check the child on. Thus it might be a list of all the activities available in the nursery school program, with spaces beside each activity to check whether the child participates in it. Or it could be a list of various ways children cope with anxiety or a list of all the children in school, with places to fill in for the child's close companions and those whom he particularly avoids.

A checklist may also be used to assess whether an educational goal is being reached. When writing this kind of checklist, the teacher should list the educational goal first and then define several kinds of behaviors that are likely to be present when the goal is accomplished.

Thus when the staff of our Children's Center chose the general goal of fostering emotional health in the children, the following behaviors were selected as representing coping behaviors related to emotional health: able to express liking for other children and adults, able to express anger in a way that does not damage people or equipment, able to confront an adult directly when the adult has caused the child to feel angry, able to maintain sustained friendships with other children.

Next, the process of making the checklist was refined by including measures of how often the behavior occurred. For our purposes we selected the following categories of frequency: *no opportunity to observe, hardly ever, about half the time,* and *usually* as being quantitative measures we could all understand. The addition of these measures of frequency changed our modest checklist into a more useful measure—a rating scale.

Since we knew how desirable it is to assess the child's abilities shortly after he begins school as well as at midyear and year's end, we found it helpful to allow space for the three evaluation periods on one sheet of paper. This made comparison simpler and also reduced the bulkiness of the file for each youngster.

Finally, additional items were added to cover other aspects of emotional and social behavior that the staff felt were important. The student should bear in mind that there is nothing holy about this particular list; other staffs would select other items suited to their own goals and children.

The final form of our chart looked like the one shown on pp. 288 and 289.

Suggestions about compiling checklists. Although it is often helpful to go through the checklists of other schools in order to garner ideas, each school should really develop its own set, because each school has its own list of educational goals, and the checklists should be designed to fit these goals. It is astonishingly easy to be trapped into evaluating children on skills that have not been emphasized in the curriculum. Results of such mismatched evaluations can only be disappointing.

The teacher should be as explicit and clear as possible when describing the behaviors that will be evaluated. For example, suppose that the following educational objective has been selected as a worthy one by the school: "Following an initial period of adjustment, the child will demonstrate emotional independence by tolerating separation from meaningful family members during his day at nursery school." Which of the following checklist items should be selected as the most explicit one to use as a measure that the child is achieving independence?

1. The child rarely demonstrates his anxiety.
2. The child can wave goodbye to his mother without undue stress.
3. The child enters into a nursery school activity within 10 minutes after his mother's departure.
4. The child exhibits a favorable attitude toward his teachers.

Numbers 1 and 4 are not clearly related

Santa Barbara City College Children's Center

SOCIAL-EMOTIONAL COMPETENCE SCALE

Child's name _____ Last _____ First _____ Middle _____ Birth date _____

Self-confidence

	Not able to observe	Hardly ever	About half the time	Usually	Not able to observe	Hardly ever	About half the time	Usually	Not able to observe	Hardly ever	About half the time	Usually
Able to hold his own when challenged (confident, not unduly intimidated)												
Likes to try new things												
Not overly sensitive to reprimand or correction												
Able to adjust to change in routines or people in the nursery school												
TOTAL												

Autonomy and dependence

	Not able to observe	Hardly ever	About half the time	Usually	Not able to observe	Hardly ever	About half the time	Usually	Not able to observe	Hardly ever	About half the time	Usually
Enters into nursery school activity within 10 minutes after mother's departure												
Spends more time with own age group than with adults												
Relates to more than one adult at school												
Appears independent – when given the opportunity, able to make decisions for himself												
TOTAL												

Social competence

Able to share teacher with others

Willing to bargain in order to attain goals

Able to share when he has enough for himself

Able to show or express concern for other people

TOTAL

Coping techniques

Able to express liking for other children and adults

Able to express anger in a way that does not damage people or equipment

Able to confront adult directly when adult has caused child to feel angry

Able to maintain sustained friendships with other children

TOTAL

GRAND TOTAL

Pretest

Date

Recorder

Midtest

Date

Recorder

Posttest

Date

Recorder

to the stated goal. Number 2 is probably a good item to use, although the phrase "without undue stress" may vary in interpretation from teacher to teacher. Number 3 is the clearest statement of the four and should be included on the checklist.

When writing such lists, the teacher must also keep them within reason in terms of developmental levels. It can be frustrating and discouraging to both child and teacher if she expects behavior that lies beyond his developmental ability to achieve. For this reason, it cannot be recommended too strongly that developmental charts be consulted when checklists are being constructed. Where such material is not available, the lists should be based on recommendations of experienced early childhood teachers.

Before writing checklist items, one should also decide whether they will be used in parent conferences. If they will be (and they can be very useful in this regard), it is wise to phrase them in a truthful yet not derogatory way. For example, the same general behavior is described in both of the following items, but consider which one would be more palatable to a parent. In one, the child is described as "hardly ever able to adjust to change in routines or people at nursery school"; in the second, the child is described as "rigid and inflexible in adjustment patterns—adapts poorly to change."

One final admonition about the construction of checklists must be added. If the list is to be used in the manner suggested at the end of this chapter to summarize data for fiscal reports, it is necessary to phrase the behavior items so they are all positive behaviors that the teacher desires to have increase during the school year. An item should be phrased "able to share teacher with others" rather than "clings to teacher, fights other children off from her." If a positive goal form is not followed and a mixture of positive and negative descriptions is used, some of the behaviors will be marked as increasing and others as decreasing during the year. The result would be that the losses and gains cancel each other out, and no improvement could be revealed by the final scores.

USE OF THE INFORMATION THAT HAS BEEN COLLECTED
Developing a prescriptive curriculum

For the individual child's well-being, the most important use of checklists, observations, and interviews is the use of the material to identify strengths and difficulties so that learning activities may be prescribed that will help the youngster develop as well as he is able to.

Thus when the teacher looked over the checklist shown on the following page, she was alerted to the fact that Jeannie had several "hardly ever" ratings on a portion of her Social-Emotional Competence Scale. A further perusal of the anecdotal records contributed to the picture of a 4-year-old girl who was new to school and who, though appearing to like the other children, stuck close to the teacher and was unable to share whatever she played with. The parent interview added the information that Jeannie was an only child who lived in a neighborhood where there were no other children. When these sources of information were put together, Jeannie emerged as being a socially inexperienced 4-year-old rather than the "spoiled brat" she might have seemed at face value. The information not only increased the teacher's understanding but also her liking for the little girl and made it possible to plan a curriculum that was built on Jeannie's liking of other people and that sought to develop her confidence and trust so that she gradually became able to let go of teachers and equipment more easily.

Making reports to the family

Preparation for a parent conference is much easier when records have been kept in a systematic manner. The material is already at the teacher's fingertips and needs only to be reviewed before the family's arrival. Such records may be referred to in a general, summarizing way or in terms of more specific behaviors as the occasion and the teacher's courage warrant. Many teachers find these reports invalu-

Santa Barbara City College Children's Center

SOCIAL-EMOTIONAL COMPETENCE SCALE

Child's name _____ Last _____ First: **Jeannie** Middle _____

Birth date __July 1, 1970__ Present age 4–2

Pretest

Self-confidence	Not able to observe	Hardly ever	About half the time	Usually
Able to hold his own when challenged (confident, not unduly intimidated)		✓		
Likes to try new things			✓	
Not overly sensitive to reprimand or correction		✓		
Able to adjust to change in routines or people in the nursery school		✓		
TOTAL		3	1	

Autonomy and dependence	Not able to observe	Hardly ever	About half the time	Usually
Enters into nursery school activity within 10 minutes after mother's departure			✓	
Spends more time with own age group than with adults			✓	
Relates to more than one adult at school		✓		
Appears independent—when given the opportunity, able to make decisions for himself	✓			
TOTAL	1	1	2	

Pretest Date __9/1/74__ Recorder __M.S.__

Midtest Date _____ Recorder _____

Posttest Date _____ Recorder _____

able as well as satisfying to use as points of reference when reviewing the year's progress with the parents.

Preparing summarizing reports for official boards and funding agencies

A useful method of summarizing data that is relatively easy for all teachers, even those not trained in statistics, to use is the simple numerical summary of checklist material. In this method, answers are tallied for the various categories on the checklists, and the totals are converted to percents to simplify drawing comparisons.

Computing a numerical summary for a checklist. Only checklists of children who have remained throughout all three testing periods should be used. If there are more than ten children in each age group, it may be worthwhile to sort the children into the smaller groups and compute the percent for separate ages. This separation will demonstrate change between categories more clearly.

Step 1 Tally (count up) answers for each category on a master sheet. For example, tally all the answers in the "not able to observe" category for the Self-Confidence Pretest; next, tally answers for the "hardly ever" category, and so forth.

Step 2 Add the number of tallies in each column.

Step 3 Add the totals of the four columns for the Pretest together to obtain the total number of answers given in all the columns. (This same total is used in the Midtest and Posttest calculations.)

Step 4 Find the percent of replies for each column by dividing the number of answers in each column by the total number of answers for all the Pretest columns.

Step 5 Repeat this process to calculate the percent replies for the Midtest and Posttest.

Once the percents have been calculated, they may be used to draw a variety of comparisons among the results of the test periods. Thus if the chart shown on p.293 were used in a fiscal report, it could be pointed out that although only 38% of the children were rated as usually appearing to be self-confident in September, by May the percent had increased to 62. Or the analysis might be phrased, "The percent of 4-year-old children who rated high on measures of self-confidence almost doubled in the period from September to May."

Although the teacher will no doubt wish to attribute such a favorable change to her educational program, it must be emphasized that this method draws no comparisons between her group and a control group not undergoing instruction. Thus it documents change but does not provide evidence that the change could not be due to other influences, such as maturation. If the teacher wishes to be on safer scientific ground, she will need to use a control group and more sophisticated statistical methods to obtain such evidence.

Using statistical methods for the analysis of data. It is important to know that methods that are vastly superior to the scheme proposed above exist for the statistical analysis of data. In particular, such techniques as *t*-tests and the analysis of variance are helpful. These methods are superior because they may be used to determine whether there is a significant difference between pretest, midtest, and posttest results or between the test results of the school population and those of a control group.

Although these techniques usually lie beyond the expertise of the nursery school teacher, she should realize that such techniques have been developed and are of real value in assessing data. Occasionally, a statistician can be prevailed upon to carry such calculations out for the teacher.

SUMMARY

Evaluation is a valuable process that nursery school teachers can use for the purposes of describing children or for measuring changes in their behavior.

Practical methods of recording behavior and evaluating it include the use of parent interviews, commercially developed tests, anecdotal records, and checklists.

COMPUTATION OF PERCENT REPRESENTATION IN VARIOUS CATEGORIES OF A CHECKLIST

Self-confidence	Pretest				Midtest				Posttest			
	Not able to observe	Hardly ever	About half the time	Usually	Not able to observe	Hardly ever	About half the time	Usually	Not able to observe	Hardly ever	About half the time	Usually
Able to hold his own when challenged (confident, not unduly intimidated)	1	2	7	5	0	2	7	6	0	1	6	8
Likes to try new things	2	2	6	5	0	0	8	7	0	0	6	9
Not overly sensitive to reprimand or correction	0	4	4	7	0	3	3	9	0	2	2	11
Able to adjust to change in routines or people in the nursery school	0	1	8	6	0	1	7	7	0	0	6	9
Number of tallies in each column	3	9	25	23	0	6	25	29	0	3	20	37
Column answer divided by total	.05	.15	.42	.38	0	.10	.42	.48	0	.05	.33	.62
Percent of replies in each category	5%	15%	42%	38%	0%	10%	42%	48%	0%	5%	33%	62%

Number of participating children = 15
Total answers for pretest = 60

$$\text{Percent} = \frac{\text{Number of answers in column}}{\text{Total number of answers in pretest, midtest, or posttest}}$$

Systematically carried out evaluation results in increased knowledge of the individual child. It facilitates the planning of a prescriptive curriculum, makes reporting to parents a simple matter, and provides useful data on which to base reports to advisory boards and funding agencies.

QUESTIONS AND ACTIVITIES

1. Testing and keeping checklists are a lot of work and are also time consuming. Are these activities really worth the time and trouble they take? What other methods of identifying skills or lags might be employed in place of these ones which would be as satisfactory?

2. *Problem:* Your school is funded by a state that requires that you administer a variety of pretests and posttests to the children to determine the effectiveness of the program. This year, you are horrified to discover that posttest results indicate the children have made little improvement in language development when compared with the national norm included with the test information. You are in charge of the program. What would you do about this result?

3. In your opinion, what should become of evaluative records once the child has left the preschool? Should they be forwarded to his next school, for example? Should they be destroyed? Should they be saved for a number of years? Think carefully about the pros and cons of taking any of these actions.

4. Assess the needs of some youngsters in your school as they have been revealed by your evaluation materials. On the basis of these findings, suggest activities that you feel could be used to develop the youngsters' weaker areas by drawing on their strengths as identified by the evaluation procedures.

5. Do you feel that the results of tests and records about the child should be available to parents upon request?

REFERENCES FOR FURTHER READING

References of General Interest

Ginsberg, H. *The myth of the deprived child.* Englewood Cliffs, N. J.: Prentice-Hall, Inc., 1972. Ginsberg attacks the use of intelligence tests as a means of determining the true mental abilities of children who come from minority groups or from families of low income.

Hodges, W. L., McCandless, B. R., Spicker, H. H., and Craig, I. S. *Diagnostic teaching for preschool children.* Arlington, Va.: Council for Exceptional Children, 1971. In this short book the authors describe a research study where the results of standardized tests were used for the purpose of identifying deficits in development in a group of preschool children. It is a good example of how a prescriptive curriculum can be developed to counteract deficits.

Lambert, N. M. The present status of the culture-fair testing movement. In J. T. Flynn and H. Garber (Eds.), *Assessing behavior: readings in educational and psychological measurement.* Reading, Mass.: Addison-Wesley Publishing Co., Inc., 1967. Lambert succinctly reviews the problems and status of the culture-fair testing movement. A perusal of this article should help the student gain an appreciation of the difficulties encountered in constructing tests that are unbiased and that do not favor a particular cultural or ethnic group.

Leshan, E. J. *The conspiracy against childhood.* New York: Atheneum Publishers, 1971. This is a popular presentation of the case against forcing development in children. The chapter entitled "Any Dope Can Have a High IQ" is particularly apropos to read in connection with the topic of evaluation.

Murphy, L. B. *Personality in young children: methods for the study of personality in young children.* Vol. I. New York: Basic Books, Inc., Publishers, 1956. Volume I contains an interesting description of various open situations that can be used for the purpose of evaluating young children. These include the use of miniature life toys, sensory toys, dough and cold cream, painting, the Rorschach test and play situations. The discussion is based on the responses of particular children. The interpretations are first rate, and the book supports the philosophy that it is not always necessary to resort to an intelligence test to measure children adequately.

Resources for the Evaluation of Commercial Tests

Buros, O. K. (Ed.) *The seventh mental measurements yearbook.* Highland Park, N. J.: Gryphon Press, 1972. This is the classic reference in the field of test evaluation. A massive two-volume work, it contains descriptions and tough-minded assessments of tests in print that are written by authorities in the field. It also lists books concerned with testing. One of Buros' avowed intentions is upgrading the quality of published tests, a process he reports to be discouragingly slow.

Educational Testing Service. *Test collection bulletin.* Princeton, N. J.: The Service, many dates. The ETS bulletin lists new tests acquired for their test library. It includes a brief description of each test and marks ones that are especially suitable for children from birth to age 9 years. No estimate of test quality is included. Since the bulletin is issued four times a year, it is a good way to keep abreast of new tests coming on the market.

Hoepfner, R., Stern, C., and Nummedal, S. G. *CSE-ECRC preschool/kindergarten test evaluations.* Los Angeles: School Evaluation Project, Center for the Study of Evaluation and the Early Childhood Research Center, 1971. This publication is a compendium of tests appropriate for use in preschool and kindergarten. The tests are evaluated in terms of meaningfulness, examinee appropriateness, administrative usability, and quality of standardization. Although the reader may be appalled at the general low quality of the reported tests, this is an invaluable reference because it is simple to use and very explicit.

Plakos, J. *Tests in use in Title VII bilingual education projects.* Fort Worth, Tex.: National Consortia for Bilingual Education, 1971. Testing minority children or children who come from families of the poor often presents special problems, and the reader would do well to bear the following quotation in mind when seeking tests appropriate to such youngsters: "It is recognized . . . that any standardized testing done among subgroups of the general population, such as Mexican-American, is at best hazardous and at worst untenable" (Palomares and Cummins, 1968, p. 3). The Plakos reference lists all tests used during 1970 in bilingual programs funded under Title VII. It notes whether the test is available in Spanish or English, its purpose, and the age group it is appropriate to but gives no estimate of the quality of the test itself. To the best of my knowledge, no such reference is yet available of tests appropriate to black children or children of other minority groups.

Sources of Suggestions for and Examples of Checklist Items

Dillman, C. M., and Rahmlow, H. F. *Writing instructional objectives.* Belmont, Calif.: Fearon Publishers, 1972. Dillman and Rahmlow explain how to develop test items to evaluate whether an objective is being achieved.

Instructional Objectives Exchange. *Early childhood education.* Los Angeles: The Exchange, no date. A sample test item is given for each objective listed in the book.

For the Advanced Student

Smith, M. S., and Bissell, J. S. Report analysis: the impact of Head Start. *Harvard Educational Review,* 1970, **14**, 51-104. The authors assess the Westinghouse Head Start report (Cicerelli, Evans, and Schiller, 1969) and criticize the study on the basis that tests and methods of evaluation employed did not fit the goals of the Head Start program.

Thorndike, R. L., and Hagen, E. *Measurement and evaluation in psychology and education.* (3rd ed.) New York: John Wiley & Sons, Inc., 1969. This is a basic, comprehensive textbook on measurement and evaluation. The chapter on rating scales makes very informative reading for teachers who are developing checklists.

PART **NINE**

What lies ahead?

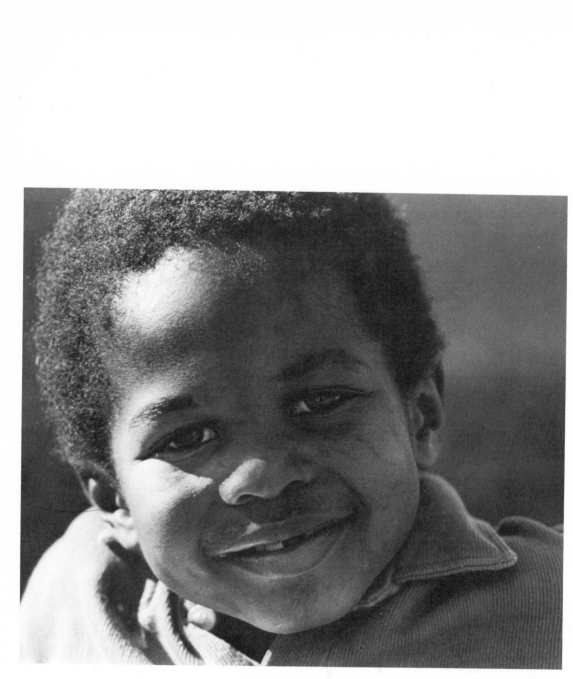

Los Niños Head Start

CHAPTER 21

Recent trends in early childhood education

It is very difficult to define or to measure the most important aspects of quality in a child-development program. We can require a staff-child ratio, but it is difficult to mandate that the staff care about the children, feel each child individually reaching out to the people and things in his environment, and respond warmly and lovingly. It is hard to define, measure, and regulate the important intangible qualities we want so much; it is impossible to legislate what goes on in the human hearts we are so concerned about. The law is an imperfect way to run society, but it is the best way we have found.

Regulation alone, and even regulation combined with funds, will not produce quality. The only real monitor is the concern of the community; the only real power base for regulation is strong public support.*

We live in the midst of change, and it is interesting to reflect, as this book draws to a close, on what trends we may be dealing with in the future because, after all, a beginning textbook is only that—a beginning. The teacher who has mastered the fundamentals must always look ahead to see what she should turn to next. So it is well to pause and consider what trends are developing and to ask ourselves what concerns we will be facing in the coming years.

Of course, many of these issues have already been reviewed in this volume. Such things as cross-cultural education, the role of evaluation and of cognitive development, and the inclusion of the excep-

tional child will continue to concern us in the coming decade just as building emotional health, fostering creativity, following sound routines, and building healthy bodies will remain eternally important. But we must also be aware of the shifts in emphasis and new trends that are now taking place.

CHILD ADVOCACY MOVEMENT

The White House Conference of 1970 (Beck, 1973; Ward, Akers, Hines, and Eggleston, 1971) reflected, once again, a concern for the rights of children, and there is an interesting movement developing at present that seeks to identify injustices to children and to remedy them. This is the Child Advocacy movement, which has been defined as "a matter of dedication to a point of view. Its only common denominator is a generalized commitment to children's rights and to improving so-

---

*From Morgan, G. G. Regulation of early childhood programs.In D.N. McFadden (Ed.), *Planning for action.* Columbus, Ohio: Battelle Memorial Institute, 1972. P. 178.

cial provisions for children" (Kahn, Kamerman, and McGowan, 1973, p. 84). At this time, concerns of this movement include such activities as investigating why children are excluded from school (Task Force on Children Out of School, 1970), working to provide input from minority groups into the decision-making process (Black Child Development Institute, 1972), teaching parents how to act as advocates for their children (United Bronx Parents, 1973), and agitating for better-quality children's television (Action for Children's Television, 1973). The broadness and diversity of concerns are evident from even this partial list, and the method of approach varies from case to class action and from focussing on a single concern to working on several related issues at the same time.

Coupled with the recognition that children have rights that require protection goes an increased interest in and knowledgeability about legislation. The time is past when parents and teachers of young children can afford to remain ignorant of what is happening in Washington or in various state capitols across the nation, and many organizations are beginning to take note of this fact. For example, *Young Children,* which is the official publication of the National Association for the Education of Young Children, has recently begun a series of inserts about legislation that it carries in every issue.

At present it appears that the most vital issue on the legislative front is not only the provision of additional child care and early education opportunities but also the implementation and maintenance of standards that will help assure that the care provided is nurturing and generative rather than merely custodial. *It is a terrible mistake to assume that any child care is better than no child care or to assume that once mediocre legislation has been passed, it can be easily modified to produce quality programs.* Young children are too vulnerable and precious to be subjected to crowded, underequipped environments staffed by ignorant, though well-meaning caretakers. But this may come about unless parents and teachers

take time to understand legislative matters, become acquainted with their elected representatives, and help these people understand the importance of adequate legislation and licensing. (Refer to the references at the end of the chapter for further information on this subject.)

INCREASED DEMAND FOR SERVICES TO YOUNG CHILDREN

The past decade has witnessed a marked increase in the number of young children participating in preschool programs. For example, enrollment in preprimary education increased from 30% of 3- to 5-year-olds in the early 1960s (Schloss, 1966) to 43% by 1971 (Barker, 1972). But despite this increase, which has been largely due to the advent of "compensatory" programs such as Head Start, there remain many young children who need care and learning opportunities but who are not receiving them.

Adequate day care was emphasized at the 1970 White House Conference as the most pressing need in child care. It was estimated in 1970 that more than 4,000,000 working mothers had young children under the age of 6, but even at that time there were only 640,000 licensed day care spaces available. The situation is likely to become even more serious, since the Labor Department predicts that by 1980 5,300,000 mothers of small children will be in the labor force. Eight out of ten of these families do not qualify for publicly supported day care, even though five of every eight who do not qualify cannot afford private care (Education Commission of the States, 1971).

If adequate care is to be provided for these children, it is highly probable that some form of institutional financial support, perhaps combined with a sliding scale of parent fees, will have to be provided. Such support could be obtained from union dues (Steinfels, 1973), industry (Stein, 1973), or government support at federal, state, or local levels (Auerbach, 1973; Education Commission of the States, 1971).

Several states already offer financial support for some preschool programs.

New Jersey, for example, includes 4-year-olds in its kindergarten programs, and California may pass legislation to accomplish this in 1975 (Riles, 1974). Six states (California, Connecticut, Iowa, New Jersey, Virginia, and Washington) plus American Samoa are currently providing some financial support for various kinds of preschool programs, ranging from compensatory programs to children's centers (Education Commission of the States, 1971). The federal government funds Project Head Start and, indirectly through Title IV-A, supports services for additional youngsters as well. So the concept of governmental support is not as far fetched as it might seem. Perhaps the rising tide of feminism will prove to be the most effective force in overcoming resistance among industry and union management to the idea of providing child care while mothers are on the job.

The children of migrant workers are desperately in need of child care service. At best, the preschool services for children of migrant workers range from specially constructed day care centers open during the harvest season to mobile units that follow the workers as they move from crop to crop (Sunderlin, Osborn, and Cohen, 1971). At worst, service is nonexistent, and very young children spend long hours alone in shacks or locked in cars at the edge of the fields. The problem of the migrant worker is widespread (only Alaska, Hawaii, and Rhode Island report no use of migrant labor), and the needs for better housing, health, and employment standards go far beyond provision of preschool care, although child care is most certainly an important area to consider.

Statistics on migrant services make fascinating reading. Over and over the states are able to list the number of children served (which ranges from 30 in Arkansas to 4,489 in Texas) but just as consistently list as "unknown" the number of children not served (Education Commission of the States, 1972). Of course, as child advocates are quick to point out, as long as the number of migrant children who require care remains "unknown," it is impossible to determine how much service is needed.

Infant care is being investigated as another area of possible service to children. As a result of early, shocking studies on the effect of institutionalization on infant development (Bowlby, 1951; Spitz, 1945), day care personnel in the United States did all they could to further the well-being of very young children and infants by keeping them in the home. More recent research appears to indicate that merely spending time away from the mother's care is not the damaging factor. Rather, it is the possible lack of environmental stimulation and lack of personal, individualized care often characteristic of understaffed, ill-informed institutional settings that lie at the heart of marasmic decline (Casler, 1968).

With these newer findings in mind, the possibility of providing infant care outside the home is once again being investigated (Caldwell and others, 1970; Frank Porter Graham Child Development Center, no date; Garber and Heber, 1973; Keister, 1970). These meticulously supervised, carefully controlled studies report promising findings, and there is no denying that there is a very real need for such infant care among women who find they must work outside the home when their children are very young.

However, we must never forget that the younger the child is, the more vulnerable he is to environmental insult and the less able he is to protect himself from malign conditions. We cannot depend on the possibility that parents will always be good judges of child care or infant care situations. I hear frequent tales of parents in my own community who simply call and enroll their youngsters in nursery schools without asking anything beyond the price and who express surprise when invited to visit. Inspection and licensing regulations do not necessarily ensure good care. Some states do not license nursery schools at all (Grotberg, Chapman, and Lazar, 1971), and even in those where licensing is in effect, quality of care provided varies widely (Keyserling, 1972). If these circumstances are true of preschool care, is it not likely that they would also be true of infant care? Yet poor infant care may have even more serious consequences for development than poor preschool care does. For this reason infant care should still be regarded with caution and championed as a cause only if strong safeguards are built into the program and knowledgeable people are on hand to provide continuing supervision, guidance, and encouragement for the staff.

INCREASED FLEXIBILITY AND VARIETY IN TYPES OF SERVICE AND INSTRUCTION

New patterns of service, such as franchised child care (Bank of America, 1969, 1970; H. Brown, 1971; Newsweek, 1972), education by means of television (Ball and Bogatz, 1972; Ratliff and Ratliff, 1972; Sprigle, 1971), and evening and overnight care, are also being investigated to meet changing needs.

Of particular interest to students is the increasing trend toward offering child care on campuses—a movement that extends from the university (Ravenscroft, 1973) to the junior college level. For example, a recent survey revealed that 46 of 98 community colleges in California already offer some form of child care on their campuses (Hendrick, 1974). Although considerable notoriety and radical political activity has attended the formation of some campus child care facilities (Simmons and Chayes, 1973), it is not true that the child care movement is necessarily the pawn of a few radical students. Offering child care is a popular cause with most students, and good services for children can come about as a result of this enthusiasm if early childhood personnel on campus are willing to take the risk of making friends with sponsors of these movements and helping them learn about what quality child care entails.

Still another innovative pattern of service is the move toward educating children in the home itself (Gordon, 1969; Gray and Klaus, 1970; Schaefer, 1970; Weikart and Lambie, 1968). An interesting variation of this idea is the Home Start program, which is getting under way under the auspices of Head Start. In this program, neighborhood mothers receive training and financial support and welcome small groups of youngsters into their homes for learning activities (O'Keefe, 1973).

Many home tutoring programs are based on the idea of a weekly visitor who brings materials for the children to use but who also focusses on drawing the mother in so that she gradually adds to her personal repertoire ideas and activities that enhance her youngster's growth. For example, when the mother herself understands how important it is to develop language competence in young children and also understands in simple, practical ways how she can foster this ability in her children, a positive, continuing influence has been built into her children's lives. The long-term benefits of this approach to the family are obvious.

INCREASED FLEXIBILITY IN APPROACHES TO TEACHER TRAINING

Accompanying increased demands for flexibility in patterns of care and instruction has come an interest in new patterns of teacher training. Junior colleges are offering training in the first two years of undergraduate work, which equips many people with sound training in early childhood education so that they qualify for jobs as teachers and aides in a wide variety of nursery school programs.

Television consortia are springing up that seek to offer high quality educational programs to be viewed at home and taken for unit credit at various colleges. Packaged programs of taped lectures and discussions are now more readily available, and films appear to be more numerous.

On a national level the concept of the Child Development Associate is gaining ground as an alternative way of educating teachers (Young Children, 1973). A Child Development Associate would qualify for her degree by demonstrating actual competence with young children instead of by taking a specified number of college level courses. I believe that this approach has great merit, providing that various competencies prove to be measurable and the process of identifying them can be achieved without requiring an unreasonable amount of time or money. If the approach is successful, awarding credentials based on competence should result in an increased variety of educational options for students, combined with higher quality interaction between children and the staff who serve them—both highly desirable outcomes.

INCREASED RECOGNITION OF THE IMPORTANCE OF PARENTING

Along with the increasing interest in home visiting and home education go an acknowledgment of the enduring importance of parental influence (Gordon, 1969; Schaefer, 1972; White, 1973) and an increasing concern about effective ways to link home and school more closely and to educate parents. Many schools now try to narrow the gap by asking parents to be resource people, to participate with the children during the day, or to serve in decision-making capacities on policy-making boards (Knitzer, 1972). Some teachers are also becoming more attuned to the contributions families make to educating their young children and are more appreciative of these contributions.

Parent education is taking many new forms, ranging from courses on parenting and family life offered at the high school level (Lazar and Chapman, 1972) to intensive tutoring of mothers of infants (Heber, Garber, Harrington, Hoffman, and Falender, 1972). In addition, the old standby parent cooperatives that have played a valuable role in educating families for many years continue to operate effectively and to gain in popularity (Taylor, 1954), since many of the new campus child care centers operate on parent cooperative principles. Finally, the staff of many nursery schools and day care centers also work hard to provide stimulating, helpful parent meetings intended to broaden the parents' knowledge of child behavior and help them gain skills in living with their youngsters.

TREND TOWARD A BETTER SENSE OF PROPORTION

We have already seen that school doors are being opened for parents and that increased recognition of the importance of their influence in the life of the child is developing. The work of Christopher Jencks (1972) also reminds us that education is at best only a partial influence on the family and society and that many avenues must be explored and economic policies modified if the cycle of poverty is to be broken.

We are also being reminded that the education of the adolescent is both valuable and important (Rohwer, 1971; McCurdy, 1974); some research even indicates that apparent deficits that occur at younger ages may be made up at later stages of development (Kagan and Klein, 1972; Kagan, Klein, Haith, and Morrison, 1973).

Although these findings may at first glance seem threatening to early childhood teachers who have fought so long for a modicum of recognition, it is only sensible to acknowledge that the entire future of the child's life does not rest solely on the two or at the most three years he is in an early childhood program. Such findings need not be taken to imply that early childhood education does not have an important contribution to make in fostering the well-being of young children and their families—it does. But such reports as those mentioned above help us maintain a sense of proportion as well as retain a feeling of responsibility for bringing about all the good things we can for the children in our care.

RECOGNITION OF THE NEED FOR BETTER RESEARCH

Research has been cited throughout this book wherever possible to help substantiate opinions of what constitutes sound educational practice with young children. The citations have not been as numerous as one might wish, nor do they offer the comfort of replication. Moreover, the studies have often been characterized by small sample size and, in some of the earlier studies, by naive design.

The needs in this area are clear. Many fields remain to be explored (Almy, 1973; Datta, 1973; Grotberg, Chapman, and Lazar, 1971; LaCrosse, Lee, Litman, Ogilvie, Stodlosky, and White, 1970), and the need is particularly great for replicated studies using carefully randomized samples of adequate size. Longitudinal studies are still in very short supply, and we continue to explore areas that can be easily counted and measured and to ignore more difficult but possibly more significant and relevant areas, such as play, which cannot be quantified so easily. We also need to know a great deal more about children who are functioning well and what benign circumstances in their lives have made this possible. Finally, there is a need for systematic exploration of topics so that we will not have to depend on hunt-and-peck results that must be fitted into the larger pattern of needed knowledge like pieces of a jigsaw puzzle.

Yet, with all these failings, we seem on firmer ground today with research than we were in the past. More areas are being investigated, and designs and statistical methods are increasing in sophistication and rigor. We must remain careful, however, that we employ these techniques to investigate things that really matter.

TWO GUIDELINES TO REMEMBER

With so much to do and so many problems to solve, the reader may well wonder if there are any general principles to keep in mind that will help her in making decisions for the future. There are at least two that are helpful to remember.

First, there will be a continuing need for teachers to remain open to new ideas and continued growth. We must beware of becoming trapped in congealing philosophy. Lillian Katz (1974) said it well: "We must proceed—having enough skepticism to keep on learning, but with enough confidence to keep on acting." If I could leave students with only one thought about this, it would be, "Do not forget to question, but do not allow doubt to paralyze your ability to act."

The second guideline to remember is, "When in doubt about the value of a decision, put the child's welfare first." In the press of other concerns, whether it be legislation, teacher training, or the search for a "perfect" educational model, there is a real risk that in the struggle we will lose sight of the most important person of all—that small, vulnerable individual filled with fascinating complexities and bewildering contradictions whom we have named "the preschool child."

It is, after all, this child's well-being that we must put ahead of every other concern in early childhood education. And when policies are made or compromises suggested, then we must unhesitatingly apply the yardstick of what will be of maximum benefit to him as we make decisions that affect his future.

QUESTIONS

1. By the time you read this chapter on trends, even newer ones will be arising. What additional ones are you aware of that have developed in the field of early childhood education?
2. Are there any activities in your local community that reflect the Child Advocacy movement? Share with the class how these gained impetus and whether the advocacy activities appear to be producing positive changes in the lives of children.
3. Some people feel that the growth of day care and other early childhood programs is a threat to the home life of the child and will contribute to the destruction of family life by weakening bonds between its members. Explain why you do or do not agree with this point of view.
4. Many women now champion the cause of infant care outside the home as one of women's fundamental rights. If you were asked to be on a panel to discuss the desirability of infant care for very young children, what position would you take? Be sure to state your reasons for your point of view.
5. *Problem:* You have two young children of your own and, like many other students, you need child care badly in order to continue your education. The licensing restrictions for child care are clearly defined and enforced in your state and require such things as a fenced yard, a toilet for every 7 children, 35 square feet of indoor and 75 square feet of outdoor space for every child, and some units of early childhood education for the teachers. You are desperately interested in starting a day care center, but these restrictions obviously increase the cost and difficulty of beginning it. Under these circumstances, do you feel it would be all right for the center to "just begin" and go underground? What might the alternatives be to doing this?

REFERENCES FOR FURTHER READING
Child Advocacy

Day Care and Child Development Council of America. *Directory for the child care advocate.* Washington, D. C.: The Council, 1973. The directory lists 36 nationwide organizations involved in monitoring legislation pertaining to children and also lists government agencies and members of Congress.

Edelman, P. B. Report analysis: the Massachusetts reports: advocacy for children. *Harvard Educational Review,* 1973, **43**(4), 639-652. This is an analysis of the successes and limitations of the work of the Task Force on Children described below; informative.

Kahn, A. J., Kamerman, S. B., and McGowan, B. G. *Child advocacy: report of a national baseline study.* Washington, D. C.: U. S. Department of Health, Education, and Welfare, Office of Child Development, Children's Bureau, 1973. The authors present a well-written description of what the Child Advocacy movement is all about and how it operates.

Task Force on Children Out of School. *The way we go to school.* Boston: Beacon Press, 1970. This relatively early example of the Child Advocacy movement documents a study of children who are out of school in Boston. Assuming that other cities may have problems similar to Boston's, we should pay attention to this strong evidence that a Child Advocacy program is seriously needed.

Legislation

Action for children's cause. *Young Children,* 1973–1974, **28** and **29,** all issues. This is a series of inserts in each issue of *Young Children* which provide specific guidelines for understanding and working with legislation.

Licensing

Morgan, G. G. Regulation of early childhood programs. In D. N. McFadden (Ed.), *Planning for action.* Columbus, Ohio: Battelle Memorial Institute, 1972. Morgan provides a thoughtful and comprehensive discussion of the problems and issues concerning licensing at all levels, from the local fire marshal up through the federal government; an indispensable, authoritative reference.

United States Department of Health, Education, and Welfare. *Guides for day care licensing.* Washington, D. C.: The Department, Office of Child Development, 1973. These are the latest set of recommendations for day care standards published by the federal government.

Day Care

Allen, S. B., Edelman, M. W., Hansen, O., and others. *Perspectives on child care.* Washington, D. C.: National Association for the Education of Young Children, 1972. The authors emphasize the need for adequate care and discuss this problem in relation to legislation and finances.

Education Commission of the States, Task Force on Early Childhood Education. *Early childhood development: alternatives for program implementation in the states.* Denver, Colo.: The Commission, 1971. This gold mine of material includes summaries of alternative ways to educate young children, estimates of operating costs, suggestions for different ways to include early childhood education in state budgets, lists of teacher certification requirements, and state funding efforts.

Roby, P. *Child care—who cares? Foreign and domestic infant and early childhood development policies.* New York: Basic Books, Inc., Publishers, 1973. In this collection of articles about day care, Roby considers many aspects of the problem, including the need for service, child care trends in the United States, and child care abroad; *excellent.*

Migrant Education

Education Commission of the States, Task Force on Early Childhood Education. *Early childhood programs for migrants: alternatives for the states.* Denver, Colo.: The Commission, 1972. In this fact-filled, interesting publication from the Task Force, state and federal funding for migrant preschoolers is discussed, and a survey of child care service presently available is presented.

Sunderlin, S., Osborn, K., and Cohen, M. D. *Migrant children: their education.* Washington, D. C.: Association for Childhood Education International, 1971. The authors discuss appropriate curriculum and describe several programs now in operation for migrant children; interesting and readable.

Infant Care

Dittman, L. L. (Ed.) *Early child care: the new perspectives.* New York: Atherton Press, 1968. Dittman concentrates on very young children and infants, includes a number of outstanding articles on the education of the very young, presents several points of view, and concludes with descriptions of innovative programs that were then current for infants.

Dittman, L. L. *The infants we care for.* Washington, D. C.: National Association for the Education of Young Children, 1973. This is a useful reference with which to begin the study of infant care, either in terms of home visits or of setting up a center for care away from home. Helpful bibliographies are included at the end of each chapter.

Franchised Child Care

Child Welfare League of America. *Small children as a small business: a primer for potential investors in day care centers.* Washington, D. C.: The League, 1971. Plain, truthful suggestions and advice for people who are considering investing in the child care business are given. This work should be read and carefully considered before making any commitments or signing any agreements.

Educational Television for Children

Ball, S., and Bogatz, G. A. *Research on Sesame Street: some implications for compensatory education.* Princeton, N. J.: Educational Testing Service, 1972. Ball and Bogatz report research on Sesame Street, where the findings were primarily positive.

Ratliff, A. R., and Ratliff, R. G. Sesame Street: magic or malevolence? *Young Children,* 1972, **27**(4), 199-204. The authors question some of the affective values children may be learning from Sesame Street, particularly in the area of aggression.

Sprigle, H. A. Can poverty children live on "Sesame Street"? *Young Children,* 1971, **26**(4), 202-218. Sprigle questions whether the educational goals cited by the producers of this series are being attained by them, bases comments on a research study.

Parent Involvement

Black Child Development Institute. From a black perspective: optimum conditions for minority involvement in quality child development programming. In Roby, P. *Child care —who cares? Foreign and domestic infant and early childhood development policies.* New York: Basic Books, Inc., Publishers, 1973. A good set of recommendations is given for specific ways to help black families gain strength and representation in early childhood programs. The suggestions would also apply very well to families from other minority groups.

McFadden, D. N. (Ed.) *Planning for action.* Columbus, Ohio: Battelle Memorial Institute, 1972. There are two good chapters in which parent involvement is discussed, with an emphasis on the role of parents as educational decision makers.

Project Head Start. *Parent involvement: a workbook of training tips for Head Start staff.* Number 10A. Washington, D. C.: Office of Economic Opportunity, 1969. Pamphlet no. 6180-12. This manual contains suggestions for helping parent groups participate in decision-making activities as well as with their children at home and in school.

Steinfels, M. O'B. *Who's minding the children? The history and politics of day care in America.* New York: Simon & Schuster, Inc., 1973. Chapter six, "What Is It Like to Use Day Care?" contains a frank description of how one group of parents involved themselves actively with day care staff. It should be read by all teachers to help them see their program from the vantage point of parents who are often afraid to speak up directly.

Research

Datta, L. *New directions for early childhood development programs: some findings from research.* Urbana, Ill.: ERIC Clearinghouse on Early Childhood Education and the University of Illinois, 1973. Datta reviews recent findings and makes recommendations for further research; a well-documented, useful publication.

Grotberg, E. (Director), Chapman, J. E., and Lazar, J. B. (Eds.) *A review of the present status and future needs in day care research.* Washington, D. C.: Education Resources Division, Capitol Publications, 1971. Research findings that are particularly relevant to work in day care are given.

LaCrosse, E. R., Lee, P. C., Litman, F., Ogilvie, D. M., Stodlosky, S. S., and White, B. L. The first six years of life: a report on current research and educational practice. *Genetic Psychology Monographs,* 1970, **82**, 161-266. The authors review recent research in many areas having to do with young children and make recommendations for further research that would be beneficial.

References*

Action for Children's Television. In A. J. Kahn, S. B. Kamerman, and B. G. McGowan (Eds.), *Child advocacy: report of a national baseline study.* Washington, D. C.: U. S. Dept. of H.E.W., Office of Child Development, Children's Bureau, 1973.

Adams, M. *Mental retardation and its social dimensions.* New York: Columbia University Press, 1971.

Alexander, A. M. *The money world of your preschooler.* East Lansing, Mich.: Cooperative Extension Service, Michigan State University, 1967.

Allen, K., Hart, B., Buell, J. S., Harris, F. R., and Wolf, M. M. Effects of social reinforcement on isolate behavior of a nursery school child. *Child Development,* 1964, **35**(2), 511-518.

Allen, Lady of Hurtwood. *Planning for play.* Cambridge, Mass.: The M.I.T. Press, 1968.

Allen, Lady of Hurtwood, Flekkoy, M. S., Sigsgaard, J., and Skard, A. G. *Space for play: the youngest children.* Copenhagen: World Organization for Early Childhood Education, 1964.

Allen, S. V., Edelman, M. W., Hansen, O., and others. *Perspectives on child care.* Washington, D. C.: N.A.E.Y.C., 1972.

Almy, M. Spontaneous play: an avenue for intellectual development. *Young Children,* 1967, **22**, 265-277.

Almy, M. *Early childhood play: selected readings related to cognition and motivation.* New York: Simon & Schuster, Inc., 1968.

Almy, M. *Early childhood research: second thoughts and next steps.* Urbana, Ill.: ERIC Clearinghouse on Early Childhood Education and University of Illinois, 1973.

Almy, M., Chittenden, E., and Miller, P. *Young children's thinking.* New York: Teachers College Press, 1966.

American National Red Cross. *Standard first aid and personal safety.* Garden City, N. Y.: Doubleday & Co., Inc., 1973.

Andrews, G. *Creative rhythmic movement for children.* Englewood Cliffs, N. J.: Prentice-Hall, Inc., 1954.

Andry, A. C., and Scheep, S. *How babies are made.* New York: Time-Life Books, 1968.

Arnheim, D. D., and Pestolesi, R. A. *Developing motor behavior in children: a balanced approach to elementary physical education.* St. Louis: The C. V. Mosby Co., 1973.

Ashton-Warner, S. *Teacher.* New York: Bantam Books, Inc., 1965.

Auerbach, S. Federally sponsored day care. In P. Roby (Ed.), *Child care—who cares? Foreign and domestic infant and early childhood development policies.* New York: Basic Books, Inc., Publishers, 1973.

Axline, V. M. *Dibs: in search of self.* Boston: Houghton Mifflin Co., 1964.

Axline, V. M. *Play therapy.* (Rev. ed.) New York: Ballantine Books, Inc., 1969.

Baker, K. R. *Let's play outdoors.* Washington, D. C.: N.A.E.Y.C., 1969.

Bakwin, H., and Bakwin, R. M. *Behavior disorders in children.* (4th ed.) Philadelphia: W. B. Saunders Co., 1972.

Ball, S., and Bogatz, G. A. *Research on Sesame Street: some implications for compensatory education.* Princeton, N. J.: Educational Testing Service, 1972.

Bambara, T. C. Black English. In *Curriculum*

---

*For the full names and addresses of organizations refer to Appendix B.

approaches from a black perspective. Washington, D. C.: Black Child Development Institute, 1973.

Bandura, A. *Aggression: a social learning analysis.* Englewood Cliffs, N. J.: Prentice-Hall, Inc., 1973.

Bandura, A., Grusec, J. E., and Menlove, F. L. Vicarious extinction of avoidance behavior. *Journal of Personality & Social Psychology,* 1967, **5.** 16-23.

Bandura, A., and Huston, A. C. Identification as a process of incidental learning. *Journal of Abnormal Social Psychology,* 1961, **63,** 311-318.

Bandura, A., and Menlove, F. L. Factors determining vicarious extinction of avoidance behavior through symbolic modeling. *Journal of Personality & Social Psychology,* 1968, **8,** 99-108.

Bandura, A., and Walters, R. H. Aggression. In H. W. Stevenson (Ed.), *Child psychology.* 62nd Yearbook, *National Social Studies Education.* Chicago: University of Chicago Press, 1963.

Bank of America. Day nurseries for preschoolers. *Small Business Reporter,* 1969, **8,** 10.

Bank of America. Franchising. *Small Business Reporter,* 1970, **9,** 9.

Bank Street College. *Early childhood discovery materials.* New York: The Macmillan Co., 1968.

Barker, L. A. *Preprimary enrollment October 1971.* Washington, D. C.: National Center for Educational Statistics, Office of Education, U. S. Dept. of H.E.W. 1972.

Bartlett, E. J. Selecting preschool language programs. In C. B. Cazden (Ed.), *Language in early childhood education.* Washington: D. C.: N.A.E.Y.C. 1972.

Bates, B. *Project Head Start, 1969: a descriptive report of programs and participants.* Washington, D. C.: Office of Child Development, U. S. Dept. of H.E.W., 1972.

Baumrind, D. Socialization and instrumental competence in young children. In W. W. Hartup (Ed.), *The young child: reviews of research.* Vol. 2. Washington, D. C.: N.A.E.Y.C., 1972.

Beard, R. *An outline of Piaget's developmental psychology for students and teachers.* New York: The New American Library Inc., 1972.

Beck, R. The White House Conferences on children: an historical perspective. *Harvard Educational Review,* 1973, **43**(4), 653-668.

Beiswenger, H. Luria's model of the verbal control of behavior. *Merrill-Palmer Quarterly,* 1968, **14**(4), 267-284.

Bender, J. Have you ever thought of a prop box?

In K. R. Baker (Ed.), *Ideas that work with young children.* Washington, D. C.: N.A.E.Y.C., 1972.

Bengtsson, A. (Ed.) *Adventure playgrounds.* New York: Praeger Publishers, Inc., 1972.

Bereiter, C. *Academic preschool, Champaign, Illinois.* Washington, D. C.: U. S. Govt. Printing Office, 1969.

Bereiter, C., and Englemann, S. *Teaching disadvantaged children in the preschool.* Englewood Cliffs, N. J.: Prentice-Hall, Inc., 1966.

Bernbaum, M. *Early language development: an abstract bibliography.* Urbana, Ill.: ERIC Clearinghouse on Early Childhood Education, October, 1971 (a).

Bernbaum, M. *Early childhood programs for non–English speaking children.* Urbana, Ill.: ERIC Clearinghouse on Early Childhood Education, December, 1971 (b).

Bernstein, B. Language and social class. *British Journal of Sociology,* 1960, **11,** 271-276.

Beyer, E. *Teaching young children.* New York: The Bobbs-Merrill Co., Inc., 1968.

Biller, H. B. Father absence, maternal encouragement and sex role development in kindergarten-age boys. *Child Development,* 1969, **40,** 539-546.

Birch, H. G., and Gussow, J. D. *Disadvantaged children: health, nutrition and school failure.* New York: Harcourt Brace Jovanovich, Inc., 1970.

Bissell, J. S. The cognitive effects of preschool programs for disadvantaged children. In J. L. Frost (Ed.), *Revisiting early childhood education: readings.* New York: Holt, Rinehart and Winston, Inc., 1973.

Black Child Development Institute. *Annual Report 1972.* Washington, D. C.: The Institute, 1972.

Black Child Development Institute. From a black perspective: optimum conditions for minority involvement in quality child-development programming. In P. Roby (Ed.), *Child care—who cares? Foreign and domestic infant and early childhood development policies.* New York: Basic Books, Inc., Publishers, 1973.

Bland, J. C. *Art of the young child: 3 to 5 years.* The Museum of Modern Art. Garden City, N. Y.: Doubleday & Co., Inc., 1957.

Blank, M., and Solomon, F. A. A tutorial language program to develop abstract thinking in socially disadvantaged preschool children. *Child Development,* 1968, **39**(1), 379-390.

Blank, M., and Solomon, F. A. How shall the disadvantaged child be taught? *Child Development,* 1969, **40**(1), 48-61.

Block, J., and Martin, B. Predicting the behavior

of children under frustration. *Journal of Abnormal Social Psychology,* 1955, **51**, 281-285.

Bloom, B. S. *Stability and change in human characteristics.* New York: John Wiley & Sons, Inc., 1964.

Bloom, B. S., Englehart, M. D., Furst, E. J., Hill, W. H., and Krathwohl, D. R. *Taxonomy of educational objectives.* New York: David McKay Co., Inc., 1956.

Borke, H. Interpersonal perception of young children: egocentrism or empathy? *Developmental Psychology,* 1971, **5**(2), 263-269.

Bowlby, J. Maternal care and mental health. *World Health Organization Monographs,* 1951, No 2.

Bowley, A. H., and Gardner, L. *The young handicapped child: educational guidance for the young cerebral palsied, deaf, blind, and autistic child.* (2nd ed.) Edinburgh: E. & S. Livingstone, 1969.

Bowser, P., and Eckstein, J. *A pinch of soul: fast and fancy soul cookery for today's hostess.* New York: Avon Books, 1970.

Braine, M. D. S. The ontogeny of English phrase structure: the first phrase, *Language,* 1963, **39**, 1-13.

Braun, S. J., and Lasher, M. G. *Preparing teachers to work with disturbed preschoolers.* Cambridge, Mass.: Nimrod Press, 1972.

Brearley, M. & Hitchfield, E. *A guide to reading Piaget.* New York: Schocken Books Inc., 1966.

Briggs, D. C. *Your child's self esteem: the key to his life.* Garden City, N. Y.: Doubleday & Co., Inc., 1970.

Bromberg, S. L. A beginning teacher works with parents. In K. R. Baker (Ed.), *Ideas that work with young children.* Washington, D. C.: N.A.E.Y.C., 1972.

Bronfenbrenner, U. Preface. In H. Chauncey (Ed.), *Soviet preschool education.* Vol. 2. *Teacher's commentary.* New York: Holt, Rinehart and Winston, Inc., 1969.

Bronfenbrenner, U. *Two worlds of childhood: U. S. and U. S. S. R.* New York: Simon & Schuster, Inc., 1970.

Brooks, M. Helping the child amputee. *News Letter of the Association for the Care of Children in Hospitals,* 1973, **1**(1), 1-4.

Brown, D. G. *Behavior modification in child and school mental health: an annotated bibliography on applications with parents and teachers.* Rockville, Md.: National Institute of Mental Health, 1971.

Brown, H. *Legislative statement of Harold Brown on investigation of franchising, with attachments.* Washington, D. C.: C.W.L.A., 1971.

Brown, M., and Plihal, J. *Evaluation materials for use in teaching child development.* Minneapolis, Minn.: Burgess Publishing Co., 1966.

Brown, R. *A first language: the early stages.* Cambridge, Mass.: Harvard University Press, 1973.

Brown, R., and Bellugi, U. Three processes in the child's acquisition of syntax. *Harvard Educational Review,* 1964, **34**, 133-151.

Bruner, J. S. The course of cognitive growth. *American Psychologist,* 1964, **19**, 1-15.

Bruner, J. S. On the conservation of liquids. In J. S. Bruner, R. R. Olver, P. M. Greenfield, and others. *Studies in cognitive growth.* New York: John Wiley & Sons, Inc., 1966.

Bruner, J. S. *Poverty and childhood.* Detroit: Merrill-Palmer Institute, 1970.

Buchanan, R., and Mullins, J. B. Integration of a spina bifida child in a kindergarten for normal children. *Young Children,* 1968, **23**(6), 339-344.

Buckle, D., and Lebovici, S. *Child guidance centers.* Geneva: World Health Organization, 1960.

Budke, W. E., Bettis, G. E., and Beasley, G. F. *Career education practice.* Columbus, Ohio: ERIC Clearinghouse on Vocational and Technical Education, Ohio State University, 1972.

Buros, O. K. (Ed.) *The seventh mental measurements yearbook.* Highland Park, N. J.: Gryphon Press, 1972.

Butler A. L. *Current research in early childhood education: a compilation and analysis for program planners.* Washington, D. C.: American Association of Elementary-Kindergarten-Nursery Educators, 1970.

Buttolph, E. G. *Music without the piano.* New York: Early Childhood Education Council of N. Y., 1968.

Caldwell, B. M. What is the optimal learning environment for the young child? *American Journal of Orthopsychiatry,* 1967, **37**, 1.

Caldwell, B. M. The importance of beginning early. In J. B. Jorden and R. F. Dailey (Eds.), *Not all little red wagons are red.* Arlington, Va.: Council for Exceptional Children, 1973.

Caldwell, B. M., and Richmond, J. Appendix B: a "typical day" for the groups at the Children's Center. In L. L. Dittman (Ed.), *Early child care: the new perspectives.* New York: Atherton Press, 1968.

Caldwell, B. M., and others. Infant day care and attachment. *American Journal of Orthopsychiatry,* 1970, **40**, 397-412.

Carmichael, V. *Science experiences for young children.* Los Angeles: Southern California Association for the Education of Young Children, 1969.

Carson, R. *The sense of wonder.* Harper & Row, Publishers, 1956.

Carter, J. L. *Language stimulation program, Auburn, Alabama.* Washington, D. C.: U. S. Govt. Printing Office, 1969.

Casler, L. Perceptual deprivation in institutional settings. In G. Newton and S. Levine (Eds.), *Early experience and behavior.* Springfield, Ill.: Charles C Thomas, Publisher, 1968.

Cazden, C. B. Subcultural differences in child language: an interdisciplinary review. *Merrill-Palmer Quarterly,* 1966, **12**, 3.

Cazden, C. B. Children's questions: their forms, functions and roles in education. *Young Children,* 1970, **25**(4), 202-220.

Cazden, C. B. *Language in early childhood education.* Washington, D. C.: N.A.E.Y.C., 1972 (a).

Cazden, C. B. *Child language and education.* New York: Holt, Rinehart and Winston, Inc., 1972 (b).

Cherry, C. *Creative movement for the developing child: a nursery school handbook for non-musicians.* (Rev. ed.) Belmont, Calif.: Fearon Press, 1971.

Child Advocacy System Project. In A. J. Kahn, S. B. Kamerman, and B. G. McGowan. *Child advocacy: report of a national baseline study.* Washington, D. C.: U. S. Dept. of H.E.W., Office of Child Development, Children's Bureau, 1973.

Child Development Group of Mississippi. *From the ground up: ideas for playground and indoor equipment to build for a community Head Start program.* Jackson, Miss.: KIPCO, 1967.

Child Development Staff. *Programs for infants and young children. Part II: nutrition.* Washington, D. C.: Appalachian Regional Commission, 1970.

Child Study Association of America. *What to tell your children about sex.* New York: Pocket Books, 1968.

Child Welfare League of America. *Small children as a small business: a primer for potential investors in day care centers.* Washington, D. C.: C.W.L.A., 1971.

Chittenden, G. E., Murphy, M. N., and Williams, B. *Essentials of nursery education.* Washington, D. C.: N.A.E.Y.C., no date.

Chukovsky, K. *From two to five.* Translated by M. Morton. Berkeley: University of California Press, 1968.

Cicerelli, V. G., Evans, J. W., and Schiller, J. S. *The impact of Head Start on children's cognitive and affective development. Preliminary report.* Washington, D. C.: Office of Economic Opportunity, 1969.

Clark, A. N. *Journey to the people.* New York: The Viking Press, Inc., 1969.

Clark, K. B. *Prejudice and your child* (2nd ed.) Boston: Beacon Press, 1963.

Cohen, D. H., and Stern, V. S. *Observing and recording the behavior of young children.* New York: Teachers College Press, 1958.

Cohen, S. How to alleviate the first-year shock of teaching emotionally disturbed children. In M. S. Auleta (Ed.), *Foundations of early childhood education: readings.* New York: Random House, Inc., 1969.

Cole, M., and Bruner, J. S. Preliminaries to a theory of cultural differences. In I. J. Gordon (Ed.), *Early childhood education: the seventy-first yearbook of the National Society for the Study of Education, part II.* Chicago: University of Chicago Press, 1972.

Coles, R. *Children of crisis: a study of courage and fear.* New York: Dell Publishing Co., 1967.

Combs, A. W. *Perceiving behaving becoming: a new focus for education, Yearbook, 1962.* Washington, D. C.: Association for Supervision & Curriculum Development, 1962.

Combs, A. W. *Educational accountability: beyond behavioral objectives.* Washington, D. C.: Association for Supervision and Curriculum Development, 1972.

Committee for Early Childhood. The fundamental learning needs of today's young children, *Young Children,* 1970, **25**(6), 326-335.

Conner, F. P., and Talbot, M. E. *An experimental curriculum for young mentally retarded children.* New York: Teachers College Press, 1970.

Coopersmith, S. *The antecedents of self esteem.* San Francisco: W. H. Freeman and Co., Publishers, 1967.

Corrado, J., and Reed, J. *Play—with a difference.* New York: The Play School Association, 1970.

Cox, F. N., and Campbell, D. Young children in a new situation, with and without their mothers. *Child Development,* 1968, **39**, 123-131.

Cratty, B. J. *Perceptual and motor development in infants and children.* New York: The Macmillan Co. 1970 (a).

Cratty, B. J. *Some educational implications of movement.* Seattle: Special Child Publications, 1970 (b).

Cratty, B. J. *Intelligence in action: physical activities for enhancing intellectual abilities.* Englewood Cliffs, N. J.: Prentice-Hall, Inc., 1973.

Cross-Cultural Family Center. *A multi-cultural curriculum for today's young children: an outgrowth of a cross-cultural nursery school.* San Francisco: The Center, 1969.

Curry, N. E., and Arnaud, S. (Eds.) *Play: the child strives toward self-realization.* Washington, D. C.: N.A.E.Y.C., 1971.

Dalton, M. M. A visual survey of 5,000 school children. *Journal of Educational Research,* 1943, **37**, 81-94.

Dashe, M. *Children with special problems: a manual for day care centers.* Washington, D. C.: D.C.C.D.C.A., 1972.

Datta, L. *New directions for early childhood development programs: some findings from research.* Urbana, Ill.: ERIC Clearinghouse on Early Childhood Education and the University of Illinois, 1973.

Davis, C. M. Results of the self selection of diets by young children. *Canadian Medical Association Journal,* 1939, **41**, 257-261.

Dawe, H. C. An analysis of two hundred quarrels of preschool children. *Child Development,* 1934, **5**, 139-157.

Day Care and Child Development Council of America. *Multiethnic reading and audio-visual material for young children: annotated bibliography,* Publication No. 101. Washington, D. C.: D.C.C.D.C.A., 1972.

Day Care and Child Development Council of America. *Directory for the child care advocate.* Washington, D. C.: D.C.C.D.C.A, 1973.

De Bono, E. *Lateral thinking: creativity step by step.* New York: Harper & Row, Publishers, 1970.

De Bono, E. *The dog exercising machine.* New York: Simon & Schuster, Inc., 1970.

De Grazia, S. *Of time, work, and leisure.* New York: The Twentieth Century Fund, 1962.

DeNevi, D. The education of a genius: analyzing major influences on the life of America's greatest architect. *Young Children,* 1968, **23**(4), 233-239.

Dennis, W. Causes of retardation among institutional children: Iran. *Journal of Genetic Psychology,* 1960, **96**, 47-59.

Deutsch, M. The role of social class in language development and cognition. In E. M. Bower (Ed.), *Orthopsychiatry and education.* Detroit: Wayne State University Press, 1971.

Deutsch, M., Katz, I., and Jensen, A. R. *Social class, race, and psychological development.* New York: Holt, Rinehart, and Winston, Inc., 1968.

D'Evelyn, K. E. *Individual parent-teacher conferences.* New York: Teachers College Press, 1963.

D'Evelyn, K. E. *Developing mentally healthy children.* Washington, D. C.: American Association of Elementary-Kindergarten-Nursery Educators, 1970.

Dillman, C. M., and Rahmlow, H. F. *Writing instructional objectives.* Fearon Publishers, 1972.

DiLorenzo, L. T., and Salter, R. An evaluative study of prekindergarten programs for educationally disadvantaged children. Followup and replication. *Exceptional Children,* 1968, **35**(2), 111-121.

Dinkmeyer, D. C. *Child development: the emerging self.* Englewood Cliffs, N. J.: Prentice-Hall, Inc., 1965.

Dittman, L. L. *The mentally retarded child at home: a manual for parents.* Washington, D. C.: U. S. Dept. of H.E.W., Children's Bureau, 1959.

Dittman, L. L. (Ed.) *Early child care: the new perspectives.* New York: Atherton Press, 1968.

Dittman, L. L. *The infants we care for.* Washington, D. C.: N.A.E.Y.C., 1973.

Dunn, L. M. (Ed.) *Exceptional children in the schools: special education in transition.* (2nd ed.) New York: Holt, Rinehart and Winston, Inc., 1973.

Dworkin, A. G. Stereotypes and self-images held by native born and foreign born Mexican-Americans. *Sociology and Social Research,* 1965, **49**, 214-224.

Ebbick, F. N. Learning from play in other cultures. *Childhood Education,* 1971, **48**, 2.

Ebel, R. L. Behavorial objectives: a close look. *Phi Delta Kappan,* November 1970, 171-173.

Edelman, P. B. Report analysis: the Massachusetts reports: advocacy for children. *Harvard Educational Review,* 1973, **43**(4), 639-652.

Education Commission of the States, Task Force on Early Childhood Education. *Early childhood development: alternatives for program implementation in the states.* Denver, Colo.; the Commission, 1971.

Education Commission of the States, Task Force on Early Childhood Education. *Early childhood programs for migrants: alternatives for the states.* Denver, Colo.: The Commission, 1972.

Education Service Center, Region XIII. *Information and materials to teach the cultural heritage of the Mexican-American child.* Austin, Tex.: Dissemination Center for Bilingual Bicultural Education, 1972.

Educational Facilities Laboratory. *Found: spaces and equipment for children's centers: a report from Educational Facilities Laboratory, 1972.* New York: Educational Facilities Laboratory. 1972.

Educational Testing Service. *Test Collection Bulletin.* Princeton, N. J.: The Service, many dates.

Eisner, E. Instructional and expressive educational objectives: their formulation and use in curriculum. In W. J. Popham, E. W. Eisner, H. J. Sullivan, and L. L. Tyler (Eds.), *Instructional Objectives.* Chicago: Rand McNally & Co., American Educational Research Association, 1969.

El'Konin, D. B. Some results of the study of the psychological development of preschool-age children. In M. Cole and I. Maltzman (Eds.), *A handbook of contemporary Soviet psychology.* New York: Basic Books, Inc., Publishers, 1969.

Ellingson, C., and Cass, J. *Directory of facilities for the learning-disabled and handicapped.* New York: Harper & Row, Publishers, 1972.

Elliot, O., and King, J. A. *Psychological Reports,* 1960, **6**, 391.

Engel, R. C. *Language motivating experiences for young children.* Van Nuys, Calif.: DFA Publishers, 1968.

Engel, R. C., and Gold, B. The early childhood unit—a lot of room for children to grow. *Teaching Exceptional Children,* 1974, **6**(2), 59-67.

Erikson, E. H. *Childhood and society.* New York: W. W. Norton & Co., Inc., 1950.

Erikson, E. H. *Young man Luther.* New York: W. W. Norton & Co., Inc., 1958.

Erikson, E. H. Identity and the life cycle. *Psychological Issues,* **1**, 1, Monograph 1, 1959.

Erikson, E. H. *Childhood and society.* (2nd ed.) New York: W. W. Norton & Co., Inc., 1963.

Erikson, E. H. A healthy personality for every child. In R. H. Anderson and H. G. Shane (Eds.), *As the twig is bent: readings in early childhood education.* Boston: Houghton Mifflin Co., 1971.

Eron, L. D., Walder, L. O., and Lefkowitz, M. M. *Learning of aggression in children.* Boston: Little, Brown and Co., 1971.

Eron, L. D., Walder, L. O., Toigo, L., and Lefkowitz, M. M. Social class, parental punishment for aggression and child aggression. *Child Development,* 1963, **34**, 849-867.

Ervin-Tripp, S. Language development. In L. W. Hoffman and M. L. Hoffman (Eds.), *Review of child development research.* Vol. 2. New York: Russell Sage Foundation, 1966.

Estvan, F. J. The social perception of nursery-school children. *Elementary School Journal,* 1966, **66**, 7.

Estvan, F. J. Teaching the very young: procedures for developing inquiry skills. In R. H. Anderson and H. G. Shane (Eds.), *As the twig is bent: readings in early childhood education.* Boston: Houghton Mifflin Co., 1971.

Evans, E. *Contemporary influences in early childhood education.* New York: Holt, Rinehart and Winston, Inc., 1971.

Evans, E. K. *The beginning of life: how babies are born.* New York: Crowell Collier and Macmillan, Inc., 1972.

Fein, G., and Clarke-Stewart, A. *Day care in context.* New York: John Wiley & Sons, Inc., 1973.

Ferreira, N. J. *The mother-child cookbook.* Menlo Park, Calif.: Pacific Coast Publishers, 1969.

Feshbach, N. Sex differences in children's modes of aggressive responses towards outsiders. *Merrill-Palmer Quarterly,* 1969, **15**, 249-258.

Feshbach, N., and Feshbach, S. Children's aggression. In W. W. Hartup (Ed.), *The young child: reviews of research.* Vol. 2. Washington, D. C.: N.A.E.Y.C., 1972.

Flavell, J. H. *The developmental psychology of Jean Piaget.* New York, Van Nostrand Reinhold Co., 1963.

Flavell, J. H. Role-taking and communication skills in children. *Young Children,* 1966, **21**, 164-177.

Flavell, J. H., Botkin, P. T., Fry, C. L., Wright, J. W., and Jarvis, P. E. *The development of role-taking and communication skills in children.* New York: John Wiley & Sons, Inc., 1968.

Fleming, G. A. (Ed.) *Children's dance.* Washington, D. C.: American Association for Health, Physical Education, and Recreation, 1973.

Forbes, J. *The education of the culturally different: a multicultural approach.* Washington, D. C.: U. S. Govt. Printing Office, 1968.

Forrester, F. *Preschool program, Fresno, California.* Washington, D. C.: U. S. Govt. Printing Office, 1969.

Foster, C. J. *Developing responsibility in children.* Chicago: Science Research Associates, 1953.

Fowler, W. On the value of both play and structure in early education. *Young Children,* 1971, **27**(1), 24-36.

Frank, L. K. Play is valid. *Childhood Education,* 1968, **44**, 433-440.

Frank, L. K. Tactile communication. In C. B. Kopp (Ed.), *Readings in early development: for occupational and physical therapy students.* Springfield, Ill.: Charles C Thomas, Publisher, 1971.

Frank Porter Graham Child Development Center. *Perspectives: a progress report on child care.* Chapel Hill, N. C.: University of North Carolina, no date.

Friedberg, M. P. *Playgrounds for city children.* Washington, D. C.: A.C.E.I., 1969.

Fromm, E. Selfishness and self-love. *Psychiatry,* 1939, **2**, 507-523.

Furman, R. A. Experiences in nursery school consultations. In K. R. Baker (Ed), *Ideas that work with young children.* Washington, D. C.: N.A.E.Y.C., 1972.

Furman, R. A., and Katan, A. K. *The therapeutic nursery school.* New York: International Universities Press, 1969.

Gagné, R. Contributions of learning to human development. *Psychological Review,* 1968, **73**(3), 177-185.

Galambos, J. W. *A guide to discipline.* Washington, D. C.: N.A.E.Y.C., 1969.

Gallagher, J. J., and Bradley, R. H. Early identification of developmental difficulties. In I. J. Gordon (Ed.), *Early childhood education: the seventy-first yearbook of the National Society for the Study of Education, part II.* Chicago: University of Chicago Press, 1972.

Garber, H., and Heber, R. *The Milwaukee project: early intervention as a technique to prevent mental retardation.* National Leadership Institute, Teacher Education/Early Childhood, University of Connecticut, Storrs, Connecticut, 1973.

Gearheart, B. R. *Learning disabilities: educational strategies.* St. Louis: The C. V. Mosby Co., 1973.

Gerhardt, L. A. *Moving and knowing: the young child orients himself in space.* Englewood Cliffs, N. J.: Prentice-Hall, Inc., 1973.

Gerlach, N. S., and Sullivan, H. J. *Constructing statements of outcomes.* Inglewood, Calif.: Southwest Regional Laboratory for Educational Research & Development, 1967.

Gesell, A., Halverson, H. M., Thompson, H., and Ilg, F. *The first five years of life: a guide to the study of the preschool child.* New York: Harper & Row, Publishers, 1940.

Getzels, J. W., and Jackson, P. W. *Creativity and intelligence.* New York: John Wiley & Sons, Inc., 1962.

Ginott, H. *Teacher and child.* New York: The Macmillan Co., 1972.

Ginsberg, H. *The myth of the deprived child.* Englewood Cliffs, N. J.: Prentice-Hall, Inc., 1972.

Glassman, L., and Erickson, D. *A selected guide to government agencies concerned with exceptional children.* Arlington, Va.: IMC/RMC Network, 1972.

Glockner, M. *Integrating handicapped children into regular classrooms.* Urbana, Ill.: University of Illinois and ERIC Clearinghouse on Early Childhood Education, 1973.

Glueck, S., and Glueck, E. *Unraveling juvenile delinquency.* Cambridge, Mass.: Harvard University Press, 1950.

Goldberg, S., and Lewis, M. Play behavior in the year-old infant: early sex differences. *Child Development,* 1969, **40**, 21-31.

Goodman, M. E. *Race awareness in young children.* New York: Crowell Collier and Macmillan, Inc., 1964.

Goodman, W. When you meet a blind person. In S. A. Kirk and F. E. Lord (Eds.), *Exceptional children: educational resources and perspectives.* Boston: Houghton Mifflin Co., 1974.

Gordon, E. W. Compensatory education: Evaluation in perspective. *IRCD Bulletin,* 1970, **6**, 5.

Gordon, I. J. *Parent involvement in compensatory education.* Urbana, Ill.: University of Illinois and ERIC Clearinghouse on Early Childhood Education, no date.

Gordon, I. J. Stimulation via parent education. *Children,* 1969 (a), **16**, 57-59.

Gordon, I. J. The beginnings of the self: the problem of the nurturing environment. *Phi Delta Kappan,* 1969 (b), **50**, 375-378.

Gordon, I. J. *Children's views of themselves.* (Rev. ed.) Washington, D. C.: A.C.E.I., 1972.

Gordon, I. J., and others. *Reaching the child through parent education: the Florida approach.* Jacksonville, Fla.: Institute for Development of Human Resources, 1969.

Gotkin, L. G. The telephone call: the direct line from teacher to family. In K. R. Baker (Ed.), *Ideas that work with young children.* Washington, D. C.: N.A.E.Y.C., 1972.

Gowan, J. C. *Development of the creative individual.* San Diego: Robert R. Knapp, 1972.

Grams, A. *Sex education: a guide for teachers and parents.* Danville, Ill.: The Interstate Printers & Publishers, Inc., 1969.

Granato, S., and Krone, E. *8 —Serving children with special needs.* Washington, D. C.: U. S. Dept. of H.E.W., Office of Child Development, 1972.

Grant, L. *What do I need? How much does it cost?* Carpinteria, Calif.: Lou Grant, 1971.

Gray, S. W., and Klaus, R. A. The early training project and its general rationale. In R. D. Hess and R. M. Bear (Eds.), *Early education.* Chicago: Aldine Publishing Co., 1968.

Gray, S. W., and Klaus, R. A. The early training project: a seventh year report. *Child Development,* 1970, **41**, 909-924.

Green, E. H. Group play and quarreling among preschool children. *Child Development,* 1933, **4**, 302-307.

Greenberg, P. J. Competition in children: an experimental study. *American Journal of Psychology,* 1932, **44**, 221-249.

Greenberg, P. *The Devil has slippery shoes: a biased biography of the Child Development*

Group of Mississippi. New York: The Macmillan Co., 1970.

Griffin, L. *Multi-ethnic books for young children: annotated bibliography for parents and teachers.* Washington, D. C.: N.A.E.Y.C., no date.

Grinspoon, L., and Singer, S. L. Amphetamines in the treatment of hyperkinetic children. *Harvard Educational Review,* 1973, **43**(4), 515-555.

Grost, A. *Genius in residence.* Englewood Cliffs, N. J.: Prentice-Hall, Inc., 1970.

Grotberg, E. (Director), Chapman, J. E., and Lazar, J. B. *A review of the present status and future needs in day care research.* Washington, D. C.: Education Resources Division, Capitol Publications, 1971.

Gruenberg, S. M. *The wonderful story of how you were born.* Garden City, N. Y.: Doubleday & Co., Inc., 1970.

Guilford, J. P. A system of psychomotor abilities. *American Journal of Psychology,* 1958, **71**, 146-147.

Guilford, J. P. *The nature of human intelligence.* New York: McGraw-Hill Book Co., 1967.

Guilford, J. P., and Hoepfner, R. *The analysis of intelligence.* New York: McGraw-Hill Book Co., 1971.

Gussow, J. D. Bodies, brains and poverty: poor children and the schools. *ERIC-IRCD Bulletin,* 1970, **6**(3), 1-20.

Hagman, E. P. The companions of preschool children. *University of Iowa Studies of Child Welfare,* 1933, **7**(4).

Halliday, C. *The visually impaired child: growth, learning and development: infancy to school age.* Louisville, Ky.: American Printing House for the Blind, 1971.

Harley, R. K. Children with visual disabilities. In L. M. Dunn (Ed.), *Exceptional children in the schools: special education in transition.* (2nd ed.) New York: Holt, Rinehart and Winston, Inc., 1973.

Hartley, R. E., Frank, L. K., and Goldenson, R. M. *Understanding children's play.* New York: Columbia University Press, 1952.

Hartup, W. W., and Coates, B. Imitation of a peer as a function of reinforcement from the peer group and rewardingness of the model. *Child Development,* 1967, **38**, 1003-1016.

Harvard Educational Review. The rights of children: parts I and II. *Harvard Educational Review,* 1973, **43**(4); 1974, **44**(1).

Hawkridge, D., Chalupsky, A., and Roberts, A. *A study of selected exemplary programs for the education of disadvantaged children.* Palo Alto, Calif.: American Institute for Research in the Behavioral Sciences, 1968.

Heber, R. Modification in the manual on terminology and classifications in mental retardation. *American Journal of Mental Deficiency,* 1961, **46**, 499-501.

Heber, R., Garber, H., Harrington, S., Hoffman, C., and Falender, C. *Rehabilitation of families at risk for mental retardation: progress report.* Madison, Wisc.: Rehabilitation Research and Training Center, University of Wisconsin, 1972.

Hegeler, S. *Peter and Caroline: a child asks about childbirth and sex.* New York: Abelard-Schuman Limited, 1957.

Hellmuth, J. (Ed.) *Disadvantaged child: Head Start and early intervention.* Vol. 2. New York: Brunner/Mazel, Inc., 1968.

Hellmuth, J. (Ed.) *Disadvantaged child: compensatory education, a national debate,* Vol. 3. New York: Brunner/Mazel, Inc., 1970.

Hendrick, J. B. The pleasures of meaningful work. *Young Children,* 1967, **22**, 373-380.

Hendrick, J. B. Aggression: what to do about it. *Young Children,* 1968, **23**, 298-305.

Hendrick, J. B. What mothers need. *Young Children,* 1970, **25**, 109-114.

Hendrick, J. B. *The cognitive development of the economically disadvantaged Mexican-American and Anglo-American four-year-old: teaching the concepts of grouping, ordering, perceiving common connections, and matching by means of semantic and figural materials.* (Doctoral dissertation, University of California at Santa Barbara.) Santa Barbara, Calif., 1973.

Hendrick, J. B. *An analysis and summary of a survey of child care needs and child care services available on California community college campuses as of March, 1974.* Santa Barbara, Calif.: Santa Barbara City College and the California Association for the Education of Young Children, 1974.

Herron, R. E., and Sutton-Smith, B. *Child's play.* New York: John Wiley & Sons, Inc., 1971.

Hess, E. H. In L. Uhr and J. G. Miller (Eds.), *Drugs and behavior.* New York: John Wiley & Sons, Inc., 1960.

Hildebrand, V. *Introduction to early childhood education.* New York: The Macmillan Co., 1971.

Hilgard, E. R., and Bower, G. H. *Theories of learning.* (3rd ed.) New York: Appleton-Century-Crofts, 1966.

Hill, R. B. *The strengths of black families.* New York: Emerson Hall, 1971.

Hirsch, E. S. *Transition periods: stumbling blocks of education.* New York: Early Childhood Education Council of N. Y., 1972.

Hodgden, L., Koetter, J., Laforse, B., McCord,

S., and Schramm, D. *School before six: a diagnostic approach.* St. Ann, Miss.: Central Midwest Regional Educational Laboratory, 1970.

Hodges, B. W. *How babies are born: the story of birth for children.* New York: Essandess Special Editions, 1967.

Hodges, W. L., McCandless, B. R., Spicker, H. H., and Craig, I. S. *Diagnostic teaching for preschool children.* Arlington, Va.: Council for Exceptional Children, 1971.

Hoepfner, R., Stern, C., and Nummedal, S. G. *CSE-ECRC preschool/kindergarten test evaluations.* Los Angeles: School Evaluation Project, Center for the Study of Evaluation and the Early Childhood Research Center, 1971.

Hofsteater, H. T. An experiment in preschool education: an autobiographical case study. In S. A. Kirk and F. E. Lord (Eds.), *Exceptional children: educational resources and perspectives.* Boston: Houghton Mifflin Co., 1974.

Holt, J.: *How children fail.* New York: Dell Publishing Co., Inc., 1964.

Hoppe, R. A., Milton, G. A., and Simmel, E. C. *Early experiences and the process of socialization.* New York: Academic Press, Inc., 1970.

Horowitz, F. D. Social reinforcement effects on child behavior. In W. W. Hartup and N. L. Smothergill (Eds.), *The young child: reviews of research,* Vol. 1. Washington, D. C.: N.A.E.Y.C., 1967.

Howe, P. S. *Basic nutrition in health and disease.* (5th ed.) Philadelphia: W. B. Saunders Co., 1971.

Hughes, M. M., and Sanchez, G. I. *Learning a new language.* Washington, D. C.: A.C.E.I., 1957.

Hunt, J. McV. *Intelligence and experience.* New York: The Ronald Press Co., 1961.

Hunter, M., Schucman, H., and Friedlander, G. *The retarded child from birth to five: a multidisciplinary program for child and family.* New York: The John Day Co., Inc., 1972.

Hymes, J. L. *Early childhood education: an introduction to the profession.* Washington, D. C.: N.A.E.Y.C., 1968 (a).

Hymes, J. L. *Teaching the child under six.* Columbus, Ohio: Charles E. Merrill Publishing Co., 1968 (b).

Ingalls, A. J., and Salerno, M. C. *Maternal and child health nursing.* (2nd ed.) St. Louis: The C. V. Mosby Co., 1971.

Inhelder, B. *Recent trends in Genevan research.* Paper presented at Temple University, fall 1968.

Instructional Objectives Exchange. *Early childhood education.* Los Angeles: The Exchange, no date.

Ireland, R. R. The care and education of preschool nonwhites in the Republic of South Africa. In B. C. Mills (Ed.), *Understanding the young child and his curriculum.* New York: The Macmillan Co., 1972.

Jackson, P. W., and Wolfson, B. J. Varieties of constraint in a nursery school. *Young Children,* 1968, **23**(6), 358-368.

Janis, M. G. *A two-year-old goes to nursery school: a case study of separation reactions.* New York: N.A.E.Y.C., 1966.

Jefferson, B. *Teaching art to children: content and viewpoint.* (3rd ed.) Boston: Allyn & Bacon, Inc., 1969.

Jencks, C. *Inequality: a reassessment of the effect of family and schooling in America.* New York: Basic Books, Inc., Publishers, 1972.

Jensen, A. R. How much can we boost I.Q. and scholastic achievment? *Harvard Educational Review,* 1969, **39**(1), complete issue.

Jersild, A. *When teachers face themselves.* New York: Teachers College Press, 1955.

John, V. P., and Horner, V. M. *Early childhood bilingual education.* New York: Modern Languages Association of America, 1971.

Johnson, H. M. *The art of block building.* New York: Bank Street College of Education, 1933.

Joint Commission on the Mental Health of Children. *Crisis in child mental health: challenge for the 1970's.* New York: Harper & Row, Publishers, 1970.

Joint Commission on the Mental Health of Children. *Mental health: from infancy through adolescence: reports of Task Forces I, II, and III and the Committeees on Education and Religion.* New York: Harper & Row, Publishers, 1973.

Jones, E. *What is music for young children?* Washington, D. C.: N.A.E.Y.C., 1958.

Jordan, J. B. OCD urges special education's support for new Head Start services to handicapped children. *Exceptional Children,* 1973, **40**, 1.

Jordan, J. B., and Darley, R. F. *Not all little red wagons are red: the exceptional child's early years.* Arlington, Va.: Council for Exceptional Children, 1973.

Joyce, M. *First steps in teaching creative dance: a handbook for teachers of children kindergarten through sixth grade.* Palo Alto, Calif.: National Press Books, 1973.

Kagan, J. *Creativity and learning.* Boston: Houghton Mifflin Co., 1967.

Kagan, J., and Klein, R. E. Cross-cultural perspectives on early development. Paper presented to the American Association for the

Advancement of Science, Washington, D. C., December 1972.

Kagan, J., Klein, R. E., Haith, M. M., and Morrison, F. J. Memory and meaning in two cultures. *Child Development,* 1973, **44**(1), 221-223.

Kahn, A. J., Kamerman, S. B., and McGowan, B. G. *Child advocacy: report of a national baseline study.* Washington, D. C.: U. S. Dept. of H.E.W., Office of Child Development, Children's Bureau, 1973.

Kamii, C. Evaluation of learning in preschool education: socioemotional, perceptual-motor and cognitive development. In B. S. Bloom, J. T. Hastings, and G. Madans (Eds.), *Handbook on formative and summative evaluation of student learning.* New York: McGraw-Hill Co., 1971.

Kamii, C. A sketch of the Piaget-derived preschool curriculum developed by the Ypsilanti Early Education Program. In S. J. Braun and E. P. Edwards. *History and theory of early childhood education.* Worthington, Ohio: Charles A. Jones Publishing Co., 1972.

Kanner, L. Early infantile autism. *Journal of Pediatrics,* 1944, **25**, 211-217.

Karnes, M. B. *Helping young children develop language skills: a book of activities.* Washington, D. C.: Council for Exceptional Children, 1968.

Karnes, M. B., Teska, J. A., and Hodgins, A. S. The effects of four programs of classroom intervention on the intellectual and language development of four-year-old disadvantaged children. *American Journal of Orthopsychiatry,* 1970, **40**(1), 58-76.

Katz, L. G. Children and teachers in two types of Head Start classes. *Young Children,* 1969, **24**(6), 342-349.

Katz, L. G. Condition with caution. 1972 (a), *Young Children,* **27**, 5.

Katz, L. G. *Research on open education: problems and issues.* Urbana, Ill.: ERIC Clearinghouse on Early Childhood Education, 1972 (b).

Katz, L. G. Keynote address and closing address. California Association for the Education of Young Children. San Diego, Calif., March 1974.

Keats, E. J. *Whistle for Willie.* New York: The Viking Press, Inc., 1964.

Keister, M. E. *A demonstration project: group care of infants and toddlers. Final report submitted to the Children's Bureau.* Greensboro, N. C.: University of North Carolina, 1970.

Kellogg, R. *Analyzing children's art.* Palo Alto, Calif.: National Press Books, 1969.

Kessen, W. *The child.* New York: John Wiley & Sons, Inc., 1965.

Kessler, J. W. *Psychopathology of childhood.* Englewood Cliffs, N. J.: Prentice-Hall, Inc., 1966.

Kessler, J. W., Gridth, A., and Smith, E. Separation reaction in young mildly retarded children. Paper presented at the annual convention of the American Orthopsychiatric Association, Boston, 1968.

Keyserling, M. D. The magnitude of day care needed. In S. V. Allen, M. W. Edelmann, O. Hansen and others (Eds.), *Perspectives on child care.* Washington, D. C.: N.A.E.Y.C., 1972.

King, K. E., and Kerber, A. *The sociology of early childhood education.* New York: American Book Co., 1968.

Kirk, S. A. *Educating exceptional children.* (2nd ed.) Boston: Houghton Mifflin Co., 1972.

Kirk, S. A., Karnes, M. B., and Kirk, W. D. *You and your retarded child: a manual for parents of retarded children.* (2nd ed.) Palo Alto, Calif.: Pacific Books, Publishers, 1968.

Kirkhart, R., and Kirkhart, E. The bruised self: mending in the early years. In K. Yamamoto (Ed.), *The child and his image: self concept in the early years.* Boston: Houghton Mifflin Co., 1972.

Klein, J. Planned variation in Head Start programs. *Children,* 1971, **18**(1), 8-12.

Kliman, G. *Psychological emergencies of childhood.* New York: Grune & Stratton, Inc., 1968.

Knitzer, J. Parental involvement: the elixir of change. In D. N. McFadden (Ed.), *Planning for action.* Washington, D. C.: N.A.E.Y.C., 1972.

Kohlberg, L. A cognitive-developmental analysis of children's sex-role concept and attitudes. *Genetic Psychological Monographs,* 1966, **75**, 128.

Kohlberg, L. Stage and sequence: the cognitive-developmental approach to socialization. In D. A. Goslin (Ed.), *Handbook of socialization and research.* Chicago: Rand McNally & Co., 1969.

Kraft, I., Fuschillo, J., and Herzog, E. *Prelude to school: an evaluation of an inner-city preschool program.* Washington, D. C.: U. S. Govt. Printing Office, 1968.

Krathwohl, D. R., Bloom, B. S., and Masia., B. B. *Taxonomy of educational objectives, handbook II.* New York:David McKay Co., Inc., 1964.

Krebs, D. L. Altruism: an examination of the concept and a review of the literature. *Psychological Bulletin,* 1970, **73**, 258-302.

Kritchevsky, S., Prescott, E., and Walling, L. *Physical space: planning environments for young children.* Washington, D. C.: N.A.E.Y.C., 1969.

Laban, R. *The mastery of movement.* (2nd ed.) London: MacDonald & Evans, 1960.

Labov, W. The logic of nonstandard English. In F. Williams (Ed.), *Language and poverty.* Chicago: Markham Publishing Co., 1970.

LaCrosse, E. R., Lee, P. C., Litman, F., Ogilvie, D. M., Stodlosky, S. S., and White, B. L. The first six years of life: a report on current research and educational practice. *Genetic Psychology Monographs,* 1970, **82**, 161-266.

Lambert, N. M. The present status of the culture-fair testing movement. In J. T. Flynn and H. Garber (Eds.), *Assessing behavior: readings in educational and psychological measurement.* Reading, Mass.: Addison-Wesley Publishing Co., Inc., 1967.

Lambert, W. E., and Klineberg, O. The development of children's views of foreign peoples. In M. D. Cohen (Ed.), *Learning to live as neighbors.* Washington, D. C.: A.C.E.I., 1972.

Landreth, C., and Johnson, B. C. Young children's responses to a picture inset test designed to reveal reactions to persons of different skin color. *Child Development,* 1953, **24**, 63-80.

Lane, M., Elzey, F. F., and Lewis, M. S. *Nurseries in cross-cultural education: final report.* Washington, D. C.: National Institutes of Mental Health, 1971.

Latimer, B. I. (Ed.) *Starting out right: choosing books about black people for young children, pre-school through third grade.* Washington, D. C.: D.C.C.D.C.A., 1972.

Lavatelli, C. S. *Early childhood curriculum: a Piaget program.* Boston: American Science and Engineering, Inc., 1970 (a).

Lavatelli, C. S. *Piaget's theory applied to an early childhood curriculum.* Boston: American Science and Engineering, Inc., 1970 (b).

Lavatelli, C. S. (Ed.) *Language training in early childhood education.* Urbana, Ill.: University of Illinois and ERIC Clearinghouse on Early Childhood Education, 1971.

Lawrence, T. M. (Ed.) *Teaching Exceptional Children,* 1971, **3**, 3.

Lazar, J. B., and Chapman, J. E. *A review of the present status and research needs of programs to develop parenting skills.* OCD Grant #CB-107, April 1972.

League of Women Voters. *Food for all.* Washington, D. C.: The League, 1972.

Lee, B. N., and Merrill, M. D. *Writing complete affective objectives: a short course.* Belmont, Calif.: Wadsworth Publishing Co. Inc., 1972.

Leithwood, K. A., and Fowler, W. Complex motor learning in four-year-olds. *Child Development,* 1971, **42**, 781-792.

LeShan, E. J. *The conspiracy against childhood.* New York: Atheneum Publishers, 1971.

Levenstein, P. Cognitive growth in preschoolers through verbal interaction with mothers. *Journal of Orthopsychiatry,* **40**(3), 426-432.

Lewis, M. M. *Language, thought and personality.* New York: Basic Books, Inc., Publishers, 1963.

Lichtenberg, P., and Norton, D. G. *Cognitive and mental development in the first five years of life: a review of recent research.* Rockville, Md.: National Institutes of Mental Health, 1970.

Lieberman, J. N. Playfulness and divergent thinking ability: an investigation of their relationship at the kindergarten level. In M. Almy (Ed.), *Early childhood play: selected readings related to cognition and motivation.* New York: Simon & Schuster, Inc., 1968.

Lindsay, Z. *Art and the handicapped child.* New York: Van Nostrand Reinhold Co., 1972.

Lombard, A., and Stern, C. Effect of verbalization on young children's learning of a manipulative skill. *Young Children,* 1970, **25**(5), 282-288.

Looff, D. H. *Appalachia's children: the challenge of mental health.* Lexington, Ky.: University of Kentucky Press, 1971.

Lorenz, K. *On aggression.* Translated by M. K. Wilson. New York: Harcourt Brace Jovanovich, Inc., 1966.

Lowenfeld, B. *The visually handicapped child in school.* New York: The John Day Co., Inc., 1973.

Lowenfeld, V. *Your child and his art: a guide for parents.* The Macmillan Co., 1954.

Lystad, M. H. *Social aspects of alienation: an annotated bibliography.* Chevy Chase, Md.: National Institutes of Mental Health, 1969.

Maccoby, E. E. (Ed.) *The development of sex differences.* Stanford, Calif.: Stanford University Press, 1966.

Maccoby, E. E., and Zellner, M. *Experiments in primary education: aspects of Project Follow-Through.* New York: Harcourt Brace Jovanovich, Inc., 1970.

MacEwan, P. T. *Liberating young children from sex roles: experiences in day care centers, playgroups, and free schools.* Boston, New England Free Press, 1972.

Macfarlane, J. W. Study of personality development. In R. G. Barker, J. S. Kounin, and H. F. Wright (Eds.), *Child behavior and development.* New York: McGraw-Hill Book Co., 1943.

Macnamara, J. *Bilingualism in primary education: a study of Irish experience.* Edinburgh: Edinburgh University Press, 1966.

Mager, R. F. *Preparing instructional objectives.* Belmont, Calif.: Fearon Publishers, 1962.

Maier, H. W. *Three theories of child develop-*

ment. New York: Harper & Row, Publishers, 1965.

Margolin, E. Conservation of self expression and aesthetic sensitivity in young children. *Young Children,* 1968, **23,** 155-160.

Margolin, E. *Sociocultural elements in early childhood education.* New York: The Macmillan Co., 1974.

Markun, P. M. *Parenting.* Washington, D. C.: A.C.E.I., 1973.

Marland, S. P. (Submitter). *Education of the gifted and talented.* Washington, D. C.: U. S. Office of Education, 1972.

Martinson, R. A. *Educational programs for gifted pupils.* Sacramento, Calif.: California State Department of Education, 1961.

Martinson, R. A. Children with superior cognitive abilities. In L. M. Dunn (Ed.), *Exceptional children in the schools: special education in transition.* New York: Holt, Rinehart and Winston, Inc., 1973.

Marzollo, J., and Lloyd, J. *Learning through play.* New York: Harper & Row, Publishers, 1972.

Maslow, A. *Eupsychian management.* Homewood, Ill.: Dorsey Press, 1965.

Matterson, E. M. *Play and playthings for the preschool child.* Baltimore, Md.: Penguin Books Inc., 1965.

Maudry, M., and Nekula, M. Social relations between children of the same age during the first two years of life. *Journal of Genetic Psychology,* 1939, **54,** 193-215.

May, R. *The meaning of anxiety.* New York: The Ronald Press Co., 1950.

Maynard, F. *Guiding your child to a more creative life.* Garden City, N. Y.: Doubleday & Co., Inc., 1973.

McCandless, B. R., and Evans, E. D. *Children and youth: psychosocial development.* Hinsdale, Ill.: Dryden Press, 1973.

McCarthy, D. Language development in children. In L. Carmichael (Ed.), *Manual of child psychology.* (2nd ed.) New York: John Wiley & Sons, Inc., 1954.

McCord, W., McCord, J., and Howard, A. Familial correlates of aggression in non-delinquent male children. *Journal of Abnormal Social Psychology,* 1961, **62,** 79-93.

McCurdy, J. Research puts new emphasis on teen-age education. *Los Angeles Times,* Feb. 17, 1974, part II, 1 & 6.

McFadden, D. N. (Ed.) *Planning for action.* Columbus, Ohio: Battelle Memorial Institute, 1972.

McGraw, M. B. Later development of children specially trained during infancy: Johnny and Jimmy at school age. In R. N. Singer (Ed.), *Readings in motor learning.* Philadelphia: Lea & Febiger, 1972.

Meeker, M. N. *The structure of intellect: its interpretation and uses.* Columbus, Ohio: Charles E. Merrill Publishing Co., 1969.

Meeker, M. N., Sexton, K., and Richardson, M. O. *SOI abilities workbook.* Los Angeles: Loyola-Marymount University, 1970.

Menninger Clinic Children's Division. *Disturbed children.* San Francisco: Jossey-Bass, Inc., Publishers, 1969.

Menyuk, P. Syntactic structures in the language of children. *Child Development,* 1963, **34,** 407-422.

Michal-Smith, H. *The exceptional child in the normal nursery.* New York: Early Childhood Education Council of N. Y., 1966.

Midlarsky, E., and Bryan, J. H. Training charity in children. *Journal of Personality and Social Psychology,* 1967, **5,** 405-415.

Miel, A., and Kiester, E. *The shortchanged children of suburbia.* New York: Institute of Human Relations Press, The American Jewish Committee, 1967.

Milhollan, F., and Forisha, B. E. *From Skinner to Rogers: contrasting approaches to education.* Lincoln, Neb.: Professional Educator Publications, 1972.

Millar, S. *The psychology of play.* Baltimore, Md.: Penguin Books Inc., 1968.

Mischel, W., and Grusec, J. Determinants of the rehearsal and transmission of neutral and aversive behaviors. *Journal of Personality and Social Psychology,* 1966, **3,** 197-205.

Mitchell, E. The learning of sex roles through toys and books. *Young Children,* 1971, **28**(4), 226-232.

Moffitt, M. W. *Woodworking for children.* New York: Early childhood Education Council of N. Y., no date.

Moffitt, M. W., and Omwake, E. *The intellectual content of play.* New York: New York State Association for the Education of Young Children, no date.

Monahan, R. *Free and inexpensive materials for preschool and early childhood.* Belmont, Calif.: Lear Siegler/Fearon Publishers, 1973.

Montagu, A. *Touching: the human significance of the skin.* New York: Columbia University Press, 1971.

Montessori, M. *The discovery of the child.* Translated by M. J. Costelloe. Notre Dame, Ind.: Fides Publishers, Inc., 1967.

Moor, P. What teachers are saying—about the young blind child. *The Journal of Nursery Education,* 1960, **15,** 2.

Moore, O. K., and Anderson, A. R. The Responsive Environments Project. In R. C. Hess and R. M. Bear (Eds.), *Early education,* Chicago: Aldine Publishing Co., 1968.

Morgan, G. G. Regulation of early childhood programs. In D. N. McFadden (Ed.), *Plan-*

ning for action. Columbus, Ohio: Battelle Memorial Institute, 1972.

Morland, J. K. Racial acceptance and preference of nursery school children in a southern city. In A. R. Brown (Ed.), *Prejudice in children.* Springfield, Ill.: Charles C Thomas, Publisher, 1972.

Moskovitz, S. Behavioral objectives: new ways to fail children? *Young Children,* 1973, **28**(4), 232-235.

Moss, H. Sex, age and state as determinants of mother-infant interaction. *Merrill-Palmer Quarterly,* 1967, **13**(1), 19-36.

Moustakas, C. *The authentic teacher: sensitivity and awareness in the classroom.* Cambridge, Mass.: Howard A. Doyle, 1966.

Murphy, L. B. *Personality in young children: methods for the study of personality in young children.* Vol. 1. New York: Basic Books, Inc., Publishers, 1956.

Murphy, L. B., and Leeper, E. M. *Away from bedlam.* Washington, D. C.: U. S. Dept. of H.E.W., Office of Child Development, 1970 (a).

Murphy, L. B., and Leeper, E. M. *The vulnerable child.* Washington, D. C.: U. S. Dept. of H.E.W., Office of Child Development, 1970 (b).

Murphy, L. B., and Leeper, E. M. *More than a teacher.* Washington, D. C.: U. S. Dept. of H.E.W., Office of Child Development, 1970 (c).

Murray, F. B. Acquisition of conservation through social interaction. *Developmental Psychology,* 1972, **6**, 1-6.

Mussen, P. H., Conger, J. J., and Kagan, J. *Child development and personality.* New York: Harper & Row, Publishers, 1969.

Mussen, P., and Parker, A. Mother nurturance and girls' incidental imitative learning. *Journal of Personality and Social Psychology,* 1965, **2**, 94-97.

Mycue, E. de los S. *Young children with handicaps, part I. Emotional disturbance and specific learning disabilities.* Urbana, Ill.: College of Education Curriculum Laboratory, 1973 (a).

Mycue, E. de los S. *Young children with handicaps, part II. Physically handicapped.* Urbana, Ill.: University of Illinois and ERIC Clearinghouse on Early Childhood Education, 1973 (b).

Mycue, E de los S. *Young children with handicaps, part III. Educable and trainable mentally handicapped: an abstract bibliography.* Urbana, Ill.: University of Illinois and ERIC Clearinghouse on Early Childhood Education, 1973 (c).

Mycue, E. de los S. *Young children with handicaps: part IV. Resources: directories, news-letters, bibliographies, and general information: an abstract bibliography.* Urbana, Ill.: University of Illinois and ERIC Clearinghouse on Early Childhood Education, 1973 (d).

National Institute of Neurological Diseases and Stroke. *Learning to talk: speech, hearing and language problems in the pre-school child.* Washington, D. C.: U. S. Dept. of H.E.W., 1969.

Nedler S., and Sebera, P. Intervention strategies for Spanish-speaking children. *Child Development,* 1971, **42**, 259-267.

Neff, W. S. *Work and human behavior.* New York: Atherton Press, 1968.

Neill, A. S. *Summerhill.* New York: Hart Publishing Co., Inc., 1960.

Neisser, E. G. *Your child's sense of responsibility.* New York: Public Affairs Pamphlets, 1957. Pamphlet no. 254.

Nelson, W. E., Vaughan, V. C. III, and McKay, R. J. *Textbook of pediatrics.* (9th ed.) Philadelphia: W. B. Saunders Co., 1969.

Neuman, D. Sciencing for young children. In K. R. Baker (Ed.), *Ideas that work with young children.* Washington, D. C.: N.A.E.Y.C., 1972.

Newsweek. Enterprise: the child-care business. *Newsweek,* May 29, 1972.

Nicolaysen, M. Dominion in children's play: its meaning and management. In K. R. Baker (Ed.), *Ideas that work with young children.* Washington, D. C.: N.A.E.Y.C., 1972.

Northcott, W. H. Candidate for integration: a hearing impaired child in a regular nursery school. *Young Children,* 1970, **25**(6), 367-380.

O'Connell, D. *Multiply handicapped children: a bibliography.* Urbana, Ill.: University of Illinois and ERIC Clearinghouse on Early Childhood Education, 1973.

O'Keefe, R. A. Home Start: partnership with parents. *Children Today,* Jan.-Feb., 1973, 12-16.

Orata, P. T. The Iloilo experiment in education through the vernacular. In *The use of vernacular languages in education.* Monographs on Fundamental Education, VIII. Paris: U.N.E.S.C.O., 1953.

Orpet, R. E., and Meyers, C. E. Six Structure-of-Intellect hypotheses in six-year-old children. *Journal of Educational Psychology,* 1966, **57**, 341-346.

Otis, N. B., and McCandless, B. R. Responses to repeated frustrations of young children differentiated according to need area. *Journal of Abnormal Social Psychology,* 1955, **50**, 349-353.

Page, P. *Campus day care: issues and resources.* Washington, D. C.: C.W.L.A., 1971.

Palomares, V. H., and Cummins, E. J. *Assess-*

ment of rural Mexican-American pupils, preschool and grades one through six. Sacramento, Calif.: California State Department of Education, 1968.

Parke, R. D. (Ed.) *Recent trends in social learning theory.* New York: Academic Press, Inc., 1972 (a).

Parke, R. D. Some effects of punishment on children's behavior. In W. W. Hartup (Ed.), *The young child: reviews of research,* Vol. 2. Washington, D. C.: N.A.E.Y.C., 1972 (b).

Parten, M. B. Social participation among preschool children. *Journal of Abnormal Social Psychology,* 1932, **27,** 243-269.

Parten, M. B., and Newhall, S. Social behavior of preschool children. In R. Barker (Ed.), *Child behavior and development.* New York: McGraw-Hill Book Co., 1943.

Patterson, G. R., Littman, R. A., and Bricker, W. Assertive behavior in children: a step toward a theory of aggression. *Monographs of the Society for Research in Child Development,* 1967, **32**(5), 1-43.

Peters, A. deH. Health support in day care. In E. Grotberg (Ed.), *Day care: resources for decisions.* Washington, D. C.: Office of Economic Opportunity, 1971.

Peters, A. deH. The delivery of health and social services to child and family in a daytime program. In D. N. McFadden (Ed.), *Planning for action.* Columbus, Ohio: Battelle Memorial Institute, 1972.

Petersham, M., and Petersham, M. *The circus baby.* New York: The Macmillan Co., 1950.

Peterson, D., Gonzalez, A., Hendrick, J., Johnson, C., Miller, M., Rhodes, D., Statucki, M., and Wilson, K. *Educational objectives for the Santa Barbara City College Children's Center:* unpublished report to the California State Department of Education. Santa Barbara, Calif.: Santa Barbara City College, 1973.

Petty, W. T., and Starkey, R. J. Oral language and personal and social development. In W. T. Petty (Ed.), *Research in oral language.* Champaign, Ill.: National Council of Teachers of English, 1967.

Piaget, J. *The language and thought of the child.* New York: Harcourt Brace Jovanovich, Inc., 1926.

Piaget, J. *The child's conception of physical causality.* London: Routledge & Kegan Paul, 1930.

Piaget, J. *The psychology of intelligence.* London: Routledge & Kegan Paul, 1950.

Piaget, J. *Play, dreams and imitation in childhood.* Translated by C. Gattegno and F. M. Hodgson. New York: W. W. Norton & Co., Inc., 1962.

Piaget, J. *The origins of intelligence in children.* New York: W. W. Norton & Co., Inc., 1963.

Piaget, J. *The child's conception of number.* New York: W. W. Norton & Co., Inc., 1965.

Piaget, J., and Inhelder, B. *The child's conception of space.* New York: W. W. Norton & Co., Inc., 1967.

Piaget, J., and Inhelder, B. *The psychology of the child.* Translated by H. Weaver. New York: Basic Books, Inc., Publishers, 1969.

Pickler, E. Some contributions to the study of the gross motor development of children. *Journal of Genetic Psychology,* 1968, **113,** 27-39.

Piper, M. R. *Sunset Mexican cookbook.* Menlo Park, Calif.: Lane Magazine & Book Co., 1969.

Pitcher, E. G., and Ames, L. B. *The guidance nursery school.* New York: Harper & Row, Publishers, 1964.

Pitcher, E. G., Lasher, M. G., Feinburg, S., and Hammond, N. C. *Helping young children learn.* Columbus, Ohio: Charles E. Merrill Publishing Co., 1966.

Pitcher, E. G., and Prelinger, E. *Children tell stories: an analysis of fantasy.* New York: International Universities Press, 1963.

Plakos, J. *Tests in use in Title VII Bilingual Education Projects.* Forth Worth, Tex.: National Consortia for Bilingual Education, 1971.

Popham, W. J., Eisner, E. W., Sullivan, H. J., and Tyler, L. L. *Instructional objectives.* Chicago: Rand McNally & Co., 1969.

Porter, J. D. R. *Black child, white child: the development of racial attitudes.* Garden City, N. Y.: Doubleday & Co., Inc., 1970.

Project Head Start. *Parent involvement: a workbook of training tips for Head Start staff.* Number 10A. Washington, D. C.: Office of Economic Opportunity, 1969.

Publications Committee, N.A.E.Y.C.. *Water, sand and mud as play materials.* Washington, D. C.: N.A.E.Y.C., 1959.

Ratliff, A. R., and Ratliff, R. G. Sesame Street: magic or malevolence? *Young Children,* 1972, **27**(4), 199-204.

Ravenscroft, P. Day care on campus. *Day Care and Early Education,* 1973, **1**(2), 22-25.

Read, K. H. *The nursery school: a human relationships laboratory.* (5th ed.) Philadelphia: W. B. Saunders Co., 1971.

Redl, F. *When we deal with children.* New York: The Free Press, 1966.

Redl, F., and Wattenberg, W. W. *Mental hygiene in teaching.* (2nd ed.) New York: Harcourt Brace Jovanovich, Inc., 1959.

Redl, F., and Wineman, D. *Children who hate.* New York: The Free Press, 1951.

Redl, F., and Wineman, D. *Controls from within.* New York: The Free Press, 1952.

Reese, H. W., and Lipsitt, L. P. *Experimental child psychology.* New York: Academic Press, Inc., 1970.

Reif, T. F., and Stollak, G. E. *Sensitivity to young children: training and its effects.* East Lansing, Mich.: Michigan State University Press, 1972.

Rey, H. A. *Curious George.* Boston: Houghton Mifflin Co., 1941.

Riles, W. Keynote address. California Association for the Education of Young Children, San Diego, March 1974.

Riley, J. E. The self-concept and sex-role behavior of third and fourth grade boys. *Dissertation Abstracts,* 1966, **27,** 680.

Robb, M. D., Mushier, C. L., Bogard, D. A., and Blann, M. E. (Eds.) *Foundations and practices in perceptual motor learning—a quest for understanding.* American Association for Health, Physical Education, and Recreation, 1971.

Robb, P. *Epilepsy: a review of basic and clinical research.* Washington, D. C.: U. S. Dept. of H.E.W., National Institute of Neurological Diseases and Blindness, 1965.

Roby, P. *Child care—who cares? Foreign and domestic infant and early childhood development policies.* New York: Basic Books, Inc., Publishers, 1973.

Rogers, C. R. *On becoming a person.* Boston: Houghton Mifflin Co., 1961.

Rogers, C. R., and Dymond, R. F. *Psychotherapy and personality change.* Chicago: University of Chicago Press, 1954.

Rohwer, W. D. Prime time for education: early childhood or adolescence? *Harvard Educational Review,* 1971, **41**(3), 316-341.

Rosecrans, C. J. Play—the language of children. *Mental Hygiene,* 1968, **52,** 367-373.

Rosenhan, D. Prosocial behavior of children. In W. W. Hartup (Ed.), *The young child, reviews of research.* Vol. 2. Washington, D. C.: N.A.E.Y.C., 1972.

Rosenthal, R., and Jacobson, L. *Pygmalion in the classroom: teacher expectation and pupil's intellectual development.* New York: Holt, Rinehart and Winston, Inc., 1968.

Rowan, B. *The children we see.* New York: Holt, Rinehart and Winston, Inc., 1973.

Ruebush, B. K. *Children's behavior as a function of anxiety and defensiveness.* Unpublished doctoral dissertation, Yale University, 1960.

Ruebush, B. K. Anxiety. In H. W. Stevenson (Ed.), *Child psychology, part I. 62nd Yearbook of the National Society for the Study of Education.* Chicago: University of Chicago Press, 1963.

Rutherford, E., and Mussen, P. Generosity in nursery school boys. *Child Development,* 1968, **39,** 755-765.

Rutter, M. Behavioral and cognitive characteristics of a series of psychotic children. In J. K. Wing (Ed.), *Early childhood autism: clinical, educational and social aspects.* New York: Pergamon Press, Inc., 1966.

Saario, T., Jacklin, C. N., and Tittle, C. K. Sex role stereotyping in the public schools. *Harvard Educational Review,* 1973, **43**(3), 386-416.

Sander, E. When are speech sounds learned? *Journal of Speech and Hearing Disorders,* 1972, **37,** 1.

Schaefer, E. S. A home tutoring program. *Children,* March-April 1969, 59-61.

Schaefer, E. S. Need for early and continuing education. In V. Denenberg (Ed.), *Education of the infant and young child.* New York: Academic Press, Inc., 1970.

Schaefer, E. S. Parents as educators: evidence for cross-sectional, longitudinal and intervention research. *Young Children,* 1972, **27**(4), 227-239.

Schattner, R. *An early childhood curriculum for multiply handicapped children.* New York: Intext Press, 1971.

Scheffield, M., and Bewley, S. *Where do babies come from?* New York: Alfred A. Knopf, Inc., 1972.

Schima, M., and Bolian, P. *The magic of life.* Englewood Cliffs, N. J.: Prentice-Hall, Inc., 1970.

Schloss, S. *Nursery-kindergarten enrollment of children under six: October, 1965.* Washington, D. C.: National Center for Education Statistics, Office of Education, U. S. Dept. of H.E.W., 1966.

Schwarz, J. C., and Wynn, R. The effects of mother presence and previsits on children's emotional reaction to starting nursery school. *Child Development,* 1971, **42,** 871-881.

Scott, M. *Some parameters of teacher effectiveness as assessed by an ecological approach.* DARCEE Papers & Reports, George Peabody College, 1969.

Scrimshaw, N. S. Early malnutrition and central nervous system function. *Merrill-Palmer Quarterly,* 1969, **15**(4), 375-388.

Sears, R. R. Relation of early socialization experiences to self-concepts and gender role in middle childhood. *Child Development,* 1970, **41,** 267-290.

Sears, R. R., Maccoby, E., and Levin, H. *Pat-

terns of child rearing. New York: Harper & Row, Publishers, 1957.

Seefeldt, C. *A curriculum for child care centers.* Columbus, Ohio: Charles E. Merrill Publishing Co., 1973.

Shaffer, H. B. *Emotionally disturbed children.* Washington, D. C.: Educational Research Reports, 1973.

Sharp, E. *Thinking is child's play.* New York: E. P. Dutton & Co., Inc., 1969.

Shaw, C. R. *The psychiatric disorders of childhood.* New York: Appleton-Century-Crofts, 1966.

Sheviakov, G. *Anger in children.* Washington, D. C.: American Association of Elementary-Kindergarten-Nursery Educators, 1969.

Shriner, T. H. Economically deprived: aspects of language skills. In L. E. Travis (Ed.), *Handbook of speech pathology and audiology.* New York: Appleton-Century-Crofts, 1971.

Siegel, L. S. Development of the concept of seriation. *Developmental Psychology,* 1972, **6,** 135-137.

Sigel, I. E. The Piagetian system and the world of education. In D. Elkind and J. H. Flavell (Eds.), *Studies in cognitive development.* New York: Oxford University Press, 1969.

Sigel, I. E., and Hooper, F. H. (Eds.) *Logical thinking in children: research based on Piaget's theory.* New York: Holt, Rinehart and Winston, Inc., 1968.

Sigel, I. E., and McBane, B. Cognitive competence and level of symbolization among five-year-old children. In J. Hellmuth (Ed.), *The disadvantaged child.* Vol. 1. Seattle: Special Child Publications, 1967.

Sigel, I. E., Starr, R., Secrist, A., Jackson, J. P., and Hill, E. Social and emotional development of young children. In J. L. Frost (Ed.), *Revisiting early childhood education: readings.* Holt, Rinehart and Winston, Inc., 1973.

Simmons, A. S., and Chayes, A. H. University day care. In P. Roby (Ed.), *Day care—who cares? Foreign and domestic infant and early childhood development policies.* New York: Basic Books, Inc., Publishers, 1973.

Sinclair, C. B. *Movement of the young child: ages two to six.* Columbus, Ohio: Charles E. Merrill Publishing Co., 1973.

Singer, J. L. (Ed.) *The control of aggression and violence: cognitive and physiological factors.* New York: Academic Press, Inc., 1971.

Sitkei, E. G., and Meyers, C. E. Comparative Structure of Intellect in middle and lower-class four-year-olds of two ethnic groups. *Developmental Psychology,* 1969, **1,** 592-604.

Smart, M. S., and Smart, R. C. *Child develop-ment and relationships.* (2nd ed.) New York: The Macmillan Co., 1972.

Smedslund, J. Les origines sociales de la centration. In F. Bresson and M. de Montmalin (Eds.), *Psychologie et épistemologie génetiques.* Paris: Dunod, 1966.

Smilansky, S. *The effects of sociodramatic play on disadvantaged children.* New York: John Wiley & Sons, Inc., 1968.

Smith, H. Standard or nonstandard: is there an answer? *Elementary English,* Feb. 1973, 225-234 (a).

Smith, H. Black English: considerations and approaches. *The English Journal,* Feb. 1973, 311-318 (b).

Smith, J. A. *Setting conditions for creative teaching in the elementary school.* Boston: Allyn & Bacon, Inc., 1966.

Smith, M. S., and Bissell, J. S. Report analysis: the impact of Head Start. *Harvard Educational Review,* 1970, **14,** 51-104.

Snyder, A. *Dauntless women.* Washington, D. C.: A.C.E.I., 1972.

Solomon, P., Kubzansky, P. E., Leiderman, P. H., Mendelson, J. H., Trumbull, R., and Wexler, D. *Sensory deprivation.* Cambridge, Mass.: Harvard University Press, 1965.

Southwick, C. H. (Ed.) *Animal aggression: selected readings.* New York: Van Nostrand Reinhold Co., 1970.

Sparling, J. J., and Sparling, M. C. How to talk to a scribbler. *Young Children,* 1973, **28**(6), 333-341.

Spitz, R. A. Hospitalism: an inquiry into the genesis of psychiatric conditions in early childhood. *The psychoanalytic study of the child,* Vol. 1. New York: International Universities Press, 1945.

Spock, B., and Lerrigo, M. O. *Caring for your disabled child.* New York: The Macmillan Co., 1965.

Spodeck, B., Andrews, P., Lee, M., Riley, J., and White, D. *A black curriculum for early childhood education: teaching units.* Urbana, Ill.: University of Illinois, 1971.

Sprigle, H. A. Can poverty children live on "Sesame Street"? *Young Children,* 1971, **26**(4), 202-218.

Starks, E. B. *Blockbuilding, blockbuilding, blockbuilding.* Washington, D. C.: American Association of Elementary-Kindergarten-Nursery Educators, 1960.

Starkweather, E. K., and Cowling, F. G. The measurement of conforming and nonconforming behavior in preschool children. In R. Mooney and T. Razik (Eds.), *Explorations in creativity.* New York: Harper & Row, Publishers, 1967.

Stein, S. The company cares for children. In P.

Roby (Ed.), *Child care—who cares? Foreign and domestic infant and early childhood development policies.* New York: Basic Books, Inc., Publishers, 1973.

Steinfels, M. O'B. *Who's minding the children? The history and politics of day care in America.* New York: Simon & Schuster, Inc., 1973.

Stent, M. D., Hazard, W. R., and Revlin, H. N. *Cultural pluralism in education: mandate for change.* New York: Appleton-Century-Crofts, 1973.

Stevens, C. *The birth of Sunset's kittens.* New York: Young Scott, 1969.

Stevenson, H. W., and Stevenson, N. G. Social interaction in an interracial nursery school. *Genetic Psychology Monographs,* 1960, **61**, 41-75.

Stevenson, H. W., and Stewart, E. C. A developmental study of racial awareness in young children. *Child Development,* 1958, **29**, 400-409.

Stone, J. C., and DeNevi, D. P. (Eds.), *Teaching multicultural populations: five heritages.* New York: Van Nostrand Reinhold Co., 1971.

Stott, L. H., and Ball, R. S. Consistency and change in ascendance-submission in the social interaction of children. *Child Development,* 1957, **28**, 259-272.

Stott, L. H., and Ball, R. S. Infant and preschool mental tests: review and evaluation. *Monographs of the Society for Research in Child Development,* 1965, **30**, 3 (serial no. 101).

Strain, F. B. *New patterns in sex teaching.* New York: Appleton-Century-Crofts, 1940.

Sunderlin, S., and Gray, N. *Equipment and supplies: tested and approved for preschool/school/home.* Washington, D. C.: A.C.E.I., 1968.

Sunderlin, S., Osborn, K., and Cohen, M. D. *Migrant children: their education.* Washington, D. C.: A.C.E.I., 1971.

Sunderlin, S., and Wills, B. (Eds.) *Nutrition and intellectual growth in children.* Washington, D. C.: A.C.E.I., 1969.

Sutton-Smith, B. The role of play in cognitive development. *Young Children,* 1967, **22**, 361-370.

Sutton-Smith, B. A syntax for play and games. In R. E. Herron and B. Sutton-Smith (Eds.), *Child's play.* New York: John Wiley & Sons, Inc., 1971.

Sutton-Smith, B. *Child psychology.* Englewood Cliffs, N. J.: Prentice-Hall, Inc., 1973.

Sutton-Smith, B., and Rosenberg, B. G. Sixty years of historical change in the game preferences of American children. *Journal of American Folklore,* 1961, **74**, 17-46.

Tarnay, E. D. *What does the nursery school teacher teach?* Washington, D. C.: N.A.E.Y.C., 1965.

Task Force on Children Out of School. *The way we go to school.* Boston: Beacon Press, 1970.

Taylor, K. W. *Parent cooperative nursery schools.* New York: Teachers College Press, 1954.

Terman, L. M., Baldwin, B. T., and Bronson, E. *Mental and physical traits of a thousand gifted children: genetic studies of genius.* Vol. 1. Stanford: Stanford University Press, 1925.

Thomas, S. B. *Malnutrition, cognitive development and learning.* Urbana, Ill.: ERIC Clearinghouse on Early Childhood Education, 1972.

Thompson, G. G. The social and emotional development of preschool children under two types of educational programs. *Psychological Monographs,* 1944, **56**(5), 1-29.

Thorndike, R. L., and Hagen, E. *Measurement and evaluation in psychology and education.* (3rd ed.) New York: John Wiley & Sons, Inc., 1969.

Torrance, E. P. *Guiding creative talent.* Englewood Cliffs, N. J.: Prentice-Hall, Inc., 1962.

Torrance, E. P. Adventuring in creativity. *Childhood Education,* October 1963, **83**.

Torrance, E. P. *Creativity.* Belmont, Calif.: Fearon Publishers, 1969.

Torrance, E. P. Freedom to manipulate objects and question-asking performance of six-year-olds. *Young Children,* 1970(a), **26**(2), 93-97.

Torrance, E. P. *Encouraging creativity in the classroom.* Dubuque, Iowa: William C. Brown Co., Publishers, 1970(b).

Travis, L. E. *Handbook of speech pathology and audiology.* New York: Appleton-Century-Crofts, 1971.

Trieschman, A. E., Whittaker, J. K., and Brendtro, L. K. *The other 23 hours.* Chicago: Aldine Publishing Co., 1969.

Truax, C. B., and Tatum, C. D. An extension from the effective psychotherapeutic model to constructive personality change in preschool children. *Childhood Education,* 1966, **42**, 456-62.

Tyler, R. W. A generalized technique for constructing achievement tests. In R. W. Tyler (Ed.), *Constructing achievement tests.* Columbus, Ohio: Bureau of Educational Research, 1934.

Tyler, R. W. *Basic principles of curriculum and instruction.* Chicago: University of Chicago Press, 1950.

United Bronx Parents. In A. J. Kahn, S. B. Kamerman, and B. G. McGowan. *Child advocacy: report of a national baseline study.* Washington, D. C.: U. S. Dept. of H.E.W.,

Office of Child Development, Children's Bureau, 1973.

United States Commission on Civil Rights. *Teachers and students: differences in teacher interaction with Mexican-American and Anglo students. Report V: Mexican-American education study.* Washington, D. C.: U. S. Commission on Civil Rights, 1973.

United States Department of Agriculture. *Project Head Start Community Action Program: food buying guide and recipes.* Washington, D. C.: Office of Economic Opportunity, 1967.

United States Department of Health, Education, and Welfare. *United States immunization survey: 1972.* Washington, D. C.: Center for Disease Control, Public Health Service, 1973(a).

United States Department of Health, Education, and Welfare. *Quantity recipes for child care centers.* Washington, D. C.: U.S. Gov. Printing Office, 1973(b).

United States Department of Health, Education, and Welfare. *Guides for day care licensing.* Washington, D. C.: U.S. Dept. of H.E.W., Office of Child Development, 1973(c).

United States Office of Education and the National Institute of Mental Health. *Mental health and learning: when community mental health centers and school systems collaborate.* Washington, D. C.: U.S. Dept. of H.E.W., 1973.

Utzinger, R. C. *Some European nursery schools and playgrounds.* New York: Educational Facilities Laboratory and the Architectural Research Laboratory of the University of Michigan, 1970.

Valentine, C. W. *The normal child and his abnormalities.* (3rd ed.) Baltimore: Penguin Books Inc., 1956.

Van Riper, C. *Speech correction: principles and methods.* (5th ed.) Englewood Cliffs, N. J.: Prentice-Hall, Inc., 1972.

Varma, V. P. *Stresses in children.* New York: Crane, Russak & Co., 1973.

Vaughn, G. *Mummy, I don't feel well: a pictorial guide to common childhood illnesses.* London: Berkeley Graphics, 1970.

Waatjen, W. B., and Leeper, R. R. (Eds.) *Learning and mental health in the school.* Washington, D. C.: Association for Supervision and Curriculum Development, 1966.

Wallach, M. A., and Kogan, N. *Modes of thinking in young children: a study of the creativity—intelligence distinction.* New York: Holt, Rinehart and Winston, Inc., 1965.

Walsh, A. M. *Self-concepts of bright boys with learning difficulties.* New York: Teachers College Press, 1956.

Ward, E. H., Akers, M., Hines, R. P., and Eggleston, P. The 1970 White House Conference on Children—reports by N.A.E.Y.C. official delegates. *Young Children,* 1971, **26**(4), 194-201.

Ward, W. C. Creativity in young children. *Child Development,* 1968, **39,** 737-754.

Watson, G. Some personality differences in children related to strict or permissive parental discipline. *Journal of Psychology,* 1957, **44,** 227-249.

Watson, J. D. *The double helix: being a personal account of the discovery of the structure of DNA.* New York: Atheneum Publishers, 1968.

Webb, L. *Children with special needs in the infants' school.* London: Collins Fontana Books, 1969.

Weber, E. *The kindergarten: its encounter with educational thought in America.* New York: Teachers College Press, 1969.

Weber, E. *Early childhood education: perspectives on change.* Worthington, Ohio: Charles A. Jones Publishing Co., 1970.

Weikart, D. P. (Ed.) *Preschool intervention: a preliminary report of the Perry Preschool Project.* Ann Arbor, Mich.: University of Michigan Press, 1967.

Weikart, D. P. *Relationship of curriculum, teaching, and learning in preschool education.* Ypsilanti, Mich.: HiScope Educational Research Foundation, 1971.

Weikart, D. P., and Lambie, D. Z. Preschool intervention through a home teaching program. In J. Hellmuth (Ed.), *The disadvantaged child,* Vol. 2. New York: Brunner/Mazel, 1968.

Weikart, D. P., and Lambie, D. Z. Early enrichment in infants. In V. Denenberg (Ed.), *Education of the infant and young child.* New York: Academic Press, Inc., 1970.

Weikart, D. P., Rogers, L., Adcock, C., and McClelland, D. *The cognitively oriented curriculum: a framework for preschool teachers.* Washington, D. C.: N.A.E.Y.C., 1971.

Wender, P. H. *The hyperactive child: a handbook for parents.* New York: Crown Publishers, Inc., 1973.

Werner, N. E., and Evans, I. M. Perception of prejudice in Mexican-American preschool children. In N. N. Wagner, and M. J. Haug. *Chicano: social and psychological perspectives.* St. Louis: The C. V. Mosby Co., 1971.

White, B. L. Informal education during the first months of life. In R. D. Hess and R. M. Bear (Eds.), *Early education.* Chicago: Aldine Publishing Co., 1968.

White, B. L. *Human infants: experience and psychological development.* Englewood Cliffs, N. J.: Prentice-Hall, Inc., 1971.

White, B. L. Closing address. Los Angeles: California Association for the Education of Young Children, March 1973.

White, D. *Multi-ethnic books for Head Start children, part I. Black and integrated literature.* Urbana, Ill.: ERIC Clearinghouse on Early Childhood Education, 1969.

White, R. W. Motivation reconsidered: the concept of competence. In M. Almy (Ed.), *Early childhood play: selected readings related to cognition and motivation.* New York: Simon & Schuster, Inc., 1968.

White, R. W. *The enterprise of living: growth and organization in personality.* New York: Holt, Rinehart and Winston, Inc., 1972.

Wickstrom, R. L. *Fundamental motor patterns.* Philadelphia: Lea & Febiger, 1970.

Wilder, A., Sendak, M., and Engvick, W. *Lullabies and nightsongs.* New York: Harper & Row, Publishers, 1965.

Wilson, J. A. R., Robeck, M. C., and Michael, W. B. *Psychological foundations of learning and teaching.* New York: McGraw-Hill Book Co., 1969.

Winder, C. L., and Rau, L. Parental attitudes associated with social deviance in preadolescent boys. *Journal of Abnormal Social Psychology,* 1962, **64**, 418-424.

Wing, J. K. (Ed.) *Early childhood autism: clinical, educational and social aspects.* New York: Pergamon Press, Inc., 1966.

Wittes, G., and Radin, N. *Ypsilanti home and school handbooks: helping your child to learn: the learning through play approach.* San Rafael, Calif.: Dimensions Publishing Co., 1969(a).

Wittes, G., and Radin, N. *Ypsilanti home and school handbooks: helping your child to learn: the nurturance approach.* San Rafael, Calif.: Dimensions Publishing Co., 1969(b).

Wittes, G., and Radin, N. *Ypsilanti home and school handbooks: helping your child to learn: the reinforcement approach.* San Rafael, Calif.: Dimensions Publishing Co., 1969(c).

World Health Organization. *Deprivation of maternal care: a reassessment of its effects.* Geneva: World Health Organization, 1962.

Wylie, R. *The self-concept.* Lincoln, Neb.: University of Nebraska Press, 1961.

Yarrow, L. J. The effect of antecedent frustration on projective play. *Psychological Monographs,* 1948, **62**, 6.

Yarrow, L. J. Separation from parents during early childhood. In M. L. Hoffman and L. W. Hoffman (Eds.), *Review of child development research.* Vol. 1. New York: Russell Sage Foundation, 1964.

Young Children. The development of the Child Development Associate (CDA) Program. *Young Children,* 1973, **28**(3), 139-145.

Young Children. Action for children's cause. *Young Children,* 1973-1974, **28, 29,** all issues.

Zimmerman, B. J., and Bergan, J. R. Intellectual operations in teacher question asking behavior. *Merrill-Palmer Quarterly,* 1971, **17**(1), 19-26.

Zintz, M. V. *Education across cultures* (2nd ed.) Dubuque, Iowa: Kendall Hunt Publishing Co., 1969.

Zion, G. *Dear garbage man.* New York, Harper & Row, Publishers, 1957.

Zirkel, P. A. Self-concept and the disadvantage of ethnic group membership and mixture. *Review of Educational Research,* 1971, **41**(3), 211-226.

APPENDIX A

Table A. Communicable childhood diseases*

Disease	Infectious agent and general description	Importance	Mode of transmission	Communicable period	Incubation period	Symptoms	Treatment and nursing care	Prevention
Bacillary dysentery (shigellosis)	Shigella dysenteriae and Shigella paradysenteriae Acute inflammation of colon	Extremely widespread in areas with poor sanitary facilities and hygiene practices Disease often severe in infancy but often mild after age 3 yr.	Direct or indirect contact with feces of infected patients or carriers Contaminated food, water, and flies play important role	As long as patients or carriers harbor organisms (as determined by stool or rectal swab cultures) Healthy carriers common; they should not become food handlers In areas where sanitary treatment of sewage is not routine, stools should be disinfected	1-7 days (usually 3-4 days)	Mild to severe diarrhea; in severe cases blood, mucus, and pus may be seen in stool Abdominal pain, fever, and prostration may be present	Treatment depends on severity of infection Ampicillin drug of choice; chloramphenicol; tetracycline (used after age 8 yr.); furazolidone Paregoric and bismuth may help control diarrhea Keep patient warm; oral fluids may be restricted; intravenous therapy may be necessary to prevent dehydration	Attack appears to confer limited immunity No preventive known other than improved individual and community hygiene
Chicken pox (varicella)	Virus capable of causing varicella or herpes zoster Mild, chiefly cutaneous infectious disease Varicella – response to primary infection Herpes zoster-	Very common, highly contagious, usually mild disease Complications other than secondary infection from scratching rare; however, encephalitis	Direct or indirect contact with secretions from mouth or moist skin lesions of varicella or herpes zoster	Approximately 24 hr. before rash appears until 7 days after its onset; dried crusts not contagious	10-21 days (usually 14 days)	Slight fever; malaise; rapidly progressing papulovesiculopustular skin eruption in all stages of development, first appearing on trunk and scalp	Keep fingernails short and clean to minimize secondary infections caused by scratching Calamine lotion, oral antihistaminics reduce pruritus	None; immune after one attack Immune serum globulin (ISG) or hyperimmune zoster globulin for the corticosteroid-treated child or others at increased risk

Continued.

	reactivation (in debilitated persons or persons receiving immunosuppressive therapy) possible. Overwhelming severe infection seen in children receiving immunosuppressive therapy. *CAUTION: Contact!*					
Diphtheria	*Corynebacterium diphtheriae* (Klebs-Löffler bacillus). Severe, acute infectious disease of upper respiratory tract and perhaps skin. Toxins produced may affect nervous system and heart. Rarely seen because of routine childhood immunization, more comprehensive public health regulations, and enforcement of milk standards and carrier control. 5%-10% mortality. Serious complications include neuritis, paralysis, and myocarditis	Direct or indirect contact with secretions from respiratory tract or skin lesions of patient or carrier. As long as virulent organisms are present in discharges and lesions. Isolation until satisfactory nose and throat cultures obtained; contacts may be isolated	2-6 days	Depend on type and part of upper respiratory area inflamed. Formation of fibrinous false membrane, which may or may not be visible in throat or nose. Nausea, possible muscle paralysis, and heart complications	Administration of analgesics, antitoxin, erythromycin (preferred), and penicillin. Absolute bed rest; gentle throat irrigations; bland, soft diet; humidification. Possible need for tracheotomy. Watch for muscle weakness	Immunity after one attack, but person may be immune without history of disease. Immunity determined by Schick test. Routine primary schedule—DTP booster injection on exposure
German measles (rubella, 3-day measles)	Virus. Acute infectious disease characterized chiefly by rose-colored macular rash and lymph node enlargement. Very common, frequently occurring in epidemic form. Complications rare for victim but may cause deformities of fetus if contracted by pregnant woman during first trimester	Usually direct contact with secretions from mouth and nose. May be acquired in utero. From 1 wk. before rash appears until approximately 5 days after its onset	14-21 days (usually 18 days)	Rose-colored macular rash occurring first on face, then on all body parts; enlargement and tenderness of lymph nodes; mild fever	Supportive nursing care with good personal hygiene	Rubella vaccine. Immune after one attack

*From Ingalls, A. J., and Salerno, M. C. *Maternal and child health nursing.* (2nd ed.) St. Louis: The C. V. Mosby Co., 1971.

Table A. Communicable childhood diseases — cont'd

Disease	Infectious agent and general description	Importance	Mode of transmission	Communicable period	Incubation period	Symptoms	Treatment and nursing care	Prevention
Herpes zoster (shingles)	Virus Same virus causes both chicken pox (varicella) and herpes zoster	Overwhelming severe infection seen in children receiving immunosuppressive therapy CAUTION: Contact!	Direct or indirect contact with secretions from mouth or moist skin lesions Zoster less contagious, but susceptible children exposed to zoster lesions may develop chicken pox	Approximately 24 hr before rash appears until 7 days after its onset	10-21 days (usually 14 days)	Zoster lesions confined to skin over sensory nerves and preceded by local pain, itching, and burning Meningismus associated with cranial nerve involvement	Cut fingernails to prevent scratching Analgesics, sedation, thiamine; prednisone in severe cases; wet compresses to lesions	Usually immune after first attack Rarely, second attack seen in some individuals
Measles (rubeola, or 2-week, or red measles)	Virus Acute infection characterized by moderately high fever, inflammation of mucous membranes of respiratory tract, and macular rash	Very common highly infectious disease frequently occurring in epidemic form Possible serious complications include pneumonia, otitis media, conjunctivitis, and encephalitis	Direct or indirect contact with secretions from nose and throat, perhaps airborne May be acquired in utero	From time of "cold symptoms" until about 5 days after rash appears	About 10 days	Catarrhal symptoms, like a common cold; conjunctivitis; photophobia Fever followed by macular, blotchy rash involving entire body Koplik's spots (eruption on mucous membrane of mouth) diagnostic	Antibiotics (to prevent complications) Aspirin and tepid sponge baths for severe cases; various soothing lotions Boric acid eye irrigations; protection from bright lights—eyeshade Observation for onset of pneumonia or ear infection	Live measles vaccine, immune serum globulin (ISG) lessens disease Usually immune after first attack
Meningococcal meningitis (cerebrospinal fever)	Neisseria meningitidis (N. intracellularis) Meningococcus Serious, acute disease caused by bacteria that invade bloodstream and even-	Occurs fairly often where concentrations of people are found (army bases, schools) because of healthy carriers Very severe or relatively mild	Direct contact with patient or carrier by droplet spread Organism may be found in urine	As long as meningococci are found in nose and mouth Usually not infectious after 24 hr. of appropriate therapy	1-7 days (usually 4 days)	Sudden onset of fever, chills, headache, and vomiting (convulsions fairly common in children) Cutaneous petechial hemor-	Spinal tap and culture needed to confirm diagnosis Temperature control; penicillin G, ampicillin, analgesics, and sedatives Watch for clinical	Extent of immunity after attack unknown Sulfonamides have been used prophylactically during epidemics

Disease	Cause and Description	Complications	Transmission	Period of Communicability	Incubation Period	Symptoms	Treatment and Care	Immunization
	tually meninges, causing fever and central nervous system inflammation Mortality depends on early diagnosis and treatment Complications include hydrocephalus, arthritis, blindness, deafness, impairment of intellect, and cerebral palsy					rhages; stiffness of neck; opisthotonus; joint pain; possibly delirium; convulsions	Maintain dim, quiet atmosphere; turn gently; watch for constipation and urinary retention; attention to fluid balance signs of increasing intracranial pressure or meningeal irritation and eye and ear involvement	No immunization available
Mononucleosis, infectious (glandular fever)	Virus? Mildly contagious disease characterized by increase in monocyte-type white cell in blood, lymph node enlargement, fever, and fatigue Heterophil agglutinin studies positive fairly late in course of disease Isolation not recommended*	Typically, disease of teen-agers or young adults Trauma may rarely cause ruptured spleen; hepatitis in 8%-10% of cases May involve prolonged convalescence	Probably droplets from nose and throat, saliva, or intimate contact	Not known Probably only during acute stage	Unknown (probably 2-6 wk.)	Sore throat, malaise, depression, enlarged spleen, liver, and lymph nodes Possible jaundice with liver damage	Symptomatic, no specific therapy known Bed rest, high carbohydrate, protein intake Possible use of corticosteroids with severe throat involvement and airway obstruction	
Mumps (infectious parotitis)	Virus Acute infectious disease causing inflammation of salivary glands and, at times, testes and ovaries	Possible serious consequences for male after puberty, when an attack is more severe; sterility can be complication Meningitis or encephalitis occur infrequently Mild pancreatitis may be encountered	Direct or indirect contact with patient by droplet spread	From several days before apparent infection until swelling disappears	14-21 days (usually 18 days)	Tender swelling chiefly of parotid glands in front of and below ear Headache; moderate fever; pain on swallowing	Bed rest; bland, soft diet; analgesics; warm or cold applications to swollen glands Watch for tenderness of testes—scrotal support may be necessary Observe for abdominal pain and signs of complications	Mumps vaccine Usually immune after first attack Immune serum globulin (ISG) may help those exposed to have milder cases or avoid symptoms

*Report of the Committee on Infectious Diseases, ed. 16, Evanston, Ill., 1970, American Academy of Pediatrics.

Table A. Communicable childhood diseases—cont'd

Disease	Infectious agent and general description	Importance	Mode of transmission	Communicable period	Incubation period	Symptoms	Treatment and nursing care	Prevention

Poliomyelitis (infantile paralysis)	Virus
	Acute infectious disease, may occur in many forms and degrees of severity
	Attacks primarily gastrointestinal and nervous systems; may cause muscular paralysis
		New cases uncommon since vaccine
		When paralysis takes place, many complications may occur involving respiratory, musculoskeletal, urinary, and digestive systems
			Direct or indirect contact with pharyngeal secretions and feces of infected persons (many infected persons have no symptoms)	Communicable for indefinite period before onset of symptoms
				Usually isolated for 7 days after onset or until fever subsides
				Virus may persist in stool for weeks; local sewage facilities should be evaluated
				Careful personal hygiene needed
					7-12 days?	Variable; may include diarrhea, constipation, emesis, painful stiff neck, rigid back, tender skeletal muscles, and respiratory distress
						Cranial nerve involvement
						Three main types
						1. Inapparent infection,
						2. Nonparalytic, and
						3. Paralytic
						  a. Spinal, affecting skeletal muscles and diaphragm
						  b. Bulbar, affecting swallowing, facial muscles, and respiration,
						  c. Mixed
							No specific treatment known
							Supportive treatment depends on patient needs; bed rest, hot packs to relieve muscle spasms, observation for respiratory or bulbar involvement
							Possible tracheotomy and respiratory support; observation for constipation and urinary retention
							Gentle positioning; physical and occupational therapy
								Routine primary schedule and boosters; OPV (Sabin-oral) optimum immunization schedule; IPV (Salk-injections) primary schedule plus repeated biennial booster doses

Rabies (hydrophobia)	Virus Only one nonfatal case reported, acute infectious encephalitis, causing convulsions and muscle paralysis	Exceedingly dangerous Household pets may acquire rabies through bite of rabid wild animals All dogs should be immunized periodically; cats	Bite of rabid animals or entry of infected saliva through previous break in skin or mucous membrane	During clinical course of disease plus 3-5 days before appearance of symptoms	Usually 2-6 wk.	Mental depression, headaches, restlessness, and fever Progresses to painful spasms of throat muscles, especially when attempting to drink	No effective treatment known Supportive nursing care to help prevent convulsions; analgesics; death usually occurs in about 7 days	Vaccination of dogs; 10-day confinement of any dog who has bitten human Laboratory investigation of brain of dog that dies during this period; if

		may also be carriers, but impractical to insist on immunization				Delirium, convulsions, and coma		rabies is diagnosed, person bitten must receive rabies vaccine
Smallpox (variola)	Virus. Highly contagious infection involving constitutional symptoms—fever and characteristic scarring rash; may occur in severe or mild forms	There should be no cases of smallpox in United States; preventive vaccine has been known and available over 100 yr., but not everyone maintains protection, every year cases occur. Mortality 20%-50%. Complications include secondary infection, bronchitis, and bronchopneumonia	Direct or indirect contact with secretions from skin lesions or mouth; airborne for short distances	From first appearance of illness until all crusts disappear	10-14 days (usually 12 days)	Sudden onset of high fever with flulike symptoms; rash appears in 3-4 days, involving normally exposed parts of body, face, arms, and upper chest. Rash progresses to deeply seated pustules, all at about same stage of development, leaving typical scars. Photophobia	No specific treatment. Antibiotics used to avoid secondary infection. Procedures to relieve fever and itching. Possible blood transfusions. Shield eyes from light; special oral hygiene; encourage nutritious fluids; attention to fluid balance. Deodorizing procedures for patient and room	Routine primary immunization smallpox vaccination. Booster at school age and every 10 yr. Permanent immunity usually follows first attack
Staphylococcal infections	Coagulase-positive staphylococci (*Micrococcus pyogenes*, var. *aureus*) pus-producing coccus. Descriptions variable	Found almost everywhere; causes many hospital infections; does not respond well to usual antibiotic therapy; extremely difficult to control; anyone may be carrier at intervals. Complications include skin lesions, pneumonia, wound infections, osteomyelitis, arthritis, meningitis, and food poisoning	Depends on body area infected. Asymptomatic nasal carriers common. May be airborne. Direct or indirect contact with infected secretions	As long as lesions drain or carrier state persists	Variable; 1-2 days to several weeks	Depend on area infected. Fever and characteristic signs of inflammation typical	Antibiotics according to drug sensitivity pattern of organism; methicillin, oxacillin. Topical antibiotics: bacitracin, neomycin, polymyxin	No immunization generally available and effective. Good hygiene and aseptic technique best preventive

Continued.

Table A. Communicable childhood diseases — cont'd

Disease	Infectious agent and general description	Importance	Mode of transmission	Communicable period	Incubation period	Symptoms	Treatment and nursing care	Prevention
Streptococcal infections	Strains of hemolytic streptococci Diseases include septic sore throat, scarlet fever (scarlatina), erysipelas, impetigo, puerperal fever	Interrelated group of infections; septic sore throat probably most common Early complications include otitis media May cause serious complications — nephritis and rheumatic fever, with possible arthritis and carditis	In septic sore throat and scarlet fever, direct or indirect contact with nasopharyngeal secretions from infected patient; probably airborne In erysipelas, impetigo, and puerperal fever, direct or indirect contact with discharges from skin or reproductive tract	Variable Carrier state possible	2-5 days	Depend on manifestations Septic sore throat, severe pharyngitis and fever Scarlet fever, pharyngitis, fever, and fine reddish rash and strawberry tongue Erysipelas, tender, red skin lesions and fever often recurrent Puerperal fever	Depends on manifestation Penicillin for at least 10 days	No artificial immunization available Penicillin prophylaxis may be used with special groups Good asepsis important
Tetanus (lockjaw)	Bacillus *Clostridium tetani* Acute infectious disease attacking chiefly nervous system Wounds deprived of good oxygen supply especially vulnerable	Always considered in event of burns, automobile accidents, or puncture wounds Mortality rate of about 35%	Entrance of spores into wounds through contaminated soil Person-to-person transmission unlikely unless discharges from infected wound contaminate open lesion	Infectious, but only potentially communicable if draining wound present	3-21 days (usually 8 days)	Irritability, rigidity, painful muscle spasms, and inability to open mouth Exhaustion and respiratory difficulty	Antitoxin and sedation plus muscle relaxant Quiet, dim room Possible suction and tracheotomy Observation of fluid balance; watch for constipation and respiratory distress; protect from self-injury during convulsions	Routine primary immunization booster at school age and Td every 10 yr.
Tuberculosis	*Myobacterium tuberculosis* (tubercle bacillus) Typically chronic infection that	Serious world health problem, particularly in economically deprived areas Infants and young	Direct or indirect contact with infected patients; body excretions or droplet spread	As long as organism is discharged in sputum or other body excretions Communicability	From infection to primary lesion, 2-10 wk. Time of ap-	Active pulmonary tuberculosis: anorexia, weight loss, night sweats, afternoon fever, cough and dysp-	Several drugs may prevent growth of organism, including streptomycin (STM), para-aminosali-	BCG vaccine to build up immunity in high-risk populations advised by some Early detection

Disease	Characteristics	Public health importance and complications	Mode of transmission	Period of communicability	Incubation period	Symptoms and diagnosis	Treatment and nursing care	Prevention and immunity
(Tuberculosis, continued)	may affect many body organs Human type most often causes pulmonary infection Bovine type causes much of tuberculosis affecting areas outside lungs	children very susceptible Pulmonary complications, hemoptysis, spontaneous pneumothorax, or spread to other organs with varied symptoms; possible orthopedic problems	(depending on type) Respiratory tuberculosis often airborne; bovine type may result from drinking milk from infected cows (now rare in U. S.)	may be reduced by medication, therapy, and teaching cough control and asepsis to patients Body often walls off a primary infection, controlling spread and preventing active disease	pearance of active symptoms variable	nea, fatigue, and hemoptysis; in children dyspnea and cough often absent Diagnosis based on symptoms and microscopic studies of sputum, gastric washings, and chest x-ray examination	cylic acid (PAS), and isoniazid (INH) Nursing care includes provision for mental and physical rest; nutritious diet; observation for toxic drug reactions and increasing respiratory distress; provision for and instructions in personal hygiene; moral support	and control of known cases through periodic x-ray examination, possible skin tests, and close medical supervision
Typhoid fever (enteric fever)	*Salmonella typhosa*, a bacillus (many types have been identified) Relatively severe febrile systemic infection with symptoms involving lymphoid tissues, intestine, and spleen, which may be accompanied by complete prostration and delirium Condition has prolonged course and convalescence	Always of potential public health importance when community hygiene breaks down Carrier states may persist Complications include intestinal hemorrhage and perforation, thrombosis, cardiac failure, and cholecystitis	Direct or indirect contact with urine and feces of infected patients and carriers Food and water supplies may be infected by contaminated *flies* or unsuspected *carriers*; community sewage facilities should be evaluated; excreta may have to be disinfected before being added to local system	As long as typhoid organism appears in feces or urine 2%-5% of those affected become permanent carriers	1-3 wk. (usually 2 wk.)	In children symptoms may be atypical, may at first resemble upper respiratory infection; intestinal tract becomes inflamed and even ulcerated; spleen enlarges; fever mounts; pulse relatively slow; rash, "rose spots" may be present	Chloramphenicol and supportive nursing care; liquid to bland, soft diet as tolerated; bed rest Watch for abdominal distention and hemorrhage; small enemas may be ordered; observation of fluid balance	Immunity usually acquired after one attack Triple vaccine against forms of paratyphoid as well as typhoid available

Continued.

333

Table A. Communicable childhood diseases — cont'd

Disease	Infectious agent and general description	Importance	Mode of transmission	Communicable period	Incubation period	Symptoms	Treatment and nursing care	Prevention
Whooping cough (pertussis)	*Bordetella pertussis* (pertussis bacillus) Acute infection of respiratory tract, characterized by paroxysmal cough ending in "whoop," often accompanied by vomiting	Severe disease in infants, may terminate fatally Complications include bronchopneumonia and convulsions, widespread hemorrhages, hernia, and possible activation of pulmonary tuberculosis	Direct or indirect contact with nasopharyngeal secretions of infected patients (droplet infection)	From 7 days after exposure to 3 wk. after onset of typical cough Greatest in catarrhal stage before onset of paroxysms	5-21 days (usually within 10 days)	Early symptoms resemble typical common cold Cough worsens and may become violent and paroxysmal Vomiting may be caused by coughing or nervous system irritation; cough may linger after convalescence	Diagnosis confirmed with bacterial studies of exposed cough plates and presence of leukocytosis Immune serum globulin; erythromycin antibiotic of choice; provision for rest and quiet; sedatives Light nutritious diet; judicious fluid intake to prevent dehydration; weight determinations Observation for onset of respiratory distress or other complications	Immunity produce after one attack Routine primary schedule plus boosters

APPENDIX B

EDUCATIONAL ORGANIZATIONS, NEWSLETTERS, AND JOURNALS ASSOCIATED WITH EARLY CHILDHOOD

Educational Organizations

A.C.E.I.
*Association for Childhood Education
  International*
3615 Wisconsin Avenue, N. W.
Washington, D. C. 20016

American Montessori Society
175 Fifth Avenue
New York, N. Y. 10010

C.W.L.A.
Child Welfare League of America, Inc.
44 East 23rd Street
New York, N. Y. 10010

D.C.C.D.C.A.
*Day Care and Child Development Council of
  America, Inc.*
1401 K. Street, N. W.
Washington, D. C. 20005

*Early Childhood Education Council of New
  York City*
196 Bleeker Street
New York, N. Y. 10012

Education Development Center
Early Childhood Education Study
55 Chapel Street
Newton, Mass. 02150

*American Association of Elementary-
  Kindergarten-Nursery Educators*
1201 16th Street
Washington, D. C. 20036

ERIC/ECE
*Educational Resources Information
  Center/Early Childhood Education*
805 West Pennsylvania Avenue
Urbana, Ill. 61801

N.A.E.Y.C.
*National Association for the Education of
  Young Children*
1834 Connecticut Avenue, N. W.
Washington, D. C. 20009

U. S. Dept. of H.E.W.
*United States Department of Health,
  Education, and Welfare*
Office of Child Development
Children's Bureau
Washington, D. C. 20201

Newsletters

The Black Child Advocate
Black Child Development Institute
1028 Connecticut Avenue, N. W., Suite 514
Washington, D. C. 20036

ERIC/ECE Newsletter
805 West Pennsylvania Avenue
Urbana, Ill. 61801

Report on Preschool Education
Capitol Publications, Inc.
Suite G-12
2430 Pennsylvania Avenue, N. W.
Washington, D. C. 20037

Today's Child
Roosevelt, N. J. 08555

Journals

Childhood Education
A.C.E.I.
3615 Wisconsin Avenue, N. W.
Washington, D. C. 20016

Children Today
U. S. Dept. of H.E.W.
Office of Child Development
Children's Bureau
Superintendent of Documents
U. S. Government Printing Office
Washington, D. C. 20402

Child Development
Society for Research in Child Development
University of Chicago Press
5801 Ellis Avenue
Chicago, Ill. 60637

Developmental Psychology
American Psychological Association
1200 Seventeenth Street, N. W.
Washington, D. C. 20036

Harvard Educational Review
Longfellow Hall
13 Appian Way
Cambridge, Mass. 02138

*Merrill-Palmer Quarterly of Behavior and
   Development*
Merrill-Palmer Institute

71 East Ferry Avenue
Detroit, Mich. 48202

Young Children
N.A.E.Y.C.
1834 Connecticut Avenue, N. W.
Washington, D. C. 20009

APPENDIX C

A BEGINNING LIST OF FREE MATERIALS AND RESOURCES*

Empty ribbon rolls	Gift wrapping section of department stores
Wood shavings	Building scrap piles, carpentry shops
Material remnants	Interior design stores, upholsterers, clothing manufacturers
Scraps of suede and leather	Leather good stores
Boxes and pieces of Styrofoam	Throwaways from drug stores, five and tens, radio and television shops
Computer paper used on one side, or cards	Almost anywhere computers are used
Empty bolts from material	Textile stores

---

*Suggested by the Principles and Practices class, 1972, of Santa Barbara City College. See also Hodgen, Koetter, Laforse, McCord, and Schramm, 1970, for an additional helpful list.

Large appliance boxes	Almost all appliance stores are delighted to get rid of these
Cardboard rolls	Textile stores
Natural materials for collage	Seed pods, pebbles, leaves, and cones abound
Feathers	Bird refuge
Wood scraps	Carpenters and cabinet shops
Burlap	Horse-boarding barns
Small cardboard boxes	Dime stores, hearing-aid stores, department and stationery stores
Ticker tape and newsprint rolls and ends	Local newspaper office
Wallpaper sample books	Wallpaper stores
Art papers of various sizes and colors	Print shops
5-gallon ice cream containers	Drive-ins and ice cream stores
Rug scraps	Carpet stores and installers
One- or two-day animal loans	Local pet shops

APPENDIX D

ACTIVITIES TO DEVELOP AUDITORY DISCRIMINATION*

Have the children put their heads down on the table. Display on a nearby shelf or table various instruments: xylophone, cymbals, tambourine, bells, and so forth. While they have their heads down, play one instrument. Children can take turns making the sounds for others to identify.

I was in the kitchen at the sink, and D. was standing at the kitchen gate. He was swinging the gate back and forth so that it would bang against the stopper. As it got louder and louder I was about to tell him to stop when I decided to use this situation for auditory discrimination. We were promptly joined by two other children. First we listened to how loud the gate could bang shut. Then I asked them if they could make it very quiet so that there wasn't any noise. We did these two opposites several times. Then we started very quietly and got louder and louder and louder. We tried this with our feet stamping on the floor and also clapping our hands. First we did it loud then quiet, then quiet and louder, and then as loud as we could.

Under the table I made different sounds and asked the children to identify them. I used a bell, sandpaper rubbed together, two blocks hit together, scissors opening and closing, and tearing paper. Then I asked one child to make his own sound and let the rest of the children guess what it was.

Using one sound, have the children shut their eyes while you move about the room, and ask the children to point to where you are. Then let the children be the sound makers.

*Suggested by the Language and Cognitive Development class, 1973, of Santa Barbara City College.

Record on a tape recorder familiar sounds such as a car starting, water running, train, door shutting, refrigerator door opening or closing, or a toilet flushing (if you use this last one, do it at the end, as it tends to break up the group). Stop at each sound and have the children identify it. For older children play a series of sounds, and see how many they can remember.

I put several things in a box, one at a time, and had the children listen to the sounds: a tennis ball, tooth brush, piece of metal, and a comb. Then I put the box behind my back, put one of the objects in the box, brought it in front of me and rattled it. The children guessed what made the noise.

With my children we listened to the sounds around us when we were outside. We heard the leaves blowing, other children yelling, a car going by, and sand falling. It was fun and made the children really aware of the sounds around them.

I used a triangle with a wooden stick and a metal one. The children listened while I showed them the sticks; then I had them close their eyes and tell me which stick I had used.

Using a xylophone, strike a middle note, then play other notes and ask the children if the new note is higher or lower than the middle one. Also, for degree of loudness, strike the notes hard or lightly and ask the children if the sound is loud or soft.

Material. Cans with tops, small nails, rice, beans, salt.

I made up two cans of each material. I had all the cans on the table and went around and asked the children to pick one and shake it. Then I asked them to try and find one that sounded exactly the same. Then we opened the cans to see if the cans really did contain the same ingredient. The children enjoyed playing this and wanted to have many turns.

Material. Six bottles, same size; one spoon; water

Take two bottles and put the same volume of water in them, then two other bottles with the same volume of water, and finally two more. I covered the bottles with contact paper so the children couldn't see how much water each bottle held. Taking turns, the children tried to pick out sounds that matched by hitting the bottle with the spoon. If we were in doubt that the tones matched, we poured the water out and measured it.

APPENDIX E

DEFINITIONS OF THE PARAMETERS AND CATEGORIES OF THE STRUCTURE OF INTELLECT*

Formal definitions of the parameters and their categories are given below . . . . Letter symbols applied to the various categories are also given here. Their use will be explained later.

Operations

Major kinds of intellectual activities or processes; things that the organism does in the processing of information, information being defined as "that which the organism discriminates."

Cognition (C). Immediate discovery, awareness, rediscovery, or recognition of information in its various forms; comprehension or understanding.

Memory (M). Fixation of newly gained information in storage. The operation of memory is to be distinguished from the memory store.

Divergent production (D). Generation of logical alternatives from given information, where the emphasis is upon variety, quantity, and relevance of output from the same source. Likely to involve transfer recall (instigated by new cues).

Convergent production (N). Generation of logical conclusions from given information, where emphasis is upon achieving unique or conventionally best outcomes. It is likely that the given (cue) information fully determines the outcome, as in mathematics and logic.

Evaluation (E). Comparison of items of information in terms of variables and making judgments concerning criterion satisfaction (correctness, identity, consistency, etc.).

Contents

Broad, substantive, basic kinds of areas of information.

Figural (F). Pertaining to information in concrete form, as perceived or as recalled in the form of images. The term "figural" minimally implies figure-ground perceptual organization. Different sense modalities may be involved—visual, auditory, kinesthetic, and perhaps others.

Symbolic (S). Pertaining to information in the form of denotative signs having no significance in and of themselves, such as letters, numbers, musical notations, codes, and words (as ordered letter combinations).

Semantic (M). Pertaining to information in the form of conceptions or mental constructs to which words are often applied, hence most notable in verbal thinking and verbal communication, but not necessarily dependent upon words. Meaningful pictures also convey semantic information.

Behavioral (B). Pertaining to information, essentially nonfigural and nonverbal, involved in human interactions, where the attitudes, needs, desires, moods, intentions, perceptions, thoughts, etc. of others and of ourselves are involved.

Products

Basic forms that information takes in the organism's processing of it.

Units (U). Relatively segregated or circumscribed items or "chunks" of information having "thing" character. May be close to Gestalt psychology's "figure on a ground."

*From Guilford, J. P. *The analysis of intelligence.* New York: © 1971, McGraw-Hill Book Co. Pp. 20 and 21. Used with permission of McGraw-Hill Book Co.

Classes (C). Conceptions underlying sets of items of information grouped by virtue of their common properties.

Relations (R). Connections between items of information based upon variables or points of contact that apply to them. Relational connections are more definable than implicational connections.

Systems (S). Organized or structured aggregates of items of information; complexes of interrelated or interacting parts.

Transformation (T). Charges of various kinds (redefinitions, shifts, transitions, or modifications) in existing information.

Implications (I). Circumstantial connections between items of information, as by virtue of contiguity, or any condition that promotes "belongingness."

The SI code system

The code letters for the 15 SI categories and their use will now be explained. Each SI ability is often designated in terms of its special trigram, composed of a letter for each of its parameters—its operation, content, and product, in that order. For example, CMS is a shorthand expression for "cognition of semantic systems," and EFT is the label for "evaluation of figural transformations." Some letters happen to be used twice, but never for categories of the same parameter—for example, MMR means "memory for semantic relations," and NSS means "convergent production of symbolic systems." Keeping in mind the order of the three parameters in a trigram should help the reader avoid confusions. The code system is summarized here for convenient reference:

Operation	*Content*	*Product*
C—cognition	F—figural	U—unit
M—memory	S—symbolic	C—class
D—divergent production	M—semantic	R—relation
N—convergent production	B—behavioral	S—system
E—evaluation		T—transformation
		I—implication

Author index

Subject index